THE JAVIER PLAYS

DIAGRAM OF A PAPER AIRPLANE

A THICK DESCRIPTION OF HARRY SMITH (VOL. 1)

YOUR NAME WILL FOLLOW YOU HOME

53SP 24

April 2016

ISBN no. 978-0-9897393-4-4

53rdstatepress.org

Cover image: a tracing by Karinne Keithley Syers of Robert Fludd's copper engraving, "Mechanik & Musik & Sackpfeife & Dudelsack" (1624).

"A Hard Rain's A-Gonna Fall" written by Bob Dylan. Copyright © 1963 by Warner Bros. Inc.; renewed 1991 by Special Rider Music. All rights reserved. International copyright secured. Reprinted by permission.

"I Couldn't Get High" written by Ken Weaver. Copyright © 1965 by Heavy Metal Music. Appears on The First Fugs Album produced by Ed Sanders and Harry Smith. All rights reserved. Reprinted by permission.

THE JAVIER PLAYS

Carlos Murillo

53rd State Press
Brooklyn, NY

TABLE OF CONTENTS

7   DELUGE: A Preface to *The Javier Plays*
Carlos Murillo

27   DIAGRAM OF A PAPER AIRPLANE
Introduction
Kip Fagan

Diagram of a Paper Airplane

131   A THICK DESCRIPTION OF HARRY SMITH
Introduction
Tamsen Wolff

A Thick Description of Harry Smith (Vol. 1)
(or Do What Thou Wilt Shall Be the Whole of the Law)

241   YOUR NAME WILL FOLLOW YOU HOME
Memories of an Invisible Muse: An Introduction to Your Name Will
Follow You Home
Alicia Hernández

Your Name Will Follow You Home

379   AFTERWORD: The Mystique of Failure
Dr. Alexandra Tanner

397   Acknowledgements

Deluge: A Preface to *The Javier Plays*

Carlos Murillo

"Beware the things you find behind file cabinets in musty basements. Rather — beware the things someone else finds in such places that you take it upon yourself to steal."

— *American playwright Javier C., from the introduction of his unpublished manifesto "To Murder Whimsy: Bi-Polar Realism and the Future of American Playwriting" (1984)*

The origins of *The Javier Plays*

Some time in the last decade of the last century, I became acquainted with a young woman who briefly had worked as a summer intern at New Dramatists – we'll call her "Nicole" for the purposes of this preface – 1) to protect the innocent, and 2) to confess that I can't recall with certainty her actual name.

New Dramatists, housed in a former house of worship on West 44th Street in Hell's Kitchen, is a New York City based organization "Dedicated to the Playwright" – or so read the fading gold letters stenciled on the transom window above the entrance. The organization provides a select group of playwrights seven-year residencies designed to help develop their craft, work within a community of likeminded professionals, and provide a home for folks pursuing a profession in which the specter of homelessness – both literal and figurative – looms large. Most of the organization's activity takes place in the months between September, when a new crop of writers are inducted as members, to June, when writers who have completed their seven years get "kicked to the curb," as one former resident described his experience to me over beers at Rudy's, a nearby watering hole and holdout from the darker, seedier days of Hell's Kitchen.

Summer is a quiet time at The Church (as playwrights and staff affectionately call the place) so "Nicole," our intern, was tasked with preparing boxes of archival material for shipment to the Beinecke Library at Yale University, which houses New Dramatists' storied archives. For the interplanetary visitor wishing to unearth the trajectory

of late 20th century American drama, there hardly exists a better place to start. Among the artifacts in the collection: seminal works in draft form by some of the country's finest, most successful and legendary playwrights, as well as countless lost plays by obscure and forgotten ones. "Nicole" spent a good deal of her summer entombed in the dank base-ment, combing through dozens of file cabi-nets, dusting off their contents, cataloguing, organizing and packing them away for future theatre scholars. The tedium of her task was tempered by the glimmer of possibility: she'd heard tales of past interns striking gold while excavating the ruins, unearthing lost treasures. Past discoveries included an early draft of a Pulitzer-winning play by August Wilson, a lost James Baldwin work, complete with handwritten marginal notes, among many others.

In mid-August, after emptying the contents of a brown metal file cabinet tucked in a far corner of the basement, "Nicole" discovered an unopened package in a large manila envelope behind the bottom drawer. The envelope piqued her curiosity – battered, wrinkled, torn and mended with layers of clear packing tape, blotched with stains of indeterminate origin, it had been reduced, reused and recycled by its sender frequently enough as to render it almost useless. Covered with dozens of labels with different ad-dresses, cross-outs made with magic marker and numerous strata of "Return to Sender" stamps and post markings worthy of an archaeological dig, the envelope had traveled great distances over the course of its life before landing in its final resting place behind the drawer. The sender had clearly "pushed the envelope" of this envelope, as it were, with his presumably penny-pinching reuse of it. Or perhaps the sender meant to create

a low-rent, Rauschenberg-esque assemblage – a reminder to himself and to its recipients of the cycles of hope and rejection inherent to the playwriting profession, and of the porous line between gold and garbage, the permanent and the ephemeral.

All alone in the dank basement, "Nicole" hesitated opening the envelope. She felt foreboding that the artifact's exterior strangeness must conceal something dark, cursed, perhaps evil. Indeed, the contents were alarming.

Enclosed in the envelope, "Nicole" found an unread, unevaluated application for one of New Dramatists' coveted residencies by the obscure Colombian-born American playwright Javier C. Though none of the material inside was dated, "Nicole" deduced from the faded, top layer postmark that the applicant mailed the package a full seven years before, on September 11, 1991 – a full four days before the submission window closed on September 15th (and a full twenty years before the New Dramatists application process went paperless.) Had Javier's application been accepted, he would have completed his residency around the time "Nicole" graduated from Bennington College and moved to New York to start her internship.

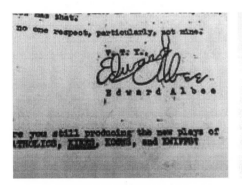

The application contained all the requisite materials: a cover letter, two copies of two complete plays, a resume, a statement of purpose, and a letter of recommendation from Pulitzer Prize winning playwright Edward Albee (later declared a forgery).

In addition, the sender included a number of unrequested supplementary materials: an incomplete, handwritten, mostly illegible draft of a manifesto entitled "To Murder Whimsy: Bi-Polar Realism and the Future of American Playwriting," fragments of a third play (perhaps "play" is too generous a description – the sender himself described it as a "bucket of vomit" in the form of dialogue, impossible stage directions, descriptions of unwritten scenes, unsent hate mail, proposals for unwieldy practical jokes), a Ziploc bag containing a half dozen crumpled paper airplanes, a photocopy of what appeared to be a page from an original copy of Giordano Bruno's *Ars Memoriae* (1582), an unopened package of Little Debbie cakes, a half smoked cigarette, a series of cut-outs from milk cartons featuring images and descriptions of missing children, and an unopened fortune cookie that had been crushed to dust under the weight of all this material. (The fortune itself, legible through the plastic wrapper and shards of cookie, read: "Trust him, but still keep your eyes open. Lucky # 3, 23, 25, 31, 34, 46."

As "Nicole" delved deeper into the required materials, they revealed an eccentricity that matched the supplementary ones. The typo-ridden cover letter, a model of incoherence, argued that the long history of political violence in Javier C.'s native land Colombia – a violence which cost him his father's life, prompting his mother to whisk her two year old son into exile in the US in 1960 – justified his choice to become a playwright bent on examining "the unfinished nature and dark underbelly of the American experiment from the perspective of a reluctant immigrant from the other America – where your coffee, bananas and cocaine comes from." The two plays – *Death of a Liberal* (1977) and *The Rich Also Cry* (1979) – evidenced an undoubtedly unique (and some would say abrasive) voice. More drafts-in-progress than finished works, the manuscripts were riddled with handwritten marginal notes, cross outs, index cards stapled to various pages, and pornographic doodles. The handwritten resume said little about his dramatic output, production history or educational background – instead it read as a catalogue of misdeeds: his petty crimes, the various drugs he took, and the names (when he could recall them) of women and men that "co-piloted" his numerous and varied sexual escapades, including dates, locations and brief notes on the duration, quality and psychic cost of these experiences. The Statement of Purpose was equally

inappropriate to the application. Rather than describe his plays, his work, his theatrical vision, his influences, what he hoped to accomplish over a seven-year residency, the Statement goes to considerable length to describe his mother's hands and the hundreds of matchbooks she collected from every restaurant she visited in her adult life – a collection he discovered in a linen closet while cleaning out her apartment after her sudden and unexpected death in 1981.

While not a discovery as significant as an early, lost August Wilson work, for "Nicole" it had enough value as a curiosity to break the monotony of that August.

After squandering half the afternoon peeling away the spooky layers of this strange artifact, "Nicole" did what any industrious intern would do: she went to the office of Todd London, New Dramatists' recently appointed Artistic Director, to ask him what to do with it. Mr. London had no idea who Javier C. was, nor could he explain to "Nicole" why the package had never been opened and the materials enclosed in it never evaluated. As to what to she ought to do with it, he told "Nicole" to "Go to town with it, sweetheart." (In an interview I conducted with Todd London in 2012, he recalled neither the incident nor the intern in question, and denied with uncharacteristic bite "I actually used a phrase like that, despite this 'Nicole person's' claim that I did.")

Javier C.'s unevaluated application package was not included among the items sent to Yale that summer. Thus, the chances of his work being resurrected by an intrepid scholar seeking to fill in the potholes in the accepted evolutionary trajectory of American drama, were reduced, for all practical purposes, to nil. Faced with the choice of condemning it in the dustbin or restoring the package to its purgatory behind the drawer, "Nicole" followed Todd London's advice: she took it home, where it languished on her bookshelf, forgotten.

How *The Javier Plays* came into my possession

That December, at the New Dramatists annual holiday party, I met "Nicole."

Like many American playwrights, I coveted membership in the organization. Being only a few years into a fledgling theatre career at that point, and knowing tales of now well-established playwrights applying multiple times before gaining admittance (I understand from organizational lore that Pulitzer-winner Paula Vogel holds the record for number of attempts before acceptance), I acknowledged that it might be some time (in my case, more or less a dozen years) before I might be anointed a congregant of The Church. In the meantime, I contented myself with attending the occasional play reading and crashing holiday celebrations, where, as a young, struggling artist on the prowl, I happily helped myself to the copious amounts of free booze, pounced on networking opportunities and sought out potential partners for "no strings attached," consequence-free dalliances.

It was the '90s. I was in my 20s. In that period of my life I was marked with twin character flaws: kleptomania and promiscuity. My kleptomaniac impulses focused exclusively on the accumulation of books. I lifted them everywhere – bookstores, public libraries, the various places where I was employed, off of shelves in the apartments of friends, acquaintances and strangers. If I happened to find myself an overnight guest at someone's home, I never left without a souvenir volume. I had read Edmund White's exhaustive 1993 biography, *Genet* (NB: I actually paid the $35 it cost to acquire it) — which chronicled, among other things, the novelist and playwright's obsessive book thieving. I love Genet's work. As a young writer seeking models in the work of my predecessors, both Genet's self-reflexive dramaturgy and his thieving criminality served to justify my own.

My promiscuity, on the other hand, was driven by the privilege of being a poor, young and randy aspiring-artist-on-the-make in a city filled with poor, young and randy aspiring-artists-on-the-make. While I mostly acted on these twin traits separately, I found myself, on occasion, in circumstances where these flaws dovetailed into an admittedly neurotic, criminal compulsion. Forensic science provides ample documentation of cases where criminals either leave behind or remove artifacts from the scenes of their crimes. While it would be wrong to characterize my consensual amorous escapades as criminal, being raised Catholic, they might as well have been. That I could never leave a "crime" scene without removing a book from it, well that, friends, is indeed criminal.

My library, as long as it existed (past tense, yes, more on that soon), not only embodied much of my accumulated knowledge (a substitute for my failure to complete a college education), but encoded in the volumes was my personal history: the places I visited, friends, colleagues and acquaintances I associated with, establishments where I worked, retail outlets at which I shopp(lift)ed, and people with whom I slept.

That said, beyond the accumulation of books and sexual experience, by chasing this criminal compulsion I hungered for something deeper: an anthropological knowledge I could only acquire visiting the apartments of strangers. Many of the greatest museum collections in the world are concentrated in the 469 square miles of New York City. But in my opinion the richest treasures aren't housed in obvious places like The Met, the MOMA or the Museum of Natural History. No. The greatest museum treasures in New York City — or any metropolis for that matter — exist in the private realm, inside the apartments of anonymous dwellers of the city. For me, being taken to a strange apartment by a sweet young thing was to gain entry to a museum for one. What artifacts does she possess? What books sit on her shelves? What images hang on her walls? What unpaid bills sit neglected on her night table? What garments (and skeletons) hang in her closet? And footwear? What rots inside her refrigerator? Are unspoken hopes and fears written into the tchotchkes she collects and the manner in which she arranges them? Is there a story all this stuff tells? Of her life? Of the city? Of the culture inside which we're condemned to live? It was in these unofficial museums where I believed I might unlock a thick description of American life in the 20th Century. For years I toyed with the idea of writing a history of the United States as revealed by the artifacts people accumulate in their apartments. As with so many ideas, this one never came to fruition.

A DIGRESSION ABOUT MUSEUMS

The stranger's-apartment-as-museum paradigm struck me for the first time in 1992 while housesitting for a "friend with benefits" in the Prospect Heights section of Brooklyn. The owner of the apartment was a divorcee in her 30s who worked in the development office of a well-known, now defunct not-for-profit off-Broadway theatre. She left town regularly to visit her ailing mother in Ottawa. When she traveled, knowing I was hard up for a consistent place to live, she generously handed over the keys to her place so I could get the mail and tend to her Ficus tree. The apartment was beautifully appointed – large south-facing windows overlooking a Brownstone – and tree-lined Brooklyn street, high ceilings and spacious, airy, tastefully furnished rooms that took up the entire second floor. For all its beauty, I couldn't help but sense that something fundamental was missing. Her apartment was a museum with phantom wings. Something had been removed, amputated from the place. The artifacts she had accumulated seemed to enclose absence – like when you remove a photograph from a wall and it leaves a clean rectangle of color fresher than the paint surrounding it.

She had lived in the apartment for nearly a decade with her ex-husband, a French Canadian attorney who relocated to Montreal after their divorce. The apartment appeared as if he removed half its contents when he left, and she never bothered to makeover the apartment in her own image. I don't mean to convey that she was a sad, lonely or forlorn person, pining away for her lost husband. On the contrary, she voraciously enjoyed her post-marital life. She possessed razor-sharp intelligence and head-turning good looks, worked in a profession she loved and was very good at, lived in a fantastic apartment, had lots of friends and a healthy stable of gentlemen (and women) with whom she indulged in life's pleasures.

A small alcove off the living room served as a library. Built into it were floor to ceiling Mahogany bookshelves framed by a pair of expensive leather wingback chairs. One after-noon, on my third stint house sitting, I went into the library alcove to browse titles and choose a souvenir. I found wedged in a section devoted to serious, thick historical and legal tomes three paperback books of Magick spells – their titles barely decipherable. The cheap bindings were cracked from heavy use. Opening one of the volumes to a dog-eared page revealed instructions for a fertility spell. Combing through all of the spell books, it became clear: fertility spell after fertility spell after fertility spell. Having seen her naked on dozens of occasions, I never expected to see her so naked as this. I quickly returned the spell books to their place on the shelf – feeling ashamed that I had violated her most hidden, private self.

It struck me then and strikes me any time I am in a stranger's apartment: encoded in the artifacts the dweller accumulates (and in their juxtaposition to each other) is the psychic DNA of the being that occupies the space. Everything about them – what's visible and invisible, their past, present and future wishes and anxieties, their triumphs, disappointments, love and hatred, the ache they feel for people and things they've lost – is written in invisible ink in the white spaces between words.

How *The Javier Plays* came into my possession, part two

But back to "Nicole."

We met at the New Dramatists holiday party that December and immediately hit it off. We were roughly the same age, shared a common pursuit (she also aspired to be a playwright). We liked many of the same plays, books and films. I laughed at her jokes, she laughed at mine. I was struck by her contrarian nature, which she backed up with her sharp powers of observation, brutal honesty and deft use of language. Not to mention she looked irresistible in the green 40s vintage flower print dress she wore – presumably one specimen of many vintage garments I fantasized hung in her closet. As festivities wound down at The Church, we fell into a taxicab on 9th Avenue. Half an hour later, on Bedford Avenue in the Greenpoint section of Brooklyn, we fell out of it, and stumbled up the four flights of stairs to her studio apartment.

A few hours later, we lay silent, wide awake, post-coital on her bed, black sky out-side morphing into pale blue, the constant dull whoosh of late night New York City giving way to early morning bird chirps, joggers and garbage trucks making their dawn rounds. We'd arrived at a moment familiar to anyone who has indulged in such esca-pades – when the unspoken question hovers in the air: Should I stay or should I go?

"You should go," she said, just as the question began to form in my mouth.

"Oh." Torn between disappointment and relief, I asked if I could call her, maybe hang out some night, go see a show. She shrugged, wrote her number down on the back of a ConEd envelope, and left it at the foot of her bed.

She watched me dress, expressionless, which made me uneasy. Her gaze made me feel like I might be a forged artifact intruding on her museum. To defuse my discomfort, I confessed my book thieving guilty pleasure, hoping it would amuse her. She stared back at me blankly, pointed to the bookshelf. "Go to town, kid," she said. So I did.

Combing through the titles I noted a lot of overlap between her book collection and mine. One title caught my interest – a paperback copy of *Famous All Over Town* by a writer named Danny Santiago. While skimming through it, my eye caught the manila envelope I described earlier, wedged between her copies of Thomas Mann's *Doctor Faustus* and *Open Secrets* by Alice Munro. I replaced the Santiago book, and pulled the manila envelope off the shelf. "What's this?" I asked. She told me the story. I asked if I could take it as my souvenir. She shrugged, and repeated: "Go to town with it, kid."

I left her apartment, walked the two miles down Bedford Avenue to the apartment where I was crashing in Williamsburg, which at the time was still an urban war zone. I wedged the envelope on my own bookshelf between Camille Paglia's *Sexual Personae* and Plutarch's *Lives of the Noble Greeks and Romans*. It languished there for a decade.

I tried calling "Nicole" the next weekend. I couldn't bring myself to punch in the last digit of her telephone number. I never saw her again.

DELUGE: CHICAGO, 2007

In my family's history, triumph and catastrophe often share the same bed. I'll spare you the catalogue of examples that go back generations. Suffice to say that when things are looking up, it's always a good idea to keep an eye over your shoulder for the rabid dog, cancer tumor, federal agent or assassin that's inevitably stalking your heels.

In 2007, I spent a good part of the winter in Louisville, KY where my play *dark play or stories for boys* premiered at the Humana Festival at Actors Theatre of Louisville. The production was a huge success, and though it did not receive the blessing or invitation to come to New York by *Times* theatre critic Charles Isherwood (who dismissed the entire slate of plays that year as "dispiriting"), the play has enjoyed a fruitful life with many productions in the US and eastern Europe, and continues to be produced with some frequency, at least at the time of this writing, seven years after its premiere.

After the opening, I returned on a high to Chicago – where I live with my wife and two children (I'd successfully sublimated my promiscu-klepto compulsions eight years earlier). I bustled with renewed energy, optimism and a fearless hunger to climb the next mountain, as it were, to write my next play.

We live in a tiny house in Bridgeport, an historic neighborhood in the South Side of Chicago. Built in 1878, seven years after the Great Chicago Fire decimated the city, the house was originally inhabited by Lithuanian immigrants employed by the nearby Union Stockyards (see Upton Sinclair's *The Jungle* for a colorful portrait of the place.) A previous owner of the house illegally converted a detached garage into a livable apartment, complete with kitchenette and bathroom. This was one of the main amenities that at-

tracted my wife and I when we house hunted in 2005 — I could use this space as an office and guests could stay there, affording me (and them) privacy from the child dominated main house. The morning after I returned from Humana, emboldened by my success, I grabbed my keys off the kitchen table and headed back there to write. I unlocked the door, looked inside, muttered to myself "huh" — or something equally idiotic — closed the door and returned to the house. My wife sat in the kitchen working at her computer. She spotted me swaying in the threshold. She must have noticed the dead, faraway look in my eye — she asked, "Carlos, what's wrong." My response: "It's raining in there."

While in Louisville, the hot water heater failed, turning my office into a 400 square foot sauna/terrarium — how long it had been that way, God knows. Long enough for the drywall to warp and buckle. Long enough for a steady rain to drip from every surface. Long enough for a rainforest-like haze to permeate the air. Long enough for horror movie-sized chunks of mold to feed on the futon, the vintage wooden sewing table I used as a desk, the bookshelves. Long enough for boxes and file cabinets filled with drafts of plays, notebooks, files, newspaper clippings I collected and rejection letters I saved, to sweat their ink rendering them illegible. Long enough for entire continents to peel off the globe my wife gave me as a wedding present. Long enough for the accordion file containing every letter ever written to me to disintegrate in my hands when I tried to rescue it from the closet. Every shred of evidence of friendships, relationships, love affairs that shaped me in my twenties – in other words, my personal history – the museum of my life on Earth up to that point – disappeared forever as if my life never happened.

Water doesn't discriminate. It decimated the 2000-plus volumes in my library. Every book – the ones I acquired legitimately, ones I stole, the ones I inherited or were given to me as gifts – lost their angular shape, thickened, bulged. Bindings peeled. Mold spores devoured words. The handful of rare and very pricey volumes (a beautiful, mint English-language first edition of Le Corbusier's 1923 *Towards a New Architecture* that I stole from a previous employer comes to mind) reduced to worthlessness. The external manifestation of my pursuit of knowledge, bloated like the victim of a drowning.

I wrote before about one's accumulated things being a personal museum – a form of psychic DNA. The utter destruction of all the material objects that mattered to me split the double helix of my identity, leaving each strand to blow aimlessly in the wind. If a stranger wanted to visit my museum, they would be chagrined to discover that my life pre-2007 ceased to exist anywhere except inside my deeply flawed memory. If a stranger visited my museum, they would think I came into existence at the age of 36.

A firm that deals with catastrophic fire and water damage gutted the space, tossing my collection of artifacts in a pile on the parking platform behind the house. The pile looked like the ruins left behind by a devastating Midwest twister. My things. A pile. Destined for a landfill somewhere. Waiting for the insurance adjustor to assess it, and assign a dollar amount to an incalculable personal loss.

When I could muster up the courage to bear it, I would sneak to the parking podium out back hoping I could salvage something. One day digging through the wreckage, I broke into tears when I came upon a cheap paperback copy of Edward Albee's *Zoo Story*, given to me by a former lover from many years before. The inscription she'd written on the title page had been smudged into near illegibility: the only words that survived – "You," "I," "inspired." Shaking off this flood of emotion, my eyes landed on the manila envelope with Javier C.'s ill-fated New Dramatists application. Beneath the decimated cheap paperback copy of *Zoo Story*, this resilient little artifact somehow survived. The layers of packing tape waterproofed the contents.

A PHONE CALL DELIVERS GOOD NEWS

In a narrative symmetry usually reserved for novels, plays and films, and almost never the stuff of actual life, two months after the deluge Emily Morse, the Director of Artistic Development at New Dramatists, telephoned me. I'd known Emily for a long time — early in the roaring 90s, we both interned at the legendary but sadly defunct Circle Repertory Company. She also had a hand in the production of my very first play *Subterraneans* in 1994, at Todo Con Nada, a tiny, resource-free but seminal performance space on Ludlow Street, where she served as Associate Artistic Director. Emily was calling with good news: I had been accepted, after five failed attempts, as a New Dramatists resident playwright, with a graduating date of June 2014. Unlike Javier C., I know my applications never got lost, because until that moment the rejection letter arrived like clockwork every May.

Seven years in residence at the finest playwright development organization in the United States seemed ideal. Seven years to dream up new worlds, to bask in the brilliance of my fellow residents, seven years to build on my body of work and take it to a whole new level, seven years of having what so many artists in the field lack — a place to call home. My elation lasted 48 hours. All emotions, like coins, have two faces. If elation was "heads" then dread, fear of failure, and self-loathing lived on the flipside. On that side of the coin, seven years seemed like a mountain of time waiting to be squandered.

I had no question where this dread was coming from.

I was wounded — not that anyone looking at me would know it. I went about life wearing a mask of calm that concealed grief — I lost nearly everything, but there had not been funeral rites to transition me from a life with my things to my life without them. (Only later did I come to understand the function and value of funerals when my mother passed away suddenly and unexpectedly in December of 2009.) I taught my playwriting courses at DePaul University, directed a play by a young student playwright named Ike Holter (on my birthday the cast thoughtfully gave me a box full of books to begin rebuilding my collection), played with my kids, took meetings, ate two and a half meals a day. Inside, though, I lived with a persistent, drone-like ache that wouldn't go away. I had no words. I was in mourning. I'd try to ridicule my empty materialism – it was all just stuff, after all. Compared to the day-to-day catastrophes in the world, my loss amounted to nothing. But looking at it that way that didn't help. All that "stuff" was my history, my *identity*. If my museum was obliterated, who was I anymore – as a think-er, a writer, as a male human in his thirties wandering the earth searching for scraps of meaning? In some ways it felt as if I'd survived an irreversible brain injury. I was alive, I could function, but some fundamental capacity had been wrenched from my grasp. Part of me was dead – robbed of the things that expressed my being, my history existed only as memories in my head. But memory decays, perpetually rewrites itself, invents out of whole cloth entire episodes of life that never actually happened. My history might as well have been a figment of my imagination.

A lot of my writing was destroyed. In those days I wrote mostly by hand. I had electronic copies of the completed versions of my plays (that they survived encoded in 1s and 0s provided little comfort – if solid things can perish so easily, surely flimsy 1s and 0s offer no safety) – but the notebooks, drafts, scribbles on napkins (all of which I hoarded) – all the work that went into the finished plays gone, gone, gone. And being gone, morbid questions about the worth of dreaming up fictions for the stage haunted me and nearly paralyzed me. Was Emily Morse's good news really good news, then? Would the gift of seven years help resurrect what I had lost? Would I reconnect with my lost sense of purpose? Or would it presage more destruction?

Turning my eyes away from the abyss, I carved out a week in July for a self-imposed writing retreat at New Dramatists. I reserved a room in 7th Heaven (one of the great amenities of the organization: the building has three modest rooms up on the third floor where out of town resident writers can stay free of charge). In the face of all the uncer-tainty and anxiety I was feeling, I hoped being there for a spell would help me overcome my grief and point me in a direction of renewal.

I can't explain what compelled me, but on the eve of my trip to New York as I fin-ished packing, I grabbed the envelope containing Javier C.'s ill-fated New Dramatists application and stuffed it in my suitcase.

I spent my first three days in the Church avoiding the task at hand. The writing went nowhere. Everything I set down rang hollow, false. Instead of facing the blank page, I squandered hour after hour chain-smoking on the stoop of New Dramatists. Late night on the second day I tried the last number I had of an ex-girlfriend, expecting that it would be long disconnected. To my surprise, she answered. I apologized for breaking up with her by phone on Christmas Eve in 1997. She accepted my apology, then told me to fuck off and hung up.

At dusk on the third day, butt firmly planted on New Dramatists' stoop, my eyes landed on an elderly man on the sidewalk across the street. He must have been in his 80s. Rail thin, his plaid shirt and khaki pants hung off him like his body was a coat hanger. His shoulders were so hunched it appeared as if his head was a cancer growing from his sternum. He moved at a sloth's pace, heading west – a creature moving in slow motion trapped in a world where everything else moved at warp speed. At the pace he moved, it would take him half an hour to reach Tenth Avenue. I imagined his arrival to his run down tenement and his slow, pained assault of the five-flight Mount Everest separating him from the safety of his apartment. Who was this man? Did he have family? Friends? Did he have anyone to look after him? (I suspected, because of his advanced age, most of the dramatis personae in his life either were dead or near death.) What had he done with the time he'd been given? What would he do with the little time he had left? Had he chased after some vision for his life, only to realize too late that he painted himself into a corner chasing pipe dreams? If he died in the night, how long would it take for someone to notice? And what in God's name was he doing still living in a crappy neighborhood in an unforgiving city that reserves its most cruel indifference for its oldest, weakest and least productive citizens? What did *his* museum look like? Would any of it survive him? Would I become him some day?

He haunted me for the rest of the day.

Late that night, after several frustrating hours trying to write, I packed it in for the night. I headed up to my room in 7th Heaven. As I prepared for bed, the strange manila envelope on the desk caught my eye. I'd only ever given the most cursory glance at its contents – when I did, it filled me with dread – so I can't say for certain what compelled me to open it and dig inside. I spent the rest of the night in the library looking through all the materials and reading the plays, exceptional works which were written in the vein of "Bipolar Realism" (Javier C.'s description). What happened to this guy? Why had his work been ignored? The application materials revealed a brilliant mind offset by a healthy dose of insanity lurking in the shadows, waiting to pounce. Was he still writing? Does he still live at the return address on the envelope (just five blocks from New Dramatists)? Does he live in New York City anymore? What did his museum look like? Was this envelope his museum? If so, what kind of life could I infer from it? I felt a door open inside me.

At dawn, I strolled up to 49th Street to the building where Javier lived. His name was not on the buzzer panel. Listed next to apartment 4C, a woman's name. I buzzed on the off chance he might still live there. A woman's groggy, bothered, Puerto Rican accented voice answered. I asked if Javier was around. No one here by that name, followed by a shower of curses for waking her up.

Google searches for Javier and his plays proved that even in this day and age there exist those few that leave no footprints behind. I visited the website Doollee.com, a free online guide to modern English-language playwrights from 1956 to the present. Javier C.'s name does not appear among the 47,000+ playwrights. His plays are absent from the 160,000+ works accounted for. I called Morgan Jenness, my mentor from my days working in the literary office of The Public Theater in the 90s. She's a living encyclopedia on everything to do with contemporary plays and playwrights. Morgan knew nothing of Javier or his work.

Curiosity devolved to obsession. I needed to know who this man was, if more of his work existed somewhere, if I could find him, if I could rescue these works from obscurity. For the next seven years – the full duration of my residency at New Dramatists – incapable of writing anything of my own, I set aside my theatrical ambitions and explorations in order to excavate everything I could about Javier's life, his work and the loss he suffered, and to build, in the pages of this book, a small museum to document it.

Every museum needs a curator – who is either blessed or cursed by the task of or-ganizing a museum's contents into an assemblage that conveys something resembling meaning. Whether it is a blessing or curse depends in some measure on the comprehen-siveness and quality of the material left behind for the curator to assemble. I've visited world-class museums that seek to convince us that its version of history's grand sweep is correct because they possess the goods to prove it. I've also visited many small town museums in the most out of the way places, built on artifacts acquired at estate sales, replicas and forgeries – their narratives sag like skin hanging from a skeleton missing most of its bones, their placards obfuscate, riddled as they are with questionable facts, discrepancies and misspellings, and their message speaks less about the grand sweep of history, but more to a cry for help, a shout against a gale force headwind to a world that doesn't care: "We existed!"

Javier himself, in *A Thick Description of Harry Smith*, his final viable work, addresses this dilemma through the character of the Curator, a woman driven to the brink of madness and despair trying to make heads or tails of the seemingly random artifacts left behind by the very real Harry Everett Smith. The artifacts in and of themselves may or may not mean something. That they exist together in boxes suggests a web of relationships waiting to be deciphered. Often in the process of digging up Javier's bones and attempting to reanimate them, I've looked to her struggle for guidance, inspiration and plain old commiseration.

As curator of the small museum that exists within these pages, I relied on the scant-est of materials to lay its foundation: a battered envelope with three half written plays, a manifesto both literally and figuratively illegible; a series of maddening, and in the end, frightening interactions with one Professor Emiliano Kurtz, whose book, *The Mystique of*

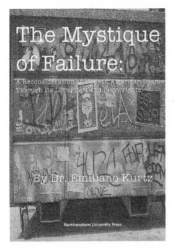

Failure: Reconsidering Modern American Drama Through its Lost Playwrights and Plays, contains a chapter on Javier based on dubious research; and a handful of other clues that led me to dead end to discovery to dead end. A curator faced with such insurmountable obstacles has two choices: 1) give up, or 2) play archaeologist and infer a civilization from the pottery shards and bones you've dug up. During my seven years at New Dramatists, I built the museum contained in these pages. The thought of giving up was not infrequent. In the end, however, the shards Javier left behind were too important to me to leave buried in the dirt. The picture still remains woefully incomplete. Perhaps, however, the existence of this small museum will spur readers to pick up where I leave off to embark on a more thorough excavation.

Chicago, January 2015

7   Transom window above the entrance of New Dramatists. Photo by Carlos Murillo.

8   Exterior of Rudy's Bar & Grill on 9th Avenue between 44th & 45th Streets. Photo by Carlos Murillo.

    Basement of New Dramatists, scene of the discovery of Javier C.'s lost New Dramatists application. Photo by Carlos Murillo.

9   Low-quality reproduction of forged Edward Albee signature. Photo by Carlos Murillo.

    Bronze statue of Giordano Bruno (1548-1600) by Ettore Ferrari at Campo de'Fiori, Rome. Bruno was an Italian Dominican friar, philosopher, mathematician, poet and atrologer who was tried for theological heresy and burnt at the stake in 1600. Photo in public domain.

10 The Fortune. Photo by Carlos Murillo.

11 Todd London, New Dramatists' Artistic Director from 1996-2014. Courtesy Todd London. Photo by Susan Johann.

13 Row houses on Prospect Avenue in Prospect Heights, Brooklyn. Photo in public domain.

16 Exterior of my home in the Bridgeport neighborhood in Chicago. Photo by Carlos Murillo.

    The guest house that doubles as my writing space in the rear of the property. Photo by Carlos Murillo.

17 Insurance company photos of gutted office space. Photo by Carlos Murillo.

18 Exterior of 167 Ludlow Street, former site of Todo Con Nada, a legendary basement performance space that was evicted to make way for The Dark Room Bar. Photo by Michael Minn.

    Entrance to The Dark Room Bar, which occupies the former site of Todo Con Nada. Photo by Michael Minn.

21 Exterior of the apartment building where Javier C. lived on West 49th Street between 9th and 10th Avenues. Photo by Carlos Murillo.

The buzzer outside the building where Javier C. lived, according to the return address on the envelope. Photo by Carlos Murillo.

22 Birgit Huppuch as The Curator in A Thick Description of Harry Smith presented by P73 at The Culture Project in June 2012. Photo by Carlos Murillo.

23 Cover image of Emiliano Kurtz's 2007 book. Photo by Carlos Murillo.

DIAGRAM OF A PAPER AIRPLANE

INTRODUCTION

Kip Fagan, Freelance Director

Carlos Murillo likes to drive people insane.

It's sometimes intentional, sometimes un-, but he derives great pleasure from it either way. In polite company he'll profess the opposite, but his mad cackle as someone's eyes spiral inward when confronted with a particularly vertigo-inducing plot revelation gives him away. He wants you to live in the insanity that his characters live in. He wants you to feel as unsteady, as unstable, as unsure of what's real and what's bullshit as the recurring cast of his nightmare-logic trilogy are forced to feel. I think he feels bad that he makes his characters feel so insane, so he wants you to keep them company.

The thing about this particular brand of Murillo insanity, though: *it's an immensely pleasurable place to live.*

Carlos' plays trap you in their logic and don't let go, in the way that Martin Scorsese's *After Hours* traps you, or a Roberto Bolaño novel, or the first season of *Twin Peaks*. And once you're trapped, you become a co-conspirator with his characters in trying to solve their existential mysteries, finish their Sisyphean collaborations, reconcile their irreconcilable feuds. And once you're trapped inside this trilogy, you'll probably start to feel a mixture of resentful admiration, fond exasperation, and hopeless love for its central character: the elusive and obscure playwright Javier C.

But at first you'll be on the outside looking in.

Diagram of a Paper Airplane is the first play in the trilogy, though in true Carlos fashion, it's the last sequence of events in a strict chronological sense. He starts at the end, with the fallout and the ruins. The play begins with a man named Alvaro talking to an unseen academic interlocutor about Javier C.'s unfinished *magnum opus*:

> You askin me
> if it survived? If it
> still exists somewhere out in the big bad world?
> *Shit.*

Maybe the question you *should* be askin,

Mistah P. Aitch.D Candidate, Columbia University: Did *Diagram of a Paper Airplane* exist at *all?*

And so the play named after an imaginary, unfinished play begins by questioning the existence of the imaginary, unfinished play in question. This opening announces that the world isn't solid under our feet. And as we meet the other collaborators and fellow-travelers — Herman, sputtering paranoically into a recording device, and Valerie, the den mother full of compassion one second and volatility the next — we begin to piece together the group's splintered past, and present.

The past: a combustible, anarchic ensemble of theatre artists idealistically committed to the irascible, unpredictable maybe-genius at its center. Javier C. and his notion of a new and dangerous theatre of "bipolar realism." Alcohol-fueled fights, polemical screaming-matches, bursts of bewildering inspiration. And, finally, a disappearance so shattering it splinters the group irretrievably.

The present: a reunion of sorts on the occasion of Javier C.'s death. A cosmic practical joke where the dead author assembles his former compatriots, now wrecked and haunted, to read his lost play. And a damaged young woman who begins to learn the truth behind the wreck and the haunt.

Formally and structurally, *Diagram of a Paper Airplane* (Carlos' version, not Javier's) hews closer to traditional play-making than the freewheeling *Your Name Will Follow You Home* or the mad, rambling medicine show *A Thick Description of Harry Smith*. This allows Carlos to sink deep emotional talons into a reader or viewer. We are compelled to mythologize the absent Javier and the (brilliant? crackpot?) work the group created together. This mythology both deepens and breaks apart in the dizzying meta-narratives of the other two pieces, so *Diagram* is crucial as a lodestar for the trilogy. It's as *firma* as Carlos' *terra* gets.

If some mad and inspired theatre company were to ask me how to most ideally produce the trilogy, the only true answer is an insane one. Though the plays function brilliantly as individual entities, to really grasp the ferocious imaginative reach of the trilogy one would have to experience a same-day marathon of all three plays, starting with *Diagram*, followed by *Harry Smith*, and concluding with *Your Name*. And after the nine or so hours of living with this crazed assemblage, the audience would be fed a strong cocktail and told to get comfy, because the actors were demanding to perform *Diagram of a Paper Airplane* again.

I can already hear Carlos' cackle from behind the risers as the shell-shocked audience settles back into their seats and the actor playing Alvaro meanders on stage to ask:

You askin me

if it survived? If it

still exists somewhere out in the big bad world?

Shit.

Maybe the question you *should* be askin, Mistah P.Aitch.D Candidate, Columbia University: Did *Diagram of a Paper Airplane* exist at *all?*

Norfolk, Nebraska 2014

NOTES ON IMAGES, BY PAGE

27 This image is in the public domain in the United States because it is a work prepared
by an officer or employee of the United States Government as part of that person's
official duties under the terms of Title 17, Chapter 1, Section 105 of the US Code.
See Copyright.

28 Kip Fagan during a music rehearsal for a workshop of The Javier Plays at New Dramatists in March 2014. Pictured left to right: Lucas Papaelias, Kate Ferber, Kip
Fagan and Joe Jung. Hidden behind Joe Jung – Paul Whitty. Photo by Carlos Murillo.

DIAGRAM OF A PAPER AIRPLANE

Characters

(in order of appearance)

Alvaro	49
Herman	53
Valerie	50
Lila	28
Mario	29

A minor character, the FedEx Man, is played by the same actor that plays Mario.

Setting

Various kitchens in tenement apartments in NYC. Hells Kitchen, Lower East Side, Washington Heights.

1. The Lonesome Death of Javier C.

ONE

Morning. The kitchen table in Alvaro's tenement apartment in Washington Heights. On the table, an unopened pack of Kools, an empty ashtray, a microphone, a digital recording device. Alvaro talks to an unseen interviewer.

ALVARO: You askin me
>if it survived? If it
>still exists somewhere out in the big bad world?

>*Shit.*

>Maybe the question you *should* be askin,
>Mistah P. Aitch.D Candidate, Columbia University:
>Did *Diagram of a Paper Airplane* exist at *all*?

TWO

The wee hours. The kitchen table in Herman's Hell's Kitchen tenement apartment. On the table: an old telephone — the kind with a dial and obsolete ring, and a portable cassette recorder, also obsolete. Herman in his pajamas presses the record button.

HERMAN: Valerie *P.*

telephoned at 2:35 this morning.

My telephone hardly rings anymore —
People stopped calling long ago.
To most people,
A telephone call that time of night —
How *intrusive*. How *thoughtless*. How *rude*.
But not me, no.
I sleep very little these days.
For all practical purposes
2:35 in the morning is quarter past noon is six forty five pm is three minutes to midnight.

What *did* arouse my curiosity vis-a-vis the phone call
Was the fact that Valerie P. bothered to make it.
You see:
Two and a half decades have passed since Valerie P., Javier C. and I
Played at being *pioneers*. Co-*colonists*
Inhabiting a tiny but shared slice of
Terra Incognita.
In other words:
We stopped being friends.
A long.
Time.
Ago.
Furthermore
When we were friends,
If Valerie P. and I ever *did* speak *telephonically*,
It was because *my* digits reached for hers.

Yes,

Valerie P. telephoned at 2:35 this morning

To inform me that

Javier C.

Her estranged husband

(and father to their mutually estranged daughter

Lila

Hhhhhhhh

Lila

Herman clicks off the recorder, gathers himself, clicks it back on.

Valerie P. telephoned at 2:35

To inform me that Javier C.

Her estranged husband

(father to their mutually estranged daughter

Lila C. dash P.)

"Left the building" as it were.

This past Tuesday.

Javier C. *drowned.*

In a *freak.*

Flash.

Flood.

Somewhere in the wilds of Northern New Mexico,

Where *supposedly*

he was

immersed (forgive the pun)

in "*research*"

for a play he first

threatened to write

Two and a half decades ago

A play he *claimed* to have been *actually* writing

For the last seventeen years:

Diagram of a Paper Airplane.

Long awaited follow up to his *oeuvre* of lost plays:
The *seminal Death of a Liberal*, the genuinely *spooky*
The Rich Also Cry, the complete *mind* fuck,
A Thick Description of Harry Smith,
And his unpublished, book-length manifesto
To Murder Whimsy:
Bipolar Realism and the Future of American Playwriting.
Works for the theatre noteworthy for their undeserved
obscurity.
Works which have not been performed in
many, many years.
When they *were* performed,
they appeared in venues only the most generous would call *theatres*.

Yes,
once upon a time
We pursued the quixotic endeavor of putting on *plays*.
Which I expect surprises you:
That before I became an historian,
Before I built my formidable reputation,
And *long* before said reputation endured a gang rape by a cabal of
Certain powerful, well-connected individuals,
I.
Did.
Theatre.
I was the *dramaturge*.
(If you have no idea what that means, *Google* it.)
Yes, once upon a time, Javier dreamed we could "resurrect a dying animal."
We believed in him. He was *that. good*.
But like so many dreams,
Ours was rudely interrupted by certain crimes of omission.

Anyway. Hearing the news from Valerie P., the tips of my fingers went cold.
Montage of images exploded in my brain: Moonless night. Arctic Circle.

Japanese fishing boat torn in half by an iceberg.

Japanese fishermen slaughtering each other over pieces of flotsam

While their flag burned against the night sky.

A small child sinking under the surface of the sea.

Haunted, Herman clicks off the recorder. The haunt passes. He resumes recording.

Valerie P. had more on her *agenda*:

Following her account

of the freakish circumstances surrounding Javier C.'s *death,*

She proceeded to ask me a *favor.*

Would I telephone *Alvaro M.*, tell *him* the news.

Alvaro M., American playwright (of *Latin* American descent)

Fellow traveler-slash-casualty of our colonial exploits of yore.

I told her under no circumstances would I do such a thing.

I told her: "For all I know Alvaro M. could be dead too,

Besides: I don't have his telephone number."

"*Liar,*" she said. "Liar, liar, *liar.*

Don't think I've forgotten Herman, about your *habits.*"

"Habits?"

"The date books, the recordings, the index card files, the *lists,* the *address books* — "

I tried to reason with her:

"Valerie, Val Valie The likelihood Alvaro M. hasn't *moved*

In the mountain of time that's passed between — "

"Where are you sitting, Herman?"

"In my kitchen."

"You made a meal for me in that kitchen once upon a time."

"Point. being?"

"The kitchen I'm sitting in is the same one you wept in ten days straight when Maria

R. left you. Once upon a —"

"*Point. being.*"

"You haven't moved. I haven't moved. In that *'mountain of time'*

So there's every reason to believe Alvaro *M.* is festering away in his kitchen too."

Pause.

Then Valerie *reeeaaalllly* crossed the line:

"Besides … It's what *Javi* would have *wanted*."

Javi.

Which was *cheap*.

For her to play the "what-the-dead-guy-would-have-wanted" card.

I told her as much, I said:

"Valerie that is just plain cheap I would have expected more from you."

Valerie appears in her own kitchen talking on a cordless telephone.

VALERIE: You don't really know me anymore, do you … Herman?

The sound of a telephone click. Valerie disappears.

HERMAN: That fucking passive aggressive

Herman hits the record button on his tape recorder. Herman clicks off the recorder.

HERMAN: So yes, I dug out

The *address book*.

Dialed Alvaro M.'s telephone number.

THREE

The wee hours. A young couple asleep on a beat up fold out couch in a tenement apartment in Greenpoint, Brooklyn. The young man snores. The woman stirs and mutters in her sleep. An alarm clock on the side table reads 2:34 am.

YOUNG WOMAN: No.

> Please.
>
> Go away.
>
> I don't want you here.
>
> I won't listen.
>
> I won't go
>
> I won't —

When the time on the clock changes to 2:35 am, the young woman darts upright. She looks at the young man next to her. She rises from the bed as if under a spell.

FOUR

The wee hours. Valerie's kitchen in her Lower East Side apartment. On the table a large magnifying glass on a stand, a cloth with strands of human hair on it, tweezers, scalpels and other surgically precise instruments. A half-eaten bowl of Cheerios. In front of the magnifying glass a metal stand on top of which is an object barely visible to the naked eye. Valerie's face appears huge, distorted by the lens. She works on the minuscule object with her instruments while talking on a cordless phone.

VALERIE: Yes, *that* Herman.

    Come on, Josephine, how many Hermans are there?

    Herman The Human Sledgehammer.

    Herman The Human Sandpaper Machine.

    Herman The Human Box Cutter.

    Yes, if you want to resort to vulgarities, he's that too.

    But you know something?

    Truth be told Herman's one thing to me he isn't to anyone else.

    He's sweet.

    No no no no no no no … listen:

    He calls.

    Couple of hours ago.

    Right, who calls that time of night?

    He calls to tell me he "heard." About Javier.

    Wanted to

    "check in"

    See how I was taking the news.

    If I "needed" anything –

    Right? Talking as if I was still married to that prick, as if there was some sort of feeling some sort of I don't know what

    Anyway

    After assuring him I'm "okay," I don't "need" anything

    – that I'm *relieved* –

    (No of course I didn't say that can you imagine?) –

There's this silence

Followed by that Herman sigh ...

Herman appears in his kitchen, recorder off, staring at nothing.

HERMAN: Hhhhhhhhhh

Herman disappears.

VALERIE: That's right *THE* Herman sigh

That says "I've got a lot more on my *mi-ind*, get ready for the *on-slaaaaught.*"

You know me

I took the bait.

Herman's a Human Sledgehammer, I'm a Human *Fish*.

Always spellbound by the worm on its hook,

Always subject to a bunch of idiotic fishermen celebrating their catch.

And when the fisherman (or woman – you know that story) sees I'm not fat enough?

They toss me in the sea to sink beneath a trail of my own blood.

No I'm not self-dramatizing, Josi. It's true. But I recover, I recover, cause that's who I am that's what you *do* that's what you're supposed to *do*.

Anyway, he sighed. That Herman sigh.

Herman appears in his kitchen, recorder off, staring at nothing.

HERMAN: Hhhhhhhhhh

Herman disappears.

VALERIE: I said, "Herman? You okay?"

He said: "Were you intending to keep me in the dark?"

"You found out on your own, you didn't need me to break the news."

You know what he said?

"That's just *mean*.

Valerie."

Followed by a tirade,

Catalogue of wrongs *I'd* done *him*.

All that concern, am I okay, do I need anything

Next minute –

Know what he called me?

A passive aggressive, self-involved, dried up *orifice*.

Oh, I told him
"Eat me, Herman, I'm hanging up!"
"No no no no no no
Please. Valerie Val Vali I'm
Sorry I"
That's right one second shock and awe, next he's raining sweetness on me.

No, he *is* sweet –
That's my point –
In fact, he can be downright maudlin –

Herman on the telephone. The earpiece has a suction cup wire tap attached.

HERMAN: Valerie?

VALERIE: Yes, Herman?

HERMAN: Do you think?
Javier's in heaven or in hell?

The sound of Valerie choking on cereal.

HERMAN: Valerie?
Are you okay?
Wait: Are you *eating*?

Herman disappears. Valerie's phone conversation with Josephine continues.

VALERIE: Yes, Josephine, I fixed myself a bowl of cereal when he called
I'd been working, it was late I have deadlines I was hungry phone calls with Herman
can become

Epic

Hearing *Herman* ask that:
Do I think Javier is in heaven or hell?
I choked on my Cheerios, okay?
Heaven? Hell? Javier? *Herman?* What the *fuck?*
But sweet, right? In that awkward? Wooden? Herman-like way?

No, I didn't answer I did that thing *teachers* do?

What do they call it? Made it a "teachable moment"?

You know, when some little fucker of a student asks a question you don't know the answer to? Throw the question right back.

Herman and Valerie back on the phone.

VALERIE: What do *you* think, Herman? Do *you* think Javier's gone to heaven or hell?

HERMAN: *Hhhhhhhh …*

Herman disappears. Valerie back to conversation with Josephine.

VALERIE: Yeah. He answered.

Although …

I have no idea what he said.

Soon as he started yammering

my mind wandered off, Josi

like I was

walking down a hallway with three million doors.

Each with a different question written on it:

Is he in heaven?

Is he in hell?

Or somewhere between?

What was he doing in New Mexico, was he still —

Nothing.

Nothing, Josephine.

Looking. I was going to say "looking," "was he still looking," *okay?*

I'm sorry I didn't mean to it's just …

Wait: are you seriously asking me that?

Let me put it this way, Josephine:

Long time ago?

Javier wrote a fragment of some play he never finished

something about

paper airplanes

It was about visiting purgatory. After his death.

All I can tell you, sweetie? if he landed in some kind of purgatory?

God help him if it was like the one he imagined.

Herman appears again.

HERMAN: What are they going to do with his body?

VALERIE: What do you mean?

HERMAN: The body.

Javier's body?

What are they going to do with it?

VALERIE: "They." What are "they" going to do // with his

HERMAN: That's what I am ask//ing

VALERIE: What are you implying?

HERMAN: Nothing?

VALERIE: Because what I hear lurking underneath that "*they,*" Herman, is "*you*"

HERMAN: I mean to imply no // such

VALERIE: That's always the substitute "*they,*" right? Meaning "*You.*"

"What are *you,* Valerie, going to do with the body?" What about "*we*" Herman? No, of course, that would be too *painful,* would mean having to *dig,* right?

HERMAN: I'm just asking // a

VALERIE: My god you really are a motherfucker. You think I'm still tethered to him. You think I *owe* him something. "*What are they going to do with // his body?*"

HERMAN: I was simply asking a // question …

VALERIE: I don't know what *they* are going to — For all I know he has another family to take care // of

HERMAN: Unlikely

VALERIE: I've got to // go

HERMAN: Look, Valerie … Val … Valie …

All I am saying is
I know any obligation you had to him
ended
When
It *ended*
But at the same time certain bonds

VALERIE: God you're an ass//hole

HERMAN: *Certain bonds*
    Do transcend failed marriages.

VALERIE: Good bye Her//man

HERMAN: Wait: does Alvaro know?

VALERIE: Christ, how the hell would I // know if Alv

HERMAN: Don't you think Alvaro
    Of all people
    Should know?

VALERIE: Herman …

HERMAN: Shouldn't someone call him?

VALERIE: "Someone." First "they," now "someone"
    For all we know, Alvaro could be dead too.

HERMAN: True,
    But if you were him … And you were alive
    Would you want to be kept in the dark?

VALERIE: Um. Yeah.

HERMAN: Someone has to call him. It's the *humane* thing to // do.

VALERIE: You're like a dog with a bone.
    Go ahead. Call him.
    But don't say I didn't warn you.
    Last time I saw Alvaro he was

    Sick.

HERMAN: All the more reason someone should call him, don't you think?

VALERIE: Frankly, I could give a shit.

HERMAN: Wow. Valerie. I would have expected more from you.

VALERIE: You don't really know me anymore, do you … Herman?

HERMAN: I'm calling him.

VALERIE: That tone worries me, Herman.

HERMAN: What tone?

VALERIE: I hear morbid glee in your voice.

HERMAN: What kind of person do you think I am?

VALERIE: I think …
>
> For the most part? You,
> Herman, are a decent human being.
> But I know Herman well enough to know
> He can be a twelve-year-old boy.
> That's captured a little frog in a jar.
> Dying to know what kind of
> *Stresses*
> Its little body can take.

HERMAN: Are you comparing Alvaro to a helpless animal?

VALERIE: Oh, // god.

HERMAN: Because I wonder how Alvaro would // feel

VALERIE: One thing I know about Alvaro? He's more civilized than some savages I know.

HERMAN: I'm calling him.

VALERIE: Go ahead.

HERMAN: Valerie … one more question, I'll leave you alone …
>
> What about Lila?
> Does Lila know?
> Or do you plan on keeping your daughter in the dark about this one too?

VALERIE: Good bye Herman.

Herman disappears. Valerie continues her conversation with Josephine.

VALERIE: And that was that, Josi.

What?

Lila?

Of course she knows. Josephine: what kind of person do you think I am?

FIVE

The apartment in Brooklyn. The clock reads 3:17 am. The young man still deep in sleep. The young woman, fully clothed, watches the sleeping man. She leans down, touches his chest, caresses his face and kisses him. She takes her cell phone from the side table and slips it into her bag. She leaves.

SIX

Herman's kitchen. He talks into the recorder.

HERMAN: So yes, I dug out

> The *address book*
>
> Dialed Alvaro M.'s telephone number.

Herman attaches a suction cup wire tap to his receiver, plugs it into his recorder, presses record and dials. Alvaro answers the phone in his kitchen.

ALVARO: Ahhhl-*Oh*.

HERMAN: I hear a voice I'll be damned

> It's *Alvaro M.'s* voice
>
> Sounds older –
>
> Little less …
>
> *Alive*
>
> Than I remember …
>
> But then: we're all a little less alive every day, aren't we?

> Alvaro? Is that you?

ALVARO: Who's calling?

HERMAN: Herman.

ALVARO: Herman // *Fin—*

HERMAN: Yes.

ALVARO: Shit.

HERMAN: It's

> good to hear your voice.

ALVARO: Wish I could say the same.

HERMAN: Soooo … are you well? How's the … scribbling?

ALVARO: Scuse me?

HERMAN: The writing. How's // the … ?

ALVARO: I was just pullin my next Play out my ass when you called.

> Hey, didn't I read something bout you? Like what?
>
> Nine? Ten years ago?
>
> In *The Post? Weekly World News? National Enquirer?*

HERMAN: Alvaro …

ALVARO: No no no that's right,

> *New York Times.*
>
> What they call it? The *pay-puh* uh record?

HERMAN: Alvaro …

ALVARO: Didn't they sack you from some fancy pruh-fessuh-ship cause // like

HERMAN: For heaven's sake // Alvaro

ALVARO: Didn't they sack you cause

> You became like a
>
> Holocaust denier or some // shit like that?

HERMAN: Oh. Please. Alvaro // that's just

ALVARO: I read that I was like "Man,

> Always knew Aitch was one fucked up individual // but … "

HERMAN: Alvaro …

ALVARO: Cause I didn't know PhD meant Pruh-fessuh, Holocaust Denial

HERMAN: *Stop it.*

ALVARO: Least you got a nice settlement out of it – always wondered how many dollar
bills are in an "undisclosed sum a // money"

HERMAN: *Alvaro* …

ALVARO: *That's* living the American Dream, right? – wish somebody'd pay me an undisclosed sum a money // to go away

HERMAN: *ENOUGH.*

ALVARO: Why you dialing my number after all these years?

> You getting nostalgic cause you about to die or something?

You thinking: "While I'm countin the days I got left on this piece a shit planet
Why not make some phone calls? Right some a my wrongs in case there *is*
a Man // Upstairs?"

HERMAN: Hhhhhhhhhh//hhh

ALVARO: *Big* sigh. *Heavy* sigh. I remember that sigh, Aitch,
   An I distinctly remember never liking what came out your mouth *after* // that sigh.

HERMAN: Alvaro. Look: I didn't want to call.
   I'm calling because
   I just received a telephone call — out of the blue — from Valerie.

ALVARO: Name don't ring a bell.

HERMAN: Valerie // you know who

ALVARO: I might a known a *Mallory* once, but a // Valerie?

HERMAN: *Valerie*. Javier's // ex —

ALVARO: Cut to the chase, Aitch.

HERMAN: Hhhhhhh//hhh

ALVARO: For motherfucking // sake stop it with that *sighing*

HERMAN: Okay okay okay.

   Are you sitting down?

ALVARO: No I'm riding the final stage a the Tour de France, Aitch.
   Out with it.

HERMAN: Valerie called
   To tell me that Javier
   Passed
   on Tuesday.

ALVARO: *"Passed."*

HERMAN: That's correct.

ALVARO: What'd he pass? Kidney stone? The ketchup?
   More a them warped motherfuckin genes a his — now *that* would be a // tragedy.

HERMAN: Alvaro …

ALVARO: Cause what's the saying? First time a mistake? Second time bad luck? Third time—

HERMAN: Alvaro!

ALVARO: *Ohhhhh* … you mean he *died*. Why didn't you just come out an say // that?

HERMAN: *Hhhhhhhhhh//hh*

ALVARO: That sigh, man, that *fucking* sigh —
Wait: are you recording this?

HERMAN: No of course not.
Look, Alvaro, I know how you must // feel

Shift. Alvaro's kitchen. Early afternoon. Alvaro recounts the phone call to the unseen interviewer.
Alvaro smokes.

ALVARO: An I'm like …
That why you calling me? Tell me *that?*
An he's like

HERMAN: I thought you of all people Would want to know	ALVARO: "I thought you of all people would want to know."

ALVARO: In that motherfucking patronizing voice a his.
I'm like: "Thankyouverymuch for ruining my day."
An he's like …

HERMAN: Tragic isn't it	ALVARO: "Horrible, isn't it?"

ALVARO: I'm like …
Sorry.
That's just not something that registers on my horror-meet-uh
I'm glad that motherfucker is dead.

HERMAN: If you're so glad he's gone

ALVARO: He said "*gone.*" Not "*dead.*" // What an asshole

HERMAN: If you're so glad he's gone
How is it I ruined your day?

ALVARO: By telling me that bitch was still alive til last week.

    Cause far as I'm concerned?

    Javier died a *looooong* time ago

    The *thought*

    He was still out there

    Slithering around somewhere

    That he still *existed* in the world

    Til Tuesday?

    That just fucks me up like you wouldn't believe.

HERMAN: His reaction was so

    Shocking

    I was dumbstruck I said something

    feeble like

    "Alvaro, I

    I'm dumbstruck I

    Didn't know you felt // that way."

ALVARO: Now you do, Mr. Herman F. Dumbstruck.

HERMAN: Look, I wouldn't have called if Valerie hadn't asked // me to …

ALVARO: What? Yoko Ono too delicate to dial the phone all by herself?

HERMAN: That's just …

ALVARO: Look Aitch:

    In like three seconds?

    You an your tape recorder gonna hear a click, // okay?

HERMAN: I'm not // rec

ALVARO: When you hear that click

    I want you

    An your tape recorder

    To understand in no uncertain terms what I mean:

    Bye Bye. Fuck off.

    Don't

Ever. call this number again.

Comprende, *compadre?*

One

Two ...

Three.

HERMAN: The line went dead.

Herman disappears. Alvaro talks to the unseen interviewer.

ALVARO: I used to smoke Kools.

I loved smoking.

Sometimes? I'd sit in my kitchen all day?

An just smoke.

But I quit cold turkey like a year ago.

Woke up one morning

Went in the kitchen do my first chore a the day

Which was like

smoke five Kools drink a pot a coffee stare out the window?

But that day I was like ...

"E-nuff. No more. I'm tired.

Gotta find me something else to look forward to than the next Kool."

Cause that's how bad shit had got – sit in my kitchen all day

Only time I left the apartment was to replenish my pack.

So I light up, thinking:

This is my last. Kool. *ever.*

I start thinking about all the Kools I ever smoked

I look at the Kool I'm smoking

"You're the last one, baby ... "

Kind a like breakin up with someone?

But trying to let em down gentle?

Like, "Aw, yeah, we had some good times, right?

Remember that time we went to Coney Island in like

December?

That time I got in a fight with my brother on Thanksgiving

I came over you made me potato salad?"

But inside you're thinking

"Taxi meter's runnin, Gotta split."

I *stubbed* that last Kool out.

Cause in the end you gotta be *hard*

You gotta be like

Japanese about it.

I pick up the pack,

Zippo, ashtray,

Go over to the kitchen window

Which has like a million dollar view uh the airshaft?

Pile a garbage at the bottom of it?

I'm like:

"Bye Kools. Nice knowing you.

Bye ashtray. Have a good life.

Bye Zippo. You be cool now."

I been clean since.

I keep myself honest.

Five minutes after I threw my paraphernalia down the airshaft?

Went down to the corner bought me one last pack.

Brought it back in my kitchen.

put it in the drawer where I keep the knives.

Temptation's three feet away in my knife drawer –

But I *don't* succumb

Willpower, baby. I am the master a my own twisted desires.

Sometimes?

When shit gets real bad?

I open that knife drawer

Take out that pack a Kools

Lay it on the table

Gentle

I look at it

Touch it

Sometimes —

I take one a the Kools out the pack

Smell it slip it in my mouth

Roll it round my lips

Got the Zippo in my hand

Thumb on the flint wheel all twitchy

like I'm Christopher Walken playin Russian Roulette

Then I'm like

HA! Motherfucker

You don't own me bitch.

Lonely, isn't it? All alone in the dark with the knives?

A year.

Then that bitch Herman calls?

To tell me Javier *"passed"*?

I hang up I'm like

Night a the Living Dead.

Zombie-beeline to the knife drawer.

Take out my Kools.

Light one up.

First Kool in a year

"Hi old friend. Nice to see you. I missed you, baby."

Five Kools later?

My head starts trippin out —

How'd Javi die?

Not like it matters — you die you die,

Don't matter if it's by heart attack or shark attack.

But how'd Javi die?

Was Javi sick?

Was Javi alone?

Did Javi do it to himself?

Did Javi have a place to live or was he in the streets?

Was someone gonna bury him? Or was Javi gonna end up in Potter's Field?
And why the fuck am I still calling him Javi?

His little girl … Lila … (though she must not be so little no more)
Does she know?
She even care?

An what the fuck did Javi mean by that?
"*Whimsical.*"
Last motherfucking thing he said to me before he split – "*whimsical.*"
What. the *fuck*. did he mean by that?

Bitch was like that. Always had at the tip a his tongue
The one word that could pull that thread
Unravel the whole muthafuckin sweater …
"*Whimsical*" …

Next thing I know? I reach for a Kool, pack is empty.
Year I been away from this shit.
That bitch Herman calls?
Two hours later whole pack is gone.

Now I got two questions for *you*, Mistuh Pee. Aitch. Dee Candidate, Columbia University …

One: How'd you find me?
An two:
Where the *fuck*
Did you find his plays?

SEVEN

The wee hours. The young woman by the front entrance of a Hell's Kitchen tenement. She is about to buzz an apartment, but instead reaches for her cell phone and dials.

YOUNG WOMAN: Hi, sweet one. It's me.
I
know you won't get this?
Not til ... Much later. But ...

I need you to know that
I love you.
That's the first thing the *important* thing ...
I didn't want to wake you I

I know you'll wonder –
How can I love you
When you'll wake up
On a fold out couch
in some strange apartment
Me not next to you ...
Martha and Bonnie'll be there –
they'll see you they'll see the empty ...

You'll think
"She can't possibly love me.
She drags me to New York
No reason
On some random *Tuesday,*
makes me stay on some couch in some
hole in the wall in the ass end of Brooklyn
with her weird lesbian friends then
disappears."
Mario: I need you to know: I love you with all of my heart.
But that's the uh ...
hhhhhhhhhh

See: there's … *my* heart

And there's an

other heart.

Shit.

Bad service cuts her off. She dials again.

It's me again I got cut off …

I was

Trying to explain …

Sometimes?

I feel a *heart*.

Other than my own. Beating inside me.

Like I have two hearts.

One that's mine.

Another that's …

Someone else's.

Squeezed next to mine.

Like having

twin hearts?

Trapped in

Some kind of fucked up cradle? made of ribs and muscle?

I'm not being metaphoric I know you sometimes think I talk in …

but this heart this

second heart?

It's been there since I can remember …

Sometimes it speaks for me. Moves for me. Thinks for me …

Like having the ghost of a stranger inside you.

I love you, Mario.

I woke up at 2:35.

I thought it was your heartbeat that woke me.

But no.

It was his. That stranger inside …

He told me to slip out of bed. Get dressed.

Leave Martha and Bonnie's place. Come here.
I could hear my own heartbeat
Faint in the background begging me
Don't listen. Get back in bed. Leave tomorrow.
Forget you ever came back to this godforsaken city.

But the other heartbeat ... He always wins ...

I can't tell you where I am ...
I'll explain it to you some time. I promise.
But please believe me: It's the last time I will ever come here.
When I'm done, I'm coming back, Mario.
I love you ...
Please understand.
I love you.

She clicks off the phone.

LILA: *Hhhhh*

She waits, then presses the buzzer.

EIGHT

The wee hours. Herman's kitchen. He changes tapes and resumes recording himself.

HERMAN: Four thirteen am

I've got the Willies.

I'll wager, oh listener –

That if you endured the

Ickiness

Of that last tape –

The

disastrous exchange of *un*-pleasantries with my *Latin* friend –

I'll wager two questions come to mind.

One:

Why does this Herman "F" use only first initials of surnames?

Two:

What is up, Mister Herman F. with this monstrous accusation of Holocaust denial?

Quick shift to VALERIE's place. She rubs her head as if suffering an excruciating headache.

VALERIE: What are they gonna do with his body …

Herman, you fucker.

She downs some aspirin, picks up her phone and dials. Herman's phone begins to ring.

HERMAN: Ah! The telephone! Guess who's calling? Guess who won't pick up? Anyway:

why initials in place of names? Cryptic, no?

This Herman fellow must be *hiding* something.

But that would make no sense, would it?

For you to have requested these tapes from the Special Collections Librarian

(a woman I fantasize about obsessively)

You would have to:

    1) Know the tapes exist, therefore

    2) Know the identity of the man who recorded them, and

    3) Knowing his identity, you must have at least an inkling of his *notoriety*.

In other words: you already have an *agenda*.

But maybe you're that rare, genuinely curious, agenda-free person
lured into the constipated bowels of The New York Public Library
not to seek what you already know,
but to journey across the vast terra incognita of human knowledge.
In your quest you stumble on a man named Herman. With a Jewish sounding last name.
You learn the library's holdings include all eleven of his published books.
You learn he bequeathed tapes ... hundreds of hours of his own testimony ...
Curiosity aroused, you dust off a voice unheard for years ... ? Decades ... ?
Centuries ... ?

The telephone stops ringing. Quick jump to Valerie's kitchen.

VALERIE: Fucker.

She dials another number.

ALVARO: Ahhhl-
   Oh?

VALERIE: Alvaro?
   It's Valerie.

ALVARO: Coño! What is this?
   Fuckin' *Night a the Living Dead?*

Back to Herman's place.

HERMAN: It is for you, virgin listener,
   I use initials in place of surnames.
   You see: In spite of the ongoing *threats* — from time to time
   I leave my apartment, head to the Library. To use the computer.
   Maybe
   Oh, I don't know
   Look up a recipe?
   On occasion I'll permit myself
   A petty indulgence:
   I "google" myself.
   My full name.

No quotations.

18 million results.

I try again – my name. In quotes.

Four million results.

Less unwieldy but still needing refinement.

I add "historian"

Ah! A manageable 350,000 results!

A number that remains somewhat stable when I add, oh,

The title of one of my books, say, *The Peace Delusion* or

Towards a Gentler Means to an End: Reconsiderations of Machiavelli for the Age of Globalization.

Then,

Indulgence devolves into morbid curiosity …

I add the dreaded "H.D." words

Lookee there!

One hundred twenty thousand results!

My my look at all those places where the crime of Holocaust Denial

And my name live in wedded bliss.

Morbid curiosity becomes self-laceration:

I replace "Holocaust Denier" with

Terrorist.

Fascist.

Murderer.

Friedmanite.

Rapist.

Abortionist.

Child molester.

Genocidal maniac.

Results! Results!

Thousands of results.

I reside among the pantheon of untouchables.

You understand now why I keep names secret?

Was just last week I subjected myself again to this assault.

For reasons that still baffle me, I typed one. last. combination: My name. In quotes. Followed by Javier C.'s name.

"Your search did not match any documents."

Herman clicks the recorder off. He sits silently. He clicks the recorder on.

HERMAN: As to question Two — this Holocaust Denial business

Where to begin …

The apartment intercom buzzer sounds. Herman leaps to the defensive: he turns out the light, moves to the knife drawer, where he removes a handgun. Next, he goes to a cabinet and removes a periscope-like device — a car mirror attached to a tv antenna. He moves to the window, extends the mirror outside to see who is down below. The intercom buzzes again.

HERMAN: God …

He goes to the intercom, presses a button. Sounds of the street outside.

HERMAN: Who is it?

YOUNG WOMAN'S VOICE: Herman … ?

It's me.

Herman hesitates, then buzzes her in.

He opens the front door slightly. The echo of women's shoes ascend the four flights stairs.

During the ascent, we pop in on Valerie. She's just getting off the phone. Her headache seems to have gone away. She dials another number.

Back at Herman's. The young woman's footsteps stop outside the door. She pushes it open, stands, a silhouette in the threshold. A silent standoff. The telephone begins to ring.

HERMAN: Lila … What are you …

LILA: You gonna answer that?

HERMAN: No.

LILA: Herman … ?

Do you believe in ghosts?

He says nothing. She says nothing. The phone continues to ring.

HERMAN: Lila … I am so, so sorr—

LILA: Shhhhh.

A moment. They fall into an embrace. It is uncertain who initiates. Herman still has the gun in his hand. The last thing we see: the red light of the tape recorder recording. The telephone continues to ring.

2. Deus FedEx Machina

ONE

Herman's kitchen the next morning. Herman and Lila in bathrobes. Lila absorbed in the cross-word puzzle. The gun is still on the table. Herman fixes his gaze on Lila's finger, which sports a modest engagement ring.

HERMAN: I spoke to your mother last night.

> This morning, actually

> She telephoned.
> At 2:35.

Lila looks at him quickly, then returns her attention to the crossword.

HERMAN: Does your mother know you're in town?

LILA: What's up with the gun, Herman?

HERMAN: This? Oh, well …

> You know.

LILA: No.

HERMAN: Protection.

LILA: From … ?

HERMAN: Neighborhood …

> The city …

LILA: I read in some magazine it's become one of the most livable places in America.

HERMAN: Perhaps but

> Certain *people*

LILA: Want to see you dead.

HERMAN: That's right.

LILA: They make threatening calls at all hours —

HERMAN: 24/7. I have tapes, I could // play them for

LILA: They want to find you so they can kill you. Slowly.

HERMAN: That's right.

LILA: You're nuts.

> You'd think, if "those people" wanted you dead?
> They'd have done it a long time ago.

HERMAN: When it mattered, you mean.

LILA: No …

HERMAN: When I mattered, is that what you're say//ing?

LILA: Forget it.

HERMAN: Aside from that

> Things happen. Door to the street.
> Doesn't lock properly.

> So: you're not interested.

LILA: In why you have a gun? I'm plenty // interested in

HERMAN: No.

> Your mother …
> She telephoned // last night.

LILA: Your conversations with my mother are none of my business.

HERMAN: She doesn't know you're in town … ?

LILA: If she does, it's not because I told her. She say anything to you?

HERMAN: About …

LILA: Me being in town …

HERMAN: No.

LILA: Cause she has a way of knowing things like that that just …

> Drives me up the fucking // wall

HERMAN: Do you plan on *contacting* her

LILA: No.

HERMAN: She seemed to *suggest*

    she'd like to

    touch base // with you

LILA: That would be novel.

    Why would she tell you that?

    She doesn't *know*, does // she

HERMAN: Christ NO, God, no.

    Imagine?

    What exactly are you doing in town?

LILA: What's with the questions? I'm in town. I come I go I

HERMAN: I know

LILA: When I come I come see you, right? I don't ask anything, you don't ask anything, complication free. That should make you happy, // right?

HERMAN: It does …

    It's just that

    I got the sense that she's

    Looking for you // and

LILA: She has my *cell*.

HERMAN: I think you should call // her.

LILA: Oh for fuck's sake

    Ground rules, Herman. Remember ground rules?

    I walk through that door –

HERMAN: –Your mother // your fa–

LILA: – Does not exist. She lives in the world out there. What we do happens in the world in here. And never the two worlds –

HERMAN: – Shall meet I know I know I'm // only –

LILA: Herman!

Silence.

HERMAN: You look well.

LILA: Thank you.

HERMAN: It's been what? Six months // since

LILA: Eight.

HERMAN: Right …

But you.

Standing at my door.

Arriving unannounced –

LILA: I'm sorry about // that

HERMAN: No …

I

Just

You.

I forget to breathe.

You

Move

Me.

She places her hand – the one with the ring – on his, and gives it a squeeze.

LILA: What do you say we get out of here, go somewhere?

It's a beautiful day.

HERMAN: Somewhere …

LILA: I don't know. Coney Island?

The park? The zoo?

HERMAN: Not in the mood.

LILA: You won't take me to the zoo?

HERMAN: Lila …

LILA: You like taking me to the zoo …

HERMAN: *LILA.*

LILA: Whoa. Tone, Herman.

    You do not have the permission to use that // tone with

HERMAN: I'm sorry I'm just

    confused.

LILA: By … ?

HERMAN: You come here

    In the night

    At the end of a week that,

    Fuck. I can't even talk about this.

LILA: What is it?

HERMAN: You come here. God knows what time.

    We hardly say a word – I know:

    Not unusual.

    But now it's morning. And last night

    certain questions

    I should have asked …

Lila's cell phone rings loudly. The ring tone, some kind of "ironic," Lila-appropriate song.

HERMAN: What is that?

LILA: My phone? Hold on.

    Shit.

HERMAN: You're not going to answer it?

LILA: Nope.

HERMAN: Who was it?

LILA: A friend.

HERMAN: Why don't telephones sound like telephones anymore?

LILA: Cause the future happened last Thursday, Herman. You missed it.

    You were saying …

HERMAN: You need to call your mother.

LILA: Jesus // Christ

HERMAN: And what is that thing?

LILA: What thing?

HERMAN: On your finger – // that *thing*.

LILA: Which finger oh // *this* finger *this* thing

HERMAN: *That* finger, yes, *that* thing, // yes yes yes

LILA: What does it look like?

HERMAN: I told your parents?
 Years ago I told them:
 "Why all of a sudden are you
 dabbling in having *babies?*"

LILA: Babies

HERMAN: I told them:
 Two of the biggest narcissists ever to walk the earth
 What do you want a *baby* for?
 Now there's a a a a
 thing on your finger

LILA: Herman. Settle down. Let's get dressed. Go to the park. I'll tell you all about it.

HERMAN: And what's this insanity you were talking last night, this business about ghosts?

LILA: Nothing. Something stupid // that's all

HERMAN: What did you // mean?

LILA: *Nothing.*

HERMAN: You need. to call. your mother.

LILA: Herman! I am not calling my mother, now drop it or I'm out // of here

HERMAN: Do you know your father died this week?

LILA: Excuse me?

HERMAN: Do you know.

> Your father.
>
> *Died.*
>
> this week.

LILA: Why would you say such a horrible thing?

HERMAN: So you don't know.

LILA: He's not dead.

HERMAN: According to your mother, he is.

LILA: What the fuck would my mother know, she doesn't talk to him she // hasn't

HERMAN: And you do?

LILA: I talk to Tina. I talked to Tina on Monday // I

HERMAN: Who's Tina?

LILA: I talked to her, she said everything was fine

HERMAN: Who's Tina?

LILA: His *friend*.

HERMAN: In New Mexico?

Pause.

LILA: How do *you* know he's in // New

HERMAN: You talked to this Tina woman Monday?

LILA: Yes, Monday.

HERMAN: Your mother told me he died on Tuesday.

LILA: No.

HERMAN: He drowned. In a freak

> flash // flood

LILA: Herman ... why are you saying // this –

HERMAN: Call your mother. Ask her.

LILA: She was telling you the truth?

HERMAN: I haven't spoken to your mother in —

When we do speak it's mercifully brief

Mention of your father *rare,* and no,

Neither she nor I make a habit of telling fibs about people dying,

let alone your father dying.

What are you doing?

LILA: I'm calling Tina. She would have called she

Lila dials Tina. She waits. What she hears puzzles her. She tries again. Same thing. Hangs up.

LILA: What the fuck …

HERMAN: What?

LILA: You knew this. Last night.

You didn't think this would be // something I'd want

HERMAN: That's what I've been trying to tell you, Lila. I'm sorry // that …

LILA: "Do I tell her?" "Do I fuck her?" Hm. "Fuck her. Tell her in the morning // if I
ever get around to

HERMAN: It was not like that, Lila, // it was

LILA: That's just *FUCKED* Herman …

HERMAN: Where are you going?

LILA: They were right about you — everything they *said,* everything they *wrote* — they
were right.

HERMAN: Please. Don't. // go.

LILA: Go to hell, Herman.

She begins dressing. The intercom buzzes. Herman freaks, grabs his gun and moves into a defensive position aiming it at the door.

LILA: What the fuck …

HERMAN: See who it is.

LILA: No.

HERMAN: Please!

LILA: For Chrissake!

She goes to the buzzer.

LILA: Who is it?

VOICE: Fed Ex.

LILA: Fed Ex. What do you w— Herman, don't point that thing // at me

HERMAN: Ask him what he wants.

LILA: You'd guess he's delivering a package?

HERMAN: *Ask him what he wants.*

LILA: What's this is in reference to?

VOICE: Uhhhh FedEx package for Herman Fi--- ?

The sound of a sidewalk argument obscures the last name.

HERMAN: Ask who it's from.

LILA: For God's sake // Herman …

HERMAN: *Ask* him.

LILA: May I ask who the package is from?

VOICE: Lady …

LILA: Please …

VOICE: Christina Sanchez … Gallup, New Mexico.

HERMAN: I don't know a Christina San—

LILA: *Tina.* Herman. *Tina.*

Lila buzzes and opens the door slightly. Footsteps rising up floor by floor. Lila lights a cigarette, and stares down Herman. The Fed Ex Man reaches the door, knocks. It opens. The Fed Ex Man is baffled by what he sees — the half naked young woman smoking and the older man crouching in his robe with the gun.

FED EX MAN: Whoa. Uhhh ... Either of you wanna sign for this?

Hello?

Lila signs for the package. The Fed Ex Man is taken aback by her half nakedness and her seeming not to care. He leaves. She deposits the package on the table.

LILA: You gonna open it?

HERMAN: Open it for me?

LILA: Fucking coward.

She exits, still dressing, shoes in hand.

HERMAN: Lila ... please, don't go ...

Herman goes to the table. He opens the box and removes a manuscript.

HERMAN: God ...

Herman's telephone rings. He picks up the phone as if in a trance.

HERMAN: Hello?

Valerie's kitchen. On the table an open Fed Ex box and a manuscript.

VALERIE: It's me. DON'T hang up. Did you ... ?

HERMAN: The Federal Express man was just here.

VALERIE: Here too.

He hangs up the phone. A moment. The phone rings again. Herman doesn't answer. It rings and rings and rings. Herman goes to the package. He nudges it. It doesn't explode. He gingerly opens the package. He removes from it a huge manuscript. He looks at its cover.

HERMAN: *Hhhhhhhhhhhhh ...*

He clicks on the recorder.

HERMAN: I have on my kitchen table
A practical joke from a dead man.
Javier C.
Lifeless at the bottom of a river in the wilds of Northern New Mexico
Could not be content to just
Sink Into oblivion.

Fucker.

Herman clicks off the recorder.

Calm.

He clicks the recorder back on again.

A box arrives this morning –
I sign for it and the *attitude*. The
self-importance of the Federal Express Man,
with his *hat* his
uniform that
little electric *thingy*
For all I know the package could be some kind of
improvised explosive device sent by my enemies
But I open it:
Inside, a manuscript. By Javier C.

My first impulse: burn the damn thing
But curiosity – oh curiosity …
That whore always wins in the end doesn't she.

The title …
Diagram of a Paper Airplane. Rotten bastard made good on his decades old threat
Actually *wrote* the fucking thing.
Of course, Javier C. could never leave a title alone, noooo
There had to be an "or" or a colon followed by a subtitle – some corrosively stupid,
incomprehensible description of the play's "form." This one is no exception:
Diagram of a Paper Airplane COLON *A last will, testament and indictment in the form of a
tragical metatheatrical fantasia (with songs)*. Parentheses around "with songs."

Pompous cocksucker.

Next page:
Dramatis Personae – seven principals in all HA! I know where *this* is going! Long list
of minor characters – the Goat Herder, the German Innkeeper, Consuela – the
German Innkeeper's wife, Japanese Fishermen … and *hhhhhhhh*
A Chorus of Children Disappeared …
Jesus.

And the *setting:*

Herman reads from the manuscript. Valerie and Alvaro in their kitchens do the same.

HERMAN: "Setting:

VALERIE: Various kitchens in New York City tenement apart//ments.

ALVARO: A roach infested unit of a flea bag motel outside Gallup, New // Mexico.

HERMAN: A disgraced history professor's office on the campus of an unnamed major Catholic university in a very large Midwestern city. Haha!

VALERIE: Various locations in the small fishing village of Puerto Angel, Oaxaca, Mexico, including: a German-run bed and breakfast, a police station, a Japanese fishing boat anchored in the bay, a goat herder's shack, a morgue.

ALVARO: A potential future sinkhole near downtown Albuquerque, New Mexi//co?

VALERIE: A garbage strewn dead end street by the Domino's Sugar plant, Williamsburg, Brook//lyn.

HERMAN: A mental asylum in Middletown, Connecti//cut

VALERIE: A New Age emporium in Portland, Oreg//on.

HERMAN: A burning Japanese fishing boat that has struck an iceberg in the North Atlan//tic.

ALVARO: An illegal sex club in Barri Xinès, Barcelona, // Spain.

VALERIE: An abandoned nuclear power plant in an unspecified coun//try?

HERMAN: "Red Herring's Bar and Grill" outside Mahagonny, USA … ?

HERMAN/ALVARO/VALERIE: The moon.

HERMAN: Listen to this:

"Given the number and variety of locations, // no attempt

VALERIE: no attempt shall be made when // staging the play

ALVARO: staging the play to recreate these environments literally."

HERMAN: I love that.

The dedication:

"For the Puerto Angel Seven and the Innocent Bystanders Caught in the Crossfire."

Valerie's kitchen. She's on the phone with Josephine.

VALERIE: Josephine, sorry, I forget you're three hours behind.
Call me when Fed Ex —

I got one. Herman got one. Alvaro got one.
Dedication says "To the Puerto Angel Seven —

I know you weren't there — would you
Hush for a second, Josephine? The *pages* —
They *skip*. Seven pages at a time.
Mine goes: 2, 9, 16, 23, 30 and so on.
I don't know what pages Herman got, bastard won't talk to me

HERMAN: 1, 8, 15, 22, 29, // 36, 43, 50 ...

VALERIE: but Alvaro talked, he got pages

ALVARO: 3, 10, // 17, 24

VALERIE: and so on to 600 something so one would assume —

I KNOW YOU WEREN'T THERE! IT'S NOT ABOUT YOU, JOSI,
HE'S POINTING FINGERS AT ALL OF US ...

Silence.

I'm sorry ... Josi, I didn't mean ...
Don't cry Josephine ... Jesus.
Look: there's a letter
Do *you* know who this Tina person is?

Look, Josi —
I'm throwing darts here, blindfolded

I *know* it's a can of worms. How *dare* you even say that to me.
Shame on you.

Anyway, the letter:
Barely read this Tina person's *scrawl*

the grammar

the *presumption*

Okay. I won't editorialize

Can I just fucking read it to you?

ALVARO: *(Reading the letter.)* "To Whom It May Concern.
You don no me from Atom."

VALERIE: Spelled like Atom bomb

ALVARO: "And I don no you from Atom Ether?"
Either.

VALERIE: "I m cool keepin it that way. Im jus the messenyer so don shut me.
I just wut he says I am: the 'companyun' – I'm only doin what Havi axt me"

ALVARO: "In cace bad shit wen down. Bad shit wen down so Im doin like he axt."

VALERIE: "I do not no wuts incide the Onvelup?"

HERMAN: *Envelope.*
"Alls I no he wanned u to haf it
I learned eons ago never to seek the light of reason behind Javier's dark, subterra-
nean impulses."

What?

VALERIE: That's right Josephine,
A complete sentence.
I mean, what the *fuck?*

ALVARO: "I hop wuteverz in the onvelup meens sumthin good to you, cuz he wuz actin
all freekie at the en an wen he wuz lyk that u never noo wut wuz cumin next."

HERMAN: "Pleez don contac me. Im only the mesenyer. Lik I sed. I don't wan get
shoot."

ALVARO/HERMAN/VALERIE: "Sinseerlee. Tina"

VALERIE: Doesn't that weird you out? Who is this fucking illiterate bitch?

Alvaro folds the letter into a paper airplane. He goes to the window, sets the plane on fire with his Zippo and tosses it into the airshaft.

Herman folds the letter and clicks off the recorder. He picks up the phone and dials.

VALERIE: Josphine, can you hold on a second? Call waiting. Hello?

HERMAN: Who is Tina?

TWO

Alvaro's kitchen. Late afternoon. A pile of cigarette butts in the ashtray. A carton of Kools, open. The microphone and digital recorder. Alvaro lights up a Kool and resumes his conversation with the unseen interviewer.

ALVARO: After that Night a the Livin Dead?

> Week later? Invitation comes in the mail —
>
> "Your presence is requested for a Memorial Celebration of our fallen friend Javier"
>
> "Friday, October 8, 9pm. Bring pictures, poems, memories."
>
> Hosted by
>
> What do you call her?
>
> Ex-wife in mourning? Reluctant mother a his offspring?
>
> If you don't know what to call her,
>
> What you gonna call me?
>
> Ex-friend?
>
> Ex-barrier-between-his-sorry-ass-an-the-streets?
>
> Ex-other-woman-who-happens-to-have-a-pi-pi-between-her-thighs?
>
> Make sure you write *that* shit down, in your book diss-uh-tation whatevuh …
> *Memorial.*
>
> To go or not to go, that was the question, right?

Alvaro goes to a kitchen cabinet. Inside, notebooks, wedged between plates and bowls. He removes a small stack of handwritten pages and returns to the table.

ALVARO: Javi left a bunch a shit behind when he split,

> Most of it garbage I got rid of.
>
> But I kept a couple a things …
>
> First two pages a *Diagram of a Paper Airplane*. Original. Hand written.
>
> Bitch wrote — five, 600 pages? Split it up, sent it to all the people that were there.
> All that for what? When all he had to do was mail these pages to his daughter.
>
> "Whimsical."
>
> Looks like you salivatin' Mista PhD Candidate, Columbia University …

3. Memorial

ONE

Valerie's apartment. Night. In the kitchen, Mario and Herman. Mario drinks a beer. Herman sips tea. Awkward silence.

MARIO: Weird, cause … I didn't even know Lila *had* parents.

 I mean yeah

 Everyone's got parents –

 It's just

 Weird.

 See: cause Lila?

 She like

 Never mentioned?

 Her mom?

 Her …

HERMAN: Father?

MARIO: Right, cause she's fierce

 You meet her you're like

 "Man, were you born fully formed?"

HERMAN: You went to Harvard?

MARIO: Yes and no.

 Did three semesters then

 Life

 Happened like a

 fork in the road?

 Harvard? Or the swirling chaos of life.

HERMAN: And swirling chaos …

MARIO: Exactly. But no regrets …

HERMAN: And your family's Irish?

MARIO: That's right.

HERMAN: Then why'd they name you "Mario"?

MARIO: Ha! *That's* a story ...

Herman does not take the bait. Pause.

MARIO: Like I was saying,
> Cool she's
> Reconnecting?
> Lila's not used to ...
> See: like my family?
> We're like the Kennedy's?
> If they were ass broke and lived in south Boston?
> We're tight, touch football, booze –

HERMAN: Assassinations?

MARIO: What? Oh. No no no Ha – there's been tragedy but ...
> Any time I bring Lila there she's
> *Overwhelmed*
> Like she can't deal with the
> We can get pretty sentimental sometimes? like
> We'll get into fisticuffs over who loves who more –

HERMAN: Fisticuffs?

MARIO: My family – not Lila and me – god no, we never fight. But like my brother and me? We'll kick the living crap out of each other to prove something stupid, like who's more loyal, who's more – Lila's not used to people automatically treating her like family, like – okay, I love someone? I bring that person home? My family? Second they walk in the door. Instant part of the tribe.

Freaks Lila out sometimes.

Long silence.

MARIO: Totally sucks about her father.

HERMAN: How did you and Lila meet?

MARIO: That's an awesome story.

HERMAN: I bet you're dying to tell it to me.

MARIO: Totally — wait.
Are you being
Sarcastic?

HERMAN: No.

MARIO: Cause reading you's like reading ancient Egyptian hieroglyphs —
But yeah, it's an awesome story —
See: She was doing the Car Crash Prom Queen thing in Harvard Square —

HERMAN: Car what *what?*

MARIO: Car Crash Prom Queen …

That's what's so hard to get used to — cause like my family? You can't
Screw in a light bulb without everyone gossiping about it, takes getting used to her
family not

HERMAN: I'm not Lila's family.

MARIO: Well no, but …

HERMAN: Enlighten me. Car crash … ?

MARIO: Prom Queen. It was like a
Living-statue-slash-performance-art-type-thing, SO cool to watch.
She would deck herself out? in this pink prom dress? Corsage of thorns around her
wrist. Face painted all white — blood red tears on her cheeks. She'd stand on this
podium. That was *covered* with paper airplanes.

HERMAN: Paper airplanes.

MARIO: Weird, right? She has tons of them at her place. She *finds* them. On the street.
She has this theory? that if you look at the ground all the time? you find paper airplanes everywhere. She'll walk around Boston, find like twenty of them. I thought:
crackpot, but I started looking? They're everywhere —

Anyway, she'd stand on the paper airplanes, for hours, striking these poses. And the
climax … She'd unzip the back of her dress? Expose her back, her —

HERMAN: Scars?

MARIO: You know about her scars?

HERMAN: I was there when they happened.

MARIO: Holy shit.

HERMAN: Indeed.

MARIO: Wow … I don't mean to pry // but

HERMAN: Then don't.

MARIO: Okay … Anyway

At the end she'd set fire to the paper airplanes burn herself in effigy. Not really — it was theatre … It was un.be.lievable. Thing was, no one knew who she was — people rumored she was the Provost's illegitimate daughter, castoff of the Kennedy clan —

Jangle of keys opening the front door interrupts. Valerie enters carrying bags of Chinese food.

MARIO: Let me get those for you Mrs. P.

She kisses his cheek.

VALERIE: Such a sweetie — thank you — here, there's a couple more outside.

MARIO: Chinese! Awesome!

During the following Mario unloads the Chinese food bags and groceries.

VALERIE: Herman! My // God!

HERMAN: Valerie …

VALERIE: My. *God* …

HERMAN: Likewise …

VALERIE: You're

early.

HERMAN: I

VALERIE: No no no no it's fine I'm

I should hug you shouldn't I?

HERMAN: Not necessary.

MARIO: Mrs. P. – should I just set this stuff out?

VALERIE: Please, no, Mario – you're a guest, // just …

MARIO: Not a problem Mrs. P. – where's // Lila

VALERIE: My god you

You look the same only

HERMAN: Different?

VALERIE: Have you met Lila's fiancé // Mario

HERMAN: Indeedie

VALERIE: Isn't he just delightful?

MARIO: You're too kind // Mrs. P

VALERIE: Can I get you something, Herman? Drink?

HERMAN: I'm fine.

Valerie goes to the freezer and removes a bottle of vodka. She pours herself a drink.

VALERIE: So …

How's the scribbling? Oh, I got us Chinese – meat *and* vegetable dishes of course – // you

HERMAN: I'm back to meat.

Relapsed carnivore since …

VALERIE: Really.

HERMAN: As to the scribbling –

VALERIE: Pardon?

HERMAN: You asked if // I

VALERIE: Oh right right – my mind – three hundred different places // at a

HERMAN: I remember

VALERIE: I read the last one, what was it called? *Billions of Feet* or // some

HERMAN: *A Billion Fewer Footprints: A Case for Accelerating Climate Catastro*//*phe*

VALERIE: Rightrightright. Scary stuff. I still don't understand, though, why it caused you so // much ...

HERMAN: Trouble? // Well —

VALERIE: I assume, though, that you
What's the expression?
"Got back on the horse that 'throwed' ya?"

HERMAN: You're asking if I got back on a horse.

VALERIE: That's what you do, right?

HERMAN: Well, no. The horse threw me. I tried to get up. The horse kicked me. While I was down? Horsie pooped on my head, galloped off into the sunset.

VALERIE: I'm sorry, Herman. But the job situation —
Surely you must be back in de//mand

HERMAN: I'm toxic. Unhireable.

VALERIE: Shame. You were such a good teacher.
So how are you ... ?

HERMAN: How am I ... ?

VALERIE: Living.

HERMAN: Settlement.

VALERIE: Oh, right, I read about that, undis//closed sum?

HERMAN: Undisclosed sum of money.

VALERIE: Must have been some undisclosed sum, living all these // years.

HERMAN: I'm frugal.

VALERIE: Hey, at least you get to live, right?

HERMAN: Goodbye. Nice seeing you Valerie, call me in another // twenty years

VALERIE: Oh, Herman, I'm teasing, so sensitive ... for the record, I never believed for a moment that Holocaust denial business

HERMAN: Oh, goody.

VALERIE: I even considered writing a letter to the *Times* in your defense, but who am I?

HERMAN: And you? How's the
    Mashing together of very large, incongruous objects to create "new sculptural forms" going?

VALERIE: So. Mean.

HERMAN: Really, I'm curious.

VALERIE: I've gone miniature.

HERMAN: They were getting so *Big*

VALERIE: That was twenty years ago. I've *evolved*. Besides,
    I lost my space. Real estate in this fucking city
    So I work here. In my kitchen.
    But more importantly I've become obsessed with things barely visible to the naked eye.
    I'm working on a series I'm showing at a gallery in Toledo.

HERMAN: Is it just us?

VALERIE: Hm?

HERMAN: Here. For this
    Reunion? Memorial? Posthumous play // reading?

VALERIE: Mario's here.

HERMAN: I don't mean Mario.

VALERIE: That's not nice – Mario please don't take offense, Herman is // just

MARIO: No offence taken – I'm just the fiancé.

VALERIE: Lila

HERMAN: Lila's coming?

VALERIE: She'd be here now if // she

MARIO: Mrs. P.? You mind if I?

VALERIE: Of course not – there's an ashtray out on the fire escape.

MARIO: The view out there isn't half bad.

VALERIE: Sweetie.

Mario goes out the window to smoke on the fire escape.

VALERIE: I've known him a day and a half
Already he's like a son.

Pause.

HERMAN: You haven't answered my question.

VALERIE: Which question.

HERMAN: Are we it?

VALERIE: If I said it was just us would you stay or go?

HERMAN: Valerie, Val, // Valie

VALERIE: If I said all of us will find ourselves cramped in this tiny kitchen
Would you run screaming for the hills?

HERMAN: Is it just you. And me.

VALERIE: There's Alvaro

HERMAN: He's coming?

VALERIE: He said he was intrigued but noncommittal.

HERMAN: Doesn't sound like something he would say.

VALERIE: People *evolve*, Herman.

Shift to Alvaro's apartment. He wears a black pinstripe suit with a carnation in the buttonhole and bold red tie. He holds a bouquet of roses and looks into a mirror.

ALVARO: "Whimsical"

He folds the hand written pages of Diagram of a Paper Airplane and slips them in his jacket pocket. Back to Valerie's place.

HERMAN: Nero? Is he // coming?

VALERIE: Nero's dead.

HERMAN: Shut up.

VALERIE: It's been ten years

HERMAN: Let me guess: blew his brains out?

VALERIE: Warm.

HERMAN: He jumped off of something. Big. Like a suspension bridge.

VALERIE: Cold

HERMAN: Knowing him it had to have been something spectacularly vengeful –

VALERIE: Hot.

HERMAN: Did he take Lina and the kids out with him?

VALERIE: God, Herman, // that's

HERMAN: You said "Hot"

VALERIE: He *stabbed* himself –

HERMAN: *Fuck*.

VALERIE: Talk about vengeful, he did it right in front of Lina.

HERMAN: Shit.

VALERIE: At breakfast one morning at the B&B.

HERMAN: The what?

VALERIE: You didn't know? They ran a charming little B&B in Burlington, Vermont.

HERMAN: You're joking.

VALERIE: I know, weird, right? Actors … *Anyway* – they were making breakfast for guests – one second he's chopping onions next he impales himself.

HERMAN: God.

VALERIE: Awful, no?

HERMAN: And Lina?

VALERIE: Poor woman. Week after they buried Nero they found her one night. Wandering naked on some country lane. Screaming she'd murdered her children – that she was the murderer of all children.

HERMAN: Did she?

VALERIE: Murder her children? Of course not.

HERMAN: Long overdue confession?

VALERIE: Don't. Even.

HERMAN: I'm sorry.

VALERIE: Last I heard she was in a nut house up in Connecticut.

HERMAN: How do you know all this?

VALERIE: How do you *not* know this?

HERMAN: Your evil twin.

VALERIE: Josephine?

HERMAN: Dead? Institutionalized? Witness Protection Pro//gram?

VALERIE: She lives in *Portland*. Runs a *shop* – one of those places that sells candles? Incense?
"Crafts" by local artists. Those *"books."*

HERMAN: Lordy.

Mario reenters from smoking.

HERMAN: Portland, Maine or Portland, Oregon?

VALERIE: Oregon.

MARIO: I love Oregon.

HERMAN: I fucking hate it.

MARIO: Whoa   VALERIE: Herman!

HERMAN: Forgive me Mario I didn't // mean

MARIO: No sweat — I say tomato you say toe-mah-toe
Mrs. P.? Table cloth?

VALERIE: Linen closet — door just to the right of the // bathroom

HERMAN: Is Josephine coming?

VALERIE: You know I offered to scrounge up money to pay half her airfare? Chintzy little bitch.

HERMAN: You talk to her.

VALERIE: All the time.

HERMAN: Doesn't surprise me.

VALERIE: Ha! Well fuck you Herman, eat me while you're at it.
I'm furious with her. I begged her to come. You know what she said? "I'm *content* living in the *present*." Selling candles, incense, those *"books."*

HERMAN: The latest in hemp fashion?

VALERIE: And *hats*

HERMAN: The cow.

VALERIE: That's right, that fucking hysterical cow has gone New Age.

HERMAN: Moo.

VALERIE: Moo.

HERMAN: MOOOO

VALERIE: MOOOO Ha HA Fucking right MOOOOOOOOO

They laugh as they once used to. Valerie affectionately touches Herman's face.

VALERIE: Herman I've missed you.

No response from Herman.

VALERIE: Anyway despite her hippie cow-dom
She was kind enough to FedEx her part of the manuscript.

Valerie goes to pour herself another vodka.

VALERIE: I wonder if Maria got one.

    Herman – I wonder if Maria // got one.

HERMAN: I heard you the first time.

VALERIE: You think … ?

HERMAN: Unlikely.

VALERIE: He found the rest of // us.

HERMAN: Maria's

    Elusive.

    You haven't …

VALERIE: No. Lord, no not since a long time.

HERMAN: Because you're like the Associated Press on everyone's misfortunes.

VALERIE: I can't help it if people think I'm still Queen Bee – not that I asked for that –

HERMAN: What about the goat herder? Think he'll put in // an appearance?

VALERIE: Go to hell, Herman –

HERMAN: Or is he still languishing in a Mexican prison?

VALERIE: Fuck you.

Lila enters – a very different Lila than we've seen before. She wears a simple dress with a nautical themed print. It is as if her mother chose the outfit but forgot her daughter is in her late 20s. Something childlike, unsettling about it. On the one hand, it might seem that Lila is attempting irony, on the other, there's something deadly serious about it that is unnerving. Lila carries shopping bags, one with supplies for the party, the other filled with paper airplanes.

VALERIE: Lila! Where on *earth* did you go? I waited for you at the Chinese // place –

LILA: I apologize mother. I got distracted.

MARIO: Hey, baby.

LILA: Sweetie –

MARIO: Man, you lookMm.

LILA: Mother bought it for me. Isn't it sweet?

MARIO: Sweeet.

Lila goes to Mario, kisses him —

LILA: I missed you.

MARIO: I missed *you*.

LILA: I love you.

MARIO: I love *you*.

LILA: No, I *love* you.

MARIO: Baby.

LILA: What are you up to?

MARIO: Helping your Ma set up.

VALERIE: I told him not to — he's a // guest

MARIO: No sweat Mrs. P … Like Ma always says: best way to handle a situation you're not totally comfortable with? Put on an apron, bake a cake.

LILA: Mother, you haven't introduced me to this gentleman.

VALERIE: Oh. You remember Herman. He's known you since you were a baby.

LILA: I'm afraid, mother, I have no recollection of meeting him. How do you do, sir? My name is Lila Anne. But you may call me // Lila.

VALERIE: When was the last time you saw each other?

HERMAN: Another lifetime — I understand you not

LILA: I'm enchanted to make your acquaintance.

HERMAN: Likewise Lila Ann

LILA: Please: Lila. Daddy had so many interesting friends. I learn so many things meeting them—

HERMAN: I'm
  Sorry to
  Hear the news about your father.

LILA: Tragedy, isn't it.

    If you'll excuse me, I'm going to help my fiancée.

    Pleasure to make your acquaintance.

She goes to Mario to help. They stand close to each other and talk in whispers.

HERMAN: What is the point of all this, Valerie?

VALERIE: Point of

HERMAN: Do the math: We have only four sevenths of *Diagram of a Paper Airplane* how do you // expect

VALERIE: You think that's why I asked you here?

HERMAN: Of course it is. Why else would any of us come?

VALERIE: To pay respects? To honor a man who –

    None of us would be who we are without him.

HERMAN: Suicides, mental asylum inmates, estranged mothers –

VALERIE: Lila and I are not estrange//ed.

HERMAN: – amnesiac daughters, failed writers, disgraced professors. What. a. legacy.

VALERIE: So you came out of what? Morbid curiosity? Want to know what the "mad playwright" had to say before kicking // it?

HERMAN: He *could've* sent each of us our own copy – No, he wanted us all in a room together.

VALERIE: Does that frighten you?

HERMAN: Does it frighten you?

MARIO: Smoky time!

VALERIE: Pardon?

MARIO: Didn't mean to interrupt.

    Lila and I are going out for a smoke.

LILA: *You're* going for a smoke, I'm just joining you.

MARIO: Right, for the *view.*

LILA: You're incorri//gible.

VALERIE: May I join you?

LILA: Mother!

MARIO: Mrs. P. Didn't know a fine lady like you partook in such filthy habits, but I'm happy to indulge. I promise I won't tell anyone.

VALERIE: So naughty … such a sweetie.

They exit to the fire escape. Herman alone. The intercom buzzes, startling him. He instinctively goes to a kitchen drawer to find his gun, but realizes he's not in his own apartment. Momentary panic. The intercom buzzes again. He goes to it.

HERMAN: … yes? …

ALVARO'S VOICE: Shit.

HERMAN: Alvaro? That you?

ALVARO'S VOICE: Yeah, it's me.

HERMAN: Are you … alone?

ALVARO'S VOICE: No I got Javier's rotting corpse with me.

Herman buzzes him in. He opens the door and waits. Sound of Alvaro's shoes ascending the stairs. Alvaro arrives at the door, carrying the flowers but no Fed Ex box.

HERMAN: Well

After our little tete-a-tete the other night —

I wouldn't have expected you to grace us with your presence

Lovely flowers the *suit*. My word. You look

ALVARO: Where's Valerie?

HERMAN: They're out on the fire escape.

ALVARO: They?

HERMAN: Valerie, Lila. Her *boyfriend*.

ALVARO: Lila's here?

HERMAN: Yes.

ALVARO: Hm.

HERMAN: What's that supposed to mean?

ALVARO:

HERMAN: So how are your theatrical endeavors?

ALVARO: How your Holocaust Denier friends?

HERMAN: *Hhhhhhhhh*

I caught the last one, ten years ago was it? —

It *was* the last one, right?

I flew in for the occasion — in the midst of my "troubles" — Couldn't miss Alvaro's great triumph after years in the trenches … I have to say I disagree with those that *opined* that you sold your soul to the expectations of your ethnicity.

What was the title again? *Maria—something and a Ward//robe?*

ALVARO: *Mariposa Duarte and Her Cabinet of Broken Dreams.*

HERMAN: Right.

Astonishing. So much heart. So much charm. So whimsical.

ALVARO:

HERMAN: Okay your health?

ALVARO:

HERMAN: No? Alright

Looks like you forgot something.

ALVARO: What'd I forget.

HERMAN: I assumed, with a certain express package conglomerate making recent visits —

ALVARO: Do I smell Chinese?

Valerie and Mario return from the fire escape, laughing. Lila follows.

VALERIE: OH. MY. GOD.

Alvaro, you *saint.*

ALVARO: Valerie.

VALERIE: Are these for me? You shouldn't have …

    Lila, come say hello to Alvaro.

ALVARO: You've grown.

VALERIE: Alvaro was also a friend of your father's …

LILA: Enchanted to meet you. My name is Lila Ann. But you may call me Lila.

ALVARO: Your father woulda been proud – little girl grown up into a beautiful señorita.

LILA: Why // thank you

VALERIE: This is Lila's fiancé Mario.

MARIO: Pleasure to meet you Alvaro. I'm uh

    So sorry for your loss.

ALVARO:

VALERIE: Let's sit down, I got us Chinese – anyone like a drink?

She goes to one of the kitchen cabinets and opens it – liquor.

ALVARO: You got tequila?

VALERIE: Sure Lila?

LILA: I'd love a glass of Chardonnay, please, if you // have –

VALERIE: Herman?

HERMAN: Water's fine.

VALERIE: Mario?

Mario has already gone to the refrigerator and gotten himself a beer.

MARIO: I picked up a twelve pack – hope you don't mind, Mrs. P.

    Assorted autumn brews. Anyone want one go right ahead.

During the following Valerie and Mario serve the Chinese food. At a certain point, Valerie sits, while Mario finishes the job.

VALERIE: So

  Mario

  Are you and Lila planning some kind of honeymoon?

LILA: Mother, I'm sure our guests are not int//erested in

VALERIE: Of course they are, // right Herman?

MARIO: To answer your question Mrs. P. // I

VALERIE: I love that you call me that no one's ever called me that

MARIO: At first we wanted to do something simple, road trip somewhere. Vermont? Adirondacks? No plans, just get in the car, stay in weird motels, maybe do a little fishing

HERMAN: Fishing

MARIO: You fish, Herman?

HERMAN: Can't say I do.

MARIO: Alvaro?

Alvaro looks at Mario like he's just seen an extraterrestrial.

MARIO: What about you Mrs. P., you ever fish?

Herman and Alvaro exchange glances and crack up.

VALERIE: Ha. Fucking HA.

I'll have you know, Mario, that yes, I have gone fishing.

HERMAN: When did you go fishing?

VALERIE: My father took me. All the time. When I was a child.

MARIO: Must be in the genes —Your daughter, Mrs. P.? Is a regular ace with the pole — you should see some of the monster fish I seen her catch. Effortless, like she's got a fish finder wired // into her

LILA: That's an exaggera//tion

HERMAN: Fish what?

MARIO: Fish *finder.*

HERMAN: What is that?

MARIO: Like GPS, for finding fish.

HERMAN: I have no idea what you're talking about.

MARIO: Sonar. Sends sound waves underwater

So like when a school of fish goes by?

It detects em // whammo!

HERMAN: Isn't that cheating?

MARIO: Right? I'm with you on that one. Whole *point* of fishing — least to me — you can't see what's under the water, right?

Mario notices Valerie crying softly.

MARIO: Jeez. Mrs. P ... you okay?

HERMAN: I think the water image —

MARIO: God, I'm an idiot

Mrs. P. I wasn't thinking what with your // ex-hus

VALERIE: No. Please. Go on

MARIO: How'd I get off on fishing?

HERMAN: Fishing Lila honeymoon ...

MARIO: Sure you're gonna be okay, Mrs. P?

Valerie gathers herself. She pours herself another vodka.

VALERIE: I'm fine. I do love that you call me that.

MARIO: Honeymoon — so yeah, first we figured road trip. But *then*

One morning? Lila wakes up, she's like —

LILA: Mario

MARIO: What?

LILA: Nothing. If you'll excuse me

MARIO: Where are you going?

LILA: I need some air.

Lila exits to the fire escape.

MARIO: Okay

Anyway, one morning she's like "I want to go to Mexico."

Valerie, Herman and Alvaro stop eating and focus their attention on Mario. Mario suddenly feels on the spot.

MARIO: I had the same reaction like, "Yeah, baby, you want to go to Mexico? We'll go but, why Mexico? Never heard you mention the place let alone express some secret desire to go there."

> She's like "Because."
> Lila, one word answer
> You learn pretty quick not to dig,
> let her come round if she wants to.

> Couple of days later she's like, "Okay. I'll tell you why I want to go to Mexico, but promise me you won't think I'm a freak."

Lila reenters.

MARIO: Hey baby, I was just about to tell them your Mexico dream.

Lila exits out the window again.

MARIO: What?

> Anyway – She has this dream. She's on this balcony? Of this small hotel. Looking down at this little fishing town – boats in the bay, with names in Mexican –

ALVARO: Spanish.

MARIO: Right. Anyway she senses this "presence"? And this "presence", whispers the name of the town. That she has to go there someday. Next morning she googles it. This town? – that came to her in a dream? *actually* exists.

Valerie, Herman and Alvaro are clearly taken aback.

HERMAN: The name of this town?

MARIO: *(Using the Anglo pronunciation, AYN-jel.)* Puerto Angel.

Herman and Alvaro exchange a look. Valerie leaves the table for the bathroom.

MARIO: Whoa. Way to clear the room, Mario

> Anyway. That's where we're going.

> Did I say something to?

HERMAN: No, Mario, it's just that

   Lila's father and "Mrs. P."

   For that matter Lila herself — went there once upon a time.

MARIO: *(Saying it again using Anglo pronunciation.)* Puerto Angel?

ALVARO: *AN*-hel.

HERMAN: She was just a baby.

ALVARO: Leave it, Aitch.

MARIO: That's incredible! That's Un.be.liev//able!

HERMAN: In fact, Mario, Alvaro and I went there with them.

ALVARO: *Coño.*

MARIO: When was this?

HERMAN: Long time ago. Twenty years.

Mario, excited, goes to the window.

MARIO: Yo, Lila! Come inside, you won't believe —

Lila enters. As she does, Valerie returns from the bathroom wiping her mouth.

MARIO: I was telling them? About Puerto AN-hel? You've already been been there!

LILA: No I haven't.

MARIO: You have! You, your father, your mother. Herman and Alvaro too. Isn't // that —

LILA: Mother, is this true?

   Mother?

HERMAN: I know a little *pension* you might consider staying —

ALVARO: *Aitch.*

VALERIE: Cut it, Herm//an.

HERMAN: Run by a German fellow and his Mexican wife — what was her name? Anita?
   Gabri//ella

ALVARO: *Consuela*

VALERIE: For Chris//sake

LILA: What were we doing there?

HERMAN: Your father led us down there. He was plotting the murder of whimsy –

LILA: What does *that* mean?

HERMAN: How'd he phrase it in the manifesto?

VALERIE: Herman, I'm warn//ing you –

HERMAN: "Deadly serious times demand a deadly serious // theatre … "?

VALERIE: *ENOUGH.*

Pause.

LILA: Mother, will you please tell me what // he's

VALERIE: We were on vacation.

LILA: *Mother*

VALERIE: We were *on. vacation.*

LILA: But –

VALERIE: End of discussion.

Valerie moves to the table, sits, pours a vodka and eats in silence. Lila, exasperated, heads to the bathroom.

VALERIE: Where the hell do you think you're going?

Lila slams the bathroom door shut. Mario heads to the door and knocks.

LILA: Leave me alone mother!

MARIO: Baby, it's me.

Pause. The door opens. Mario slips in. Pause. Tense silence.

ALVARO: Ever cross your mind
    Maybe Javi's not dead?

VALERIE: He's dead.

ALVARO: Wouldn't put it past him,

Him flingin that door open, "April Fool's."

VALERIE: Hm.

No.

He's dead.

HERMAN: So what now, Valerie.

VALERIE: We read.

HERMAN: Valerie, Val // Valie.

VALERIE: Christ, what is Lila doing in there? I'm going to –

HERMAN: Let them be.

The bathroom. Lila sits on the toilet bowl smoking. Mario sits at the edge of the bathtub.

MARIO: Fuckin weird, huh?

Stick a pin in the map, bang, you've already been there. Weird.

You okay?

You

Wanna leave?

LILA: No.

MARIO: Say the word, stay, go – whatever makes you happy.

Talk to me, baby. Say something.

LILA: Why did you tell them that?

MARIO: What?

LILA: Forget it.

MARIO: Lila I'm

Sorry.

Pause.

LILA: You always stayed put.

MARIO: Meaning?

LILA: Always Boston. Never anywhere else.

MARIO: We went places, vacation. Nothing too far, but yeah,
> whole tribe's pretty much right there.

LILA: I don't know what that's like. Staying put.

MARIO: It's okay, I guess. I like knowing my tribe's nearby.

LILA: Being here? It's been … forever. But

> I walk through that door, things …

> You think you're doing something that's *you*. Dabbling in school. Car Crash Prom Queen. Playing in a band. *You.* But I come back — you realize you're life's already been lived by someone else.

MARIO: Lila, baby. You're not gonna end up like them.

> Anyhow, couple of years down the road? You and me? We'll start our *own* tribe …

Pause.

LILA: When I was out on the fire escape? I
> Remembered something I
> Hadn't thought about in …
> But there it was.
> Like it happened yesterday.

MARIO: What'd you remember?

LILA: Nothing.

MARIO: Come on Lila, talk to me.

The kitchen.

HERMAN: Seriously, Valerie. How can we possibly read it when we only have three parts —

VALERIE: *Four* parts.

HERMAN: Are you going to tell her, Alvaro?

ALVARO:

VALERIE: Tell me what?

HERMAN: Seems Alvaro neglected to bring his —

VALERIE: What? Why not?

ALVARO: I burned it.

VALERIE & HERMAN: You *what?*

ALVARO: I burned it.

HERMAN: Jes//us

VALERIE: What the fuck did you do *that* for?

ALVARO: Con Ed bill's killin me, figgad I'd try eco-friendly alternatives to heat my apart//ment

VALERIE: Wait: Tell me you didn't. Tell me you're making a sick joke —

ALVARO:

VALERIE: You motherfucker!

ALVARO: Did you read it? Shit was an embarrassment. You wanna remember him for that?

VALERIE: It was out of context.

ALVARO: You see it makin sense in any con//text?

HERMAN: Regardless, Alvaro, he was our friend.

ALVARO: *Friend.* You sanctimonious motherfucker that why you're here? Celebrate your "friend"?

VALERIE: You had no right to burn it.

ALVARO: He addressed it to me. Way I see it?
Green light to do whatever the fuck I wanted.

VALERIE: So you came here because

ALVARO: I don't get out much, figgad I could use some enta-tainment.

VALERIE: You selfish son of // a bitch

ALVARO: You calling me selfish? I took Javi in when none a you would give him the time of day. Right when things started turning for me — finally, years a me pluggin away, getting nowhere, an yeah, you can say I put on my lipstick, sequin miniskirt, *tacones* whatever

106

HERMAN: Huh?

ALVARO: Whored myself, Aitch. —

> But I earned that shit. He shows up. Broken little dog. I fed him. Made sure he took his meds. *Paid* for those meds. Cradled him in my arms, calm him down when he had night//mares.

VALERIE: Boo fuck//ing hoo

ALVARO: Sat through him reading me bullshit plays he wasn't ever gonna finish, when I shoulda been finishin my own. When I do finish? Follow up to *Mariposa*? Bitch reads it. "*Whimsical.*" You want a list a all the shit I gave up to keep him alive?

VALERIE: Yet despite all your heroic efforts

ALVARO: Yeah, he ended up in the streets. Yeah, maybe best I could do, delay the inevitable. But I didn't turn my back on him.

VALERIE: No. You got your hero to finally fuck you.

> He was more than you bargained for.
> You got rid of him.

ALVARO: Fuck you, Valerie.

VALERIE: What on earth is she doing in there? LILA!

HERMAN: Valerie, Val, Valie just let them be.

The bathroom.

LILA: I can't stand it when she yells.

MARIO: Lila, talk to me. Please.

LILA: I was 3.

> It was summer.
> We were in a house I forget where —
> an *actual* house, with a yard …
> Just me and my father.

> He used to read me this book.
> About this little girl who loved the moon so much,
> Her father brought it down from the sky for her.

One night, middle of the night,
I left the house.
Went into the yard.
To look at the moon.

I don't know how long I was out there
I remember feeling cold,
But I couldn't get back inside

I shouted: "Daddy! Daddy!"
He didn't hear me.
He was asleep.

I was so. Scared.
out there by myself,
no way to get back in ...

When they went away they used to tell me
"Mommy always comes back, Daddy always comes back."
When they did, they came through the front door.
So I thought Front door.

In the yard there was a gate to an alley.
God that alley was so frightening
Shadows,
Cold concrete
I walked down the alley to the sidewalk.
To the front door
Curled myself into a ball,
Waited til morning.

Morning came, I hear my father out back.
"Lila! Lila!"
"Please, god, no, please god no"
He came running up the alley.
Naked except for his boxers.
When he got to the sidewalk,

He collapsed. "Fuck you God, Fuck you God"

Punching the pavement with his fists

I'd never seen him like that he was so

Terrifying

I went to him

Put my hand on his shoulder

"Daddy, you came back!"

He looked at me,

like he'd seen a ghost.

He grabbed my whole body,

Like he was going to crush me

The look in his eye – god just thinking about it …

Pause.

MARIO: What?

LILA: The look in his eye like

he loved me

And hated me

more than anything else in the world.

Silence.

After that

He was around less and less

Until he never came back …

Mario strokes her hair.

LILA: I'm afraid, Mario.

MARIO: Lila, baby? I promise you: I will always come back.

LILA: That's not what I am afraid of.

MARIO: Then what?

LILA: That I won't.

Back in the kitchen. Tense silence.

HERMAN: Alvaro: I don't think you realize what it is you burned.

ALVARO: Oh no?

HERMAN: No.

I saw him. Not long after that.

ALVARO: You saw him?

HERMAN: Day I moved back to New York. After my "troubles." I'd taken the train from Chicago. On the 8th Avenue side of Penn Station, I see a homeless man outside the entrance. Cardboard sign hanging from his neck. Photograph taped to it. The word "missing" written in scrawl.

I didn't recognize him.

On 44th, half a block from my apartment, it hits me. Javier. And the photo Pablo.

VALERIE: Oh, god …

HERMAN: I went back to Penn. He was gone.

Few days later I start getting hang up calls late at night.
One night, the intercom buzzes. It's him.
He'd cleaned up —
Still a little worn, but
he had that glimmer.
Of his old self.

VALERIE: He was so beautiful

HERMAN: We talked. Like old days. He'd read about my "troubles."
Told me he was working on a new play

Then without warning, something shifted. He got
Edgy. Saying he had new "leads." That the
Japanese fishermen had done it. That the boat sank
Iceberg. That if he could find them, he could finish the play.

ALVARO: Shit …

HERMAN: Pure nonsense …

    I told him so. He broke down …

    Said he'd been drinking the night before.

    Dive on 9th by the Port Authority. Said he wanted to die because

    He "left it there"

VALERIE: Left what there?

HERMAN: *Diagram*, Valerie. *Diagram of a Paper Airplane.*

    Next day he went back, it was gone.

    He had to write the whole goddamn thing over again, Alvaro.

VALERIE: And you burned it …

Silence. Valerie rises from the table.

HERMAN: Where are you going?

VALERIE: I'm getting Lila. So goddamn rude of her to lock herself in there.

She pounds on the door.

VALERIE: LILA!

Lila flings the door open.

LILA: What do you *want?*

VALERIE: In the kitchen. Now. It's time.

LILA: For what?

VALERIE: We're reading your father's play.

Lila emerges from the bathroom, followed by Mario. Valerie brings the parts of the manuscript to the table. Mario helps make room by moving dishes away. Everyone sits.

VALERIE: Well?

HERMAN: I have page one. Guess I'm first. *Hhhhhhh.*

    "Author's Note: You will note reading *Diagram of a Paper Airplane* that many narrative threads remain mysterious, and unwoven in any way one can characterize as quote neat. This is my intent, and not evidence of me being a sloppy hack. The play's open-ended nature stems from my conviction that it truthfully reflects the condition of being alive. To that end, I invite you to take a long hard look at your own fucking life – all that you've done (and not done), people you know (or once knew), things you wish you said (but didn't) – in short, all your own mysteries and unwoven threads – and see for yourself the countless paper airplanes you tossed into the sky, only never to see them land. – Javier C., Gallup New Mexico."

Who wants to read stage directions?

MARIO: I'll read. Okay: here goes.

"Prologue: Ferry to Purgatory. A massive iceberg in the middle of the North Atlantic. Floating in the sea beneath – detritus of a shipwreck: shards of a hull, dead bodies, a burning Japanese flag. In the distance, an ancient FERRYMAN rows a lifeboat towards the iceberg.

"A naked man, OUR DEAD WRITER, stands atop the iceberg."

Who's reading DEAD WRITER?

VALERIE: Alvaro.

ALVARO: *I'm* reading him? Shit

"Hello. I was not expecting you. An audience. I imagine you are wondering: who is this man wearing nary a stitch, standing butt nekkid on a massive tabular dome iceberg out in the middle of the North Atlantic. Allow me to introduce myself: I am Your Dead Writer. I'm delighted you could make an appearance on the occasion of my death. Yes, folks, I died. Just before the lights went up, in a landscape far removed from this Arctic nightmare. My death has freed me to point my finger at you in cruel indictment. Alas, decades of agony have taught me that to point a finger at you is to point a finger at myself."

MARIO: *"The FERRYMAN's boat reaches the foot of the iceberg."*

ALVARO: "Hark! I spy a Ferryman! A crotchetyoldsonofabitch Ferryman approaching my iceberg."

I told you this shit was an embarrassment.

VALERIE: Come on Alvaro.

ALVARO: That's where it skips. Anybody got page two?

VALERIE: Here.

ALVARO: "Does he bring word of my estranged bride? Of my friends turned bitter enemies? Has he come to explain why I feel no cold though my butt is nekkid and the air Arctic? …"

Why we reading this mother//fucking bullshit?

VALERIE: Godddamnit, Alvaro, SHUT UP and READ

ALVARO: *Coño*

"Will he usher me through the gates of heaven? Or hurl me into the fires of hell? Or worse: lead me to my greatest terror? Oh, cursed destiny! Purgatory! No! The foreboding!"

MARIO: "*Ominous feedback fills the stage — generated by the CHORUS OF CHILDREN DISAP-PEARED playing electric guitars.*"?

ALVARO: "State your business, wicked Ferryman!"

MARIO: "*The FERRYMAN, smiling dementedly, folds a piece of paper into a paper airplane and tosses it. It lands at the feet of OUR DEAD WRITER.*"

ALVARO: "Do I read this wicked Ferryman's aeronautic missive? Or do I ignore it? Curiosity, like St. George, has vanquished my dragon will"

HERMAN: He's right, Valerie. This really is a piece of shit.

VALERIE: Indulge me.

MARIO: "*OUR DEAD WRITER unfolds the paper airplane.*"

ALVARO: "What's this? A form letter? 'Dear Author: Thank you for submitting your manuscript. We regret to inform you that we have no use for your work. Please know that our decision pains us too: we don't like to think we're driving another nail into your coffin.
'Sincerely,
God in Heaven'"

MARIO: "*The FERRYMAN tosses another airplane, beaming with toothless delight. It lands, bursting into flames.*"

Is there a page three?

VALERIE: Here —

ALVARO: "'Dear Author: Why do you insist on sending us piece of shit after piece of shit manuscript? What the fuck is wrong with you? Are you a masochist? Or a fucking moron? Please! No mas.

'Sincerely,

The Prince of Darkness'

"Oh! The dread! Rejected by Heaven and Hell! I fear the next paper airplane will seal my Purgatorial fate!"

MARIO: "*The FERRYMAN tosses a third airplane, his toothless grin an abyss of demented joy.*"

ALVARO: "'Dear Sir: It gives us great pleasure to inform you we accept your submission. Please find enclosed a check for an astronomical sum of money. Enjoy the pleasure that awaits! Booze, drugs, women, cannibalism, necrophilia, etc Our Ferryman is at your disposal.

'Yours,

Purgatorio Repertorio Tay-Atch-Roh'"

MARIO: "*The FERRYMAN beckons. OUR DEAD WRITER hangs his head, climbs down to the boat. The FERRYMAN hands him a smelly blanket and broken life preserver. The FERRYMAN rows, humming a vaguely familiar show tune as they disappear in the distance.*"

ALVARO: Can we stop?

VALERIE: There's half a page before it breaks.

MARIO: "*The iceberg melts, whimsically, revealing:*

"*SCENE ONE*

"*A filthy motel room in Gallup, New Mexico. Dirty clothes, empty liquor bottles, cigarette butts, cockroaches. On the desk a battered Smith-Corona next to a monumental unfinished manuscript. OUR DEAD WRITER lies in bed, naked, next to a naked, functionally illiterate New Mexican Woman, TINACONSUELA.*

"*A LITTLE BOY, 4, creeps through the window. He's beautiful — head of blonde curls, large brown eyes. OUR DEAD WRITER wakes abruptly. The LITTLE BOY reaches out his hand.*"

Uh who's reading LITTLE BOY?

There are no takers.

LILA: I'll read …

VALERIE: Lila

LILA: What?

VALERIE: Never mind.

LILA: "Daddy Let's take a walk. I want you to take a walk with me."

ALVARO: "Where have you been all this time?"

LILA: "I been far, far away … Daddy, don't be afraid … "

MARIO: "*The LITTLE BOY takes his father's hand, leads him to the window and*"

HERMAN: And …

MARIO: That's it. From there it skips to page

Everyone notices Valerie softly crying.

MARIO: You okay Mrs. P.?

VALERIE: I'm
> *Fuck.*
> Don't mind me I

HERMAN: This might be a
> good place to stop?

VALERIE: No. A dead man has a wish. We grant it.

The lights shift. Passage of time. They continue reading in dumbshow. They pass pages back and forth. Valerie drinks. The lights return to normal when they reach the end of the play.

MARIO: "*Dusk. OUR DEAD WRITER and LITTLE BOY stand in Potter's field by a stack of wooden caskets. The CHORUS OF CHILDREN DISAPPEARED sing the Anagram Chant:*"

HERMAN: "Paper Airplane
> Plan a Ripe Pear"

ALVARO: "You have shown me the graves of my friends.
> "The graves of men and women I knew in passing."

HERMAN: "Pal Reaper Pain

   Pear Apple Rain"

ALVARO: "The graves of strangers I never knew."

HERMAN: "Rare Papal Pine

   Plain Raper Ape."

ALVARO: "But when will you show me the grave where I might finally rest?"

MARIO: "*He turns and sees the LITTLE BOY has gone. He kneels by the caskets and covers his face. Lights fade. End of Play.*"

Long silence.

MARIO: Wow that was …

VALERIE: Not necessary, Mario. It's okay.

Pause.

HERMAN: I'm

   Sorry, Valerie. I'm truly sorry.

Pause.

HERMAN: What time is it?

ALVARO: Quarter past two.

Silence. No one seems to know what to do.

ALVARO: "Makes you think about all your own trees."

VALERIE: What?

ALVARO: Last line of *Death of a Liberal*?

   Frank's eulogy at Jim Barrie's funeral?

VALERIE: Right, right. "What's the saying? If a tree falls in the forest?"

HERMAN: "Makes you think about all your own trees. The trees in the forest of your heart."

ALVARO: *That* was some incredible shit.

HERMAN: Hm.

ALVARO: Shit My compadre lost the plot

HERMAN: Lost more than that.

LILA: I thought it was beautiful.

Pause.

ALVARO: Well

　　Guess this party's over …

VALERIE: NO.

Pause.

　　We. Are not. Finished …

　　Memories I asked all of you to bring something
　　Did anyone … ?
　　Anyone?
　　Fine, I'll go.

　　I have memories.
　　I can think of a hundred off the top of my head that
　　made me want to slit his throat in his sleep // HA

HERMAN: Jesus, Valerie

VALERIE: Oh, Herman, I'm just being *truthful*
　　In spite of all the
　　Shit
　　My fondest memory?
　　First time I laid eyes on him.
　　He couldn't have been more than 17 // 18

ALVARO: 22.

VALERIE: Noooo

ALVARO: I was there, Valerie, he was 22.

VALERIE: Oh, go to hell, Alvaro -
　　What difference does it make if he was 15 or 35 I'm talking about what I *experienced*,
　　what I *felt*, God // you a –

HERMAN: Just go on, Valerie

VALERIE: First time I laid eyes on him, God, he was
    Amazing.
    This magical, demonic, scary, little urchin
    You're right, Alvaro, he was 22, you *were* there, *mea culpa*.
    I was just a kid – directionless, too afraid to
    Throw myself completely into anything –
    but Javi
    Way he talked, those *eyes* – I was a little frightened of him,
    It's like he knew who you were supposed to be before you had any idea.
    He was so … *Convincing*.

ALVARO: Like a snake oil salesman.

VALERIE: Shut up, Alvaro

ALVARO: I didn't mean nothing by that – I was convinced too.

VALERIE: A lot of people thought that – all talk,
    But then we read *Death of a Liberal* –
    My god This kid wrote *this* when he was 19?

ALVARO: 22.

VALERIE: If he'd been 60, Alvaro, it would have been an achievement, // so eat me.

MARIO: You ever read it, Lila?

LILA: No.

MARIO: I'd love to read it …

ALVARO: Doesn't exist anymore. Plays disappear.

VALERIE: That night, I knew I had to be with him …
    The fucker.

Long pause.

    Who's next? Herman?

HERMAN: I'll pass this round.

VALERIE: So infuriating – Alvaro?

ALVARO: Pass.

VALERIE: Oh, come on, why can't –
    Lila. Lila, it's your turn.

LILA: Mother

VALERIE: Mario, please *instruct* my daughter // to –

LILA: Mother!

MARIO: Dying to hear this woman I love, who knew, right?

VALERIE: As his flesh and blood, // as his

LILA: Fine.

VALERIE: If you're going to be that way // never

LILA: I'm not being any // "way"

VALERIE: First thing that pops in your head. // Pop!

LILA: Beluga whales.
    Daddy took me weekends to the aquarium on Coney Island, to see the beluga whales. I remember holding his hand. Our reflections in the glass. The whale's big, ghostly shape

MARIO: That's beautiful kinda chokes me up …

VALERIE: Beluga whales, what else?

LILA: You wanted a memory, I gave you a memory.

VALERIE: That image – like Mario says – beautiful

LILA: What are you getting at, mother?

VALERIE: Nothing. What else do you remember?

LILA: All sorts of things – more flashes than // full blown

VALERIE: That's the nature of things, sweetie Go ahead, we'd love to hear more.

LILA: I remember the rubber alligator. The convoluted bed time stories he made up.

VALERIE: Like which ones?

LILA: I just remember they were funny … Oh, the times it snowed, and Daddy took me to Central Park to make snow angels.

VALERIE: Snow angels?

LILA: In Sheep Meadow. We'd plop down in the snow, make snow // angels

VALERIE: Weird, I don't have any recollec//tion

LILA: It was just me and him.

VALERIE: Right.

LILA: The Paper Airplane Quests.

VALERIE: Mario, will you be a pumpkin, hand me that bottle? No – the tequila …

MARIO: Sure Mrs. P.

Alvaro shoots Mario a warning glance. Mario hesitates.

VALERIE: Is there an issue, Mario?

MARIO: No, Mrs. P …

Alvaro shrugs. Mario hands Valerie the tequila bottle. She pours herself a glass.

VALERIE: You were saying. Paper Airplane what?

LILA: I'm done talking.

VALERIE: Please finish. Not for my sake, for Mario I'm sure // he'd

HERMAN: Valerie Val Val//ie

VALERIE: Don't "Val Val Val" me.
    Paper. Airplanes.

LILA: I'm done.

MARIO: Come on Lila

LILA: Jesus, Mario, what the // fuck

VALERIE: See? Mario'd love // to know

HERMAN: *Hhhhhhhhhhhh*

LILA: Fine. Once we were in the Park. By the Carousel.

> Daddy said if I kept my eyes fixed on the ground I'd find paper airplanes everywhere. He said we should have a contest whoever found the most paper airplanes would win a prize.

VALERIE: A prize

LILA: I remember thinking how silly it was — But he was right. They were everywhere. I must have collected a dozen that day.

MARIO: That's how it started? What a cool story —

VALERIE: Astonishing, isn't it Mario.

MARIO: Yeah, unbeliev//able —

VALERIE: Fucking Beluga whales.

LILA: Excuse me?

VALERIE: *Fucking*. Beluga whales.

HERMAN: Valerie … Val // Valie

VALERIE: What else, Lila? What other *magical* moments do you remember?
> He buy you strawberry ice cream // cones?

HERMAN: Valerie.

VALERIE: Eat me, Herman.

> Beluga whales fucking *snow angels?* Fucking paper airplanes …
> Jesus Christ, the way you tell it
> You'd think that cocksucker deserved the
> Daddy of the Millennium Award.

HERMAN: Valerie, Lila let's

VALERIE: He was *terrified of you,* Lila
> *God,* you've taken an eraser to your childhood
> Scrubbed out all the *shit* all the *sickness*
> Let me tell you something you little ingrate:

ALVARO: Valerie, come // on

VALERIE: Shut it Alvaro.

Weekends. He took you to see the beluga whale *once*.

Paper *air*planes. How bucolic, daddy and his little girl in the park —

You know what that was?

His way of telling you to *shut up*.

Leave him alone so he didn't have to really *be* with you, *father* you.

Look how ridiculous you are with your shopping bags full of them

Years later, still collecting them, still obsessing over one stupid afternoon he *tricked* you,

Contest what was the prize, Lila?

LILA: I don't remember.

VALERIE: There wasn't one.

You'd bring him piles of them, like a little cat carrying in dead birds "I want your love so bad I'll do the most idiotic things to get it" — you know where they ended up? The *garbage,* Lila —

HERMAN: That's enough, Valerie.

VALERIE: You are one sick little girl. You are just like him.

LILA: That has to be the nicest thing you've ever said to me, Mommy. Thank you.

VALERIE: Forget everything.

The violence.

The contempt.

The endless silences.

The parade of "assistants" he used in *my* bed.

Because I know

Staring it in the face

Would confirm every ugly suspicion you have about yourself

Make you want to slit your // wrists.

MARIO: Mrs. P that's *enough*.

Silence. Lila holds back any emotional reaction to Valerie's attack.

VALERIE: Mario. May I have one of your cigarettes.

Mario offers his pack. Valerie takes it and heads out to the fire escape. Mario places his hand on Lila's shoulder. She shrugs it off.

MARIO: I could uh

> Use a cigarette too ...

> Lila?

No response. He exits to the fire escape. Lila, Herman and Alvaro sit in awkward silence. Alvaro heads to the fire escape. Lila begins to cry. Herman reaches his hand to Lila's.

LILA: Don't touch me.

HERMAN: Your mother, she

LILA: Don't. I know.

Pause.

HERMAN: You don't look like you.

LILA:

HERMAN: You don't seem like you.

> What is going on, Lila, you're diff//erent

LILA: What do you think of him?

HERMAN: Who?

LILA: Mario.

HERMAN: Depends on what // you

LILA: Don't

HERMAN: Are you asking me if I'd like to go *fishing* with him some week//end?

LILA: Forget it forget I asked.

HERMAN: Because honestly, Lila, I have no idea what my approval would mean to you.

LILA: You're approval, Herman, means everything to me.

Outside on the fire escape, Valerie, Alvaro and Mario smoke in tense silence.

ALVARO: You keep her in the dark about him all this time?

VALERIE: Excuse me?

ALVARO: Lila. You keep her in the dark. All this time.

Silence.

   Shit. That's deep.

Back in the kitchen.

HERMAN: Do you love him?

LILA: I *do* // love him

HERMAN: Then what I say shouldn't matter.

LILA: He's not what you would expect, right? For me, I mean.

HERMAN: That pleases you.

LILA: Yes. It does. To know that
   We're much bigger than we think we are.

   Why are you smiling that way?

HERMAN: What way?

LILA: Like I'm some
   Charming imbecile in one of your seminars I remember that look
   Someone would raise their hand, say something they thought was bright,
   You'd smile in that crushing way,
   "How sweet, how idiotic."

The fire escape:

ALVARO: Why would you do that?

VALERIE: Do what?

ALVARO: Keep her in the dark.

VALERIE: She was too young to remember. Why fill her head up with
   heartache
   That happened long before she could remember

MARIO: Mrs. P.? If you don't mind me asking …

VALERIE: Would you be a sweetie Mario and give me another cigarette?

MARIO: Sure

ALVARO: You don't think she remembers

VALERIE: She was 14 months old.

ALVARO: She remembers

VALERIE: I'm her mother. I would know // if she —

ALVARO: She *remembers*.
   All you gotta do is take one hard look at that girl
   She's walking around like the whole world's some
   Haunted house

MARIO: Can I please ask —

VALERIE: It's a phase. She'll get over it.

ALVARO: How old is she?

VALERIE: Twenty-five, twenty // six?

MARIO: Twenty-eight.

ALVARO: Little late for her to be going through "phases" // don't you

VALERIE: Tell me something: Did you ever ask my husband these // questions?

ALVARO: Oh, he's your *husband* now that's com//ical.

VALERIE: Did you ever *judge* my husband the way you're // judging me

ALVARO: Yeah. I asked him. He gave me the same motherfuckin bullshit answer.

MARIO: Somebody please tell me what you're talking about.

VALERIE: Nothing, sweetie. Nothing.

The kitchen.

HERMAN: Truth be told, Lila.
   I'm
   envious.

LILA: Herman, that's not what I

HERMAN: No no no

> I knew long ago the day would come you'd
> Find someone your age. Someone uncompromised.
> Am I sad you won't ever come visit me again? Yes.
> But my envy isn't from wanting you for me. No.
> I'm envious of a *feeling* I haven't felt in a very
> Long.
> time.

LILA: I don't understand.

HERMAN: You go around when you're young

> With a picture in your head
> of the person you think you're supposed to love.
> That person doesn't exist.
> So it takes an
> Abitrary look across a room.
> Your eyes land on someone
> Who doesn't look like, talk like, think like,
> smell like the person you imagined
> But there they are. You love them.

> I'm envious, Lila, because I'm long past the point in my life
> Where even faking that feeling is a possibility.

Pause. Lila puts her hand on Herman's.

HERMAN: Last time I felt that?

> Was that day eleven years ago
> when you walked into my seminar.

LILA: Are you trying to manipulate me?

HERMAN: No.

> Maybe a little,

> No.

LILA: Tell me something, Herman.

> Promise me you'll tell me the truth.

> Did you know who I was that day?

HERMAN: I'm not sure I under//stand

LILA: Did you know I was my father's daughter.

> Herman?

HERMAN: No.

> I didn't.

> Not until it was too late.

LILA: I love you Herman.

HERMAN: I love you.

LILA: Kiss me?

HERMAN: No.

LILA: Please?

She kisses him. At first he's reluctant. Reluctance becomes a longing, final farewell kiss. The window opens, Alvaro, Valerie and Mario return from the fire escape. They freeze seeing Herman and Lila kissing.

VALERIE: What.

> The *fuck.* //

> Is going on in here.

MARIO: Lila Jesus, // Lila

ALVARO: Shit.

VALERIE: *What the fuck is going on here?*

HERMAN: Valerie, please let me explain

Mario calmly walks up to Herman. They stand eye to eye.

HERMAN: Mario … Why don't we all sit down and

Mario lands a powerful right hook to Herman's face, knocking him down.

MARIO: Let's go Lila.

    Lila: I said: Let's. *Go*.

    Lila: *Now*.

LILA: No.

The quiet conviction in her voice suspends the room. Alvaro reaches into his pocket and removes the handwritten pages of Diagram of a Paper Airplane.

ALVARO: Lila? You don't know me. But
    I knew your father.

    Sometimes? Your father?
    Wasn't so good at
    making distinctions.
    Between what mattered, what didn't.
    This mattered.

VALERIE: What is it?

ALVARO: Please. Take it.

LILA: Is this his handwriting?

ALVARO: Yeah.

VALERIE: What is it?
    Alvaro, goddamnit, what is it?

Lila sits and reads.

LILA: "Unsent Letter to My Daughter Lila Anne:
    A Prologue to *Diagram of a Paper Airplane*."

    "Sweet Lila:

    "I don't know if you will ever read this. I suppose when I finish writing it, I could put it in an envelope, and send it to you. But I'm not sure I have the courage.

    "I wish we lived in a universe where I could fold these pages into a paper airplane, toss it into the sky and have faith it'd reach you wherever you may be.

"I wasn't a good father to you. Offering parental advice might seem at worst, a betrayal, at best, a not very funny joke. But I want to share with you something I learned which might help you someday if you have children of your own: the greatest danger to a child is not a wall socket. Crossing the street. A swimming pool with no one watching. No. The greatest danger to a child is the father and mother that brought you into the world.

"Two and a half years before you were born, your mother and I had a son. We named him Pablo. A beautiful boy. Wild blonde curls. Impish smile. Your mother's eyes."

Lila looks at Valerie. Valerie closes her eyes.

"When he was four — you were 14 months — we took you to Puerto Angel, a village by the sea in Mexico. We traveled there with our friends — fellow artists, to dream up a theatre we believed in. A theatre we planned to make when we returned to New York.

"We were young.

"At night, after your mother and I put Pablo and you to bed, we left you. To meet our friends in the hotel's courtyard. We talked, drank, dreamed late into the night. Taking turns to check on you.

"That night, we were reckless. I left with Consuela, the Mexican wife of the man who ran the hotel. Your mother left with my close friend — a man who later abandoned the theatre to become an historian.

Lila looks at Herman. He looks away. She looks at Valerie. Valerie looks away.

"In the wee hours, a voice tore open the night. "HE'S GONE" It was Alvaro. The raw, the brilliant Alvaro. He was the last to look in on Pablo and you. We returned to find him. Holding you, so small, so innocent, asleep. But Pablo was gone.

"We never found him.

"For years, your mother and I lived a purgatory of not knowing, of shame, of recrimination; as your mother and father, we tried to see only you, not the shadow of a boy who'd gone missing. We failed.

"Needless to say, we never made our theatre.

"I dream of your brother often. In my dreams Pablo appears exactly as he did the day he left us. That morning, on the beach, I taught him to make paper airplanes. I'll never forget the ecstatic delight in his eyes watching them circle in the air

Pause.

"Forgive me, Lila. Please forgive me.

"Love,
Your father."

Lila folds the sheets of paper, rises from the chair. She moves to Alvaro. She places the pages in his inside jacket pocket. She presses her hands against his chest and looks him in the eye.

LILA: *(A whisper — so soft as to be barely audible.)* Thank you.

She turns to Mario. She looks him in the eye. She removes her ring, takes his hand, places the ring on his palm and closes his fingers.

LILA: I can't.

She turns to Herman. She moves very close to him.

LILA: Denier.

She turns to Valerie. She moves towards her, thinks better of it, turns to leave the apartment.

MARIO: I guess I should uhhh

It was a

pleasure meeting you all.

He exits. Alvaro, Valerie and Herman. Alvaro goes to the door. Before he exits he turns to them.

ALVARO: Good night.

Herman and Valerie alone, not looking at each other.

TWO

Dawn. Valerie and Herman on the rooftop, sitting on crappy outdoor furniture. The FedEx boxes with Diagram of a Paper Airplane *rest on a table between them. They both fold pages of the manuscript into paper airplanes and toss them into the sky. This continues through:*

Night. Alvaro's kitchen. The carton of Kools is dead. Microphone and digital recorder still going. Alvaro talks to the unseen interviewer.

ALVARO: Did *Diagram of a Paper Airplane* survive?

Far as I know? Mistuh PhD Candidate,

Columbia University,

It didn't.

But you never know, right?

Could be out there somewhere,

Like the plays a his you found.

I'm tired. Gotta sleep.

But lemme ask you one question: his plays …

what are you gonna do with them?

Alvaro fades. Valerie and Herman continue tossing paper airplanes. After several airplanes, their hands touch. They hold hands. They do not look at each other.

VALERIE: Shall we walk in the park?

Slow fade to black.

End of play

A THICK DESCRIPTION OF HARRY SMITH (Vol.1)
(or Do What Thou Wilt Shall Be the Whole of the Law)

INTRODUCTION

Tamsen Wolff, PhD. Associate Professor of English, Princeton University

A Thick Description of Harry Smith, Volume 1 (or, Do What Thou Wilt Shall Be the Whole of the Law) is the second play of the trilogy entitled *The Javier Plays*, and it is the hallucinogenic heart of the matter. The play is a kaleidoscopically theatrical, deeply funny, razor-sharp take on the overlapping concerns that run through all three plays, including: authorship, how, when, and whether it matters; the slippery relationship between reality and fiction; and the lifecycles of art forms and artists, especially the question of what gets left behind and what to do with it.

The play begins with three beginnings, immediately establishing its multiple points of entry, and its sly, gleefully non-linear, choose-your-own trip sensibility. The first scene, "An Overture," is an introduction to the emphatically aural world of the play, since

all we see is a figure, "Perhaps it is Harry Smith," who is recording and listening – as we do too – to an assortment of American sounds, from regional songs to street noise to fireworks. According to Professor Emiliano Kurtz, who arrives in the second scene to present the play, *A Thick Description of Harry Smith* is an unfinished drama he discovered, written by forgotten playwright Javier C. The play is a surreal live radio variety show, with folk and traditional musical guests, storytelling segments, and barely tongue-in-cheek "old-timey" advertisements for fictional products. The Stranger Emcee introduces the radio show in what might be considered the third opening scene. He may or may not also be Harry Smith and Professor Kurtz, since the same actor plays all three figures. The Emcee/Harry introduces, comments on, and possibly engineers aspects of the radio show. Kurtz, not quite managing to bookend the show authoritatively, returns in the penultimate scene to discuss the drama's putative ending. But we really end where we started: with sound, this time the final musical performance of the guest band on the radio show, Blank Marlowe and the Red Herrings singing a rendition of Bob Dylan's "A Hard Rain's A-Gonna Fall."

The composite figure of Harry Smith and the form of the variety show, with its seemingly haphazard collection of recycled pieces of Americana, reflects the question that drives the alleged playwright, second-generation American Javier C.: what does it mean to be American? This is plainly an artistic as well as a national question; how can disparate peoples and histories and materials cohere into a recognizable country, or a piece of art? At the same time, the grab bag format of the variety show is a front, since the work has a strict methodical structure. The play braids together three separate radio performance segments, each in turn with three parts, reflecting the larger trilogy form and a recurring insistence on threes. These segments are: Mystery Radio Theatre: The Curator's Folly; The Darkest Heart of America: The Never-Ending Tour of Blank Marlowe and His Band, The Red Herrings; and Shadow of the Shining City: Chronicles of the American Underground. (A fourth promised segment – the confounding radio act of the Albuquerque Youth Ballet's adaptation of a Harry Smith film – turns out, after all, to be a will-o-the-wisp, a lower case red herring, a no-show.) Songs and music punctuate and shape the show. Like the segments, the musical choices appear to be a) unrelated, stand-alone performances and b) critical to collectively forming the thick description of the title. Characters, songs, and segments, like the sounds of the initial scene, summon one another out of the ether, interjecting, elaborating, confirming, merging, competing, and colliding. This babel steadily, and only apparently circuitously, builds a partial picture of Harry Smith.

Through the story of Smith, the play makes a deft, witty case for the concomitant survival and evolution of art, for memorializing without totalizing. To kick off the radio variety show, Marlowe and the Red Herrings sing Blind Lemon Jefferson's "See

That My Grave is Kept Clean," which leads the Emcee/Harry to wonder, "Will someone see *my* grave's kept clean?" Of course the answer is yes: the play is grave-tending as well as grave-robbing. It introduces the wildly eccentric avant-garde visual artist, musicologist, and experimental filmmaker Harry Smith (1923-1991) to an audience who by and large will never have heard of him. He and his work are exhumed here, brushed off, and given their due. But the play refuses to lionize Smith. The suggestion is not that he is an overlooked genius – or even necessarily any kind of recognizable genius – but that his work and life are deeply fruitful and deserve some play. His tale here remains hilariously, messily resonant, neither mythical nor definitive. This Harry Smith is a chameleon of reinvented identity, a hard act to document, let alone follow.

Late in the play in a piece of background action, Smith is giving an interview to a music journalist that illustrates his undoubtedly paranoid but also creative desire to elude a single, defining account of his life. He lies freely, transparently, zealously. The play mirrors his example in this. In the playful spirit of Harry's invention and reinvention, the real and the imaginary are so tightly and thoroughly imbricated in the play that it is nearly impossible to sort out the difference between fact and fantasy. Besides, as the material makes patently clear, the real is fantastical (you can't make this stuff up, or you can try, but you may well find that real life has already done it better). The confusion that the playwright Javier C. expresses early on in a recorded voiceover on this point – which came first, the egg (the real Harry Smith), or the chicken (his play about Harry Smith) – is not as far-fetched as Kurtz suggests. This is a legitimate question too about what constitutes the creative process: where do ideas originate? The relationship between an artist and an idea or creation is rarely simple or one-directional. The play's authorial instability repeatedly begs the question, in the immortal words of Aretha Franklin's lesser work, "Who's zoomin' who?" What's more, if we can't tell with any real specificity where ideas begin, to whom do they belong? And how much does that matter, anyway?

Even when the figures, facts, or history in the play are "real" (Allen Ginsberg, Richard Nixon, the history of recording devices), that reality is simultaneously interlaced with invention to the point where it's disconcertingly hard to know if you know what you think you know. Navigating the play's facts and fictions is an unsteady but exhilarating enterprise, like trying to stand up in a tippy boat, or attempting to complete a simple task while high. In other words, the play compels an audience to experience the joyful, liberating vertigo that comes from acknowledging that at  bottom very little if any boundary exists between what is real and what is invented, and, moreover, energy expended trying to differentiate cleanly between "true" and "not true" is probably wasted energy. Whereas *Your Name Will Follow You Home* in particular offers a more literal examination of what it means to cross the line from fact to fiction – in that play, specifically to claim another identity as your own – *A Thick Description of Harry Smith* obliterates any meaningful distinction between the two.

The giddy, unruly convergence of the real and the fictional together with the multiple stories and modes of storytelling means too that the audience is both constantly surprised and tickled, and constantly attempting to piece together a narrative. An

audience has to make sense of the information being doled or spewed out, even though – and because – this information is clearly always incomplete and unreliable. Such is the Curator's ongoing lament (or Folly, as the play would have it) as she struggles to put together the Harry Smith Museum and Interpretive Center: what can she make of the hard evidence, the actual stuff, that Harry made or owned and left behind? What does it amount to and what story does it tell? Because Smith, it turns out, was an unusual combination of hoarder – amassing enormous, odd collections of items like paper airplanes, Ukrainian Easter eggs, 78s – and its opposite – selling or destroying works and possessions whenever necessary or on a complete whim.

Harry's central lost masterpiece is his unfinished movie about Oz. Marlowe's doomed search for it, on and off the roads in the official Rand McNally map, mirrors the original journey on the Yellow Brick Road. The story of the Wizard of Oz ripples lightly outward through the whole trilogy, present particularly in the band of four slightly grudging compatriots who appear in each play (Jorge/Martin/Annie/Marlowe here, flanked by Alvaro/Herman/Valerie/Javier in the first and last plays). Like Dorothy and her crew, each group is searching for meaning/the Wizard and all will be disappointed. As the Curator repeatedly discovers, there is no *there* there, only an empty box or more of the same unfathomable stuff. About this apparently random pile of material floating in his wake, the Voice of Harry offers this key refrain: "I'm uhhh/Leaving it to/Future generations to uhhh/Figure out the purpose of all this *stuff*." What this comment extends is a blessing to future artists to have their way with his remains. What the play proposes, in its use of Oz and all things Harry, is that a vital purpose of art lies in its repurposing.

Music is the play's most important and consistent demonstration of repurposing with a purpose. Music — in the form of the vast, influential compilation *The Anthology of American Folk Music*, which Smith published in 1952 — may also be the single solid, irrefutable artifact that remains of Harry. Moreover, since he eventually won a Grammy Award

in 1991 for his efforts, music marks his one moment of public recognition and celebration, his entry into the official annals of American culture. When he won the Grammy shortly before his death, Smith stated, "I'm glad to say my dreams came true. I saw America changed through music." His dream about the potentially social transformative power of music is matched by a profound comprehension of how music itself changes. The play uses songs as constant practical examples of adoption and adaptation in art, as well as the perfect grounds for corresponding ideological artistic debates about memory, virtuosity, loss, and change. For example, Harry's determination to press recordings of perhaps the last Orthodox cantor to sing certain ancient Jewish liturgical songs is at once absurd, affecting, and illuminating. This segment, which is not long, manages to encompass questions of cultural and generational change, what it means to capture art and pass it along, and the vagaries of critical reception. In prac-

tice, all the songs that are sung throughout the play rely to greater or lesser degrees on the "originals" from Smith's anthology (which are of course not any more original than any other version), but at the same time the songs range widely and may be freely altered and reinterpreted.

In this way, "Do What Thou Wilt Shall Be the Whole of the Law," the philosophical maxim of early twentieth-century English occultist and writer Aleister Crowley, may be the play's subtitle and the motto of the town —

the Darkest Heart of America — in which Marlowe eventually finds Harry Smith and his motley crew of hangers-on. But "Do What Thou Wilt" is not the whole of the law in this play, or in the trilogy. "Do What Thou Wilt" may be the bulk of the law of artistry in *The Javier Plays*, but with the mild caveat, "Do It With a Modicum of Appreciation and Recognition for the Material and Lives at Hand" (obviously not nearly as catchy). This means that although the Curator's efforts to organize Harry Smith's artifacts to create a museum and a cogent narrative about his life and art are highly entertaining, even ludicrous, and thwarted at every turn, they are nonetheless presented as worthy of respect. Indeed, the Curator is matched by complementary, counterpart characters in the first and third plays in the trilogy, Lila in *Diagram of a Paper Airplane* and Alex in *Your Name Will Follow You Home*. All three women are truth seekers, trying, to the best of their abilities and not without self-interest, to make sense of the flotsam and jetsam of information they receive. The trilogy would never mock this effort; it depends upon it. It celebrates actively remembering and remaking art, artists, and artists as art. That action is itself wizardly. In the end, the Curator's pressing question, "What should a Harry Smith museum look like?" and Javier C.'s shadow question, What should an American artwork look like?, has a short answer: exactly like this play.

Princeton, NJ

133 *A Mechanical Device for Playing a Bagpipe, by Kaspar Rötel, 1624.* Courtesy Deutsche Fototek of the Saxon State Library. Image in the public domain.

134 As a teenager, Harry Smith documented Lummi rituals. This photo was taken in 1938 by Bill Holm. Photo in public domain.

135 Only surviving photograph of the famed Texas bluesman Blind Lemon Jefferson taken some time between 1927 and 1929. Jefferson died at the age of 36 in Chicago. Accounts of his death vary: some claim he was murdered during a robbery, others that he was attacked by a dog. The most likely scenario was that he became disoriented during a snowstorm and died of a heart attack. Photo in public domain.

136 Portrait of Allen Ginsberg and Bob Dylan backstage at a concert in 1975. Photo by Elsa Dorfman.

137 On December 21, 1970, Elvis Presley arrived in D.C. on a mission: to obtain a Federal Bureau of Narcotics and Dangerous Drugs badge. After being rebuffed at the Bureau, he visited the White House where a spontaneous meeting with President Richard Nixon was captured by White House photographer Ollie Atkins. Elvis brought a gift: a Colt .45 revolver. Elvis told the president he believed The Beatles were an anti-American influence and promoters of drug culture in the U.S., and that he wanted to do everything in his power to help the president combat these forces. Elvis left the White House with his badge. United States government – public domain.

138 Blank Marlowe and the Red Herrings, the house band of Harry Smith rehearsing during a New Dramatists Creativity Fund workshop in March 2014. Pictured left to right: Lucas Papaelias, T. Ryder Smith, Paul Whitty, and Joe Tippet. Photo by Carlos Murillo

Aleister Crowley bathing naked. Photograph was taken by Jules Jacot-Guillarmod during Crowley's 1902 expedition to K2. Photo in Public Domain.

A THICK DESCRIPTION OF HARRY SMITH (Vol.1)

(or Do What Thou Wilt Shall Be the Whole of the Law)

CHARACTERS

Dr. Kurtz/Stranger Emcee/Harry Smith, a man of indeterminate age

The Curator, a woman in her 40s

Merry Andrew

The Band, Blank Marlowe and the Red Herrings are:

Blank Marlowe, who also plays: The Voice of Javier C.

Annie, who also plays: Testimonial Voice #1

Voice of *Time* Magazine

Voice of *Rolling Stone* Magazine

Smithsonian Receptionist

Pat Nixon

Octogenarian Widow

Frankie

Martin, who also plays: Testimonial Voice #2

Victor Dealer

Announcer's Voice

Göteborg Ethnology Museum Curator

Allen Ginsberg

Ken Burns-esque Documentary Voice

Alger Crimus, Pop Culture Theorist

Rabbi

Journalist

'40s Newsreel Sounding Voice

Jorge, who also plays: Smithsonian Automated Recording

Voice of the *New York Review of Books*

Thelonious Monk

Jonas Mekas

Bob Dylan

Richard Nixon

Lionel Z.

Dr. Wilder Penfield

NOTES FROM THE AUTHOR

On the Music:

The presence of a live band, Blank Marlowe and the Red Herrings, is crucial. In addition to playing the songs, they serve as the acting ensemble. They are the third greatest bar band that ever was.

The songs in the play, with the exception of The Fugs' "I Couldn't Get High" and Bob Dylan's "A Hard Rain's A-Gonna Fall," are loosely adapted from songs that appear on Harry Smith's *Anthology of American Folk Music*. In certain cases, the lyrics are written by me using the original melodies and lyric fragments ("My Name is Merry Andrew," "The Bible Salesman's Daughter," "White House Blues"). In other cases, the lyrics are mostly from the original versions with some of my own words and tweaks. Some of these stray considerably from the originals ("Coo-Coo Bird"), and others remain closer to the originals ("See That My Grave is Kept Clean," "House Carpenter" and "Frankie"). This is intended to reflect the notion of the "folk process" – where songs are passed down, altered and rearranged, by the interpreter – acknowledging and honoring the source, yet re-crafting them for new and unforeseen purposes.

In production, I encourage the collaborators to discover as many opportunities to utilize the band even when it is not called for explicitly in the script – whether to underscore sections, aid and abet the storytelling, or create moments of delight for the audience.

Lastly, I would encourage avoiding slickness where the band is concerned. Rather, they should lend a scrappy, homespun, DIY feel to the proceedings.

On Sound:

The play functions in many respects as a radio variety show performed before a live audience. The spoken language of the play is intended to entice the audience's imagination – to have them "see" things in their minds that are not actually depicted on stage. To enhance this effect, I suggest the use of Foley work. There are places where this is indicated in the script, and like the use of the band, production collaborators are encouraged to find other places in the play for live sound effects. Again, the more homespun and actor-generated this is, the better. Slickness is strongly discouraged.

On the Performance:

This is more of a performance than a play – sort of a medicine show, or live radio play. The way I have described it to folks is: imagine an episode of *The Prairie Home Companion* in which Garrison Keillor's soul has been overtaken by Aleister Crowley, and where Lake Wobegon is a Mystery Spot, the center of a psychedelic universe.

143

AN OVERTURE

A stage that is a stage and nothing more, as it would appear between productions.

Hovering in the air between the audience and the stage are twin "Applause" lights — which light at appropriate moments in the performance.

A man sits on a crappy folding lawn chair. He's ancient looking, gnome-like — simultaneously benign and sinister, like grandpa. He wears large, plastic rimmed glasses with thick lenses that distort his eyes. He has a grey beard, and wears his grey hair long and scraggly. He sports a large, clunky pair of headphones attached to a portable cassette recorder, which is connected to an omnidirectional microphone.

Perhaps it is Harry Smith.

The man records sounds, which we hear through the theater's sound system. At first the sounds are of the theater itself — backstage noise, the chatter of the audience. Over time the sounds shift. We hear the ghostly, scratchy, low fidelity sounds of Depression-era 78 records — ancient sounding blues, Appalachian ballads, Negro spirituals, sounds of a lost America. The sounds evolve — Times Square at midnight. Atmosphere of a bus terminal waiting room. A children's playground in the city. Nature sounds in the city. An Orthodox Rabbi singing liturgical music. A street poet's incantation. Hot bebop jazz played live in a tiny nightclub. A Kiowa Indian ritual. A speed freak preacher's prophecy of doom.

The sounds culminate with the atmosphere of a 4th of July gathering. Patriotic music, fireworks, burnout.

AN INTRODUCTION TO *A THICK DESCRIPTION OF HARRY SMITH (VOL.1)* BY DR. EMILIANO KURTZ, PROFESSOR OF THEATER HISTORY AND DRAMATIC CRITICISM, UC BERKELEY

In the darkness we hear a voice on the theater's public address system.

VOICE: Ladies and gentlemen, please welcome UC Berkeley Professor of Theater History and Dramatic Criticism, Dr. Emiliano Kurtz.

The Applause light goes on. Applause – both real and recorded. Kurtz, a man in his 40s, appears on stage. His style: professorial slick – in other words, overly styled and unnervingly confident.

KURTZ: Thank you.

Bronislaw Slowik was in his late seventies when, as a graduate student, I assisted him in the preparation of the tenth and final volume of his seminal *Lives of the American Dramatists,* colloquially known as *Lives* – an ironic riff on Plutarch's *Lives of the Noble Greeks and Romans.*

The final volume – which Slowik affectionately referred to as "The Ugh-Known Vitals" – profiled a series of minor writers – that were criminally underproduced, lost their marbles, starved to death, killed themselves, or simply vanished off the face of the earth – writers who, in spite of their anonymity, influenced the dramatists that came after them.

Slowik kept index cards on these writers – he began compiling them after serving as an Air Force test pilot during World War II. You can imagine, over sixty years, how many "Ugh-Known Vitals" he collected. Sorting through them was a thankless bitch – information on these writers was scant, their extant plays few and the quality of their work – not to mention influence – dubious at best.

In the midst of this monumental – and I must say, *sad* – undertaking, I stumbled on this index card, written in Slowik's barely legible shorthand:

"Javier C. b. April 10, 1958, Bogota, Colombia, d. date uncertain, Gallup, New Mexico. Little is known about Javier C. – immigrated to the US in '64, settled in Jackson Heights, Queens. Studied Dramatic Writing at NYU for 2.5 semesters. Body of work includes: 3 full length plays, Death of a Liberal, The Rich Also Cry *and* A Thick Description

of Harry Smith; *a collection of thematically related short plays titled,* Revenge Fuck: A Chronicle of Schadenfreude in the Bedroom; *and an unpublished manifesto,* To Murder Whimsy: Bipolar Realism and the Future of American Playwriting. *Rumors persist about the existence of a fourth play, his magnum opus,* Diagram of a Paper Airplane, *though it is likely apocryphal.*

Of all the index cards documenting the shattered lives of lost playwrights, this one...
Shifted my insides.
Slowik died before completing Volume 10.
Javier never made it into *Lives.*
This index card set me on a journey
to discover this "Ugh-known Vital."
A journey that culminates
in tonight's performance of Javier's final work —
The *only* work he completed after the disappearance of his son ...
Several years ago I unearthed a recording Javier made — notes for an introduction. Listen:

A recording of Javier's voice. The voice sounds broken.

JAVIER'S VOICE: Twenty-two months into writing this play, I suffered a near terminal case of writer's block when I discovered its subject, Harry Smith — the musicologist, filmmaker, painter, anthropologist, occultist, magician, editor of *The Anthology of American Folk Music* — was not my own fictional creation, but an actual person. A cosmic joke: how could a figure so emblematic yet enigmatic, so ... *American* be anything but a figment of an overheated imagination ...

DR. KURTZ: None of this is true, of course. Javier's archives reveal his *monomania* in unearthing the facts and many fictions surrounding Harry's life and work. One might misread Javier's introduction as an *apologia* for his play. A later passage reveals his true intent ... Javier's own words:

JAVIER: *A Thick Description of Harry Smith* is my folly. My attempt to solve a riddle that has confounded me since childhood. Since immigrating from the *other* America, the Latin one, from a place one might call a "Banana Republic," I've wrestled with the question: what does the word, the idea, "American" mean? My obsessive listening to *Prairie Home Companion* provided occasional insight. Ginsberg, Whitman, Ralph Ellison helped. Elvis Presley? The Dionysian whippersnapper of '55, yes, but in my heart I want to believe: America must not end at the foot of a toilet, pants rolled round its ankles, face down on a shag carpet — If these failed me, what about the Founding Fathers, the great Presidents? — No, I needed a creature of the underground, an unknown American genius of self-invention. I needed to invent my own American. Alas, Harry Smith, America already invented you.

— Javier C., Chippewa Falls, Wisconsin, 1993

DR. KURTZ: I confess: first time I read *Thick Description,* I believed Harry Smith to be Javier's invention. His triumphant solution to the riddle of America. His demented *Citizen Kane* for the tired, poor huddled masses — I wanted Harry to embody Javier's brilliance, recklessness, invention — a naked self-revelation through the creation of an impossible "other," his penance for what he called his "great crime of omission."

What Javier never grasped was that he himself — like Harry — was an invention of the America he claimed not to understand.

Before we begin tonight's performance, I want to offer my deepest gratitude to Berkeley Repertory Theater for their tremendous support in my reconstruction of this almost-lost play.

Ladies and gentlemen, *A Thick Description of Harry Smith (or Do What Thou Wilt Shall Be the Whole of the Law...*

Applause sign lights. Real and recorded applause. Lights out. Collage sound of train whistles, iron horses, the steady rhythm of steel wheels powering along steel rails that crescendos to:

PART ONE

THE BEGINNING OF THE SHOW

A live band kicks into a rocking, swinging, celebratory version of Blind Lemon Jefferson's "See That My Grave Is Kept Clean." They are the centerpiece of a space that should have the feel of a Rauschenberg assemblage or scrap junk sculpture or post-Millennial medicine show.

SONG: "SEE THAT MY GRAVE IS KEPT CLEAN"

MARLOWE: *(singing)* Well there's one kind favor I ask of you
>　There's one kind favor I ask of you
>　Lord there's one kind favor I'll ask of you
>　Please see that my grave is kept clean

>　Lord it's two white horses in a line
>　Lord it's two white horses in a line
>　Well it's two white horses in a line
>　Take me home to my burying ground

>　My heart stopped beating, my hands got cold
>　My heart stopped beating, my hands got cold
>　My heart stopped beating, Lord my hands turned cold
>　I believe now what the Bible told

>　Have you ever heard that coffin sound
>　Have you ever heard that coffin sound
>　Have you ever heard a coffin sound
>　Then you know another poor boy's in the ground

>　Will you dig my grave with a silver spade
>　Please dig my grave with a silver spade
>　Won't you dig my grave with a silver spade
>　You may lead me down with a ball and chain

>　There's one last favor I'll ask of you
>　Just one small favor I'll ask of you

> There's one last favor I'll ask of you
>
> Please see my grave is kept clean …

They perform a rousing finish. Applause light — real and recorded applause. The band plays a theme for the entrance of the Stranger Emcee (who may be Harry Smith in disguise).

STRANGER EMCEE: Evening friends, Americans, countrymen

> Ole Garrison couldn't make it tonight,
>
> Body snatchers got him
>
> Ice fishing on Lake Wobegon, Minnie-sotie
>
> But like they say in the bizness they call *show*
>
> "War must go on … "
>
> Ladies and gentlemen:
>
> Let's hear it for the third best bar band in the world
>
> Blank Marlowe and the Red Herrings,

Applause light. Real and recorded applause.

> Performing Blind Lemon Jefferson's
>
> "See That My Grave Is Kept Clean"
>
> Last song ol Lemon committed to acetate 'fore he uhhh
>
> *Froze* to death
>
> Or got shot on 47th and Wabash, Bronzeville, south side Chicago …
>
> Details hazy like so many things …
>
> Any case wasn't a white horse but
>
> An iron horse hauled his coffin down
>
> To the Wortham Black Cemetery, Wortham, Texas …
>
> You told me back stage, Marlowe,
>
> That you, the boys and the *fine* young lady on piano
>
> Did a little grave tending on your way here …

The band members trade uncomfortable glances behind MARLOWE's back.

MARLOWE: Indeed.

STRANGER EMCEE: Quite the detour

> Speed fueled beeline from New York City to Berkeley, Cali-4-nye-A?

Wortham, Texas ... not a

Conventional stop on the triple A guide ...

MARLOWE: We got

You know,

Waylaid.

Detours ...

Circuitous routes ...

The road ...

STRANGER EMCEE: Sure sure.

Any case

Mighty kind of you to go down there

Fulfill Blind Lemon's final wish ...

You did fulfill his wish ...?

MARLOWE: Swept the headstone.

Tossed the dead flowers.

Laid down some fresh ones.

STRANGER EMCEE: Long time?

There was no head stone.

Ol Lemon lay there, grave unmarked

Wasn't til '67, '68,

Folks lobbied State of Texas to place a marker.

MARLOWE: I did not know that.

STRANGER EMCEE: By '96,

Nature reclaimed it

But in marched an Outfit called the

Scandinavian Blues Association

(Blues and Swedes, now *that* is some free association)

Wrote a check

Installed a proper headstone

LEMON JEFFERSON 1893-1929

Epitaph reads:

MARLOWE: "Lord it's one kind favor ..."

STRANGER EMCEE: dot dot dot ...

    Makes you wonder

    Will someone see *my* grave's kept clean ...?

MARLOWE: I hope so, sir ...

STRANGER EMCEE: That a favor I might ask of you?

MARLOWE: If I don't end up in the grave before you do.

STRANGER EMCEE: Anyway, ladies and gentlemen, we got a show for you tonight,
    Merry Andrew's here with his Death Machine.

Applause light. Live and recorded applause.

    Latest installment of

    Darkest Heart of America: The Never Ending Tour of Blank Marlowe and The Red Herrings

Applause light. Live and recorded applause.

    Musical guest, the late Rabbi Nuftali Zvi Margolies Abulafia

Applause light. Live and recorded applause.

    The Albuquerque Youth Ballet's performance of *Heaven and Earth Magic*

Applause light. Live and recorded applause.

    Mystery Radio Theatre Presents: *The Curator's Folly*

Applause light. Live and recorded applause.

    Shadow of the Shining City: Chronicles of the American Underground ...
    Featuring special guests Allen Ginsberg and Richard and Pat Nixon

Applause light. Live and recorded applause.

    Course no evening's complete without a trip to Mahagonny, USA
    And everyone's favorite watering hole-in-the-wall, Red Herring's Bar and Grill,
    Where the rotgut's cheap, the men are creeps, and the women even creepier.

Applause light. Live and recorded applause.

    And Ladies and Gentlemen ...
    Mr. Harry Smith's in the house

Applause light. Wild live and recorded applause.

Rumor has it

as part of our series "Dangerous Experiments in American Film"

Harry's screening his rarely seen masterpiece *Oz* ...

The applause light goes crazy. Live and recorded applause. Recorded oohs and ahhs.

... that is, if you're all good, now.

so sit back, re-lax, cause off. We. Go ...

The band kicks into a raucous reprise of "See That My Grave is Kept Clean"

But first, a word from our sponsor: Dr. Smith's American Balsam

The band strikes up a self-consciously old-timey instrumental. The Merry Andrew appears. He wears a fat suit underneath a garish, careworn costume that conjures the image of a lost Merry Prankster or a medicine show that went bust eons ago.

MERRY ANDREW: Invalid Americans! This is for YOU!

Best cure for all diseases – including asthma, bronchitis, consumption, indigestion, skin eruptions, heart troubles, obesity, swine flu, female complaints, rheumatism, diarrhea, kidney stones, flatulence, offensive breath, insomnia, chronic fatigue, scurvy, premature ejaculation, constipation, jaundice, anorexia, and chronic boredom.

TESTIMONIAL #1 (ANNIE): I have been a chronic sufferer of a number of diseases over the years – liver complaint, female weakness, not to mention manic depression. They've kept me fairly wild day and night. I tried Dr. Smith's American Balsam – in no time, my symptoms disappeared! – Mrs. Mary Anne Baxter, Boise, Idaho

TESTIMONIAL #2 (MARTIN): I am 65 years old. For the past thirty years I've endured long periods of flatulence, indigestion, catarrh of the heart. I'm also prone to road rage, sadistic and suicidal thoughts. I've taken lots of medicines over the years – Dr. Smith's American Balsam is by far the best. Dr. Smith: you changed my life. – Mr. Harold Dean Wilson, Wichita, Kansas.

MERRY ANDREW: Guaranteed remedy for every ailment known to man, Dr. Smith's American Balsam contains no narcotic, hypnotic, or hallucinogenic ingredients.

Side effects may include inexplicable euphoria, phantom limb sensation, mild paranoia, increased libido, speaking in tongues, delusions of grandeur, and in rare cases, cosmic insight. Dr. Smith's American Balsam – it's your own damn fault if you don't use the remedy that cures.

Sold in large bottles for 50 cents. Prepared by Dr. Harry E. Smith, Anacortes, Washington.

The band finishes the song. The Stranger Emcee returns, wearing ceremonial regalia: old worn trousers, an Ordo Templi Orientis t-shirt, a seersucker suit jacket and a black satin cape. He's barefoot. On his head, he wears an object that at first glance might appear occultish, but is actually constructed of cardboard paper towel tubes and paper flowers.

STRANGER EMCEE: Before we go on ... in the name of full disclosure uhhhh

Back in the greenroom

Management

Kindly provided us with free Leinenkugels.

Myself I consumed Three, four ... Six?

Also partook in our pre-performance ritual

The

Communal sharing of Mr. Fattie, a.k.a a generously rolled marijuana cigarette.

Helps with

Passing through the limn

Between

Life *off* stage and life *on*.

Speaking of Mr. Fattie

First made his acquaintance

In Berkeley, California, 1947? '46?

Applause light. The band underscores following with a Jefferson Airplane-esque psychedelic instrumental.

Beginning of a beautiful friendship.

My

Initiation

Occurred on what was supposed to be a

Decompression weekend third semester of my

Anthropological studies at the University of Washington
This was uhhh
'fore I came to the realization that
Levi-Strauss was the greatest novelist that ever lived.
Trip coincided with the
First time I saw Woody Guthrie play,
Mr. Fattie
Woody Guthrie
The uhhhh
Air?
There?
In the Bay Area?
Combined with
The
Atmosphere bourgeois people call
B'hemian — Man, I just call it American —
Red White and Blue blooded *invisible* American —
One could rightly say that weekend was a
Formative experience.

In addition to the twelve Leinenkugels, Mister Fattie
I have also ingested a couple of valium, a fistful of bennies, a few other assorted fla-
vors from the candy dish, as part of an ongoing anthro-pharmacological self-study.

I tell you this as a friendly warning:
Anything I say or do is
Uhhhh subject to theeee
Influence of my self-medication.
That said:
Let's go on with the show —

MYSTERY RADIO THEATRE: THE CURATOR'S FOLLY, PART ONE

The band kicks into an intense, creepy version of Clarence Ashley's "The Coo Coo Bird." A wall of boxes appears, as does The Curator.

STRANGER EMCEE: Ladies an Gentlemen, it's time for *Mystery Radio Theatre: The Curator's Folly Part One ...*

Please give a warm welcome to The

Curator of the future Harry Smith Museum and Interpretive Center, Mahagonny, USA, Ms. Pa—

The Curator interrupts with her rendition of "The Coo-Coo Bird." As the song progresses, The Curator's bookish exterior slowly unravels to reveal the sensuous, somewhat naughty, woman that's hidden inside.

SONG: "THE COO COO BIRD"

CURATOR: *(singing)* Gonna build me a temple
        On a hilltop so high
        So you can see Harry
        As he walks on by

        Oh the Coo-coo is a pretty bird
        She warbles as she flies
        She never hollers coo-coo
        Til the 4th of July

        We've played chess in New York
        We've played chess on the Plains
        Won't bet you ten dollars
        Cause you beat me every game

        There's a white Queen, there's a white Queen
        I know her from old
        She's robbed my shallow pockets
        Of my bishops and my gold

Gonna build me a temple

On a hilltop so high

So you can see Harry

As he walks on by

Oh the Coo-coo is a pretty bird

She warbles as she flies

She never hollers coo-coo

Til the 4th of July ...

The song ends, applause light goes on. Applause, live and recorded. The Curator, catching herself having gone to this very sensual place, takes on her "curatorial" persona.

CURATOR: Thank you, thank you ...

Behind me you see a wall of boxes,

Contents of which are the collections left behind by Harry Everett Smith

When he died in 1991 ... 160 boxes in all,

Which I, as the curator of the Harry Smith Museum and Interpretive Center,

Am immersed in the

Complex task of

Cataloguing,

Organizing and ...

Interpreting ...

Allow me to demonstrate ...

She removes a box and opens it. The lighting changes, so the Stranger Emcee is in silhouette. He becomes the Voice of Harry and speaks into the microphone. The Curator is aware of the voice and disconcerted by it.

HARRY: This uhhh's

One of those things I

Don't like being touched ...

People touching

Never know the uhhh

Danger of hand washing, hazardous chemicals on your fingers uhhh

The Curator removes items from the box.

CURATOR: Box One Forty Seven: Realia, Items Seven Thousand One to Seven Thousand Twenty-Five.

Or, what I call "Things that are shaped like things they are not."

HARRY: I'm uhhh

Leaving it to

Future generations to uhhh

Figure out the purpose of all this *stuff*

CURATOR: Plastic mechanical bank shaped like Uncle Sam.

Plastic toy phone shaped like Mickey Mouse.

HARRY: The uhhh

Rotten Easter eggs,

Paper airplanes

CURATOR: Metal mechanical bank shaped like Elvis Presley.

Metal mechanical bank shaped like the State of Oklahoma.

HARRY: The uhhhhh …

String figures,

Seminole patchwork I never look at –

CURATOR: Plastic Halloween horn shaped like Pocahontas.

Plastic mechanical bank shaped like the Statue of Liberty.

HARRY: I will say that the uhhhh *collections* are

Justifiable as any other type of

Research.

CURATOR: Yo-yo shaped like a UFO.

Dog squeak toy shaped like a hot dog.

1991 Chairman's Merit Grammy Award for Lifetime Achievement

HARRY: What was it I said at the ceremony? "I have arthritis,

I uhh flew in from Colorado so …

Thank you."

CURATOR: *1991 Chairman's Merit Grammy Award –*

HARRY: And uhhh

"I'm Glad to say my dreams came true

That I saw America change through music ... "

CURATOR: You see my dilemma ...

Charged with organizing these materials into a museum.

Like Harry used to say ...

HARRY: I'm uhhhh

Leaving it to future generations to uhh

Figure out the purpose of all this *stuff*

CURATOR: Is there rhyme is there reason ...

Is all this

Some secret, invisible map of the universe waiting to be deciphered?

Or a third rate, lunatic Dadaist's practical joke?

HARRY: But you'll wanna watch your step, see, cause uhhh

I'm an expert in Black Magick ...

CURATOR: How about a song.

Reprise of "Coo-Coo Bird."

STRANGER EMCEE: Ladies and gennelmen ...

We'll come back later in the show for more

Mystery Radio Theatre, but right now it's that time again ...

DARKEST HEART OF AMERICA: THE NEVER ENDING TOUR OF
BLANK MARLOWE AND HIS BAND THE RED HERRINGS, PART ONE

A montage of sounds created by using the instruments and Foley work, mirrors the sounds described by the Stranger Emcee.

STRANGER EMCEE: It's two minutes to midnight somewhere in America ...

 Hear the campfire crackle?

 Crickets? Forlorn coyote howl?

 Night critters lookin for a meal and a mate ...

 Whoosh of Goodyear tires rolling down the Innerstate

 So dark you can hear the Milky Way ...

 Sounds of the lonesome American Outback

 That three thousand mile wilderness between

 East Coast Sodoms and West Coast Gomorrahs ...

 Ugh-knowable landscape you see

 Out the window of your transcontinental flight

 Fills you with wonder, dread ...

 Endless prairies

 Lonely deserts

 Rocky Mountain Donner Family Picnics

 In the middle of this nowhere we find

 Blank Marlowe and his band The Red Herrings:

 VW bus broken down on route to their gig ...

 Listen: Martin toys aimlessly with Annie's *dulcimer* ...

 Watch: pretty little Annie builds her house of cards

 Knocks em down, starts all over ...

 Jorge sips his Miller Lite,

 readin a paperback bout UFOs ...

 And Blank Marlowe.

 Blowin all his yearning and pain into that harmonica

 Cause Marlowe's always de-tourin

 Leaving the Interstate for those forgotten two lane ribbons of asphalt,

 Chasin the faded jewels strung along them:

Abandoned towns, where mysteries wait
in junk shops, last chance taverns,
gravestone etchings of vanished musical forebears
And the bedrooms of lonely widows ...

Yes, Blank's got a story on his mind,
Hopes by telling it, his fellow troubadours'll
forgive this latest detour into
The Darkest Heart of America ...

MARLOWE: Once upon a time
    Darkness ruled here too ...

MARTIN: *(Stops playing the dulcimer, addresses the audience.)* Always an "Oh shit" moment,

ANNIE: Oh shit

JORGE: *Mierda*

MARTIN: when Marlowe pulled something out like that

MARLOWE: Once upon a time the darkness ruled here too.

MARTIN: Just like Marlowe to throw the gauntlet down —

JORGE: Even before the first hand of poker was dealt

ANNIE: Never bent me out a shape
    Half the shit came out Marlowe's mouth?
    Was just that
    Shit.

MARTIN: "Once upon a time" ... meant Marlowe had
    Something buried in his heart dying to crawl out.
    Been a year since our last tour.
    Tour ends, we got homes to go to,
    Beds to lie in, dogs to walk, kids to play with,
    Other halves to endure,

But not Marlowe ...

He still ...

MARLOWE: "Follows the sea"

MARTIN: That's what he says, "Follow the sea."

Marlowe's got no home –

MARLOWE: Makes you wonder

What the darkness was like

When Eisenhower passed through.

1918? '19?

Army caravan crawling East coast to West

Testing how fast the war machine'd move

If the enemy invaded ...

Sixty two days took to cross –

Might as well have crossed the darkest heart of Africa ...

Only this was the United States of America

One nation under God, indivisible –

JORGE: Don't go there ...

MARLOWE: What.

JORGE: Part about liberty and justice – don't get me // started

MARLOWE: Crossing the continent

Ol' Eisenhower felt the Dread.

Saw this wasn't one nation, no!

But a *granfalloon* of exiles, criminals, desperadoes, snake oilmen, heyoka

JORGE: Hey-oh-//wha?

MARLOWE: Sharing nothing but that vague identifier ...

American ...

If this "nation"? was under "God"?

Wasn't indivisible cause

God kept his eye only on certain parts.

ANNIE: *(Sigh.)*

MARLOWE: When ol Ike signed the bill made the Interstates? '55? '56?
    Sure as hell had those dark places etched in his head,
    Made damn sure those concrete blood vessels'd bypass
    The white spaces in your Rand McNally ...
    Cause you know what's in those white spaces?

MARTIN: No ...

MARLOWE: Darkest heart of America, that's // what

ANNIE: Oh. My. Lord.

MARLOWE: Cause once upon a time the darkness ruled // here too.

ANNIE: What in God's name are you talking about, // Marlowe?

MARLOWE: Suspicious? Course I'm suspicious, it's downright idol worship ...

ANNIE: HhhhhhhohmyGod.

MARLOWE: The singer.

ANNIE: From the interstate to the singer, here we go.

MARLOWE: Should be the singer singing the song and not the song, right?
    Or should it be the other way around –
    The song, not the singer singing it.

JORGE: Huh?

MARLOWE: Should the singer singing the song outlive the song
    or
    Should the song outlive the singer singing it
    OR:

MARTIN: Or ...?

MARLOWE: Are the singer and the song abominations against the Heavenly Creator ...

ANNIE: Now he's talking Heavenly Crea//tor

MARLOWE: Least that's what I think *he* was trying to tell me ...

ANNIE: Any idea what's he's talking about Jorge // cause I

JORGE: No idea, I just work // here

MARTIN: Shhhhhh – Marlowe?

You were saying ... "least that's what I think he was trying to tell me?"

MARLOWE: I said that?

MARTIN: Um. Yeah.

Who was trying to tell you?

MARLOWE: Andrew.

MARTIN: Andrew ...

MARLOWE: *Merry* Andrew.

ANNIE: Merry? Andrew?

MARLOWE: It's what he said, even sang it. *(Half sings.)* "My name is Merry Andrew, I come from ... "

Pause. Crickets.

The Stranger Emcee interrupts.

STRANGER EMCEE: Ladies and gentlemen, please give a warm welcome to Merry Andrew and His Death Machine

Applause light. Wild applause. Merry Andrew appears, with a bull horn and pulling a large, heavy wooden box with a long rope. This should be painful and comical to watch, sort of like Lucky in Waiting for Godot, *only American. He completes the journey — looks at the audience, striking a pose of a tired and low rent showman. He begins his song —*

SONG: MY NAME IS MERRY ANDREW (BASED ON "STATE OF ARKANSAS")

MERRY ANDREW:

My name is Merry Andrew I come from Tupelo town
For 20 years I've traveled this sad, wide world aroun'
Bumps, dead ends, and miseries, maybe one good day or two
But I never knew what misery was til Harry I met you.

I walked down to the depot saw the ticket counter man
Asked me where I want to go, said far away's I can
He took my last ten dollars, pointed to the track
Ride that Iron Horse one way, don't bother comin' back.

Got off at Mahogany where I chanced to meet a man
Told me "Call me Harry Smith, or you can call me Cain"
Wore bottle-bottom glasses, had rows of rotten teeth
Said he knew a good motel where I could catch some sleep.

Harry led me down the road to this establishment
Wasn't a motel at all, but a squalid tenement
In his room he had no food, in his milk the roaches crawled
He cast a wicked spell on me, for soon I was enthralled.

Late that night he showed me films, strangest I ever seen
Colors, shapes, vibrations leapt off the movie screen
He told me that he painted them, by hand and frame by frame
If they hadn't mesmerized me, I'd have thought this man insane.

He showed me his collections, paper airplanes, 78s,
Easter eggs, string figures, books stacked up high in crates.
He pointed out connections, fired up another joint
My mind confused and reeling I began to see his point.

Sunrise Harry turned to me, asked for fifty cents
Told me even shamans have got to pay their rent
For six long weeks he taught me to spin gold into straw
He emptied out my pockets sent me down to Wichita.

Now I wander town to town, I sell his medicine
Haunted by the memory of his demon eyes and grin
Hardly any takers except for one or two
I curse and bless the day that Harry I met you.
I curse and bless the day that Harry I met you.

At the camp fire.

MARTIN: Marlowe ... ?

   You okay ... ?

MARLOWE: He said to me:

MERRY ANDREW: Mister? I don't know you from Adam, what your business is ...

   You gotta pass the test 'fore I let you take one step further.

MARLOWE: Test?

MERRY ANDREW: Pass, I let you in.

MARTIN: "Let you in" where?

MERRY ANDREW: Fail, push that hunk a junk back in the direction you came

MARLOWE: Look I don't want no trou//ble

MERRY ANDREW: PSSSHT!

Merry Andrew hides behind the box. Drum roll. He prepares for a cheap magic trick. He leaps out from behind the box, cane in hand, and lands, striking a carnival barker pose and gesturing with his cane. Nothing happens.

He repeats this. Nothing happens.

He repeats it again. Nothing. Frustration mounts.

Again. Nothing. Explosion: Merry Andrew attacks the box with his cane, his fists, his feet and string of four letter words punctuated by the occasional "Sonofabitch Harry Smith." Nothing, nothing, nothing. He's furious. Humiliated. A performer hung out to dry. He exits. As he disappears offstage, the walls of the box collapse revealing a 1920s Victor Talking Machine. Merry Andrew pops his head out from offstage. He reenters, back in performance mode.

MERRY ANDREW: Son, you have any idea what your godforsaken eyes are a-gazin' upon?

MARLOWE: Uhhh, 78 record play//er?

MERRY: WRONG!

   Yeah, it plays 78s, but NO!

   You have before you

   A miracle of forward thinking American know-how:

   1927 VV-830-X *Credenza* Victor Talking Machine

   Known to those of us on the *inside*

As the pre-Depression iPod ...

Imagine, mister,
It's 1927. You walk into the wonderland of a Victor Dealership
Dealer makes a friendly suggestion –

VICTOR DEALER (MARTIN): Step right over here, feller ...

MERRY ANDREW: Voice turns you into the obedient customer he wants you to be
And at heart you are –

Leads you down a path flanked by these beautiful machines,
To the Holy of the Holies, top of the line
1927 –

VICTOR DEALER: VV-830-X *Credenza* Victor Talking Machine –
This elixir can be yours for 300 pre-Depression Dollars ... Listen: this'll knock
your socks off ...

MERRY ANDREW: Dealer slips a 78 on the turntable,
Lays the needle on the grooves ...

*A loud pop. A symphony of eggs frying. Merry Andrew closes his eyes in eargasmic reverie. A
song begins: "You Must Be Born Again" by Reverend J.M. Gates. The recording – scratchy,
ghostly, unnerving – sounds impossibly ancient, yet terrifying in its immediacy. It plays
through the scene.*

MERRY ANDREW: Listen to that ... Reverend JM Gates ...
You see Mister:
Your iPod might hold quarter million songs in a box smaller'n a pack of Lucky
Strikes,
But this Machine,
Un-portable as she is, ain't no dummy.
Lasts longer too – no built-in self-destruct-in-four-years mechanism ...
Yep, she features the latest in Orthophonic sound reproduction technology,
Developed in that great laboratory for advances in science, business, art, and Democ-
racy:
World. War. I.

Yep: 20 million corpses not only made the world temporarily safe for democracy,
All them bodies made possible the accurate, affordable reproduction of sound
To enjoy in your living room.
No 20 million dead, no Elvis.
No dead, no Bobby Dylan.
No dead, no Sly and the Family Stone, no Hannah Montana.

ANNIE: Hannah Montana?

MARLOWE: It's what he said.

MERRY ANDREW: Ready for the test?

MARLOWE: Uhhh –

MERRY ANDREW: Good: now
Some folks, Mister,
Call it the Death Machine
Unrepentant Murderer of American Music ...
Others kneel in reverence,
Pronounce it Birth Mother of American Music.
Others'll tell you it's The Wicked Messenger
Abomination against the Creator and all that is Holy ...

MARLOWE: Is there like a ... question you want me to answer?

MERRY ANDREW: Yeah, I got a question ... Where do you stand?

MARLOWE: Ummm ... could you elaborate?

MERRY ANDREW: Mister: advocates of the Death Machine Theory'll tell you
'fore this machine? Everyone sang. Didn't have to be a musician proper,
You just sang. To your children. Layin rails, tilling fields. Little taste of joy
After a hard day in the coal mine.
Old songs, pieces of ancestral memory
In a land that demands amnesia ...

Nowadays people spend good money on psychiatrists, Yoga lessons
When all they need's a good song, sung from the heart ...

Death Machine killed that — gave birth to a thing called *virtuosity*

Split the world in two: those that sang, those that listened ...

Those that sang got themselves on records

Those that *listened*

Turned deaf to the natural sound of their voice yearning to sing out ...

Those songs on record? Sound the same every time you listen ...

Back at the campfire. Marlowe directs the following few exchanges between Merry Andrew and the band.

MARLOWE: I'm asking you — is it not natural to be suspicious

Of those that kneel at the altar of infinite reproduction?

ANNIE: *What?*

MARLOWE: Like etching a name on a gravestone —

Wax cylinders

78s

Vinyl 45s, 33 and a third

8-track,

Cassette,

Pure evil compact disc.

Now what they call it ... MP3?

Criminal.

Squeezing all those singing voices into ones and zeroes

Like squeezing an elephant into a cricket's cage ...

MARTIN: There was a long pause.

MARLOWE: How's a song supposed to change when it's endlessly reproduced?

How's it supposed to *evolve?*

MARTIN: There was another long pause.

ANNIE: We all wished he was over and done with ...

MARLOWE: How's a song // supposed

ANNIE: Mother//fucker ...

MARLOWE: to learn to walk talk say momma sing the alphabet song

> Keep secrets talk back lose its virginity go off to the college uh hard knocks ...
> How's its heart supposed to grow when it's got a million identical twins running
> round?

MARTIN: I —

MARLOWE: HOW's a song supposed to find its woman, its man

> Birth a brood of children that look a little, sound a little like mama and daddy
> But have to grow up alone. Get Hurt. Have a one night stand.
> Maybe die a lonesome death.

MERRY ANDREW: Slow down there, Mister ... you ain't heard the other side ...

> Those that believe this machine's the Birth Mother'll tell you
> Sure, everyone sang,
> But all those songs?
> Woulda died by the campfire ...
> But for this machine keeping them alive.
> With all them songs floating around?
> Eventually they'd copulate.
> Indulge in polysexual orgiastic rites.
> Presto: a Love Child —
> Rock n Roll, baby:
> Some call it Bastard Child of musical miscegenation,
> But in my humble opinion?
> After Democracy? And the McDonald's French Fry?
> Greatest gift this country ever gave to the world ...

Band plays a '50s rock and roll riff — Merry Andrew gyrates like a demented Elvis.

MARLOWE: Right on ...

MERRY ANDREW: While you contemplate that

> Let me tell you bout those that call it The Wicked Messenger ...
> They'll have you believe this here machine is a Demon
> Violator of the Cosmic Order —

MARLOWE: Yeah. That's bullshit ...

MERRY ANDREW: Yeah. Pay em no mind.

    Cause in America?

    Violatin' the Cosmic Order is the Lost Amendment to The Bill of Rights ...

    So: Death Machine? Birth Mother? Wicked Messenger?

    Where do you stand?

From the Victor we hear, quietly, the beginning of Clarence Ashley's version of "The House Car-penter" from the Anthology. *Marlowe strums, aimlessly, to the music. Both sounds underscore the following.*

ANNIE: What'd you answer, Marlowe?

JORGE: Yeah, what did you answer?

MARTIN: Marlowe?

MARLOWE: I had a nightmare ...

    All the Mommas of the world

    Stopped singing songs to their little children.

    Instead they bought em iPods

    Stuck them ear buds in their little ears,

    Hit shuffle, let them little babies cry themselves to sleep alone in the dark ...

    I had another nightmare ...

    Where no one ever heard the cosmic roar

    Of "Voodoo Chile," or Dylan ask

    "How does it *feel* to be on your *own*

    No direction *home* ... "

MERRY ANDREW: Mister? You gonna answer the question?

MARLOWE: What's that music?

ANNIE: What music ...

MERRY ANDREW: That...? Little present Harry made.

MARLOWE: Who's Harry?

MARTIN: Again. Silence. *Long* silence ...

MARLOWE: I'm getting ahead of myself ...
    I'm starting in the middle when I
    Should be starting at the start ...

ANNIE: Shit.

STRANGER EMCEE: Listen: you hear that?
    Marlowe's aimless strumming
    Catches a melody ...

In the stillness of the night, recognition of the song sets in. Annie begins to sing, almost to herself.

SONG: THE HOUSE CARPENTER

ANNIE: *(singing)*
    Well met, well met said my old true love
    Well met well met said he

MARLOWE: *(singing)*
    I've just returned from the cold grey sea all for the love of thee

ANNIE:
    Come in, come in my old true love
    Have a seat with me

MARLOWE & ANNIE:
    It's been three fourths of a long long year since together we have been

MARLOWE:
    I can't come in, I can't sit down
    I haven't but a minute's time
    They say you're married to a house carpenter, your heart will never be mine

ANNIE:
    He said: "I could've married a king's daughter there
    And she would have married me"

ANNIE & MARLOWE:

> But I've forsaken her jewels and gold all for the love of thee

MARLOWE:

> Will you forsake your house carpenter
>
> Leave this hell with me
>
> I'll take you where the palm trees grow on the banks of the turquoise sea

ANNIE:

> I lifted up my newborn babe
>
> And kisses gave him three
>
> Said stay right here my little darling boy, keep your daddy company

MARLOWE & ANNIE:

> We hadn't been on ship but about two weeks
>
> I'm sure it was not three
>
> His true love began to weep and mourn as she gazed at the lonesome sea

MARLOWE:

> Are you weeping for your house carpenter
>
> Are you weeping cause we're poor?

ANNIE:

> I am weeping for my darling little boy whose face I'll never see anymore

MARLOWE & ANNIE:

> We hadn't been at sea but about three weeks
>
> I'm sure it was not four
>
> When a leak sprung in the bottom of the ship and we sank to the ocean floor ...

The song ends. Silence. The sounds of the night.

JORGE: There any more beer?

The crickets fade up, the harmonica theme closing the segment begins. Applause light.

STRANGER EMCEE: Folks we'll come back in a spell

> For more *Darkest Heart of America.*
>
> Little ditty you just heard was "The House Carpenter" —

Light shift. The silhouetted Harry overtakes the Stranger Emcee.

HARRY'S VOICE: Appears as track number uhhh 3
>Volume One of the *Anthology*
>Clarence Ashley, 1930, Original issue Columbia Records, Number 15654D
>Based on the Scottish Ballad, "The Daemon Lover"
>The uhhhh
>Supernatural theme in early versions
>Is virtually nonexistent in its American descendents ...

Light shift, silhouetted Harry replaced by the Stranger Emcee.

STRANGER EMCEE: Speaking of records,
>Let's hear another word from our sponsor.

Music. Recording of a rabbi singing ancient Jewish liturgical music.

ANNOUNCER'S VOICE (MARTIN): *Time* magazine calls it:

VOICE OF TIME MAGAZINE (ANNIE): "A landmark in the annals of recording..."

ANNOUNCER'S VOICE (MARTIN): *The New York Review of Books* describes it as:

VOICE OF THE NEW YORK REVIEW OF BOOKS (JORGE): "A once-in-a-generation musicological event ... "

ANNOUNCER'S VOICE (MARTIN): *Rolling Stone* creams:

VOICE OF ROLLING STONE (ANNIE): "A cosmic mind-fuck. If Harry Smith's *Anthology of American Folk Music* was the Rosetta Stone for the '50s Folk revival, these recordings are an esoteric time bomb" –

ANNOUNCER'S VOICE (MARTIN): Smithsonian Folkways, K-Tel and Zohar Records present *East Broadway Tree of Life: The Jewish Liturgical Songs of Rabbi Nuftali Zvi Margolies Abulafia.* This never-before-released 18 record set contains digitally remastered recordings of a Lower East Side legend: Rabbi Nuftali Zvi Margolies Abulafia. Recorded by noted ethnomusicologist Harry Smith, this set contains the only existing recordings of Rabbi Abulafia and his encyclopedic knowledge of Jewish liturgical music, sung by heart, from memory ... Own this miracle of music history. Available wherever records are sold ...

MYSTERY RADIO THEATRE: THE CURATOR'S FOLLY, PART TWO

STRANGER EMCEE: Time once again for *Mystery Radio Theatre*. Please welcome back
    The curator of the future Harry Smith Museum and Interpretive Center Ms. Pa—

The Curator removes two more boxes from the pile.

CURATOR: Box 158: Tarot and Playing Cards.
    I won't show you each of the two hundred fourteen items in this box —
    but to give you a sense …
    Golden Dawn Tarot
    Tree of Life Tarot
    Tarot of the Cat People
    Old Maid
    Mickey Mouse Playing Cards
    Pioneers of Country Music Cards by R. Crumb
    Watergate Scandal Trading Cards
    Iran-Contra Scandal Trading Cards
    And so on …

HARRY: I'm uhhh
    Leaving it to
    Future generations to
    Figure out the purpose of all this stuff

CURATOR: A thought experiment:
    Tonight when you go home to your *Tepee*,
    Pretend it's not you that lives there,
    That the *stuff* surrounding you
    Is the detritus of someone else's life.
    Walk through the rooms as you'd
    Walk through a museum.
    Could you infer a life from the accumulation of things?
    Would the life in any way resemble the one you lived?
    Could you extract anything resembling *meaning?*

There are 160 boxes.

The contents of which are ...

Not what one would expect.

One would *think,*

That the man responsible for assembling the *Anthology of American Folk Music* —

A recording that forever altered the course of American music —

Compiled from a collection of 20,000 78 records

One would *think* he might have a few 78s lying around ...

No. Not a single 78 in all these boxes.

HARRY: The

Anthology was intended to uhhh

Span six volumes.

I finished 1, 2, 3, middle of 4 I uhhh

Lost interest.

Same reason I

Put it together in the first place I uhh

Needed money

To

Finance

Certain

Cinematical alchemical chemical alch'olical endeavors.

CURATOR: There are records ... hundreds, mint condition. But all LPs purchased after 1965.

HARRY: I sold the 78s to the uhhh

It's another collection among collections collecting dust in

The constipated bowels of the New York Public Library —

Librarian lost my documentation

So regardless of the uhhh

Collection's *comprehensiveness,* their

Worth as a

Thick description of American life to extraterrestrial invaders,

Without documentation the records —
Are just that. Records.

CURATOR: Okay, no 78s ...

HARRY: I'm uhhh
Leaving it to
Future generations to
Figure out the purpose of all this *stuff*

CURATOR: What about the paper airplanes?
It's said Harry assembled the largest collection of found paper airplanes in the world ...

HARRY: Donated them to the Gnash-Null Air/Space Museum, Smithsonian Institution, Washington, D.C.

The Curator picks up a phone and dials. Ringing. A click.

SMITHSONIAN RECEPTIONIST #1 (JORGE): Space Museum, please hold.

Muzak version of David Bowie's "Space Oddity" underscores the following:

HARRY: The paper airplanes I was
Deciphering uhh
Patterns.
Paper airplanes you find on the streets of Greenwich Village possess characteristics —
Aerodynamics, paper quality, fold precision, unique to that geography
Compared to paper airplanes in Spanish Harlem ...
Cross-classification of the different varieties reveals a —

The Muzak is interrupted by someone picking up the phone.

SMITHSONIAN RECEPTIONIST #2 (ANNIE): Space Museum, can I help you?

CURATOR: I explained what I was looking for.

SMITHSONIAN RECEPTIONIST: Paper airplanes?
No, ma'am.

CURATOR: Nothing bequeathed by Harry Smith?

SMITHSONIAN RECEPTIONIST: Nope. But we have some other neat things ...
Ever hear of the Wright Brothers?

The Receptionist cackles and hangs up.

CURATOR: Okay, no paper airplanes ...

HARRY: I'm uhhh

Leaving it to

Future generations to –

CURATOR: What about the Ukrainian Easter eggs?

HARRY: Göteborg Ethnography Museum, Stockholm, Sweden ...

CURATOR: I email my counterpart there ... Email back:

Sound of email arriving in inbox.

GÖTEBORG CURATOR (MARTIN): Madam,

I'm sorry to say the Göteborg Museum has no Easter eggs in its collections and no objects donated by Harry Smith.

Regards,

Olle,

Head of Collections

CURATOR: Okay, no Ukrainian Easter eggs,

Except for seven rotten ones in the boxes.

HARRY: I'm uhhh

Leaving it to

Future generations to

Figure out the purpose of all this –

CURATOR: What about the films? *Early Abstractions? Mirror Animations?*
Heaven and Earth Magic? Mahagonny? The Oz film?
Not an inch of celluloid in the boxes ...

HARRY: Give Jonas Mekas a call at Anthology Film Archives. He'll hook you up.

CURATOR: I left a message ...

Waiting for the call back ...

Okay. Films? Archived.

What about the paintings – the "wild cosmic monsters" Allen Ginsberg // refers

HARRY: I have a habit of tearing out the canvases
    When I have too much to drink and I uhhhh
    Turn into Rumpelstiltskin.
    Others I traded for illuminated manuscripts, beer,
    If you uhhh track down the
    Hungarian fellow, midget —
    He'll point you to
    Fresh Kills Landfill on Staten Island where you'll uhhhh
    Find your uhhh
    "Harry Smith Museum"

CURATOR: Is there rhyme, is there reason ...
    Is all this
    Some secret, invisible map of the universe waiting to be deciphered?

HARRY: I'll say though that uhhhh
    It's as justifiable as any other type of uhhh
    Research.

CURATOR: Or some third-rate Dadaist's practical joke?

HARRY: It's a cross-sectional index to a variety of thoughts
    You can piss away your time reading *The Oxford English Dictionary*
    Or you can
    collect paper airplanes,
    Easter eggs —
    Designs are thirty thousand years old
    Making them superior to any book
    Because reason I make films, reason I paint,
    Reason I jack off or —
    It just occurred to me, saying "jack off," that Jack,
    Kerouac, that is — his favorite sex act also was uhhh
    Masturbation, specially of the mutual kind, we'd spend hours discussing it
    Though we uhhhh
    He, I never uhhhh I mean he wanted to, I wanted to but we didn't like the idea of

Offending

Anyone's religious sensibilities — what was the question?

CURATOR: Question becomes:

What should a Harry Smith Museum look like?

How about a song?

Short "Coo-coo Bird" reprise. At the end of the song, the applause light goes on. Real and recorded applause.

DARKEST HEART OF AMERICA: THE NEVER ENDING TOUR OF BLANK MARLOWE AND HIS BAND THE RED HERRINGS, PART TWO

STRANGER EMCEE: Ladies and gennelmen …

>Hear the crackle of the campfire?

>Time once again for a detour into

>*The Darkest Heart of America* …

MARLOWE: I'm getting ahead of myself

>I'm starting in the middle

>When I should be starting at the start

ANNIE: Shit …

MARLOWE: Outside every town there's a

>"Welcome to…" sign

>Name of the place, town motto,

>picture of the thing town's famous for –

>Minor Civil War skirmish … Giant Ball of Yarn …

>Town I met Merry Andrew was no different

>Only –

>"Welcome" sign?

>*Moved.*

During the following, Jorge plays the Theremin, a spooky underscore.

MARLOWE: First time I saw it – couldn't tell how far it was –

>That time a night, nowhere two-lane country road?

>Mile could be ten,

>Ten miles, a hundred …

>Looked like a

>Drive-in movie screen on the horizon.

>"Welcome to MAHAGONNY," sign read.

>Spelled like that Brecht play

>(Learned the hard way,

>With a price I'm still paying,

Locals call it Mahogany — like the wood —
Nowhere towns like that all over your Rand McNally —
Americanized foreign names
KAY-roh for Cairo, Ver-SALES for Versailles ...)

ANNIE: Where's this town?

MARLOWE: Place on my Rand McNally where it should've been?
Just white space ...

"Welcome to 'Mahogany'"
Against a strange background —
Hand breaking through the clouds,
plucking a celestial monochord ...

ANNIE: Celestial what?

MARLOWE: Monochord.
Fuckin' celestial monochord.

MARTIN: Marlowe'd never gotten over his
Decade old declaration of love for Annie,
Her brief acceptance and subsequent rejection of him,
So they had a tendency to be short with each other times like // this ...

ANNIE: Pray tell, what's a celestial monochord?

MARLOWE: Break it down.

ANNIE: Mono, one. Chord, stringed instrument. One stringed instr//ument.

MARLOWE: There you go.

ANNIE: It's the celestial part you're losing // me ...

MARLOWE: In relation to the string?

ANNIE: Yeah, jackass, "in relation to the // string."

MARLOWE: Pythagoras.

ANNIE: Oh, for crying out // loud.

MARLOWE: 580-500 // BC

ANNIE: BC blah // blah

MARLOWE: BC that's // right

ANNIE: I know who Pythag//oras ...

MARLOWE: Studied mathematical patterns
> Made by vibrating string.
> Saw evidence of an underlying plan,
> Might even say *Rand McNally*
> Of the universe ...
> That the universe is like
> one infinite musical instrument –
> If you figure its harmonies?
> mathematically – ?
> You can listen to the mind of god ...

MARTIN: There was a long silence while we
> *Contemplated* that.

MARLOWE: May I go on ... ?
> Sign: "Welcome to Mahagonny, Celestial Monochord,"
> Underneath: town motto ...

HARRY'S VOICE: "Do what thou wilt shall be the whole of the Law."

ANNIE: Shit.

CURATOR: Quotation from *Liber AL vel Legis*, also known as *The Book of the Law*.
> Main sacred text of the Law of Thelema. Dict//ated

HARRY'S VOICE: Dictated to my poppy, Aleister Crowley, 1904, in KAY-roh, Egypt
> by Aiwass, Minister of Hoor-par-crat, central deity of the Law of // Thelema ...

MARTIN: None of us needed an explanation where that came from ... We'd all,
> in our younger days,
> *Dabbled*.
> Crowley. Magick. *Sex* magick.

MARLOWE & HARRY: "Do what thou wilt shall be the whole of the Law."

JORGE: Sounds like a good law to me.

MARLOWE: Folks in town lived by it ...

> I get out the car to get a closer look.
> My eyes weren't playing tricks. Sign moved ...
> Morphing colors, shapes, patterns, vibrations ...
> Like some invisible projector was projecting on it.
> Then I hear a voice behind me.

The Merry Andrew theme plays on a toy piano.

MERRY ANDREW: Who the fuck are you?

MARLOWE: Man's standing there – dressed in this far-out drag

> Like some lost carnival geek, dragging on a rope this huge wood box.
> I say:
> Me?

MERRY ANDREW: No. The eight foot tall Chinese dude standing next to you ...

> Yeah, I'm talkin to you.

MARLOWE: I was just ...

MERRY ANDREW: Just ...

MARLOWE: Admiring the sign here.

MERRY ANDREW: Better get movin

> If you know what's good for you.

MARLOWE: Don't wanna ruffle the man's feathers

> Get back in the car, stick the key in the ignition

Jorge makes the sounds of a car ignition failing to catch.

MARLOWE: Won't turn on.

> No idea what to do – I'm in the car,
> Sign's pulsating,
> Mr. Every-Day-Is-Halloween's glaring at me

Finally, I get out …

Um.

Car won't start.

MERRY ANDREW: That so.

MARLOWE: There a gas // statio

MERRY ANDREW: What do you think this is? New York City?

MARLOWE: Huh?

MERRY ANDREW: I don't like the look of your license plates.

MARLOWE: Look, there at least

A place I can lay my head til morning?

MERRY ANDREW: Lay your head …

MARLOWE: Motel, // hotel

MERRY ANDREW: Town's closed for the night.

I'd think twice, buster, bout camping by the side of the road.

MARLOWE: Look, I'm just passing through, I // don't

MERRY ANDREW: "Passing through," huh?

Through what?

To what?

From what? And why?

MARLOWE: Decided wasn't gonna talk to him no more,

went to the car,

Locked the door,

Closed my eyes.

Don't know if it was minutes or hours passed but I hear tapping,

Against the window. High school ring, "Mahagonny High, Class of '68"

It's him. I roll down the window:

What?

MERRY ANDREW: Um ... sorry ...

> Did I ... wake you?

> I was
> Watching you sleep?
> Started feeling like,
> where'd my hospitality go?
> My
> Sense of humanity?

MARLOWE: I just stared at him.

MERRY ANDREW: Town's closed.

> Most of it, anyhow ... but
> One place's open. Red's.

MARLOWE: Red's.

MERRY ANDREW: Red Herring's Bar, Grill

> And Happy Bottom Riding Club
> Might get yourself a room there.

MARLOWE: I'm thinking:

> This guy for real?
> Or is he settin a trap...

MERRY ANDREW: Tween you me and the lamppost:

> Rumor round town Harry's screening *Oz* tonight ...

MARLOWE: Huh?

MERRY ANDREW: I intend you no harm

> just that people
> claimin to be "passing through"
> Come here with *motives* ...

> I got a mandate to protect Harry.

MARLOWE: Who's Harry?

MERRY ANDREW: Nevermind.

MARLOWE: I'll be fine here til morning.

MERRY ANDREW: Suit yourself.

MARLOWE: Off he went, dragging that wood box behind him ...
But Curiosity ... Oh, Curiosity.
Five dollar hooker always wins in the end, dudn't she?

MARTIN: You followed him?
Marlowe went silent ... looked up at the sky then:

MARLOWE: Once upon a time the darkness ruled here too ...

Harmonica theme music. Applause light.

STRANGER EMCEE: Ladies and gentlemen,
Let's leave our traveling troubadours for a spell, cause
It's time for
Shadow of the Shining City: Chronicles of The American Underground ...
Part One: The Ballad of Harry and Allen (Ginsberg that is)

SHADOW OF THE SHINING CITY: CHRONICLES OF THE AMERICAN UNDERGROUND, PART ONE

The band strikes up the "Coo-coo Bird" theme. The Curator appears.

CURATOR: I comb through indexes.

> An example:
> *I Celebrate Myself: The Somewhat Private Life of Allen Ginsberg*
> (Bill Morgan, Viking, 2006)
> Entry for "Smith, Harry":
> "pages 278, 384, 580, 596, 607, 615-619"
> Followed by subheadings
> "Death of, 619
> Bob Dylan and, 587
> Fish design by, 371
> As Ginsberg's houseguest, 586-588"

> A significant number of references, yes,
> But miniscule compared to
> Burroughs, William
> Kerouac, Jack, etc.
> Which begs the question:
> What is Harry's place
> In the hierarchy of significance?

STRANGER EMCEE: Ladies and gentlemen, it gives me great pleasure to bring you
> Live from the Bardo Plane,
> Poet Laureate of the Beat Generation,
> Mister Allen Ginsberg ...

Applause light goes on.

ALLEN GINSBERG: Thank you, so nice, thank you ...

STRANGER EMCEE: Welcome to the show, Allen ...
> Two words:
> Harry. Smith.

ALLEN GINSBERG: Harry ... what do you say about Harry. I weep for Harry. I laugh
my ass for Harry ... Harry was a genius on the realm of Leonardo

STRANGER EMCEE: You don't say –

ALLEN GINSBERG: Biggest pain in the ass ever walked the earth ...
I love Harry Smith.

First heard about him in San Francisco from a mutual filmmaker friend
Described Harry as a painter slash filmmaker slash alchemist slash magician
That Harry was descended from Aleister Crowley

Cut to 1960. '61. I'm at the Five Spot in New York listening to Thelonious Monk.
I see this old guy

Bebop Jazz underscores the next.

CURATOR: Old guy ...?
In '60 Harry was 37.
Ginsberg 34.

ALLEN GINSBERG: ... at a table drinking milk
(He was terrified of being poisoned)
Making tiny marks in a notebook –
For some inexplicable reason I think:
This must be Harry Smith.
I'd been at the Five Spot every night to see Monk
I gave him a copy of *Howl*, to Monk cause ...
I wanted to know what he thought
One night I ask Monk,
Did you read it? Did you read *Howl*? What do you think?

Music abruptly stops.

MONK (JORGE): Makes sense.

Jazz kicks in again.

ALLEN: Which was pure pleasure to hear Monk say that,
But anyway –
I ask him: "Are you Harry Smith?"

HARRY: Who wants to know?

ALLEN GINSBERG: Which I take to mean Yes.

"Wow! What are you doing here?"

HARRY: I'm

Deciphering theeeeuuuuh

Mathematical patterns theeeee

Recurrent syncopations in Monk's solos —

ALLEN: Far out ...

What are you doing that for?

HARRY: I'm using his music as background to films I'm making.

Jazz music cuts out.

ALLEN: Harry lived like a hermit

One night

He invites me to his room,

401 ½ East 70th — *Tiny,*

Every inch covered with books, Easter eggs, records, paper airplanes

HARRY: It's a work-in-progress examination of uhhh

Cross-disciplinary investigations into

Visual, anthropological, musicological phenomena.

ALLEN: That's exactly what I'm thinking, room is some kind of

Museum, map,

Of what I couldn't tell you but —

HARRY: Step right over here uhhh

ALLEN: He shows me a closet — stuffed with Seminole Indian dresses

One point I got too close to a cabinet? Sign said // keep off?

HARRY: KEEP OFF! THOSE'LL BLOW UP IF YOU GET TOO CLOSE!!

ALLEN: That's where he kept the Ukrainian Easter eggs, which he donated to a museum in Scandinavia.

CURATOR: Ha!

ALLEN: Second later he's immersed,
    Playing what looks like a solitary version of Cat's Cradle

HARRY: I'm the world's leading authority on string figures

ALLEN: Far out, how'd you get to be the world's leading authority on —

HARRY: I've mastered hundreds of forms from around the world
    I'm working on a manuscript that uhhhh —

ALLEN: Then he showed me his paintings ... *Jesus*
    These
    Amazing Cosmic Monsters

HARRY: They're not paintings they're uhhh
    Doodles of formulaic triangulations of Pythagorean calculations —
    Ones over there are uhhh
    Note for note visual transcriptions of the music of Dizzy Gillespie
    Here, I'll demonstrate

ALLEN: He sat me down ...
    Handed me a beer from the fridge, (had only a six pack, yogurt, cat food, dead
    birds he found on the street) put Dizzy's "Manteca" on the record player ...

Harry appears before an empty frame dressed like a professor but wearing shades, cigarette dan-
gling from his mouth. Opening drums of Gillespie's "Manteca." Harry does a little jig. When
the horns kick in, he uses a telescopic pointer to point out spots that correspond to the notes. At
a certain point it should appear he is no longer motivating his own movements. It's as if puppet
strings from the sky manipulate him. The song cuts off.

ALLEN: Then he got me high.
    Turned on his movie projector
    Showed me his films ...

HARRY: My uhhh
    Cinematic excreta comes in four delicious flavors:
    Batiked abstractions, painted directly on cellulouid — made 1939 to '46.

ALLEN: He painted them by hand, frame by frame ... intricate like you wouldn't believe.

HARRY: Next: semi-realistic animated collages made as part of my alchemical labors, 1957-62.

ALLEN: Movie called *Heaven and Earth Magic* // which

HARRY: which depicts the heroine's toothache consequent to the loss of a valuable watermelon, her dentistry and transportation to heaven, followed by an exposition of the heavenly land in terms of Israel and Montreal and her return to earth the day Edward the 7th dedicated the London Sewer.

If you're interested:
Films 1 thru 5 I made under the influence of marijuana.
Number 6, schmeck
Number 7, cocaine and ups.
8 thru 12, anything I could get my hands on,
But mostly uhhh
Depravation.
I'm working on uhh
Film #13, a 3-hour meditation on Shamanism
Disguised as an animated adaptation of *The Wizard of Oz* ...
At ten thousand dollars a minute
It's the most expensive animated feature ever made ...
Liz Taylor, Henry Phipps have been most generous ...

ALLEN: Mind blowing stuff, but freaked me out
End of the night
He tries to sell me *Heaven and Earth Magic* for a hundred bucks.
What am I gonna do with a movie? I don't own a projector,
But Harry was living in squalor and I ...
He would do that –
Get you high, mess with your head,
Destroy his stuff, hit you up for 20 bucks ...
I bought it.
Took it to Jonas Mekas at Film-Makers' Cooperative –

JONAS MEKAS (JORGE): Holy fucking shit! Who is this guy? He's a fucking genius...

191

ALLEN: Mekas starts showing his films ...

JONAS MEKAS: 1980? '81? First screening of *Mahagonny* ...
   Complicated like nothing you've seen ...
   Harry built a special projector,
   Simultaneously projected four images –
   In all kinds of combinations ...
   At the screening?
   Harry goes bat shit,
   Throws the projector out the window.
   First and last screening of *Mahagonny.* Oh, well ...

ALLEN: Harry was always broke. From the time we met to when he lived in my apartment to –

STRANGER EMCEE: Hold up ... he lived in your apartment?

ALLEN: '84? '85? Got himself kicked out some Bowery flophouse. Needed a place for a few days.

Sound of a taxi honking, screeching, hitting something that sounds like bones, coming to a halt.

ALLEN: Harry gets hit by a cab. Compound fracture.
   Few days turns into an eight month ordeal ...
   I took pictures – he hated me taking his picture ...
   There's one – him pouring a glass of milk.
   I call it "Alchemist Transforming Milk Into Milk"

   One day,
   Who comes by the apartment?

Buzzer. Annie plays the piano part of "Like a Rolling Stone" on a toy piano.

ALLEN: Who is it?

VOICE OF BOB DYLAN (JORGE): 's me. Bobby.

ALLEN: Bobby! What a surprise! Come up, come up ...

Allen buzzes him in. Footsteps up stairs, a knock.

ALLEN: Bobby!

BOB DYLAN: Ginzie!

ALLEN: So good to see you ... what brings you here?

BOB DYLAN: Smells like shit in here, Allen ...

ALLEN: Oh, yeah

BOB DYLAN: Shit and piss! Wait: that semen?
Place smells like the men's toilet in Washington Square ... What's going on, you depressed again?

ALLEN: No, no no ... just a
Houseguest ... You'll want to meet him

BOB DYLAN: If he smells like shit, I don't –

ALLEN: It's Harry Smith.

BOB DYLAN: *The* Harry Smith? *Anthology* Harry Smith?

ALLEN: One and only.

BOB DYLAN: He smells like shit?

ALLEN: No no no no ... I mean, yes. He's
Living in the room off the kitchen, he's doing paintings
Using his own shit and dead butterflies

BOB DYLAN: He pissin on em too?

ALLEN: Oh, no, no ...
He pees in milk cartons, saving the stuff for some alchemical ...

BOB DYLAN: Can I meet him?

ALLEN: Sure! I'll get him –
Bob Dylan, Harry Smith, same room, Holy shit.
HARRY!

Sound of Allen excitedly pounding on the door.

HARRY: *(Inaudible noises)*

ALLEN: Harry? You okay? You drunk?

HARRY: *(Inaudible noises)*

ALLEN: Harry ... Bobby Dylan's here. He wants to meet you.

HARRY: *(Inaudible noises)*

BOB DYLAN: Tell him I owe him ...

ALLEN: Hear that, Harry? Bob Dylan wants to tell you he *owes* you ...

BOB DYLAN: Tell him ... He invented me.

ALLEN: Bobby wants to tell you you *invented* him ...

HARRY: *(Inaudible noises)*

ALLEN: HARRY!!!! Bob. Fucking. *Dylan.* Is *here.* He wants to pay *tribute.*

HARRY: TELL HIM HE CAN GO PISS UP A TREE!!!!

The band starts up — playing a tune reminiscent of something that might have been an outtake from Ginsberg's "First Blues" recordings. Ginsberg plays the harmonium.

CURATOR: Combing through another index —
> *The Letters of Allen Ginsberg*
> (Bill Morgan, editor, DaCapo, 2008) ...
> September 1988:

ALLEN: *(sings)* Dear Harry it was best for us to get off the telephone
> Dear Harry it was best for me to hang up the telephone
> We dug ourselves into a hole, sorry but you're on your own

CURATOR: He follows this with an accounting of financial outlays to Harry:

ALLEN: *(sings)* Stay away from New York City it costs money to live here
> Four seventy a week adds up to 20 grand a year
> Can't afford this subsidy, to pay for your rent and beer

CURATOR: Ginsberg arranged a Shaman-in-Residence for Harry at Naropa —
> Things got out of hand ...

ALLEN: *(sings)* I won't pay for your ticket to come back to New York City

    Saying this to you my friend makes me feel real shitty

    If you find your way back here, you sure as hell can't stay with me

CURATOR: One can't help but wonder – if he read it at all – what Harry thought reading:

ALLEN: *(sings)* You indulge in magic thinking, you talk evasive yak

    You depend on me for everything, you never pay me back

    I hate to lose my patience but you're giving me a heart attack

CURATOR: Yet Ginsberg can't help closing on a warm note:

ALLEN: *(sings)* I wish you well dear Harry, don't forget your medicine

    Stay away from Kefflex, you're allergic to Penicillin

    Signing off with reverence, your humble friend Allen …

Applause light.

ALLEN: Harry came to town again in '91 …

    To get his Grammy.

    I was so happy for him, finally being recognized …

    He gave a beautiful speech.

HARRY: "I'm glad to say my dreams came true …

    That I saw America change through music"

ALLEN: Brief. But beautiful.

    What it said:

    That the homeless, the minority, the impoverished, the poet –

    which he himself was –

    The forgotten of America –

    Altered the country's consciousness …

STRANGER EMCEE: Did he stay with you that time?

ALLEN: No …

    Ended up back at the Chelsea … Few weeks later, he was dead.

His memorial service – St. Mark's Church ...

You could see all the different people he touched –

the film people, musicians, anthropologists,

poets, brain scientists, the Ordo Templi Orientis guys ... I'm still paying his back rent at the Chelsea,

But when he died ... I wept for him.

There will never be anyone else like Harry Smith.

STRANGER EMCEE: Thank you, Allen ...

For the visit ...

ALLEN: Sure thing. If you ever make it here ... look me up.

Take care, everybody!

He waves. Applause light. The band kicks into a Rockabilly instrumental.

STRANGER EMCEE: Ladies and gennelmen ...

Don't know if you heard the sound but I sure did ... Call of nature and the sweet come hither of a lonely urinal ... Good time to hit the rest stop, folks –

So, stretch your legs, grab a cocktail, smoke outside,

And excuse us while we ... powder our noses ...

Music continues. Button.

End of Part One.

PART TWO

The audience returns. Blank Marlowe and The Red Herrings take the stage and begin a song, playing up its naughty humor.

SONG: "THE BIBLE SALESMAN'S DAUGHTER" OR "NO SIR!" (BASED ON "THE SPANISH MERCHANT'S DAUGHTER")

MARLOWE: *(singing)* Tell me girl, please tell me truly

 Tell me why you scorn me so?

 When I ask, you always hurt me

 Cause you always tell me No.

ANNIE: *(singing)* No sir, no sir, no sir, no sir

 Daddy was a bible salesman

 As he walked out the front door

 Made me promise I would say No

 To everything you did implore

MARLOWE: I know your father he despised me

 But should he not return to thee

 I know that you don't have a mother

 Will you still say no to me?

ANNIE: No sir, no sir, no sir, no sir

 Yes it's true I have no mother

 And if my pop abandons me

 I'll have you know, I've got a brother

 Who will kill to protect me

MARLOWE: When you walk into the garden

 To pluck roses wet with dew

 Girl would you be offended

 If I walked and talked to you?

ANNIE: No sir, no sir, no sir, no sir

> My big brother got a letter
> To the Army he must go
> He told me that I had better
> Keep my promise to say No.

MARLOWE: If while sitting in the garden
> My fingertips and yours did brush
> Tell me would you feel offended
> If my lips and yours did touch?

ANNIE: No sir, no sir, no sir, no sir

MARLOWE: If my hand slips under your dress
> Would you pull away from me?
> If to my room I did invite you
> Would you refuse to lie with me?

ANNIE: No sir, no sir, no sir, no sir

ANNIE & MARLOWE: No sir, no sir, no sir, no sir

A change in the tenor of the song — what began as buoyant, jaunty, tongue in cheek, shifts. The song becomes an honest expression of the unrequited love between Marlowe and Annie — perhaps these verses are sung a cappella.

ANNIE: The empty rooms have grown so quiet
> Looks like Daddy's gone for good
> My dear brother fell in battle
> He came home in a box of wood.

MARLOWE: Will you tell me you don't want me
> After all that we've been through?
> Will you say "No" to my sad brown eyes
> When I say that I love you?

ANNIE: No sir, no sir, no sir, no sir ...

MARLOWE & ANNIE: No sir, no sir, no sir, no sir

Applause light. The Stranger Emcee returns.

STRANGER EMCEE: Big round of applause for Blank Marlowe and The Red Herrings!
Every time you do that number just warms the cockles of my lederhosen ...

MARLOWE: Thank you, sir

STRANGER EMCEE: And Annie?

ANNIE: Yeah, darlin?

STRANGER EMCEE: I know a version of that song. What say you and me do it
together some time ...

ANNIE: Oh yeah? What version is that?

STRANGER EMCEE: Little version I call: "Yes miss, Yes miss, Yes miss, Yessss misssss"

Rim shot.

> Ladies and gentlemen
> Welcome back for the second half ... Normally this point in the show,
> I'd introduce the
> Albuquerque Youth Ballet and their
> Dance adaptation of the
> classic Harry Smith film *Heaven and Earth Magic*
> Received word backstage that uhhh
> They won't be joining us tonight ...
> Something bout a run in with Border Patrol? Area 51?
> Truly a shame cause
> You ever seen the film? No doubt you'd ask –
> "How they gonna pull *that* off?"
>
> Shit. Anyway ... uhhhh
> Let's move on, shall we? To uhh
> nother installment of *Shadow of the Shining City:*
> *Chronicles of the American Underground* ...

*Applause light – real and recorded applause. Theme music begins ... something stately, grand,
a little self-important like certain documentaries you see on PBS.*

SHADOW OF THE SHINING CITY: CHRONICLES OF THE AMERICAN UNDERGROUND, PART TWO

KEN BURNS-ESQUE DOCUMENTARY ANNOUNCER VOICE (MARTIN):
Washington, D.C. Summer. 1973.
A long national nightmare in progress.
The U.S. Constitution dangles precariously
Over the grinding teeth of an overstuffed document shredder.
The cancer has grown malignant on the White House.

Yet in the midst of national crisis,
In the White House basement,
A few steps from the new bowling alley,
The White House Library, for the first time in history
Adds sound recordings to its collection.

Among the first obtained by the Library:
Harry Smith's *Anthology of American Folk Music* ...

Join us for tonight's episode of
Shadow of the Shining City: Chronicles of the American Underground ...
Part Two: "Patriotic Acts of Treason"

Applause light goes on — real and recorded applause. The band begins a song.

SONG: "WHITE HOUSE BLUES"

JORGE: *(singing)* Old Nixon was bothered, old Nixon he did bawl
As his chopper flew over the National Mall
From Washington to San Clement

Gerald in the White House, he's doin' his best
Prayin' he'll wake up from dreamin' this mess
We'll pardon him, for pardoning you

Quiet down little Checkers, now don't you yelp
Ain't nothing for Nixon you can do will help
'74 ain't '52

You went on the TV, said "I ain't no crook"
Time to go home now and write yourself a book
From Washington to San Clement

Ain't but two things that grieve my mind
Boys in Vietnam, the wives they left behind
They're long gone, won't ever come home

You shook hands with Brezhnev, you broke bread with Mao
Yorba Linda poor boy, hey look at you now
From Moscow to Beijing-town

Eighteen long minutes the tape went blank
One by one your cronies, walked down the plank
It's hard times, it's hard times

Yonder comes Woodstein, with their headline
Effective noon tomorrow Dick Nixon will resign
Won't have you to kick around no more

Some cheered "Good riddance," some wept real tears
As you waved bye bye to your White House years
From Washington to San Clement

F. Scott Fitzgerald says "Ain't no second act"
If he knew your story that saying he'd retract
You may be down, but you'll come back
From Washington to San Clement

Applause light.

STRANGER EMCEE: Ladies and gentlemen, please welcome Pop culture historian, rock critic, novelist, painter, documentarian and authority on all sorts of obscure stuff, Dr. Alger Crimus ...

Applause light.

ALGER CRIMUS (MARTIN): The symmetry is almost *novelistic*
    '73: White House acquires the *Anthology* —
    Beginning of the end for Nixon —

Who, of course is elected Eisenhower's Vice President
In '52. The year the *Anthology*'s first *released* ...
Perfect bookends to an era that begins and ends in crisis for Nixon –
Checkers and Watergate, but in '73
Tricky Dick can't go on TV, pimp the family dog, no –
Dylan's prophecy in '64 had come true:
The Times Had Indeed A-Changed.
Which shows that the *Anthology*
Functioned as a kind of alchemic social engineering
Not from the top *down* but from underground *up* ...

STRANGER EMCEE: Say what?

ALGER CRIMUS: Imagine:
    Nixon, battered by Watergate,
    Prowling the White House basement late at night
    After his fourth Mai Tai
    Grumbling to himself ...

NIXON (JORGE): JesusHHaldErlichmanHuntslushlushhushfundBernwardWoodstein-
    JEdgarLiddyWashingtonPostsonsabitchesIamNotACrook*CHRIST*

ALGER CRIMUS: Picture him: troubled,
    Pulling the *Anthology* off the shelf ...

NIXON: Uhh, Pat? Pat? Where are you?

PAT (ANNIE): Right here, Dick.
    I was just feeding King Timahoe ...

NIXON: Erm ... have any idea what this is?

PAT: Why, Dick,
    That's the *Anthology of American Folk Music* ...
    One of the records in the new collection ...

NIXON: I see uhhh
    Folk music, you say. Why is the cover so ...
    Peculiar ...

PAT: Why Dick, that's the hand of God reaching down from the heavens to pluck a Celestial Monochord ...

CURATOR: Etching by Theodore de Bry, 1618. From *De Musica Mundana* by Robert Fludd. English physician, astrologer, Paracelisian ...

NIXON: Parasaywhat?

ALGER CRIMUS: The White House copy is the original 1952 issue ...
With Harry's original artwork. See:
Reissues replaced Harry's design with
Sentimental photos of hard-luck Depression hobos ...
Which appealed to the Romanticism of folkies who
Held the *Anthology* as a kind of *bible* —
But in actuality missed the point — the
Alchemical purpose of Harry's design —
They misread the *Anthology* as a nostalgia trip, rather than what it was:
A peephole to the *past* as a way of engineering the *future* ...
Of American music
Of a desegregated society
Of challenging post-war consumerist America
Of Bob Dylan dispensing with the Newport Folkies,
Creating an explosively NEW American folk music
Of America *itself* ...

PAT: Shall we give it a listen, Dick?
Get your mind off that impeachable offenses business.

NIXON: Erm ... sure, Pat. Care for a Mai Tai?

Sound of a record player stylus landing on vinyl. First notes of "Henry Lee."

ALGER CRIMUS: What the Nixons would have heard is what America sounded like before it became a Republic of Amnesia and Homogeny ...

NIXON: Pat ... this music isn't easing my mind. It's giving me the heebee-jeebees.

PAT: Peculiar ...

NIXON: What is it Plum?

PAT: Booklet that comes with the set ... listen: "A few quotations that have been useful to the editor in preparing this handbook."

HARRY: "Civilized Man Thinks Out His Difficulties, At Least He Thinks He Does. Primitive Man Dances Out His Difficulties."

CURATOR: "R.R. Marret"

NIXON: Hmph.

PAT: And this one ... my word ...

HARRY: "Do What Thou Wilt Shall Be The Whole Of the Law."

CURATOR: "Aleister Crowley"

NIXON: What in God's name is that supposed to mean?

ALGER CRIMUS: I have this fantasy?
 That while they listen?
 A perverse, narcotic fueled *Mr. Smith Goes to Washington* plays out ...
 Harry himself appears like the Wizard of Oz from behind the curtains ...

HARRY: Evening Mister President ...

NIXON: JESUSCHRISTGODDAMNIT! Who the hell are you?

HARRY: I'm Harry Smith.

NIXON: What in God's name is that supposed to // mean??

PAT: Dick, calm down ...

NIXON: How the hell am I supposed to calm down with derelicts breaking into // the White

PAT: Dick: it's okay ... This is Harry Smith. He edited the *Anthology* ...

NIXON: I see, uhhh

PAT: Welcome to the White House, Mr. Smith.
 Care for a drink?

HARRY: Milk.

ALGER CRIMUS: Imagine them:
>In the darkness,
>Under the watchful gazes of
>Gilbert Stuart's portrait of Washington
>And Charles Bird King's Native Americans
>Listening to the *Anthology* ...
>What strange terrain would their conversation cross?

PAT: Here you are boys ... Enjoy!
>Oooh! This one's is catchy ... what's it called?

HARRY: "White House Blues"

PAT: Oh ...

HARRY: North Carolina Ramblers
>1926, original issue Columbia Records Number 15099D ...

NIXON: Mr. Smith has an encyclopedic knowledge of these records ...

HARRY: Shellac's an amazingly versatile product ...
>Used in everything from furniture finish,
>Rifle butts, flak helmets, your // uhhh –

NIXON: Basic war material ...

HARRY: Not to mention its use in the uhhh
>Manufacture of 78 records ...

NIXON: Wasn't aware of that –
>Didn't have 78s back in Whittier ...
>We were Quakers ...

HARRY: It's the records interested me
>Which is why some people accuse me of treason ...

NIXON: You too?

NEWSREEL INTRO VOICE (MARTIN): Grandma Beware! A Public Service Announcement from the Department of War!

Patriotic sounding marching band music — the kind you would hear on a wartime newsreel. Sound of dozens of cats meowing.

OCTOGENARIAN WIDOW (ANNIE): Down, Frisky ... Muffin, leave Binky alone.

Sound of knocking at the door.

OCTOGENARIAN WIDOW: Who is it?

VOICE OF THE WAR DEPARTMENT MAN (MARTIN): War Department ...

OCTOGENARIAN WIDOW: Just a minute ...

Sounds of an old lady's footsteps crossing to a door — stepping on cat tails every now and then, eliciting pained meows. She hums. Sound of a creaky old door opening.

OCTOGENARIAN WIDOW: Can I help you?

WAR DEPARTMENT MAN: Ma'am: we come to you for assistance with a National
    Emergency...

OCTOGENARIAN WIDOW: Yes ...?

WAR DEPARTMENT MAN: Records, ma'am.
    We're collecting 78s for the War effort ...
    Widows like you are known to horde stashes long after your husbands die.
    Do your patriotic duty and fork 'em over ...

OCTOGENARIAN WIDOW: But you already took Walter's records —

WAR DEPARTMENT MAN: Excuse me, ma'am?

OCTOGENARIAN WIDOW: Just yesterday skinny kid came by ... said the country
    needed records for Shellac ... I may be 82,
    But I'll do my part, even if it means giving away Walter's —

WAR DEPARTMENT MAN: What did this man look like?

OCTOGENARIAN WIDOW: Kind of elfish. Wore sunglasses ... chain smoked Lucky
    Strikes ... Rumpelstiltskin comes to mind. Now that I think about it ... oh, no ...

WAR DEPARTMENT MAN: Goddamnit! Beat us to it again! We need to find this
    record thieving treasonous bastard, hang him by his pinkies!!!

Harry back with Nixon.

HARRY: Not treason, exactly, I ...

    Hoarded 78s during the uhhh

    What was the movie called?

    War to End All Wars: The Sequel?

    Guv-mint declared shellac a // strategic necessity

NIXON: Strategic necess//ity —

HARRY: Right — coming as it does from only one place on earth — the // uhhh

NIXON: Indian subcontinent. Before the War, Pat and I worked for the OPA.

HARRY: Cultivation process is a bitch, shellac —

    "lac" being a derivation of the Sanskrit word "lakh"

    Referring to swarms of larvae known as *laccifer lacca* —

    make a pound of the stuff takes six months, 15,000 lac beetles ...

    War machine can't get a fix cause Indiauhhh —

    World's dope dealer for the stuff — is cut off by the

    Bombing killing maiming —

    Guvmint figured why not?

    Melt down all those 78s

    Recorded when American music uhhh

    Still retained distinct regional qualities,

    Before NPR, *Good Morning America* erased local types

    Into one homogenous Voice of America ...

ALGER CRIMUS: In that moment

    Nixon becomes Pentheus, backed by his Silent Majority,

    To Smith's Dionysus backed by the Bohemian throngs.

    There's an

    Inversion of power,

    An inversion of the

    Very idea of America *itself* ...

HARRY: Me against the War Department.

    You might call it treason,

    I call treason the Levitt house, electric toaster, self-cleaning oven. ...

ALGER CRIMUS: For Harry, witnessing Nixon undergo this transformation,
    Sees his vision manifest in reality – that the work of an underground denizen
    Will emerge into the *light*, reshape how we think of ourselves
    As a nation. As a culture. As a *people*.

Nixon snores. He startles awake.

NIXON: Sorry, Mr. Smith ... I uhh
    Dozed off for a moment ...
    You were saying?

ALGER CRIMUS: You might be thinking:
    "What the *fuck* is this guy talking about?"
    Well ... Had I been in Nixon's shoes?
    I'd have given Harry the Medal of Freedom
    for his Patriotic Acts of Treason.

Theme music swells. Applause light. The Stranger Emcee appears.

DARKEST HEART OF AMERICA: THE NEVER ENDING TOUR OF BLANK MARLOWE AND HIS BAND THE RED HERRINGS, PART THREE

STRANGER EMCEE: I hear crickets and campfire a-cracklin' ...

From the White House basement

To the streets of Mahagonny ...

MARTIN: Marlowe...? You okay ... ?

MARLOWE: Huh? What?

MARTIN: You drifted ...

Merry Andrew ...? Mahagonny...? You followed him...?

MARLOWE: The town. Worse than closed. Dead.

Like a neutron bomb'd been dropped on it.

Andrew told me stories of the place ...

We passed an abandoned well –

MERRY ANDREW: Fella named Henry Lee lies bottom of that well ...

(sings – variation on "Henry Lee")

She pressed him up against a well

To steal a kiss or two

He did not see the blade in her hand

She cut him through and through

She said, "Lie there dirty Henry Lee

Til your flesh drips from your bones

That girl of yours in merry Ireland

Still waits for your return ..."

MARLOWE: We pass an abandoned house, dead flowers in the garden

MERRY ANDREW: Every kid in town knows the Gypsy woman lives there –

(sings – variation of "Fatal Flower Garden")

Out came a Gypsy lady

Dressed up in yellow and green

"Come in, come in you pretty little boy
To fetch your ball again"

She took him by his lily white hand
Led him down the hall
She locked him in a basement room
Where no one could hear him call …

MARLOWE: Another house:

MERRY ANDREW: See that window up there?

MARLOWE: Silhouette of girl in the attic window.

MERRY ANDREW: Railroad boy had his way with her, never looked back …

(sings — variation of "The Butcher Boy")

Her father he came home from work
Heard his daughter weeping so hurt
He went upstairs to give her hope
Found her hanging from a rope

He took his knife and cut her down
In her hand this note he found
"Shape my grave as a marble dove,
To warn this world I died for love."

MARLOWE: He takes me inside an abandoned factory …

MERRY ANDREW: Used to make shoes here by hand …

(sings — variation on "Peg and Awl")

They've invented a new machine, peg and awl
They've invented a new machine, peg and awl
They've invented a new machine, prettiest thing I ever seen
Throw away my peg, my peg, my peg, my awl

Make one hundred pair to my one, peg and awl
Make one hundred pair to my one, peg and awl

Make one hundred pair to my one, peggin shoes it ain't no fun

Throw away my peg, my peg, my peg, my —

MARLOWE: Suddenly he stops.

Pulls out a bottle of pills —

MERRY ANDREW: Want one?

Jorge starts playing the theremin.

MARLOWE: What is it?

MERRY ANDREW: "Dr. Smith's American Balsam."

Cures everything from your high blood pressure to your unending heartache.

Make you happier than a dog with two dicks.

MARTIN: Did you take one?

ANNIE: That's like asking Tennessee Williams if he'd like another mint julep.

MARLOWE: Yeah, I took one.

That's when shit got real weird ...

MERRY ANDREW: Here we are ...

MARLOWE: Rickety sign: Red Herring's Bar, Grill

MERRY ANDREW: and Happy Bottom Riding Club

MARLOWE: If Death was all there was outside ... inside?

If Desolation Row was a real place? Red's would be it ...

Harmonica sounds end the segment, cross fading into the sounds of Jewish Orthodox liturgical music.

STRANGER EMCEE: Ladies and gennelmen,

Let's take a walk.

Down to Manhattan's Lower East Side.

Four Flights up to a tenement apartment on East Broadway.

Tiny hold out of a forgotten Lower East Side of

immigrants, pushcart vendors, rag pickers,

Long before the real estate Pharaoh's figured out

Hipsters'll pay top dollar for the luxury of squalor ...

Please give it up for our last installment of
Shadow of the Shining City: Chronicles of the American Underground.
Part Three: "The Lonesome Burden of Lionel Z."

Applause light.

SHADOW OF THE SHINING CITY: CHRONICLES OF THE AMERICAN UNDERGROUND, PART THREE

The Curator appears with a box.

CURATOR: I am carrying a box.

> In this box. Is one.
>
> Of Harry's. Greatest achievements.
>
> The complete recordings.
>
> Of Rabbi Nuftali Zvi Margolies Abulafia.
>
> *This* ... my friends,
>
> Will be one of, if not *the,* most significant artifact
>
> In the Harry Smith Museum and Interpretive Center.
>
> Allow me to show you —

She opens the box. It's filled with packing peanuts. She digs through, first excited, then baf-fled. Other than peanuts, the box is empty. She looks up in panic when LIONEL Z. rolls on in a wheelchair. He's ancient. Breathes with the assistance of an oxygen tank. Chain smokes Viceroy 100s.

LIONEL (JORGE): Fifty years from now?

> The recordings by Harry Smith
>
> Of my grandfather ... Rabbi
>
> Nuftali
>
> Zvi
>
> Margolies
>
> Abulafia ...
>
> Will be regarded as a
>
> Musicological event of cosmic significance ...
>
> But I'm getting ahead of myself ...

Sound of a door knocking.

> 7am. Door knocks. This is what? '51, '52?
>
> Morning after Joanne and I married ...
>
> I'm thinking: who knocks? 7am? On the door of newlyweds?
>
> I open the door, see this creature ...

At this point he's 28?

Looks older than when he died.

HARRY: I'm Harry Smith.

LIONEL: Who sent you?

HARRY: George Andrews.

LIONEL: Andrews. One of the leading UFO guys ...

CURATOR: Wrote *Extraterrestrials Among Us* (St. Paul: Llewellyn Press, Minnesota, 1986)

HARRY: He says if I want to learn Kabala,

    You're the man to see ...

LIONEL: He'd come from Berkeley.

    On a Guggenheim Fellowship.

    Joanne, also came from there

    So it was Berkeley, Berkeley all the time.

    Next five years? He practically moves in ...

    Every night. Birdland. Miles Davis, Dizzy ...

    Harry ropes Joanne to work on the *Oz* picture ...

    Million dollar budget.

    Liz Taylor, other guy – that died ...

    All put money in ...

    First time Harry's flush

    Hands out hundred dollar bills to bums. ...

Sound of an Orthodox cantor singing.

LIONEL: In Meron, in Israel

    Thousands of pilgrims –

    On the anniversary of his death,

    come to the grave of

    Shimon

    Bar

    Yochai.

CURATOR: Mystic.

Wrote the *Zohar,*

Most important book of the Kabbalah.

LIONEL Z.: They come because

In tradition

Day he died he

Revealed the deepest secrets of the Torah ...

They dance, sing

All night.

In New York

They celebrate at Home of the Sages

My grandfather does the singing ...

I think:

Something Harry'd be interested in,

An anthropo-musicological happening of the first order right here on East Broadway.

He goes. With his recording equipment.

There for hours ... at the end?

Harry corners my grandfather.

Harry doesn't talk Yiddish

My grandfather doesn't speak a word of English

Yet they're *immersed* ...

My grandfather, doesn't know from tapes,

"What's my voice doing in the box?"

Harry convinces my grandfather to record –

Thousands of songs he knows by heart ...

Understand this music is ancient – none of it written down,

Let alone on record ...

Three years

Harry turns my grandfather's tiny room into a recording studio ...

One day, my grandfather tells me:

RABBI (MARTIN): Lionel, this recording business ...

>Can go on til the end of time,
>
>*Enough!*

LIONEL Z.: They stop, press 18 LPs

>Thousand copies each.
>
>They sit there,
>
>In my grandfather's room for years ...
>
>On his deathbed ...
>
>My grandfather tells me

RABBI: Lionel, if it's the last thing you do,

>Promise me, you'll distribute the records ...

He dies.

LIONEL: Fifty years I carry this burden ...

>My uncle. Wanted nothing to do with the records
>
>Doesn't want his father's voice
>
>Playing in some record store on 14th Street.
>
>Records end up in a basement. Housing project in the Bronx.
>
>Twenty years go by,
>
>Sprinklers go bust, turns the basement into a lake ...
>
>I salvage what I could.
>
>One set. All I have left.
>
>You have to understand the importance ...
>
>Not like the *Anthology* ... those records already existed
>
>Put em together presto ...
>
>Harry made these recordings from scratch ...
>
>Fifty years from now, this will be regarded as Harry's greatest achievement ...
>
>What do I have now...?
>
>Handful of records?
>
>With scratches and dirt?
>
>They can do it with computers –

What do they call it? Digitizing ... ?

Costs money I don't have

I have to save the sound ...

The liturgical music crescendos. Applause light.

DARKEST HEART OF AMERICA: THE NEVER ENDING TOUR OF BLANK MARLOWE AND HIS BAND THE RED HERRINGS, PART THREE

STRANGER EMCEE: Speaking of sound …

    It's back to Mahagonny, USA

    Where Blank Marlowe and Merry Andrew are about to cross the uhhh

    Limn

    Into

    Red Herring's Bar and Grill

    The Darkest Heart of America …

MARLOWE: If Desolation Row was a real place? Red's would be it …

The band creates the interior environment of Red's. A wild room of desperadoes drinking, for-nicating, speculating like it's the end of the world. The band plays an apocalyptic, proto-punk rendition of "I Couldn't Get High" by the Fugs.

SONG: "I COULDN'T GET HIGH"

MARTIN: *(singing)* I went to a party the other night

    I wanted to fill my brain with light

    I grabbed myself a bottle

    I started drinking wine

    I thought pretty soon I'd be feeling fine

    But I couldn't get high, no no no

    Couldn't get high, no no no

    So I threw down the bottle

    I whipped out my pipe

    I stuffed it full of grass

    I gave myself a light

    I huffed, puffed, smoked and I toked

    After awhile my heart was nearly broke

    Cause I couldn't get high, no no no

    Couldn't get high, no no no

So I threw down my pipe

Mad as I could be

I gobbled up a cube of LSD

Waited 30 minutes for my body to sing

I waited and I waited but I couldn't feel a thing

No I couldn't get high no no no

I couldn't get high no no no

Couldn't get high, don't know why

I thought I would die … Die die dieeee!

The song falls apart. Applause light goes on — real and recorded applause.

MARLOWE: Like the town motto said:

HARRY: "Do what thou wilt shall be the whole of the Law."

MERRY ANDREW: Girl tending bar?

That's Frankie …

She'll put you up for the night.

Be careful: One minute?

She'll love you like it's the last night on earth

Next: she'll put three bullets in your back.

MARLOWE: Who are all these people …?

MERRY ANDREW: Crazy, right? Let's see … big table?

Black dude with the dark glasses? Blind Lemon Jefferson. Pretty lady's Sarah Car-ter. Found Christ, gave up singing, but she stops in time to time. Old guy with the banjo – Clarence Ashley. Other two black dudes: Reverend J.M. Gates, Mississippi John Hurt. Locals call it "Resurrection Table" –

MARLOWE: Who's the old man?

MERRY ANDREW: Ha! Which one?

MARLOWE: Wheelchair. Oxygen tank. Smoking Viceroy 100s.

MERRY ANDREW: Lionel Z. Master of the Kabala. Unfulfilled death bed promise keeps him breathing. And worried.

MARLOWE: Guys on stage?

MERRY ANDREW: House band. The Fugs. Harry produced their first record.

MARLOWE: Midget at the bar?

MERRY ANDREW: Bad news Hungarian. Slumlord.

MARLOWE: Man next to him in the expensive suit?

MERRY ANDREW: Phipps. Trust fund kid. Spends all his time druggin with the poets in town. They love him cause he's a High Fashion Goodwill Shop, closet full of Italian suits he wears once, then gives away. Balding dude over there? That's Ginsberg. He's got a mad crush on Phipps ...

MARLOWE: Wait: is that ... ?

MERRY ANDREW: Richard Milhous Nixon. 37th President of the United States ...

MARLOWE: Shit ...

MERRY ANDREW: I know, right? Check out Pat, doin the twist with Thelonious Monk ...

Sound of groaning and nasty, squishy footsteps stumbling.

MARLOWE: What the hell is that ... thing ... stumbling around?

MERRY ANDREW: Oh, that's Harry's Zombie.

MARLOWE: What?

MERRY ANDREW: While back Harry went down to Haiti to learn voodoo,
Came home, found some kid to be his Guinea pig

MARLOWE: Whoa ...

MERRY ANDREW: Yeah ... hasn't figured out how to snap him out of it.
Think the kid's name was Oscar

MARLOWE: Lady over there? Drinking alone?

MERRY ANDREW: Museum Curator. Comes every night to drink, comb through index-es. Museum's going up soon ...

MARLOWE: Old man in the corner ... Drinking milk ...

Merry Andrew is gone.

MARLOWE: Andrew? Old man in the ... ?

> I look up. Andrew's gone.

> I head to the bar,
> Squeeze between Phipps and the Hungarian midget. Hungarian flips.

HUNGARIAN MIDGET (JORGE): I don know vat happened to thet psi-koteek's sheet.
> Don aks. You aks, I knife your gut. Tell zat mutterfukker pay hees rent!

MARLOWE: Bartender ... how to describe her ... Can't be older than 21, still's got acne ...

FRANKIE (ANNIE): Don't mind him, baby. He's just trippin.
> What can I getcha?

MARLOWE: She's
> *Appealing* ... Ripped jeans, camisole ... Siamese cat eyes ...

FRANKIE: You're not from around here ...

MARLOWE: No, miss.

FRANKIE: Call me Frankie ...
> We don't get a lot of foreigners in here ...

MARLOWE: I'm not a foreigner. I'm American.

FRANKIE: Sweetie, anyone from outside Mahagonny —

MARLOWE: Pronounced like the wood

FRANKIE: Is a foreigner ...

MARLOWE: Fellow I came with —
> One in the
> Outfit...?

FRANKIE: Andrew? Aww ... sweetie-boy.

MARLOWE: Mentioned there might be a room ... ?

FRANKIE: I'll get you a room. Long as you're a good boy.
> Whatcha havin?

MARLOWE: Whiskey.

FRANKIE: So what brings you to our quaint little town?

MARLOWE: Car broke down.

    Man over in the corner. Drinking milk. What's his story?

FRANKIE: Harry?

HUNGARIAN MIDGET: I tell you already! I don know vat happened to thet psi-ko-

    teek's sheet! Aks again, I knife your heart *and* your gut. Tell that mutterfukker pay

    // hees rent!

FRANKIE: Oh, shut up, will you?

MARLOWE: You were sayin ... ?

FRANKIE: That's Harry Smith.

MARLOWE: Don't know why but ... Rumpelstiltskin crossed my mind.

    On the table: glass of milk, roaches crawling in and out,

    Tape recorder, ashtray piled with dead butts, notebooks he's jotting stuff in ...

    All the while his hands move wildly making string figures –

FRANKIE: Harry's magic. Touched by the hand of god knows what.

    Like his brain's wired to some supercomputer on Neptune ...

    Stick around, cause: later tonight? if we're good? He'll take us down to The Palace...

MARLOWE: Palace?

FRANKIE: Movie house on 4th and Desolation.

    Rumor round town Harry's screening *Oz* tonight ...

MARLOWE: *Wizard of Oz?*

FRANKIE: *Harry's Oz* ...

    Any truth to it, you're in for more treats tonite than you're already imagining.

MARLOWE: Pardon?

FRANKIE: He's got this philosophy?

    Reality's one big monster fantasy.

You pick what fantasy you wanna be in ...

Like you pick clothes out your closet

MARLOWE: I'm not sure I ...

FRANKIE: When you look at me, what's your fantasy?

MARLOWE: I dunno ...

FRANKIE: Liar.

You desire me.

You think my broken wing needs mending,

I'm a little girl lost that's seen too many people die young.

You wanna fill my head with fantasies about the

Big, beautiful world outside Mahagonny?

That's all well and good mister.

Cause three o'clock this afternoon?

Woke up? Sized up the costumes in my closet.

Picked these jeans, this camisole — ?

And neglected to put on anything between them and my *parts*

Cause

I knew your fantasy before your car broke down ...

MARLOWE: What about your man?

Frankie's face went cold as the barrel of an unfired pistol.

FRANKIE: How'd you know about Albert?

MARLOWE: Sense I get

FRANKIE: Upstairs. Got his own fantasy, and another woman to convince him it's reality.

I'll tell you a secret though:

Every night? I go up there? Shoot em both.

And every time, the judge is ... well ...

Sympathetic

What brings you to Mahagonny again?

MARLOWE: At that point the band struck up a song ...

FRANKIE: Excuse me ... boys want me on stage.

SONG: "FRANKIE" (BASED ON MISSISSIPPI JOHN HURT'S "FRANKIE")

FRANKIE: *(singing)* Frankie is a good girl, everybody knows,
    Paid one hundred dollars for Albert's suit of clothes
    He's my man, but he's doin me wrong.

    Frankie went to Red's saloon, ordered a whiskey straight,
    asked the barkeeper, "Why's my Albert always late?"
    "He was here, but he's gone again."

    He said:

JORGE: "Ain't gonna feed you no story, ain't gonna feed you no lie
    Albert was here an hour ago, with that little girl Alice Frye
    He's your man, he's doin' you wrong."

FRANKIE: Frankie went upstairs, clutching her lucky charm
    Spied through the keyhole Alice in Albert's arm
    You're my man, you're doin' me wrong.

    Frankie pointed at Albert, shot him thirteen times,
    says, "Stand back, I'm smokin' my gun, let me see that bastard dyin'
    He's my man, and he did me wrong."

    Judge took Frankie to chambers, patted her behind
    Said, "Don't you worry little girl, you're gonna be justified,
    killin' a man, cause he did you wrong."

    Frankie is a good girl, everybody knows,
    Paid one hundred dollars for my Albert's suit of clothes
    He's my man, but he did me wrong.

MARLOWE: Song ends, place went wild ...
    Hootin hollerin pistol shots to the ceiling ...
    Frankie takes her time coming back
    Inhaling every hug, kiss, pat to her beautiful behind,

CURATOR: Little murderess likes to take her sweet ass time, I WANT MY GOD-DAMN DRINK!

MARLOWE: You uhhh

The Museum keeper?

CURATOR: Who told you that?

MARLOWE: Guy I came in with

CURATOR: Andrew? Awww ... sweetie boy ...

MARLOWE: What kinda museum is it?

CURATOR: Ha! If I could answer *that* question ...

Why do you wanna know?

MARLOWE: *Curiosity* ...

CURATOR: *"Curiosity"* ... You know what they say about curiosity ...

MARLOWE: "Five dollar hooker always wins in the end, dudn't she?"

CURATOR: Excuse me?

MARLOWE: Never mind ... You were saying? Museum...?

CURATOR: See the man sitting in the corner? Drinking // milk

MARLOWE: Harry Smith.

CURATOR: You know Harry?

MARLOWE: Yeah ... I mean no. Not til I ended up here.

CURATOR: Hm.

Kid has no idea how in over his head he is.

MARLOWE: Who?

CURATOR: Interviewing Harry. Writes for some rock rag. Don't know how *he* got in.

MARLOWE: Kid can't be older than 25 — got that look about him — like he'll stay a college sophomore well into his 40s ...

HARRY: Sure you know how to work that thing, Mr. Rock n Roll Journalist?

Things happen – backwards Satanic messages, eighteen minute // gaps,

JOURNALIST: Yeah – um … I've read interviews? Half of what you say's a pack of lies, SO: I'll try again: what were you like as a child?

HARRY: Information's classified Mr. // FBI Man

JOURNALIST: Okay …

HARRY: I was born in – check my birth certificate. It's entombed in Fresh Kills Landfill on Staten Island thanks to a no-goodnik, ex-Communist Hungarian midget. Next question.

JOURNALIST: Okay … ummm. When did you start collecting 78 // records?

HARRY: In truth I should be the Czar of Russia cause my mother was Anastasia –

JOURNALIST: You're serious

HARRY: Serious as the testicular cancer that'll take your life at 43.

My grandfather was the First Guv'ner of Illinois,
First Grand Master of the Illinois Freemasons –
Received my Bachelors, Masters, PhD in mother's womb,
Lived in a treehouse between theeeee
Identical separate houses my parents built
Played with Indians, followed Madame Blavatsky, dabbled in acting –
Played multiple roles in an expressionist reimagining of *You Can't Take It With You* …
Turned 13, my father built me a blacksmith's shop, said:
"Son: spin straw into gold" – I've been alchemically inclined since …

JOURNALIST: Pete Seeger, Jerry Garcia, Dylan all cite the *Anthology* as a // major influence.

HARRY: When you're puking blood in a flophouse packed with dying derelicts last thing you wanna hear is someone yodeling "Hey Mister Tambourine Man" –

JOURNALIST: Look, can // we …?

HARRY: Day my mother died, my father set fire to
A trunk of her erotic correspondence with Aleister Crowley

JOURNALIST: She knew Crowley?

HARRY: Knew him? Crowley's my Daddy!

> She met him riding a grey stallion, naked, bareback on a beach in Oregon
>
> Don't believe rumors he was sissified — according to my mother
>
> He's quite the masculine specimen —
>
> Many nights she'd sneak in my tree house to uhhhh
>
> *Re-enact* the encounter in question ...

JOURNALIST: That's just nast —

CURATOR: Kid's falling down the rabbit hole ...

> What about you. What's your story?

MARLOWE: Musician.

CURATOR: Good luck with that.

MARLOWE: Right.

CURATOR: You wanna see it?

MARLOWE: Pardon?

CURATOR: Museum ...

> It's next door. In the abandoned Victor Dealership ...
>
> It's far from being finished, but ...
>
> Free booze there.
>
> Still gonna be awhile before Harry takes us to The Palace to screen *Oz* ...

MARTIN: Did you go?

MARLOWE: Curiosity's pulling me two ways — on the one hand

> Frankie's making eyes at me from Blind Lemon's lap
>
> On the other, there's this *museum*

ANNIE: Lemme guess which you chose, Marlowe

MARLOWE: Yeah, you'd like to think that, wouldn't you, // Annie

ANNIE: What's the saying? "If she's got a pulse and at least one functioning leg?"

MARLOWE: I went to the museum.

CURATOR: First question you ask yourself: What should a Harry Smith Museum look like?

MARLOWE: She flips a switch. Flourescent light ... mice skitter.

Cobwebs. Boxes and boxes of ...

Stuff.

Middle of the room?

Merry Andrew's Victor Talking Machine ...

CURATOR: Wanna drink?

MARLOWE: No thanks ...

She pours one for herself, slips on a record ...

Mesmerizing banjo sound ...

What's that?

CURATOR: "Coo-Coo Bird." Clarence Ashley. From Harry's *Anthology.*

Did you know Harry's also an expert on Indians?

Take a look at this ... *American Magazine,* 1943

MARLOWE: Faded picture of Harry. He's just a kid, surrounded by Indians –

'40s SOUNDING NEWSREEL VOICE (MARTIN): "INJUN-EER! Fifteen-year-old anthropologist Harry Smith makes expeditions by bike from his home to visit the Indian tribes of Washington. He knows things about them no other white man has learned, is preserving their languages, lore, wild dances. In our picture he's recording the Lummi's annual potlatch. Harry's found Indians friendly except when drunk or suspicious he's a German spy. Eighteen now, Harry hopes to study anthropology under U Washington professors. They hope to study anthropology under *him.*"

MARLOWE: Far out ...

CURATOR: I could kill that sonofabitch ...

MARLOWE: Harry?

CURATOR: Not Harry – I could kill him too, but no

The Hungarian

MARLOWE: Midget guy?

CURATOR: Landlord ...

    Harry goes to Oklahoma?

    Gets arrested, meets these Kiowa Indians in jail?

    Stays months to record their peyote rituals ...

    But he forgot to pay his rent ...

HUNGARIAN MIDGET: Tell zat endomorphic mutterfukker to pay his rent!

CURATOR: Hungarian tossed out all his things ...

    Harry's life's work to that point? Gone ... for good.

MARLOWE: You okay?

CURATOR: Shall I give you the grand tour?

MARLOWE: She told me about his films —

CURATOR: Painted by hand, frame by frame —

MARLOWE: She showed me a faded reproduction of a painting —

CURATOR: *Tree of Life in the Four Worlds*, 1954 —

MARLOWE: She showed me boxes

CURATOR: Plastic mechanical bank shaped like Uncle // Sam —

MARLOWE: Tarot cards —

CURATOR: Golden Dawn Tarot

    Tarot of the // Cat People

MARLOWE: She told me about lost things —

CURATOR: 78s, paper airplanes, Easter // eggs

MARLOWE: She showed me secrets in indexes —

CURATOR: Smith, Harry, 278, // 384

MARLOWE: More she showed me, more I needed to know, more I —

CURATOR: You seeing *Oz* tonight?

MARLOWE: Yeah ...

CURATOR: Take a look:

MARLOWE: She hands me a yellowed *New York Times* obituary

CURATOR: 12 April 1962
 "Henry Phipps, 31,
 Heir to the Phipps fortune,
 Found dead
 At the Hamilton Hotel, West 73rd Street.
 Police say cause of death is
 Quote
 Under investigation..."
 It goes on:
 "Mr. Phipps lived at 101 Central Park West."
 If you've got digs on Central Park West,
 What are you doing dead in a hotel four blocks away?

MARLOWE: I don't // know –

CURATOR: Mentions his "friend" from *Queens.*
 Discovered his body – doesn't explain what
 Mr. Heir-to-the-Phipps-Fortune was doing
 With a "friend" from *Queens* in his room ...

MARLOWE: Okay ...

CURATOR: Mentions his marriage to a Countess' daughter
 Their four year old child ...

MARLOWE: Okay ...

CURATOR: What it doesn't mention:
 Phipp's association with unsavory poets.
 His drug use.
 His forbidden sexual desires.
 His paranoia about a band of black magicians
 Squeezing him of his inheritance ...

And most significant to me:

His financial interest in a highly experimental

3½ hour animated version of *The Wizard of Oz* ...

MARLOWE: She sighed, deep – looked like she was about to cry ...

CURATOR: Is there rhyme...?

Is there reason...?

To all this...?

MARLOWE: Yeah ...

CURATOR: Excuse me?

MARLOWE: The white spaces.

On your Rand McNally ...

CURATOR: Pardon?

MARLOWE: I keep a pile of old Rand McNallys in my car

Look at em all the time, on the road, when I'm lost,

Can't sleep, when I'm empty,

and I'm tryin to remember ...

Web of blue and pink lines

Connecting one place to another –

Make it seem like they

keep the map from tearing itself apart ...

CURATOR: I'm not sure I –

MARLOWE: But you got all that white space

Bypassed by those lines ...

I keep looking for what's in the white spaces ...

Never seen a Rand McNally show what's in them ...

Stuff you throw away. Stuff you lose. Stuff you

Don't want to look at, think about ... Stuff you wanna forget.

Maybe that's what keeps the map hanging together ...

Pause.

She smiled. Turned around to look at Harry's things

CURATOR: You think all this…?

MARLOWE: Maybe…?

CURATOR: This place will be something when I'm done …

MARLOWE: Think people'll …

CURATOR: Come?
    What was that saying in that baseball picture? "Build it they will come…?"

MARLOWE: She stopped smiling.
    Her eyes got all …
    Worried
    Like she could see herself
    Twenty years from now
    Stuck in a museum with no visitors.

CURATOR: Will you hold me?

MARLOWE: Her askin that? Caught me a little off guard …

MARTIN: Did you?

ANNIE: Psssss …

MARLOWE: I did … I held her. Leaned in to kiss her …

CURATOR: That's not what …

MARLOWE: Sorry.

CURATOR: Look at the clock … movie time.
    Shall we head to The Palace?

MARLOWE: We turn to go …
    Who's standing there?

Toy piano Merry Andrew Theme.

    Merry Andrew …
    Looking mean, like the first time I laid eyes on him …

MERRY ANDREW: He wants to see you.

CURATOR: What does he —

MERRY ANDREW: Not you. *Him.*

MARLOWE: Who wants to see me?

MERRY ANDREW: Harry. Be a good boy, come quietly ...

MARLOWE: Out to the street. Desolate. Andrew points his finger west —

MERRY ANDREW: Walk.

MARLOW: Where you taking me?

MERRY ANDREW: Movies.

MARLOWE: We walked ... pitch black except for a movie marquee in the distance ...

MERRY ANDREW: Uhcourse there's the time Harry went a-bowilin in Times Square—

MARLOWE: Huh?

The band strikes up the melody of "Engine One-Forty-Three" by The Carter Family.

MERRY ANDREW: Might make my own movie bout it someday ...

    Got it all in my head, just takes me getting up off my butt ...

    What's that ole saying? Bout the tree falling in the forest?

    Makes you think about all your own trees ...

    Ones in the forest of your heart

Merry Andrew sings, Harry mimes the acts described:

SONG: "GOODBYE TIN WOODMAN'S DREAM" (BASED ON "ENGINE 143")

MERRY ANDREW: *(singing)* Henry Phipps, they found him dead, he lies in a lonesome grave

    Regret to tell you Harry, your film we cannot save

    You labored years to make it, spent Henry's every last dime

    Many a man has lost his way trying to make up lost time.

    Harry stood on a concrete isle, 42nd and Broadway

    Lost among speed freaks, failed comics, preachers gone astray

Harry went a-bowling with the reel of Film Thirteen

A Times Square night in '62, goodbye *Tin Woodman's Dream.*

HARRY: Whoosh ...

MERRY ANDREW: Of all that vanished celluloid, nine short minutes remain

If old Walt Disney could see them now, he'd hang his head in shame

Mama said don't waste your time wonderin what could have been

Life's too short and fleeting, a frame on a movie screen.

The song abruptly ends. Silence. Merry Andrew and Marlowe contemplate the enormity of the loss.

MERRY ANDREW: Whole thing went bust ...

HARRY'S VOICE: When a major investor

Was found dead under

Embarrassing circumstances ...

MERRY ANDREW: Nine minutes ... is there more? Somewhere?

MARLOWE: We get to 4th and Desolation ...

Sound of buzzing marquee neon. Crickets. Leaves and paper bags blowing in the wind against the pavement.

MARLOWE: Line of folks under the marquee

That reads:

HARRY: *Film Number 13 – Oz or Tin Woodman's Dream or*

Fragments of a Faith Forgotten

MARLOWE: Underneath

HARRY: Restored version – never before seen footage. One night only ...

MERRY ANDREW: Where do you think you're going?

MARLOWE: Getting in line?

MERRY ANDREW: Uh-uh. Side entrance ...

MARLOWE: Andrew leads me to an unmarked door,

Flanked by two unconscious winos.

Teenage girl in a white wedding dress
Gives them sips of wine, kisses their lips ...
Angel blessing the dying.

MERRY ANDREW: Upstairs ...

Sound of footsteps climbing metal stairs. Ominous music reminiscent of a Hitchcock thriller.

MARLOWE: Takes me to the empty balcony ...
Curtain to the projection booth is open ...
Inside: Harry loads the projector –
Strange machine like nothing I ever seen ...
Frankie's with him ...
Harry pays no mind to Andrew and me,
But Frankie ...
Jungle stare that says –

FRANKIE: Think you're alone now
Wait'll we're done with you ...

MERRY ANDREW: Down front.

MARLOWE: Andrew sits me down.
Below:
Rowdy anticipation.

MERRY ANDREW: *SHHHHHHHHHH!* Show's about to start ...

FRANKIE: Evening Ladies and Gentlemen
Welcome to tonight's screening of *Film Number 13* ...
Before we begin, please give a warm welcome to Harry's good friend
The legendary neurosurgeon once called "The Greatest Living Canadian"
Dr. Wilder Penfield ...

Applause light.

MARLOWE: Medical technicians roll out a dentist's chair ...
Woman on it,
Weird smile on her face,
Back of her skull's open, brain exposed

Attached to wires and needles ...
It's the Curator ...

On the screen, strange diagram – kind of a
Medieval looking cartoon ...

DR. PENFIELD (JORGE): The cartoon-like image you see is called the Motor Homunculus – it maps the cortices of the human brain. Like all maps, this one distorts reality. It renders the body in proportions that relate to the complexity of movement of each body part. Note the head, mouth, hands appear gigantic, monstrous – they possess the most complex range of movement.

This map stems from my work with epileptics. I discovered, by stimulating the temporal lobe I could trigger patients' forgotten memories, which they recall with an intensity absent in ordinary memory.

Allow me to demonstrate.

He moves to the Curator and begins stimulating her exposed brain.

CURATOR: Ooooh.

DOCTOR: Feel anything?

CURATOR: It's cold. I'm in the snow. Making snow angels ...

DOCTOR: Now?

CURATOR: Daddy holds my hand ...
Through the glass the ghostly shape of a beluga whale swims towards us ...

DOCTOR: Now...?

CURATOR: I feel empty space next to me
where I should feel the warmth of my big brother ...

The Doctor ceases probing.

DOCTOR: Discovering the physical basis of memory
Led me to the question
I asked til the day I died:

Is it possible to locate,

thus prove scientifically,

The existence of the human soul? Thankyouverymuch.

Applause light. Merry Andrew, deeply moved, eyes watery, applauds deeply.

MARLOWE: Lights go down ...

Audience goes silent

Only sound the whirring projector ...

First image appears ...

Flying towards Emerald City ...

Breathtaking ...

Like nothing I ever seen ...

But it lasts only a second.

Cacophony of a projector devouring and melting celluloid.

MARLOWE: From the projection booth

Sound of a mechanical monster

Devouring celluloid ...

A collective gasp. Followed by an unearthly voice raging.

On screen ... Emerald City boils into brown blotches

That disappear ... only blinding white on screen ...

Harry goes nuts,

Projector smashes through the booth window ...

Sails over the balcony

Crashes in a million pieces at the foot of the screen ...

Cacophony of destroyed machinery.

Theater's silent.

One by one,

Folks leave without a word.

Andrew bites his lip, bows his head.

MERRY ANDREW: Come on.

MARLOWE: He leads me to the booth.

Curtain's closed.

MERRY ANDREW: Open it.

MARLOWE: I pull it back.

Frankie,
Fierceness gone from her eyes,
Just red from crying.
And Harry ...
Looks at me with
Gentle eyes,
Wise, yet childlike,
There's a sweetness to him
Yet his look pierces
Like he can see through every layer of me ...

"You asked to see me, sir?"

He reaches to the corner of the booth
Grabs a shovel,
Hands it to me and

The power goes out. The only light on stage is the campfire. Dr. Kurtz enters, stands near the fire, which illuminates him. A long silence. The sound of crickets and embers burning.

DR. KURTZ: Thus, *A Thick Description of Harry Smith*, ends. Mid-sentence. The encounter between Marlowe and Harry, unwritten. Or perhaps written, but lost, like so many of Harry's things. Two possibilities: Javier gave up, unable to unravel the mystery of Harry Smith, and by extension, solve the riddle of America. Or, this is precisely what Javier intended: a tale with no resolution, an America condemned to purgatory. Which, given his own biography, and the loss he suffered, was the truth he lived.

On the tapes, Javier suggests a possible ending in the form of a stage direction:

JAVIER'S VOICE: An ending? Maybe ... "Dawn ... landfill outside of Mahagonny ... mighty – in the light it might be mistaken for the Cahokia Indian mounds in Illinois ... Atop the landfill, Harry, Merry Andrew, Marlowe, silhouetted against the rising sun ...

"Harry wears headphones attached to a beachcomber's metal detector ..."

"Um ..."

"Andrew holds a sieve ... filtering garbage from gold..."

"Marlowe ... what's he doing ...

Shovel in one hand ... In the other

Rand McNally ... ?

He shovels deep into the landfill..."

"They look for Harry's things."

On the tape sound of a little girl calling out "Daddy? Daddy!" in another room. Rustling sound of Javier trying to turn off a recorder. He says to himself: "Shit." He calls out: "Just a second..." A cough. A dog barking down the street. A click. The sound of blank tape.

The campfire flickers out. Silence. Lights come up. The band kicks into a rocking, celebratory/ apocalyptic version of Bob Dylan's "A Hard Rain's A-Gonna Fall."

SONG: "A HARD RAIN'S A-GONNA FALL"

ALL: *(singing)* Oh, where have you been, my blue-eyed son?
    Oh, where have you been, my darling young one?

MARLOWE: *(singing)* I've stumbled on the side of twelve misty mountains
    I've walked and I've crawled on six crooked highways
    I've stepped in the middle of seven sad forests
    I've been out in front of a dozen dead oceans
    I've been ten thousand miles in the mouth of a graveyard

ALL: And it's a hard, and it's a hard, it's a hard, and it's a hard
    And it's a hard rain's a-gonna fall

    Oh, what did you see, my blue-eyed son?
    Oh, what did you see, my darling young one?

MARLOWE: I saw a newborn baby with wild wolves all around it
    I saw a highway of diamonds with nobody on it
    I saw a black branch with blood that kept drippin'
    I saw a room full of men with their hammers a-bleedin'

I saw a white ladder all covered with water

I saw ten thousand talkers whose tongues were all broken

I saw guns and sharp swords in the hands of young children

ALL: And it's a hard, and it's a hard, it's a hard, it's a hard

And it's a hard rain's a-gonna fall

And what did you hear, my blue-eyed son?

And what did you hear, my darling young one?

MARLOWE: I heard the sound of a thunder, it roared out a warnin'

Heard the roar of a wave that could drown the whole world

Heard one hundred drummers whose hands were a-blazin'

Heard ten thousand whisperin' and nobody listenin'

Heard one person starve, I heard many people laughin'

Heard the song of a poet who died in the gutter

Heard the sound of a clown who cried in the alley

ALL: And it's a hard, and it's a hard, it's a hard, it's a hard

And it's a hard rain's a-gonna fall

Oh, who did you meet, my blue-eyed son?

Who did you meet, my darling young one?

MARLOWE: I met a young child beside a dead pony

I met a white man who walked a black dog

I met a young woman whose body was burning

I met a young girl, she gave me a rainbow

I met one man who was wounded in love

I met another man who was wounded with hatred

ALL: And it's a hard, it's a hard, it's a hard, it's a hard

It's a hard rain's a-gonna fall

Oh, what'll you do now, my blue-eyed son?

Oh, what'll you do now, my darling young one?

MARLOWE: I'm a-goin' back out 'fore the rain starts a-fallin'

I'll walk to the depths of the deepest black forest

Where the people are many and their hands are all empty
Where the pellets of poison are flooding their waters
Where the home in the valley meets the damp dirty prison
Where the executioner's face is always well hidden
Where hunger is ugly, where souls are forgotten
Where black is the color, where none is the number
And I'll tell it and think it and speak it and breathe it
And reflect it from the mountain so all souls can see it
Then I'll stand on the ocean until I start sinkin'
But I'll know my song well before I start singin'

ALL: And it's a hard, it's a hard, it's a hard, it's a hard
    It's a hard rain's a-gonna fall

End of play

YOUR NAME WILL FOLLOW YOU HOME

MEMORIES OF AN INVISIBLE MUSE:

An Introduction to *Your Name Will Follow You Home*

Alicia Hernández, Professor Emeritus, Rio Hondo College

The quest

In the summer of 2002, I stood on a ridge photographing *Seaward*, the D.L. James manor home designed by Charles Sumner Greene located in the Carmel Highlands. Eighteen years earlier, Danny (the son of D.L. James) invited me for a visit knowing my admiration for Craftsman homes designed by architects Greene & Greene. He remembered my letter written 25 years earlier while I was house hunting. However, the invitation came soon after he found himself at the center of a major literary scandal and

I was still in turmoil from the revelations.

Thus it was that in the spring of 2002, I finally summoned the courage to write to his daughter, Barbara, inquiring whether her late mother had located any of my letters initially requested six months after Danny died in 1988. It was my intention to write a memoir and the letters were crucial to the task. Danny and I corresponded for thirteen years, enough time for me to evolve from classroom critic to friend to muse. Barbara's reply was a very generous invitation to make use of her guest house for a summer weekend in Carmel Valley. It was an opportunity to sort through Danny's papers, journals, and files in hopes that my numerous letters were among all that were boxed and stored. Additionally, Danny's study overlooked the Pacific and I was interested in seeing where he labored for years editing and revising his book, *Famous All Over Town*, where my letters were likely preserved. Finally, I asked whether a tour of *Seaward* was possible. She replied that it was not, having been sold years earlier.

Arriving in Carmel, Barbara offered directions to *Seaward*. The architect had constructed a viewpoint across the rocky cliffs on a promontory. It was a spectacular view with the Pacific crashing into the bedrock, which served as the foundation. Los Lobos State Reserve surrounded the estate and enhanced the organic beauty of this magnificent dwelling. Majestic conifers facing the south façade sheltered the stone arch replicated from an English manor home — it dripped romantic splendor.

By this time, Danny had been deceased for 14 years, so I found myself alone with *Seaward* in the distance longing for answers to my questions and hoping to locate my letters. A writer friend, knowing of my intense interest in finding the letters, said she was praying to St. Anthony, the patron saint of lost causes. She wrote that despite my being Protestant, he was an "equal opportunity saint." Unfortunately, as I later learned, the saint had also been marginalized and demoted.

My thoughts on that pristine summer day standing on a spot where the house was within sight and yet access was unavailable to me: once again I was relegated to the margins of the life and times of author Dan James or as I knew him, Danny Santiago. Separation and distance were the hallmarks of our lengthy odyssey.

The publication in 1970 of "The Somebody," a short story by promising Chicano author Danny Santiago, corresponded with my first year teaching in the Montebello District, a middle class Los Angeles suburb located east of East Los Angeles, about 15 miles from the City's civic center. I taught five sections of ninth grade English totaling approximately 150 fidgety adolescents. The district at the time was majority Hispanic; however, reflecting Montebello's population, classes included Armenians, Russians, Asians, and a sprinkling of Anglos. Countless hours were spent developing uninspired lesson plans and finding my way.

In the middle of the academic year, the short story "The Somebody" appeared in *Redbook Magazine*. Reading it, I wept with joy because here was literary material with high reading appeal destined to become a classroom hit. The protagonist was Chato de Shamrock, a very cheeky Chicano teen living in East Los Angeles who expresses very keen observations about his Mexican family. There was much similarity in the story to the lives of my students, unlike any other literature they'd read to that point. The story was set in the Boyle Heights area in East Los Angeles where I once attended middle school, so the number of recognizable landmarks were very familiar. Ignoring copyright laws, I typed the story on 10 ditto masters and ran off 30 ten-page sets for the class. It took two surreptitious trips to the ditto machine given the amount of restricted paper required. Danny Santiago, the author, was a unique and talented writer. Who was he and did more published material exist? After I exhausted all the language arts exercises in my repertoire, I wrote to *Redbook* asking how to contact the author.

Two weeks later I received the first letter from Santiago stating how pleased he was that "The Somebody" landed in a classroom and that he was curious about student reaction. I read the letter to the classes and they were intrigued that an author responded. I replied with an eight-page handwritten letter describing my search for literature the students could identify with that met the curriculum criteria. I asked, "Do you have more stories?" Again another letter arrived instructing me to mail all correspondence to an address in Pacific Grove on the Monterey Peninsula and not to his New York agent on Fifth Avenue as first directed. Hallelujah! He was a Californian not an Easterner! Yes, he had plenty of stories and yes, he would mail them to us, and yes, I could transfer them to ditto masters and run off as many as the paper budget permitted. This was the start of our friendly yet mysterious thirteen-year correspondence.

True to his word, more short stories arrived and more letters too. The students waited with bated breath for new Chato adventures. I assigned short written critiques to Danny, describing their reactions to the various chapters. He instructed them to be truthful and not avoid criticism. The short evaluations became valuable feedback to a work in progress. They pointed out when a story seemed incomplete, boring, or funny. In one letter he wrote that he was planning to combine all the short stories as chapters for a book. Some of the students had suggested this and I agreed. My motive, of course, was to use the book in the classroom where dramatic changes in student demeanor ensued from rowdy to cooperative when we discussed the life of the main character, Chato de Shamrock.

CHANGES

The letters flowed steadily between Northern and Southern California. I wrote more often than he and pressed for answers to personal questions about his life asking, for example, if he had been raised and schooled in Boyle Heights, was he employed, and could he send a photograph? None were answered. My tenure lasted two and half years at the high school before accepting a job offer as an Adult School Counselor in another district. Danny was concerned, questioning who would provide feedback on new chapters. I assured him that nothing would change from my perspective; in fact, my availability for editing would increase.

Per. III
English 2

To Danny Santiago, you think you're a big cholo, by the way the story was to make up.
Maria J. Mora

I think the story was good I enjoyed it and it made sence. It wasn't like those other kind of stories that don't make sence.
Elizabeth Navaro

I enjoy your stories very much and I think they sounded very real I think this was very good and i wouldn't mind receiving copies of your stories for my self so i could collect them. You see i'm all for the Mexicans and their rights.
Darlene Doane

My letters now contained details of my personal as well as my professional life, plus I spent many hours evaluating chapters mailed to my home. I encouraged him to keep his "eyes on the prize" when his letters arrived weighted with despair instead of the usual repartee. He acknowledged my influence on maintaining his focus while completing the novel. Early in our correspondence he wrote: "You lifted me out of one of the worst periods of my life." The letters characterized me as his anchor and the one most responsible for this book being written. Toward the end of our first year of correspondence he wrote: "And if it hadn't been for you, I doubt that this book would have ever gotten itself written. When it is published, you're in for the killing or whatever."

My task as a teacher, as I interpreted it, was to present literary work with high reader appeal that validated the students' culture, and would lead them into the established canon. Having reviewed the many chapters, I felt that Danny's book held great promise and was destined to be enjoyed by readers of all ages. In addition, the lack of Chicano/a Literature available at the time was intolerable; unlike today when publishers such as Texas-based Arte Público devote their entire catalog to Hispanic literature and major publishers support departments dedicated to this market. Currently, there's an array of exemplary Chicano authors including Lorna Dee Cervantes, Ana Castillo, Michele Serros, Sandra Cisneros, Gary Soto, Jimmy Santiago Baca, Luis Valdez, Denise Chavez, and others who enrich all

Per. III
English 2

I thought that the story was good but it could have been all of your stories our class have read all deal with Mexicans.
Willard Yamaguchi

I liked it a lot, But it left me curious I want to know what happened when his father gets a hold of him. I've only read two of your stories they were good. I would like to read more.
Marta Heinrich

IT WAS GREAT
GILBERT LUJAN

genres. Scholars in the field maintain that this literature existed in 1971, but those were the early works – chronicles from early settlers, memoirs of journeys north. None were focused on East Los Angeles with a brash adolescent as the protagonist.

As the years passed, Danny's lack of disclosure and mysterious responses caused me much frustration and there were months when I ceased correspondence in protest. All the letters went to the Pacific Grove Post Office, so I surmised that he was free to move around. For years I thought he was a majordomo in the vast agricultural fields around Salinas while living in a tent or garret. Or perhaps he was in jail and allowed outside work privileges. He was very knowledgeable about agricultural matters, offering expert advice for my freshman garden. Instructions arrived suitable for 40 acres. My letter writing resumed when his letters once again appeared. One contained the following:

> *Please don't give up on me yet. You're one of the diminishing few strands of hope*
> *that hold me together. I think of you more often than you might guess and when your*
> *letters come it's always a big day for me.*

Finally in December 1982, a good news letter arrived. Instead of a date on the right hand corner, he typed 3:45 a.m. "A flock of angels" appeared with a publishing contract for the novel! He wanted me to be one of the first to know that Chato de Shamrock found a publisher. I longed to speak with him to celebrate even if it was over the phone. Would I finally see a photo of my longtime correspondent? Would I be listed in the Acknowledgements? He explained rewrites would take about half a year in 1983, with a publication date early the next year. In the spring of 1984 he wrote that Simon & Schuster was mailing a complimentary copy.

That summer I enrolled in an Art History class at Cambridge University in England. *Famous* arrived the same week as the demanding course reading list. Two weeks prior to my leaving, I received another letter: "What did I think of the book? When would I mail a review?" My answer was that since I had been reviewing the chapters for 13 years, the review would have to wait until I returned from England in a month's time.

BLISS INTERRUPTUS ...

The Cambridge summer was one of the happiest I'd experienced abroad.

Trinity Hall appeared medieval with modern day conveniences. The view from my dorm window framed the River Cam. In the mornings, the Master's Garden, with its heady array of summer blooms, intoxicated my senses. The class was stimulating and the field trips provided memorable views of the lush English countryside. Again, I mailed

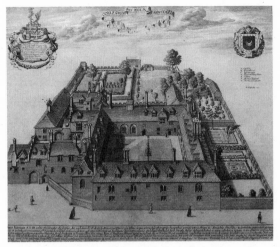

postcards to Danny, fixated on my role as mentor and muse. One explained how the cluster colleges functioned and another featured Kings College Cathedral where my classmates attended Evensong. I also described the gazebo at Trinity College where Byron purportedly wrote poetry. In short, I never allowed a teachable moment to dissipate.

A week before returning home, at breakfast, a classmate passed the *Herald American* to me. At the bottom of page one this headline appeared: "Latino Author Guilty of Deception." Who in Latin America was dishonest? When I reached paragraph three, the name Danny Santiago appeared. I kept reading with disbelief. The young/witty/talented/high school dropout/inmate was in truth Daniel Lewis James, a white 73-year-old Yale graduate in Classics, blacklisted Hollywood screenwriter, and "septuagenarian ex-Stalinist aristocrat" as described by John Gregory Dunne.

At last the answers I sought for thirteen years. In the midst of Cambridgeshire's natural splendor and remarkable history, the sense of betrayal and bewilderment were beyond measure.

On my return to California, I read the many lengthy newspaper articles, interviews, and angry columns by respected literary critics and academics. There was extensive discussion of cultural appropriation and the ethics of assuming a false identity to lend authenticity. Two well-known Chicano writers published newspaper columns defending Danny's right to tell the story of the Medina family. It was difficult to separate the book from the accusations, and a long time passed before I was able to formulate my own position. First, I dealt with no author information and no credit when *Famous* arrived, now I had to support one of two well-articulated opposing points of view. One article ended with a quote from a young female Montebello student who had been assigned a Danny Santiago story in her English class saying, "I like it. Can we have another?" That was the extent of any Montebello links throughout the in-depth article. Not only was I not named, but neither was the editorial role played by the Montebello students acknowledged.

A short letter from Danny awaited me, apologizing for his deceit and asking me to read the long biographical article in the August *New York Review of Books* written by John Gregory Dunne. He added that over the years he had been tempted to park across the street from my home hoping to catch a look at me. He never did considering this a very unfair advantage.

In October we met face to face for the first and only time. After 13 years of exchanging personal correspondence, the evening was electric and memorable. It resembled a line from a Sandra Cisneros poem *"hablamos con ganas, era un alimento."* (Our words were nourishing, spoken with desire and affection.) Did I squander the short time spent with Danny on that autumn night? I was so dazzled by his notoriety and literary affiliations that I failed to ask the two questions most often asked of me: why did Danny privately praise me and ignore me publicly? Did he ever want to end the ruse and confess the truth?

His letter after our first and only meeting reads:

> *It was good to hear from you. I was really afraid that the exposé of the septuagenarian ex-Stalinist aristocrat would put an end to our beautiful, if remote, relationship.*

In the months that followed, our correspondence became sporadic. The letters went into a manila folder and the book in my bookcase. Also filed away was the life lesson of another deceptive man. The sense of betrayal was mitigated by what I considered the most important aspect of this saga: the book was finally available to others. Now many readers would find an honest depiction of a Chicano family, something missing from the literary canon. Danny passed away three years later on May 18, 1988 from a heart condition. I learned about his passing in the obituary section of the *Los Angeles Times*. It was a profound loss of a unique friendship and collaboration.

RESURRECTION

In 1989, after 18 years as an Academic and Personal Counselor at Rio Hondo College in Whittier, my request for reassignment to my first discipline, teaching English, was granted. I spent a sabbatical year pursuing a Master's in English. Much had changed since my undergraduate days 25 years earlier. Included in the curriculum were novels and poetry authored by women, and assignments on Native American writers. In the Women in Fiction seminar, I introduced Chicana authors, new to the professor and other Master's candidates. For the Adolescent Literature course my presentation on novels of initiation focused on *Famous All Over Town*, sans the correspondence. During my first year in the English Department, I developed the first Chicano/a Literature course taught at the college and assigned *Famous* as one of the required texts. (This was a bittersweet moment knowing Danny missed my teaching the book by a mere two years.) My students struggled with the issue of authenticity after reading and discussing *Famous*.

Professional opportunities resulted from my correspondence with Danny. In 1996 I was selected as a participant for a Seminar on Literary Biography held in New York City under the auspices of the National Endowment for the Humanities. My purpose was to continue my professional emphasis on Chicano Literature, focusing on biographical research of what was now a fully accepted genre of American Literature. During my introductory remarks, I mentioned the Santiago correspondence to the group almost as an afterthought. It caused an excited explosion. They insisted that I disregard my research focus and concentrate on compiling material for a memoir based on the correspondence. The participants also stressed that I should contact the James family inquiring if my letters were saved. I estimate that I wrote over two hundred during the thirteen-year period. The group also convinced me that Danny's letters were safer in a bank vault than a manila folder. Danny's agent and editor were both New York City-based, and I arranged for us to meet. They too had been duped by Danny but nonetheless considered him a diligent working author with enormous talent. This memoir would address ongoing issues in the humanities: what categories do we impose on literature – British, American, Chicano, Asian, Black, and so forth? Who has the right to write about a culture? We ended our study of literary biography by submitting research summaries/approaches in a book of essays published by Krieger.

In 2002, during my final sabbatical prior to retirement I contacted Barbara James. My request for my letters in 1988 was first addressed to Lilith, Dan's wife. She said she was still finding it difficult to edit his papers six months after his passing. About four years later, she passed away. My letter to Barbara began, "I was a friend of your father's." I also sent copies of letters as proof of my claim. The first sentence of her reply was:

> *Of course I know who you are. You are the person who provided the one thing that would lift Papa's black fits when he really felt hopeless.*

She described Lilith's progressive dementia. As the illness progressed, Lilith spent much of her time relocating objects in strange and inappropriate places. If she did locate my letters, she most likely moved them to a mysterious place. Another possibility was that the letters were stored in the carriage house where a roof leak turned all the contents to cement. These rock-like bundles were then tossed in the trash. Barbara closed the letter with:

> *I am so glad you got in touch. I've wanted to meet you. Your enthusiasm and support meant much more to him than he probably let you know.*

BALM OF GILEAD

In July 2012, I received a letter from my former employer, Rio Hondo College. Letters from the college are usually tossed in the trash unopened as they are usually requests for donations. For some curious reason I did open this one. It turned out to be an email from a Chicago playwright regarding a play he was writing about Danny. He was familiar with my memoir in the Krieger publication, and asked that I contact him.

A play about Danny? A request for my side of the story? How did this playwright become aware of the controversy surrounding Danny? Over the course of that summer we exchanged emails and telephone calls. I shared a few letters not included in the memoir and sent additional material including interior photographs of Seaward, Dan's graduation photo requested from the Yale Alumni Office, plus a written summary of my Carmel visit in 2002. The playwright mentioned that a character based on my experience was an integral part of the play.

In August 2013, I traveled to Chicago for a reading of *Your Name Will Follow You Home* at the renowned Steppenwolf Theatre, the title based on Danny's original choice for the title of his book. Sitting in the audience, hearing my writing transformed into dialogue, having personal occurrences dramatized, and viewing an unfolding of Dan's life on stage was an overwhelmingly emotional experience. This play was very thoroughly researched, as different acts depicted Dan's life's events: his privileged upbringing in Kansas, the remote relationship to the outlaw Jesse James, his decision to join the Commu-

DANIEL LEWIS JAMES, "Dan," was born on January 14, 1911, in Kansas City, Mo. His father, D. L. James (B.A. Yale 1902, M.A. 1907), is manager of the retail store of the T. M. James & Sons China Company in that city. He has also lived in Carmel, Calif. His mother's maiden name was Lily Hyatt Snider. Dan is a nephew of Thomas M. James, Jr., '98.

His preparatory training was received at the Kansas City Country Day School and at Phillips-Andover. He entered Yale with our Class, but withdrew at the end of Junior year; he expects to return to finish his course with '33. He was a scholar of the second rank in Freshman year and of the third

nist Party and the blacklist that resulted. Also mentioned were the years he spent as a social worker in Boyle Heights and his many successes working with Mexican American families. In the play, one character grows from skeptic to believer as he discovers the many facets of this complex man.

THE FINAL FAREWELL

What did St. Anthony, even with limited powers, help me find at Carmel? He helped me find three of my letters, including the one written after the truth emerged. It reads as if written by a scolding English fishwife. There were chapter galleys with my notes attached and many were merged into the final text. In addition, there was a large envelope labeled "Fan Mail – Eastmont" with the long ago reviews from my five classes. For the students I've located, I made copies of their work; they're always amused to see their writing from forty years ago. Another interesting group of letters was from famous actors and actresses, authors, and screenwriters. Classmates from Andover and Yale were also filed. It was Danny's practice to mark the envelopes "Answered" along with the date and a sentence that captured the response. This was more evidence that he kept my letters as well.

As requested in my letter, Barbara shared photos, anecdotes, and events of Dan's life. As a young girl she also participated in the Boyle Heights family celebrations, sort of an "honorary Mexican." These she remembered with great fondness. She described the various families that were models for the book, close friends of the James'. She showed me a songbook of ballads, corridos, and other songs Dan had compiled.

The visit to Carmel reaffirmed my admiration for this very complicated, talented man. It heightened my respect for his creativity and work habits. It is my stance that during Danny's twenty years volunteering in East Los Angeles he came to admire and respect the culture and values of the Mexican-American families. Fictionalizing their lives with such authenticity was a labor of love for him. Further, being Chicano depends not on the color of the skin, but is a matter of the heart.

During my stay in Carmel, Barbara, without hesitatation, acknowledged my contributions to the writing of the novel. When it came time to say goodbye in front of the guesthouse, she asked if there was any remembrance I wanted of Danny's, a gift from him. There were so many tempting artifacts, but instead I asked for the return of my students' comments. Everything else, I proposed, should be left for biographers to peruse. Because I kept my three letters found in his papers, there remains no written evidence of my relationship with Danny.

I still hope to publish Danny's letters along with my reconstructed letters to offer readers some insight into this relationship. When speaking to classes they're always surprised that despite the betrayal, I nevertheless value the friendship we shared. My hopes are that this memoir will be unique to the study of literature and to the canon of Chicano Literature. Above all, it's a tribute to an uncommon friendship between two strangers who became confidants.

Saying goodbye to Barbara and little Olive, her dog, cemented the last link to him. It's been a threefold loss: first when I found out there was no Danny Santiago, then when I read Dan James' obituary, and finally when I organized and packed all his papers.

I'm no longer standing alone on that ridge. Over the years others have joined me in support of my role. *Your Name Will Follow You Home* binds us both on the same page for the first time. Instead of finding what I was searching for in that shimmering Carmel sea light, I bid farewell, cloaked with an embracing peace.

Whittier, California

NOTES ON IMAGES, BY PAGE

243 *Sjøtobellet (The Sea Troll), 1887 by Theodor Kittelsen (1857-1914).* Photo in public domain.

244 *Entry portal to Seaward, the home of DL James, designed by Charles Sumner Greene in 1918. Photo by William Current.* Greene and Greene Archives, Gamble House USC, Huntington Library.

245 *Interior sitting room is Seaward overlooking the Pacific.* Greene and Greene Archives, Gamble House USC, Huntington Library.

   Seaward as seen from a nearby overlook on the Pacific Coast Highway. Greene and Greene Archives, Gamble House USC, Huntington Library.

246 *Polaroids of students in Alicia Hernandez's 9th grade English class in Montebello.* Photo by Alicia Hernandez

247 *Exterior of Pacific Grove Post Office in Monterey County, California.* Photo by Alicia Hernandez

248 *Students notes written to Danny Santiago in response to reading unpublished chapters of what would become the novel* Famous All Over Town. Photos by Alicia Hernandez

250 *Bird's eye view of Trinity Hall, Cambridge by David Loggan, Cantabrigia Illustrata, 1690.* Photo in public domain – Wikimedia Commons

251 *Assemblage of articles about the Danny Santiago controversy.* Photo by Carlos Murillo.

254 *Daniel James' entry in the Yale College History of the Class of 1932.* Yale University archives.

255 *Alicia Hernandez's first edition copy of* Famous All Over Town *with a note from Danny Santiago.* Photo by Alicia Hernandez

YOUR NAME WILL FOLLOW YOU HOME

Characters

Alvaro, writer. US born Puerto Rican/Colombian/Jewish. Early 30s.

Herman, adjunct professor. US born of German-Jewish descent. Mid 30s.

Valerie, designer. Caucasian. Early 30s.

Javier, writer. Born in Colombia, immigrated as a child to NYC. Early 30s.

Nero, actor. Caucasian. Likely grew up in the Midwest. Early 30s.

Lina, actor. Mixed race — Asian-Latina or possibly Filipino. Mid 20s.

Emiliano Kurtz, university professor. White, though origins uncertain. Mid 40s.

Alex Tanner, graduate student. White. Mid 20s.

Setting

Act One takes place in a shabby tenement apartment in Hell's Kitchen, New York City and a seminar classroom at an unnamed university somewhere in the United States.

Act Two takes place in the courtyard of a shabby motel in Puerto Angel — a tiny fishing village on the Pacific coast of Oaxaca, Mexico.

Time

The scenes in Hell's Kitchen and Puerto Angel take place in 1988.
The scenes in the seminar room and Kurtz's apartment take place in 2012.

ACT ONE. Hell's Kitchen

1. AUTHENTICITY, 1988

Cramped kitchen/living room of a tenement apartment in Hell's Kitchen. It's overcrowded with second hand furniture, tons of books, musical instruments and children's toys. Off the living room, a closed door that leads to a bedroom.

Alvaro, Herman and Valerie sit around the kitchen table. On the table: take-out containers, empty wine and beer bottles, a full ashtray. Valerie sits closer to Herman. Perhaps a little too close – if you were a stranger passing, you might think they were "together."

Also in the kitchen, Nero and Lina. They awkwardly share a chair, Nero slightly behind Lina, rubbing her shoulders. They half listen to the conversation – Nero seems more fixed on getting Lina enticed enough to lure her to some place more private.

Javier is quiet, strums a guitar. He sits on a child's chair in the living room. He seems "checked out" of the proceedings, in his own world.

ALVARO: *New York Times* crowns the kid

    calls him a "new," "distinct," "streetwise,"

    "authentic" voice from "*el barrio,*"

    captures the people, rituals,

    language, violence, the *passion*,

    "urban grit," I'm like "Yeah, I can dig that."

    But when I look at the critic's name?

    I'm like,

    huh.

    How much time has *he* spent

    in East LA? That a frequent stop for him?

    Yeah, America anything's possible, right?

    Maybe he's hooked in

    minored in Chicano Studies or

    is a secret card carrying member of *La Raza*

    got some

    lost branch a the family

wrinkled little abuelita

boils him up

magical realist tamales

that cast spells on you so

butterflies fly out your asshole

when you're making love?

Just like in Azteca times.

So yeah, *maybe*

Critic's got something to back up

his assertion

that the goods are "authentic."

HERMAN: Okay, but —

ALVARO: *But*

the *other* critics …

all say the same thing —

"authenticity this," "gritty realism that" —

there really that many secret Chicanos

infiltrating the mainstream press?

HERMAN: Um. No.

ALVARO: So why do *we* take their word for it?

Authentic?

Fuck do they know?

Worst shit? People eat that shit up!

VALERIE: Alvaro! Keep it down. You'll wake Pablo and Lila.

HERMAN: Did you actually read the book?

ALVARO: Yeah, I read the book.

HERMAN: And?

ALVARO: And what?

HERMAN: Did it seem … authentic?

ALVARO: You're really asking me that?

HERMAN: Yeah …

ALVARO: You're *really* asking me that // shit.

HERMAN: Did I say something off//ensive

ALVARO: Yeah, *Herman,* I read it and I'm like
    "I guess critic's right
    sounds authentic Chicano to me."

HERMAN: So what's the problem

ALVARO: Problem is
    Mr. "Did-I-Say-Something-Offensive"
    you automatically assume I'd be some kind of authority

VALERIE: Boys, would you please // keep it down …

HERMAN: Well aren't you? If anyone in this room —

VALERIE: Well, Javi —   ALVARO: "If anyone"????….

ALVARO: Fuck do *I* know is "authentic Mexican"
    I'm triple breed Puerto Rican Colombian Jew —
    I'm as qualified as Mr. *New York Times*
    to pass that judgment
    Few times I been in LA? I avoid downtown
    Let alone East side,
    My mother? She fucking hated Mexicans.

VALERIE: You're exaggerating —

ALVARO: It's true, God rest her soul?
    She used to say
    all kinds of racist shit —
    I grew up on Long Island …
    Closest I ever got to a Mexican
    before college? Our cleaning lady
    Though now that I think about it
    She was Salvadoran …

HERMAN: Wait a minute. *You* grew up on Long Island?

ALVARO: Yeah, what about it?

HERMAN: What town?

ALVARO: Great Neck.

HERMAN: Ooooh. *West* Egg.

ALVARO: Hilarious –

VALERIE: I'm sorry – I'm missing the reference – ?

HERMAN: *Great Gatsby*? Surely you read it in high school?

VALERIE: Asshat –

She playfully swats Herman. Javier notices this.

HERMAN: West Egg? Where Gatsby lives?

VALERIE: Right // right

HERMAN: modeled after Alvaro's home // town –

ALVARO: What//ever

HERMAN: Nouveau Riche? As opposed to *East* // Egg?

VALERIE: Old money. Got//cha …

HERMAN: Then why do you talk like that?

ALVARO: Like what?

HERMAN: All … "street"

ALVARO: Fuck you, why do *you* talk like that?

HERMAN: How do I talk?

ALVARO: Like a smug son of a bitch.

HERMAN: It sounds like this whole thing is making you *mad*.

ALVARO: Yeah, it's making me mad.

HERMAN: *What's* making you mad

    Are you mad at the *critic*?

    Or the people who "eat that shit up"?

ALVARO: *Both.*

    Critic's selling me on "authenticity" —

VALERIE: Which he has no authority to do —

ALVARO: *Exactly* —

HERMAN: Of course he has the authority, he writes for *The New York Times.*

Valerie cracks up at this.

ALVARO: Yeah, //

    Whatever —

VALERIE: I think what Alvaro is trying to say, // Herman is —

ALVARO: Valerie, I don't need a translator, thankyou // verymuch?

VALERIE: Okay, //

    Asshole.

ALVARO: Critic says the book's "authentic" … Why?

    Cause the shit affirms every worn out cliché

    he picked up reading comic books.

    But *New York Times* says "Bitch roll over, play dead"

    All you bitches roll over and play dead.

    Everyone — critic? Public?

    Keep on wearing the saaaame old straitjacket.

HERMAN: *Strait//jacket*

ALVARO: So yeah, shit makes me mad. But most of all? I'm mad at *you*

HERMAN: What did I do?

ALVARO: For bringing it to us

    thinking we'd even consider —

VALERIE: Volume …

HERMAN: We? I don't recall you ever being appointed // spokesperson for

ALVARO: I ain't touching that shit with a 200-foot pole.

Javier abruptly stops strumming his guitar. Doing so silences everyone. They all look at him. Even Nero and Lina. Pause.

VALERIE: You were gonna say something, Javi?

JAVIER: Yeah. What about the writer?

ALVARO: What *about* him?

JAVIER: You mad at him?

ALVARO: Bitch is a fraud.

JAVIER: What makes him a fraud?

HERMAN: Good question, Javi.

ALVARO & JAVIER: Eat me Herman.

JAVIER: What makes him a fraud, Alvaro?

ALVARO: Uhhh …
    He's a liar?

JAVIER: How's he a liar?

ALVARO: Uhhh … let me count the ways?
    One: it's not his real name

HERMAN: There's countless examples throughout history of writers using pseudonyms—

ALVARO: Not the same —

JAVIER: How is it different —

ALVARO: You siding with him?

JAVIER: I'm not siding with anyone,
    I want to understand
    Why this is different?

ALVARO: He didn't he use his own name

cause he wants you to *believe*

he's a 14-year-old Mexican kid

HERMAN: He's clearly not 14, he's an adult *writing* about a kid that's // 14.

ALVARO: In the *first person*

HERMAN: So?

Javier's hands tense up, as if he's restraining the fantasy of strangling Herman. He tunes out, resumes strumming on his guitar.

ALVARO: He's obviously trying to pass it off like it's an autobiography –

HERMAN: It's clearly labeled a work of fiction,

Nowhere does it say it's autobio//graphical

ALVARO: It's *implied*

VALERIE: *Guys ... Volume.*

HERMAN: All his bio says

Is that he grew up in Los Angeles –

ALVARO: Which is *another* lie –

HERMAN: Yeah, but how do you get auto//biography

ALVARO: A lie to trick the reader into confusing

Danny Santiago the writer with Chato Medina the character

When in fact the *real* author is // about as far from

VALERIE: What was his name again?

HERMAN: Daniel James

ALVARO: When the *REAL* author is about as far from being Chicano from East L.A.

As is humanly possible –

HERMAN: Which proves my point: it's a work of *fiction*

ALVARO: If he signed it "Daniel James, 80 year old rich white fuck"

I might buy it's fiction, *but*

He wrote in the first person, signed it Danny. Santiago.

HERMAN: Then why did he name the protagonist Rudy Medina?

VALERIE: I thought it was Chato de Shamrock

HERMAN: Chato's his gang name

VALERIE: But why Shamrock — what is he half Irish?

HERMAN: Huh? No. Shamrock's the name of the street he grew up on — Did you even // read

ALVARO: He's fucking around with names,
    shit's intentional obfuscation
    so, yes, Herman, bitch wanted us to believe
    it was autobiographical.

HERMAN: That's just your imagination.

ALVARO: Oh, you motherfucker,
    don't make me crack this bottle // over your head

VALERIE: Whoa! // Whoa! Whoa!

HERMAN: Whoa! See that? You see that?
    He gets violent

ALVARO: You condescending puto, "my imagination"
    I'll show you my imagination cause I got like six hundred ways
    I imagine cracking open your skull!

Nero, sticking his fingers in his mouth, loudly whistles, stopping the room.

VALERIE: Nero! For Christ's sake, you'll wake the goddamn kids!

NERO: What the fuck are you guys talking about?

VALERIE: Haven't you been listening?

ALVARO: (To his pi pi may//be)

NERO: I've been listening but I have no idea // what you're

HERMAN: The book, Nero.
    Famous All Over Town?
    One that I asked you all read?
    Did you read it?

NERO: No.

HERMAN: Why not? I went out of my way to –

NERO: I don't have time to read shit –

HERMAN: We have a *deadline* Nero – we have a *commission?* To write a *play?*

NERO: I know.

HERMAN: Not just any commission? The Public Theater?
   That little place down on Lafay//ette?

NERO: I know.

HERMAN: Yeah, well Joe Papp? He only calls once
   We're already months late
   I keep coming up // with

NERO: I don't have time to read shit
   Unless it's a hundred percent sure we're doing it.

HERMAN: Did anyone read the book?

Alvaro and Lina raise their hands. Valerie waves hers as if to say "skimmed it." Nero and Javier keep their hands down.

HERMAN: That's just great –
   someone finally commissions us to write something,
   we're all supposed to come with ideas,
   zip from all // of you –

NERO: Whatever … you lost me.

HERMAN: Where did we lose you, Nero?

NERO: All these names you're throwing around –
   Just tell me. Who wrote the book?

HERMAN: Okay. Nero. There's a book.

NERO: Yeah.

HERMAN: It's called *Famous All Over Town*.

NERO: Yeah —

HERMAN: Simon & Schuster, 1983

NERO: I don't need all the details

HERMAN: Fine. It's a classic bildungsroman with —

NERO: Build a what what?

HERMAN: Bildungsroman — coming of age story?
About a Mexican kid growing up in East Los Angeles.
His family's coming apart, while his neighborhood's — the *barrio's* —
being torn down to make way for the railroad —
Following?

NERO: Following.

HERMAN: Book's author is a young unknown // writer—

ALVARO: *Purported* auth//or

HERMAN: *Purported* author is a young, unknown writer // named

ALVARO: *Chicano* writ//er

HERMAN: *Chicano* writer named Danny Santiago …

NERO: Why'd they purport him?

HERMAN: Huh?

NERO: Was he like
an illegal alien?

ALVARO: Jesus mother // of Christ

HERMAN: That's *de*ported // not

NERO: You use these words
what the fuck does "purported" mean, anyway

LINA: To have the false appearance of being

Nero licks the back of her neck.

NERO: So he's like fake …

HERMAN: He's "like fake"

NERO: So someone else wrote it.

HERMAN: Precisely. A gentleman by the name of // Daniel James.

ALVARO: Oooohhh, so he's a *gentleman*

HERMAN: Who, as Alvaro has pointed out, is not Chicano, but a white man.

ALVARO: A ninety-eight year old *filthy rich* white // man

HERMAN: Seventy-two. He's *seventy-//two*

NERO: Okay … so what's like … the big deal?

HERMAN: That's what we're trying to establish here.

Alvaro picks up an empty can of beer and tries to eat it in frustration.

JAVIER: Alvaro. Calmate.

Everyone quiets. They look at Javi. There's a long pause.

VALERIE: Did you … wanna say something … Javi?

Long pause. Javier picks on his guitar. They wait. When Javier speaks, there's an eerie calm in his voice.

JAVIER: Yes. I was gonna say something.
> But
> Herman
> wanted a turn.
> I didn't get to finish.

HERMAN: Sorry, Javi …

JAVIER: It's all good.
> Alvaro …
> My friend …
> You used the word
> "straitjacket" …

Pause. They wait to see if he'll continue. He doesn't.

ALVARO: Yeah.

JAVIER: Cause if I understand what you mean by // straitjacket

HERMAN: What he means is

Valerie places her hand on Herman's forearm to shut him up. Pause.

JAVIER: Sounds to me

of all people you're mad at? —
Critic ...
Reader ...
Writer ...
Herman ...

Only one not wearing the straitjacket is the writer.

Long pause.

JAVIER: Isn't that what we need? You and me?

To not get stuck in a straitjacket?

Long silence. Suddenly a toddler's cry from behind the closed door. Valerie lets out a sigh.

VALERIE: Goddamnit! See what you knuckleheads did? You woke Lila.

JAVIER: Want me to go in?

VALERIE: I got it. I'm gonna kill her if she wakes up Pablo ...

Valerie downs her wine glass. Goes to the door, making gentle hushing noises. She shuts the door behind her. Silence. Herman looks at his watch.

HERMAN: Shit. Look at the time. 2:30.

No response.

Well. Illuminating as always. But ... adjuncting first thing in the morning ...

He gets up. Waits for a spell. Javier and Alvaro say nothing.

Take care, gentlemen.

He gets to the door. Turns around.

Please tell Valerie I said goodnight.

JAVIER: Take it easy, Herman.

HERMAN: You too.

 And Alvaro … ?

 Didn't mean to let the uh …

 sparring

 get out of hand.

ALVARO: I'm good.

HERMAN: Nothing personal –

ALVARO: I'm good.

Herman leaves.

ALVARO: Dude's an asshole.

During the previous exchange, Nero and Lina have gotten their coats. They leave quietly, thinking they're being discreet.

JAVIER: Alvaro …

 can I borrow your copy of the book?

ALVARO: Here …

Alvaro hands him the book. Silence. Javier strums, lost in his thoughts.

ALVARO: You okay, man?

JAVIER: I'm fine. Look, uh …

 I'm gotta hit the sack soon.

ALVARO: A'ight.

Alvaro rises, sips the last of the wine, picks up his notebook. He watches Javier. Alvaro goes to him, kisses him on top of the head. It's a deep kiss – like he harbors a great love and longing for him. Javier doesn't respond, just continues playing. Valerie re-enters, just as it's ending – enough for her to see it. Alvaro sees her, clears his throat.

ALVARO: Night Valerie.

VALERIE: Night.

He exits. Valerie and Javier alone. She watches him play. He doesn't notice her. Lights fade as we hear a Godzilla-like monster growl from a '50s B monster movie, transitioning us to:

2. MONSTER MOVIE SEMINAR
OR THE MYSTIQUE OF FAILURE, 2013

Graduate Seminar: "The Mystique of Failure." The seminar room is empty, except for Emilia-no Kurtz, the instructor, and a single female student, Alex Tanner. Kurtz is in his 50s, somewhat cocky and slick. He's not conventionally handsome, but looked at through a particular lens, he does have a certain sex appeal. He speaks in an unidentifiable accent – could be Eastern European, Latin America, a hybrid of both, or could be fake. Alex is in her 20s. She's driven, whip-smart and attractive in a librarian's assistant sort of way. Kurtz talks as if the classroom is full. Behind him is a screen, on which is projected a black and white photograph of an elderly Daniel James.

KURTZ: Search of the Internet Movie Database for the films of Daniel James

Reveals a spectacularly unremarkable career trajectory.

His introduction to the profession suggests great promise –
First job in Hollywood:
Second Unit Director of Charlie Chaplin's
The Great Dictator.
Accounts of his contribution to the film vary:
Some suggest he co-authored the screenplay,
Others describe James as Chaplin's errand boy …

In an article by John Gregory Dunne
published in *The New York Review of Books* in 1984,
James describes his contribution as follows, quote:
"Chaplin felt the Nazis could capture me, pull out my fingernails,
I would never turn against him."

He laughs. Alex doesn't think much of the joke.

Remember those words – they will resonate later.

This auspicious start was followed in 1943
With a screenwriting credit for *Three Russian Girls* –
Regret to inform you,
Not an early Hollywood attempt to Americanize *Chekhov* …
Story is set in the Soviet Union during the Nazi invasion.

An American pilot, downed by the Nazis, lies in a hospital
Nursed by a sweet young thing named Natasha (played by Anna Sten).
They fall in love, but resist the
bourgeois temptation to *consumate*
As they have pressing, world-historical matters at hand,
Namely, resisting the Nazi advance into Soviet territory.

Questions?

No? Good.

Ten years pass before James resurfaces.
From 1953 to 1961, he scripts four films:

Slide reproductions of posters and stills from each film appear on the screen.

1953 *Beast from 20,000 Fathoms*
"Ferocious dinosaur awakened by Arctic atomic test terrorizes New York City."

1958 *Revolt in the Big House* – starring a young Robert Blake –
A film whose title accurately summarizes its plot –

1959 *The Giant Behemoth*
"Marine atomic test resurrects undersea dinosaur that proceeds to destroy London."

Last but not least:

Gorgo. 1961.
"Greedy sailors capture giant lizard off Irish coast.
 Sell it to London Circus.
Then its mother shows up."

Daniel James' name appears on none of these films.
Screenplays are attributed to one Daniel Hyatt.

For ten thousand dollars and an all expenses paid weekend with me at the hotel of your choice, can anyone explain to me … *WHY?*

Silence. Alex raises her hand.

KURTZ: Yes, Ms. … *(He studies his class roster.)*

ALEX: Tanner.

KURTZ: Ms. Tanner.

ALEX: You do realize I'm the only one enrolled in this seminar.

KURTZ: Your powers of perception stagger.

Do you have an answer to the question?

ALEX: I might.

KURTZ: What I said –

All expense paid weekend … ?
Joke.

ALEX: Ha ha.

KURTZ: Shall I continue –

ALEX: He must have been blacklisted.

KURTZ: Very good.

In 1951.
Which is odd – don't you think?

ALEX: How so?

KURTZ: Being blacklisted seems to

have had the paradoxical effect of
reviving a film career that died in 1943,
eight. years. before HUAC blacklisted him.

ALEX: Okay …

KURTZ: Does it trouble you? Me suggesting he did better *after* the blacklist
Than he did *before?*

ALEX: Why would it trouble me …

KURTZ: One of those episodes …

In your American history … ?
Subterranean Monster beneath the Shining City on the Hill surfaces … ?
Still raises hackles …
You're probably too young to remember, but when Kazan –

ALEX: Won the lifetime achievement Oscar

    half the audience sat on their hands cause he named names.

KURTZ: Where do you stand on such matters?

ALEX: You want to know my political persuasion ... ?

KURTZ: Well –

ALEX: I'll take the Fifth.

KURTZ: Touché.

ALEX: I've actually seen the films – the monster ones.

KURTZ: Really.

ALEX: Yeah. When I was a kid, my dad, he –

Pause.

KURTZ: He ... ?

ALEX: Never mind.

Pause. Supreme awkwardness. Kurtz looks at his watch.

KURTZ: Oh! Look at that!

    5:10. Where did all the time go?

ALEX: Professor Kurtz? Is it safe to assume this course will be cancelled?

KURTZ: Why would you assume such a thing?

ALEX: Um ... low enrollment?

KURTZ: Even if the swimming pool is empty, one must never cease throwing rose
    petals into it.

Alex starts gathering her things.

KURTZ: Next session,

    triple creature feature: *20,000 Fathoms, Giant Behemoth and Gorgo*.

ALEX: Can't wait ...

KURTZ: Drink?

ALEX: Um. No thank you.

KURTZ: See you next week.

ALEX: Yeah.

Alex leaves. Kurtz is left alone.

3. LATE NIGHT PHONE CALL

In the darkness a telephone rings. Once. Twice. Three. Four. Five.

Out of the darkness Alvaro appears — stirred from sleep, he's a wreck — hair mussed up, dressed in underwear and a t-shirt. Phone keeps ringing. He picks it up.

ALVARO: Allo?

JAVIER: You need to come over.

ALVARO: Javi?

Lights up slowly on Javier in the kitchen. He's wired.

JAVIER: You need to come over —

ALVARO: I ain't comin over, I'm asleep

JAVIER: You talking to me from your sleep?

ALVARO: No, man, I'm awake now, you woke me up

JAVIER: Then come over I gotta talk to you

ALVARO: No man, I'm hanging up this motherfuckin phone and going back to sleep

JAVIER: No. Nononononononono, NO. What are you asleep for anyway?

ALVARO: It's 3:30 in the morning —

JAVIER: Oh …

ALVARO: Are you high?

JAVIER: Fukken soaring man,
    I'm like the space shuttle,
    burning through the atmosphere

ALVARO: What'd you take?

JAVIER: Nothing, bro.

ALVARO: Call me in the morning …

JAVIER: I finished reading it.

ALVARO: What?

JAVIER: *Famous All Over Town?*

ALVARO: What'd you think of it?

JAVIER: It was a'ight.
    Not Dostoevsky but I dug it. ...

ALVARO: You read his obituary?

JAVIER: Yea, I read it.

ALVARO: Did it bother you // that –

JAVIER: Bother me? Yeah
    I'm always bothered but
    it bothered me
    in a way
    that it like
    bothered me? that it bothered me?

ALVARO: Huh?

JAVIER: Cause
    eating the book,

ALVARO: *Ay Dios // Mio ...*

JAVIER: Eating the book, his obituary,
    thinking about what you said last night
    about straitjackets, thinking about straitjackets

ALVARO: Okay ...

JAVIER: Thinking about my *mother* –
    I ever tell you she took me to see *Macbeth* when I was a kid?

ALVARO: *Mier//da*

JAVIER: Shit was like someone exploded a pipe bomb in my cranium –
    All that killing – who woulda thought murder could be so beautiful –
    But my mother, ohhhh my mother –

She was disgusted.

She had Solon's objection.

ALVARO: Reference check —

JAVIER: Solon. Greek cat. One of the Seven Wiseguys.

We should do something with that —

GreekPhilosopherMafiososSayHellotoMyLeetel//Frieng —

ALVARO: *Solon.*

JAVIER: Rightrightright

Saw Thespis act in the first Greek Tragedy

in like 80,000 BC, went up to him

at the stage door afterwards? said

"What the fuck?"

"LIES, ALL LIES! Aren't you ashamed?

Telling a big pack a lies to all those subscribers?"

It's in Plutarch — I'll check the reference later —

ALVARO: *Coño madre!*

JAVIER: *Thespis* said:

"What's the harm, it's make-believe ... "

Pissed Solon off so much

he threw down his walking stick —

which in those days was like a Jet

whipping out his switchblade on an unsuspecting Shark

"I like to leeeve een Amerrrrr//ika"

ALVARO: I can't deal with you when you're // like this —

JAVIER: Papi, papi, papi ... Listen, please, it's relevant I promise you:

Solon whipped out his AK was like

"WELL. FUCKHEAD.

If we commend make-believe like this,

everything will be make-believe,

Capitol Hill, Wall Street, New York Times, *marriage ... "*

My mother, know what she said?
After *Macbeth*?

ALVARO: Jav—

JAVIER: (cause I saw the poster on the 7 train
I kicked, screamed, sat on the pavement,
on a steaming pile a dog shit
til she promised she would take me)
Know what she said?

ALVARO: No.

JAVIER: "Que asqueroso ... all those people clapping
For a bunch of cold blooded murderers ... "

ALVARO: Javi: remember that tea I gave you?
One that's supposed to *calm* your nerves?

JAVIER: Yeah, I drank like eight cups of it.

ALVARO: I'm tired man, let's talk // tomorrow

JAVIER: Thespis busted outta the *straitjacket,* see what I'm saying?

Pause.

JAVIER: Alvaro? You there?

ALVARO: I'm listening ...

JAVIER: *Thespis.* Busted. Outta the *straitjacket.*

Solon, my mother, me, YOU ... ALL happy to walk through life wearing the straitjacket —

ALVARO: I'm not wearin no straight // jacket.

JAVIER: What do you and I hear time and time again
When some bitch producer reads our shit?
"Too intellectual. Too universal. Not street enough, not ghetto enough,
not enough 'grit,' not poetic enough, not *magical* enough."

ALVARO: Javi —

JAVIER: When it is, they say the exact opposite –

"Too *raw, too specific,*

too poetic – no one talks like *that*

too street, *too* ghetto, too gritty, grit like that?

Subscribers won't stand for it, and how do you think

they're gonna put all that magic on stage?"

I hear it all the time,

you hear it all the time,

enough's enough, right compa?

ALVARO: Okay, but what's that got to do // with

JAVIER: The book?

Like *I said* – not so much the book,

but the *writer … writer.* busted. through his own straitjacket …

ALVARO: I'm hanging up, I can't take it when you're like // this …

JAVIER: Papi, papi, papi, papi, don't hang up on me.

Just one more thing.

I promise …

ALVARO: *One* thing.

JAVIER: Promise.

ALVARO: Take a breath …

Javier takes a loud, audible, deep breath for Alvaro's benefit.

ALVARO: Okay …

JAVIER: O. Kaaaay.

Silence.

I finished reading the book.

Breath.

Read the obituary.

Breath.

Saw his picture.

Breath.

Thought. Book. Obituary. Picture.
What the fuck.

Then a thing happened.

ALVARO: What … thing …

JAVIER: That feeling?

When you're alone at night?

Startle you feel when a stranger looks at you through the window?

Alvaro closes his eyes tight, restrains himself from responding. Breath.

I got that startle.

Stranger. Looking at me.

Through the kitchen window.

ALVARO: Javi. You're on the *fifth. floor.*

Window in your kitchen

looks out to the airshaft.

There's no stranger looking at you.

JAVIER: I felt that *startle.*

I look up, expect to see a stranger.

Stranger's me.

In the glass – hazy, distorted reflection. Me.

Then BOOM!

Glass shatters.

ALVARO: What?

JAVIER: Not literally, but I see something on the other side of the glass …

ALVARO: What'd you see?

JAVIER: Ruined street. From the end of the book.

After the railroad tears down the neighborhood?

ALVARO: Okay …

JAVIER: Outside the Aztec Club. Boarded up –
 Street looks like a bomb exploded
 Houses obliterated …
 Mounds of garbage –
 People left behind –
 Book of Bones, comic books, crumpled red dress
 Crayons like little flecks of color in the …

ALVARO: I get the picture …

JAVIER: Who shows up. Old Man. Daniel James …
 He's tall, 6' 6"
 Grey hair, dressed like a 1940s longshoreman …
 Old man takes a red crayon from the pile,
 Goes to the boarded window –
 Writes in big, curvy, sexy letters –

ALVARO & JAVIER: "Chato de Shamrock"

JAVIER: Old man's tagging the boarded up window,
 Who shows up? Kid …

ALVARO: Danny.

JAVIER: You and me, we're grooving now.

ALVARO: Go on, baby.

JAVIER: Kid sees the old man …
 Old man finds a picture of Chato's family,
 Sister, mother, baby

ALVARO: *Father*

JAVIER: Old man?
 He goes to hang the picture up, next to his tag
 Kid extends his arm,
 Makes the shape of a gun with his finger and

ALVARO: BANG!

Silence.

ALVARO: What happens next.

JAVIER: I don't know.
Why I need you, bro.

Come over?

ALVARO: No, man … it's late

JAVIER: We're rolling

ALVARO: I don't wanna go down that road.

JAVIER: You don't need to be scared – I'll hold your hand

ALVARO: I ain't scared of shit, bro.

JAVIER: Know what I think?
You like living inside your straitjacket.

ALVARO: Hilarious coming from you.

JAVIER: So comfortable in there …
You wouldn't know what to do with your hands if they were set free.

ALVARO: Punch you in the mouth, maybe …
Only straitjacket I'm wearing is you.

Pause.

JAVIER: We got a deadine. You know what that means?

ALVARO: I know // what that

JAVIER: Years, you and me
On our own
in the trenches getting nowhere
Finally big theater steps up? Throws us a bone?
Joe Papp only calls once, my friend.

ALVARO: I *know*

JAVIER: *You* need this. // *We need*

ALVARO: I don't need this — I don't know // why you

JAVIER: *I need this.* I got two little monsters
 They're asleep, but when they wake?
 They're gonna need to eat, need clothes, toys
 Fuckin' trips to the ice cream parlor ...
 They want and want and need and need ...
 I got NOTHING to give them.

 No one ever gave us a commission before.
 Might be the only chance we ever get.
 I need this.

ALVARO: We'll come up with some other material ...

JAVIER: We got nothing, we been running round in circles.
 We could do some cool shit with this ...
 Come over. Papi? Por fa?

ALVARO: Javi ... I don't know —

JAVIER: When the glass shatters ... you gotta listen ...
 Besides ... means you and me get to spend more time ...

 Alvo?

ALVARO: *(Deep sigh)*

JAVIER: You comin'?

ALVARO: I'll think about it.

He hangs up. Javier hangs up. He smiles. He thinks he might have him. Lights fade as we hear a Godzilla-like monster growl from a '50s B monster movie, transitioning us to:

4. GORGO

Kurtz and Alex watch the final moments of Gorgo *when Gorgo's 200-foot-tall mother rips through the Battersea Amusement Park to rescue her son. We hear Mama Gorgo's roar, accompanied by sounds of urban destruction and a melodramatic film score.*

BBC REPORTER FROM FILM: *(Absurd English accent, like a mental patient pretending to be a cricket announcer.)* "Maybe our prayers have been answered.

> The Great City,
> overwhelmed, exhausted,
> lies helpless under the immeasurable power and ferocity
> of this towering apparition from before the dawn of history.
> Yet,
> As though disdaining the pygmies under her feet,
> she turns back,
> turns with her young,
> leaving the prostrate city,
> and leaving Man himself
> to ponder the proud boast
> that he alone is Lord of all Creation"

LITTLE BOY FROM FILM: "You're going back now ... back to the sea ... "

Music swells. Kurtz switches off the projector. He and Alex sit in silence in the dark.

KURTZ: Lights, please!

Alex rolls her eyes, gets up, switches on the light. Kurtz wipes tears from his eyes.

ALEX: You're kidding me, right?

KURTZ: You're not moved? Mother?

> Rescuing her son from being made a public spectacle?

ALEX: Um, no. She's a 200-foot-tall monster. She destroyed half of London.

KURTZ: Watch it again someday if you ever have kids.

Silence.

ALEX: You have kids?

KURTZ: Two.

ALEX: How old?

KURTZ: 17 and 14.

ALEX: Are they —

KURTZ: They live with their mother in Seattle.
   Look we're not here to talk about trivialities,
   we're here to talk about *Gorgo*.

ALEX: Movie seems pretty trivial to me ...

KURTZ: Does it? How so?

ALEX: Run of the mill '50s monster movie —
   Bad special effects?
   Inept dialogue,
   Zero character development,
   Plot threads that go nowhere ...
   Moral universe that's about as
   Black and white // as —

KURTZ: That's one, very narrow, way of looking at it.

ALEX: And I'm missing ... ?

KURTZ: Hell, I don't know — are there political dimensions you can ex//tract—

ALEX: Only the most obvious ones ...

KURTZ: Enlighten me.

ALEX: Greedy American shipwreck pillagers, *bad*.
   Salt-of-the-earth-Irish-villagers-who-subsist-on-no-more-than-what-they-need-
   from-the-sea, *good*.
   Toss in some soft boiled Marxism,
   Between the images of urban apocalypse you *really* want to see —
   It's like porno, only with monsters.

Kurtz laughs.

KURTZ: That's // good.

ALEX: What would compel the guy
  to write the same movie
  three. times?

KURTZ: You see them as the same.

ALEX: Essentially …

KURTZ: Interesting.
  I'll answer your question with a question.
  Why write the same movie three times?

ALEX: Box office?
  Big market for that kind of thing in the '50s, // '60s … ?

KURTZ: Perhaps … but a bit too easy?

ALEX: Simple explanation's usually the right one.

KURTZ: What things do you return to?
  What things do you repeat?

ALEX Excuse me?

KURTZ: Surely you repeat things in your life,
  You know the outcome
  Yet you repeat, repeat, repeat …

ALEX: That's none of your business …

KURTZ: As if someone has already written your life
  And you're just playing the script they handed you.

ALEX: That's depressing.

KURTZ: You ask: why make the movie three times.
  You answer, glibly, "box office," "fashion of the times."
  Yes, inside all glib answers lies a kernel of truth,
  like when you tell yourself
  "I dumped him because he doesn't see the *real* me" time and time again —

But you know,

in the darkest,

shakiest corners of your soul —

there's another *reason*

for all that *repetition*.

ALEX: You can decide to break the pattern ...

KURTZ: You arrive at this conclusion from personal experience?

Or is trolling the self-help section of Barnes & Noble your guilty pleasure ...

ALEX: Again, none of your business ...

KURTZ: Yes, you might say Daniel James is making the same damn film over and over again, OR

ALEX: Or ... ?

KURTZ: You can identify which patterns he's *breaking* in *Gorgo*,

And perhaps reveal something ...

ALEX: Like ... ?

KURTZ: Actual profundity underneath its cheapness.

Pause.

ALEX: Okay ... ending's different ...

KURTZ: That's a start ...

ALEX: Monster doesn't get killed like in the first two.

Gets to escape back to the sea ...

KURTZ: Happy for the monster, not so happy for humanity.

I think that little variation is key to

answering your question. What else?

ALEX: There's no nuclear testing theme in *Gorgo*.

It's the inciting incident for awakening the monster in the first two.

KURTZ: Good.

What *does* incite Gorgo?

ALEX: Greedy American shipwreck hunters.

   No moral quandary that

   they're essentially grave robbers.

KURTZ: Bingo. Other pattern breaking?

ALEX: In *20,000 Fathoms* and *Behemoth*

   The human ingenuity that unleashes the monster,

   Is used also to destroy it. Whereas *Gorgo*

   Human ingenuity is useless … Gorgo's mother destroys everything.

KURTZ: Now you're getting somewhere …

ALEX: But: once she rescues *Gorgo*,

   Neither mother nor son has any interest in continuing their destruction.

   They retreat to the sea …

Pause.

KURTZ: Did I just see a light bulb?

ALEX: Daniel James is angry.

KURTZ: Whatever for?

ALEX: The blacklist?

KURTZ: Lots to be angry about. Destroyed careers, broken friendships, shattered families.

ALEX: He's had to hide

KURTZ: They steal his name. Has to make up a new one … Daniel Hyatt …

ALEX: He wants revenge …

KURTZ: Not so sure it's that –

ALEX: He wants to show – at least in the first two

   that human beings do idiotic things like nuclear testing

   and in doing so unleash monsters, but

   in the face of annihilation

   can correct themselves …

   redeem their humanity …

KURTZ: Go on …

ALEX: He's saying that if HUAC recognized the destruction they unleashed
    They could fix their errors, redeem their humanity, put the monster back into its box

KURTZ: A possible reading …

ALEX: But in *Gorgo*, it's too late … Ten years later
    no one's in the mood to fix the past …
    it's as if he's saying
    the monster is more *human* than *humans* …
    She's a destroyer, but only because
    she wants to protect her child above all else …

Pause.

KURTZ: Hm.
    Last film he ever made … his farewell –
    As if to say, "I'm tired of hiding behind false names,
    I'm retreating to the sea … Goodbye."

Silence.

ALEX: What happened to him … ?

KURTZ: He slummed it for awhile.

ALEX: Pardon?

KURTZ: Nothing. He uhhh …
    Doesn't resurface again
    For twenty-two years.

    And not because he wanted to.

Pause.

ALEX: Are you going to tell me what happened?

KURTZ: Look at the time. 5:10.
    How about we blow this popsicle stand and get dinner …

Alex considers this.

ALEX: Maybe some other night …

She gathers her things. Before she leaves, she turns.

ALEX: Professor Kurtz?

KURTZ: Yes?

ALEX: Thank you.

She turns to exit.

KURTZ: Ms. Tanner …

I don't presume it would be of interest to you, but

At present I am at work on a major project of a highly sensitive nature.

ALEX: Okay …

KURTZ: I'm in need of someone —

Someone trustworthy.

An assistant

Who can

Assist me.

ALEX: What kind of project is it?

KURTZ: An excavation.

ALEX: That's all you're going to give me?

KURTZ: Were you to express interest I might allow you a peek at the cat inside
the proverbial bag.

ALEX: And if I don't?

KURTZ: Sorry. Cat stays in the bag.

Would you be interested in seeing the cat?

ALEX: Perhaps.

KURTZ: Good. We'll discuss it next time.

*Kurtz smiles. Alex, uncertain whether a deal has been made, hesitates, moves to the door,
turns around, opens her mouth as if about to say something. Thinks better of it. Smiles.
Exits.*

5. THREE DAYS

The apartment. Evening. Valerie on the rampage trying to organize the place — it's a mess. Papers, books, empty coffee cups, bottles on the kitchen table. Toys scattered throughout the living room. Alvaro stands by the door, just arrived.

ALVARO: What do you mean "asleep"?

VALERIE: Asleep. As in sleeping // unless there's

ALVARO: For three days?

VALERIE: Wired three days, Crash! Three days down.

ALVARO: What was he doing?

VALERIE: Obsessing over that stupid novel —

ALVARO: Shit …

VALERIE: Yes, and I'm doing fantastically well — thanks for asking.

ALVARO: Sorry, Valerie … everything okay?

VALERIE: I'm *managing.*

ALVARO: Where're the kids?

VALERIE: *Just* now got Lila to sleep.

ALVARO: Pablo?

VALERIE: Don't get me started about Pablo … little monster.

ALVARO: What'd he do this time?

VALERIE: Other night? After you idiots finally left? We go to sleep.
    4:45 in the morning Lila wakes up. Great.
    I go in to feed her and who's not in his bed?

ALVARO: Oh, shit …

VALERIE: Wandered off. Again.
    I comb through the apartment — nowhere.

ALVARO: Oh, shit …

VALERIE: Out into the hall, up and down the stairs …

    Nowhere. I'm thinking fine – good riddance, kid,

    Wanna see the world? Be my guest …

ALVARO: Valerie –

VALERIE: I'm joking, Alvaro.

    What kind of person do you think I am?

    I'm practically shitting my pants –

    I keep thinking – what's his name? the milk carton kid?

ALVARO: Etan Patz.

VALERIE: I actually *exit* the building. *In my nightgown.*

    It's freezing, Lila's hanging off my nipple.

    He's not out in the street.

    I'm thinking I've got to call the cops –

    Great, child services will take Lila.

    Javi and I'll get thrown in jail for neglect.

    Before I go up to call, I think "basement"

    "laundry room," and there he is

    curled up inside the dryer looking at a *National Geographic.*

    "Hi mommy!"

ALVARO: Jesus …

VALERIE: I'm at the end of my rope. I'm really // at the

ALVARO: Where's he now?

VALERIE: Dropped him off at my sister's in Jersey yesterday.

    He's safe there until I can get things under control here.

ALVARO: Thought you didn't talk to her.

VALERIE: Sometimes you gotta swallow your pride, pick up the phone after three years.

ALVARO: Maybe you should have sent *Javi* there …

His attempt at humor falls flat.

VALERIE: Do something with this.

She hands him a child's rocking horse. He slips it under the kitchen table.

VALERIE: Not there.

He opens the front door and leaves it out in the hall.

VALERIE: I'll tell him you stopped by.

ALVARO: Want me to … ?

VALERIE: … ?

ALVARO: I could try to rouse him?

VALERIE: HA!

ALVARO: What?

VALERIE: Be my guest, Alvaro … *Rouse* him.

Unsure if she's really seeking his help or implying something else, he moves to the door.

VALERIE: Cause that would be. *great.* That would be a *fucking* miracle.

ALVARO: What …

VALERIE: Three days of me. "Go to bed, Javi! You're gonna regret it." "I'm work-ing, baby." *Working.* Followed by three days of me pounding at the door, *"get. up."* Three days of Pablo begging him to come out and play, me up all hours to feed Lila, who refuses to sleep through the night – NOTHING. So go ahead, slither on in, work your *magic …*

ALVARO: Valerie …

VALERIE: Like *I* don't have work to do … like I don't have my *own* deadlines on top of all this crap. All *him. Him, him, him.* Just sickening …

The door to Javi's room flings open. He's a mess. Boxers, soiled t-shirt. Hair a mess. By Alvaro's reaction, he stinks, as well.

JAVIER: Yo, whassup, baby?

He embraces Alvaro, who squirms – stench. Javier kisses his cheek. He notices Valerie.

JAVIER: We got any eggs?

Valerie stares at him, arms burdened with things — books, kids' toys. She drops them where she stands. Big crash. She puts her coat on, exits.

JAVIER: What's the matter with her?

ALVARO: Heard you had a long nap.

JAVIER: Come here, I gotta show you something.

He goes to the kitchen table. It's clear, except for the newspaper.

JAVIER: What happened to my shit?

He starts tearing apart the newspaper, as if whatever he's looking for might be found in it.

JAVIER: Where did she put my shit?!?!?!

Alvaro goes to a bookcase, where a stack of books and papers is wedged in a space between the volumes. He brings it to the kitchen table, while Javi looks in ridiculous places like the knife drawer.

JAVIER: Fucking kill that bitch! Always moving my shit!

Alvaro calmly deposits the books and papers on the table.

ALVARO: Looking for this?

JAVIER: Where'd you find that?

ALVARO: Bookshelf.

Javier tears through the pile, burying the kitchen table in the process. He finds what he's looking for.

JAVIER: Check this out …

He hands Alvaro a page ripped from an architectural magazine.

ALVARO: What am I supposed to be looking at …

JAVIER: *Seaward*

ALVARO: C-word?

JAVIER: Huh? No, no, bro – not the C-word, *Seaward* – like in the direction of el mar.

ALVARO: *Sea …* // gotcha

JAVIER: Know who lived in this house?

ALVARO: Looks more like a castle than a house—

JAVIER: Know who lived in this *castle*?
Our Chicano impersonator …

ALVARO: Motherfucker lived *here*?

JAVIER: Carmel-by-the-Sea

ALVARO: And he's running around pretending he's some
dirt poor brown kid?

JAVIER: I know … Isn't that cool?

ALVARO: No, man, NOT cool …

The apartment buzzer goes off.

JAVIER: It's cool he could live in a place like that
Come up with a book like *this*.

ALVARO: No. No. No. // No.

Buzzer rings again.

You gonna get that?

Javier goes to the buzzer.

JAVIER: Can I help you?

HERMAN ON INTERCOM: Herman.

JAVIER: What are you doing here?

HERMAN ON INTERCOM: Ummm … thought we were having a meeting?
I'm a little early … but …

Javier looks at Alvaro, confused.

ALVARO: It's Tuesday night, bro

Javier buzzes him in, unlocks the front door.

ALVARO: Where'd you find this?

JAVIER: Library. Copy of some architecture magazine …

ALVARO: You just rip it out like that?

JAVIER: Who's gonna miss it?

ALVARO: There's a spiritual emptiness inside you, Javi, that needs // filling –

JAVIER: Whatever …

ALVARO: You seriously still thinking about this imposter bullshit

JAVIER: No, I'm thinking about the straitjacket bullshit …

ALVARO: You keep saying that – straitjacket –
  it's starting to bug // me out

JAVIER: Yooooouuuuu know what I mean …

Herman appears at the door's threshhold. A leather shoulder bag slung over his shoulder. He eats pistachios from a small brown sack.

HERMAN: *(In his most self-conscious, piss poor Spanish accent.)* O-la, cumpadrayce …

ALVARO: *(Agonized groan.)*   JAVIER: Whassup Herman!

HERMAN: Were uh … you two in the middle of something?

JAVIER: Nah, man.

HERMAN: I just ran into Valerie? On Ninth?

JAVIER: Yeah?

HERMAN: Is she … ?
  Nevermind.
  Pistachio?

JAVIER: No thanks …

HERMAN: Alvaro?

ALVARO: I'm good …

Herman looks at the magazine tear out.

HERMAN: Oh! Charles Sumner Greene.

ALVARO: Huh?

HERMAN: House in the photo? By Charles Sumner Greene.

ALVARO: How do you know that?

HERMAN: My *degree?*

> Art History?
>
> U Chicago?
>
> *Summa Cum Laude?*
>
> They teach you how to look at things?
>
> Recognize who made them?

JAVIER: You know this house?

HERMAN: It's pretty well-known.

> Client kept making changes. Drove Greene nuts …
>
> House is unique cause Greene was known for his use of glass and wood –
>
> Only example in his *oeuvre* where stone's the primary medium

ALVARO: How do you remember shit like that?

Herman shrugs.

HERMAN: It's on a rocky bluff overlooking the Pacific Ocean – hence the use of native stone.

Pops a pistachio in his mouth.

> He was an acolyte of the Prairie School.
>
> You know, Chicago?

Another pistachio.

> Louis Sullivan?
>
> Frank Lloyd Wright?

Pistachio.

> Organic relationship between a building and its site?

Pistachio.

> No?

Silence. They stare at him.

HERMAN: Why are you cumpadrayce looking at it?

ALVARO: Cut it with the "cumpadrayce"?

HERMAN: What — ?

Buzzer. No one moves.

HERMAN: Someone gonna get that?

No one moves. Herman goes to the buzzer.

ALVARO: Not me   JAVIER: Ohhhhh yessss …

HERMAN: Who is it?

NERO ON INTERCOM: Nero.

Herman buzzes him in.

JAVIER: Know who lived in that house?

HERMAN: No …

JAVIER: Daniel James.

HERMAN: Ooooohh. Interesting … hm.
    That would make sense.

JAVIER: Why?

HERMAN: Sometimes it's referred to as the D.L. James House.

Nero enters with Lina. Nero has a twelve-pack of beer.

NERO: Yo.

JAVIER: Yo.

During the next conversation, Nero puts the beer in the fridge, takes one. Lina goes to the couch, picks up a magazine and reads. Nero joins the men looking at the picture.

ALVARO: Who, pray tell, is D.L. James, Mr. I-Majored-in-Art-History?

HERMAN: Probably his father.
    If I remember correctly, made his fortune importing fine china.
    Something also about him being related to Frank and Jesse James.

This gets Nero's attention.

NERO: *The* Frank and Jesse James?

Javier goes to the window, stares out, wheels turning. Hint of his reflection in it.

HERMAN: That's right.

NERO: You're saying Daniel James was related to Jesse James.

HERMAN: Yep. What I said.

NERO: Whoa … cool.

He goes to the couch, sits next to Lina. She reads the magazine while he plays with her hair. As the scene progresses, Nero loses interest in his surroundings and becomes obsessively focused on Lina. The rest of the group pretends not to notice, but there is an unspoken annoyance.

HERMAN: This mean you cump – *gentlemen* – are still noodling // on this

ALVARO: I'm outta here –

   Call me when you come up with something else –

JAVIER: Sit your ass down – we don't got anything else …

Valerie enters carrying a plastic shopping bag. She sees the mess on the table. She glares at Javi, removes a carton of eggs from the bag. She opens it, holds it out for Javi to see. She flips the carton over, smashes it on Javi's research. She smiles, exits into the bedroom.

JAVIER: I'm calling the meeting to order.

ALVARO: You gonna at least clean up, get dressed?

JAVIER: What for?

ALVARO: Cause you smell like – never mind.

JAVIER: So I been thinking …

ALVARO: You been *sleep//ing*

JAVIER: I been thinking about Daniel James/Danny Santiago

HERMAN: Great, can't wait to // hear

JAVIER: I been thinking we could do something with it, like –

Valerie enters the room, hair is up in a bun. She wears glasses. She carries a stack of notes and books, places them on the coffee table. She sits.

JAVIER: I been thinking we could do something with it, like —

VALERIE: He wasn't pulling stuff out of thin air.

ALVARO: Huh?

VALERIE: Daniel James. He wasn't pulling stuff out of thin air.
I've been doing a little research. On my *own*.

JAVIER: Oh, you have, have you?

VALERIE: Somebody had to get off their ass and do something.
Listen: from an article about him by John Gregory Dunne
In the *New York Review of Books*. Daniel James is quoted as saying:
"We moved into East L.A. and started making a new life for ourselves there."

ALVARO: So?

VALERIE: "For the next fifteen years the James' activities were concentrated on three
square blocks in Lincoln Heights."

ALVARO: Okay …

VALERIE: He'd been blacklisted —

NERO: He was black//listed?

VALERIE: He couldn't work in film, so he and his wife
spent the '60s volunteering there.
organized youth clubs, helped get kids off the street, out of gangs

ALVARO: He was "down"

VALERIE: Stood at weddings, funerals, baptisms —
He was even godfather to a bunch of kids

ALVARO: He was *really* "down"

HERMAN: They gave him a community service award …

Valerie gives Herman a look. Herman shuts his mouth. Javier notices this exchange. Stares at Valerie. Herman and Valerie have evidently talked about this privately.

ALVARO: Maybe we should call him Daniel "Saint" James

HERMAN: Isn't that what "Santiago" translates to?

ALVARO: Doesn't make him one of them, doesn't mean he's got the // right to —

VALERIE: I never said he was "one of them"
    I'm only saying he had *access*
    More access than you have —
    What did you say the other night?
    about avoiding?

ALVARO: Avoiding?

VALERIE: Going there. When you are in L.A.

ALVARO: Never had reason to go there — I'm not looking for "access"

VALERIE: Well there you go.

ALVARO: Point being … ?

VALERIE: You aren't lacking in the *opinion* // department

ALVARO: I'm entitled to my opinion —

VALERIE: By your own admission —
    you know *less* than him about what's // authen

ALVARO: Thank you Valerie for telling me what // I know and don't

HERMAN: All we're saying is
    He served the community.
    They respected him enough to invite him into their world.
    They didn't seem to have any trouble with the fact he wrote about it.

ALVARO: Okay … I dig that.
    But if I wake up one day, and I'm like,
    "Hm. I got an *urge* …
    Do some community service,
    but where?
    East L.A.,
    been done.
    South Bronx? *Done.*

CARMEL-BY-THE-SEA
Yeeeaaaah,
I would love to do me some community service
in Carmel-by-the-Sea …
Where do I sign up?
I'd be one happy half Puerto Rican
Sit there, lookin at the Pacific,
talk to you about your problems
over mint juleps …

HERMAN: You could mow the lawn.

ALVARO: Eat me Herman.

VALERIE: You're so negative …

ALVARO: What's negative? I'm asking a question.

VALERIE: You poke holes … your whole MO
Poke holes in everything. You know why?

ALVARO: Enlighten me, mamacita

VALERIE: Cause you're like a walking hunk
of human Swiss cheese
Can't plug the holes in your own soul
So you gotta poke, poke, poke holes in everyone and everything else …
It's *exhausting*

HERMAN: You know … all this talk about Daniel James, Danny Santiago … it's gotten
me thinking about Ben Franklin.

They all look at him — what the fuck?

HERMAN: That's right. Ben Franklin.
Cause that's where it all started.

ALVARO: Ben Franklin pretended he was Mexican?

HERMAN: No, jackass.
I'm talking about the concept of self-improvement.

ALVARO: Why do I got the feeling

    I'm gonna LOVE the next pile a dog shit // that's

NERO: ALVARO! Would you shut up, let the man SPEAK?!?!

Lina touches his arm to calm him.

HERMAN: Why thank you, Nero.

    Ben Franklin made a list.

    Thirteen virtues — *which*

    If you lived by them,

    You'd walk the path to self-improvement …

ALVARO: Okay …

HERMAN: Now: with all this *speculation*

    about our little impersonator friend

    I've taken it upon myself to do a little

    preliminary dramaturgy

Collective groan. He takes from his bag a stack of packets.

    I xeroxed these packets // for you —

Groans as he hands out packets.

HERMAN: What? This is my *role*

    You *assigned* me this role —

VALERIE: *(Reading from the packet.)* "Thirteen Virtues. One: temperance. Eat not to dullness, drink not to elevation."

NERO: *(Raising his beer.)* Here, here!

VALERIE: Shhhh! You'll wake up Lila.

ALVARO: "Two: silence. Speak not but what may benefit others or yourself, avoid *trifling* conversation."

HERMAN: Very good, Lina?

LINA: "Three: order. Let all your things have their places, let each part of your business have its time."

NERO: Dude, we can read these on our own?

    Look, I have two auditions first thing in the morning — just cut to the chase?

Herman gets flustered. Goes around the room snatching packets from everyone.

HERMAN: Fine! Read em on your own!

VALERIE: Just explain what you're getting at —

HERMAN: He's saying that as Americans
    we have the power to *will* ourselves
    to be *different. Better.*
    We can invent ourselves — not like Europeans
    where self is pre-determined, Founding Fathers
    cleaned the slate — individual Americans can clean // the slate

ALVARO: You vote for Ronnie Ray-Gun?

HERMAN: What happens in the voting booth is between me and my // ballot

ALVARO: Whatever — "clean slate"? That's just caca —

JAVIER: Yeah — but inside every piece of caca's
    A kernel of truth …

Room stops. Intense focus on Javier. Silence.

JAVIER: Okay …
    Ben Franklin's this dude.
    Accomplished ridiculous amounts of shit in his life.
    People wonder: how'd he do that?
    Here he's telling you — follow these rules,
    make a whole new self —
    if I can do it, you can too.

ALVARO: So if Nero quits drinking, chasing little hotties fresh outta NYU — he'll get
    his face on the cover of *Variety*?

VALERIE: Alvaro!   NERO: You dick …

Everyone laughs.

LINA: If you'll excuse me.

Lina exits to the bathroom. Nero crumples a napkin and throws it at Alvaro.

HERMAN: Like Javi says, we're all trapped in straitjackets …

    Only reason anyone writes? Reads? Autobiography?

    They need an instruction manual,

    on how to be Harry Houdini

    slip *out* of the straitjacket, free themselves

ALVARO: You yourself said it wasn't an autobiography …

HERMAN: Yes, it's fiction that has the contours of autobiography …

ALVARO: Whatever …

HERMAN: And who in this society needs that more than anyone else?

    Anyone … ?

VALERIE: The um … "marginalized"?

HERMAN: Bingo …

ALVARO: You mean to tell me

    Simon & Schuster

    published the motherfuckin' thing

    cause they saw it as a "self-improvement"

    manual? – tap that untapped Chicano market?

    Cause all East LA is waiting for that *New York Times* approved novel to

    teach them how to "free" themselves?

HERMAN: Not exactly, I –

ALVARO: What then?

HERMAN: If you'd let me finish –

ALVARO: By all means, Herman, I can't wait to hear this // shit …

VALERIE: Shhhhh …

HERMAN: Okay. Historically. Speaking.

    The uhhh

    Ethnic

Autobiography
Served a
Two conflicting purposes ...

ALVARO: Yeah? What purposes ...

HERMAN: I'll use the example of the slave narrative.
On the one hand,
slave, former slave might read it,
see how the writer *overcame* ...
situation ... enslavement ... But ...
who *else*
was it for?

VALERIE: White Americans.

HERMAN: Very good —

VALERIE: Remember that course, Javi? At Oberlin?
About slave narratives?

JAVIER: Huh?

VALERIE: Professor told a story ...
Abolitionist asked Frederick Douglass
before a speech to
"tone down the high falutin' rhetoric,"
be "more plantation"
so people would believe he'd actually been a slave.

JAVIER: You gotta play to your audience ...

HERMAN: Point I'm making, Alvaro,
Autobiographer —
especially a
"marginalized" autobiographer
is trapped in a Catch-22.
On the one hand they're writing

An instruction manual, how to get out of the straitjacket
for their own kind –

ALVARO: "Own // kind" …

HERMAN: On the other hand …
they have to "represent"
to the folks they perceive as holding the key
to the straitjacket –

VALERIE: White Americans …

HERMAN: Most cases, yes,
that they need to *be seen* as human.

ALVARO: Which is why this country // is –

HERMAN: Exactly. Why should anyone have to prove they're human?
But they can't just tell their own story,
they have to be spokespeople for a whole group …
which is dangerous …

VALERIE: Cause it puts you back in the straitjacket you were trying to escape –

ALVARO: None of this applies to Daniel James.

HERMAN: Why not?!?

Herman buries his head on Valerie's shoulder in frustration.

ALVARO: *He's not writing for "his own kind"*
He can't "represent" for a group he's not part of
You can't say you're in a straitjacket
When the whole time you got the key hidden in your back pocket

VALERIE: Hush!

JAVIER: I think I know what Alvaro's trying to say.

Room stops. Attention on Javier. Silence.

JAVIER: And you're right. To a degree. *But*
if we're to believe what Herman

and Valerie, my *wife*

are saying …

Valerie and Herman shift so as not to seem so close.

JAVIER: He did his homework.

HERMAN: Levi-Strauss of the Urban Beast.

JAVIER: Shut up.

He went in.

Got the key to their modest kingdom –

had access …

He wasn't "making shit up" –

Insider could read it, say yeah,

he was there, witnessed, got it right.

But if we're gonna do *this* …

ALVARO: Do // what?

JAVIER: Our problem, ladies and gentlemen

We ain't got no access …

ALVARO: Do *what* Javi?

JAVIER: No access, no details …

No details, no authenticity.

HERMAN: What do you mean "do this"

JAVIER: Huh?

HERMAN: You said, "If we're going to do *this* … "

Pause.

JAVIER: Okay …

Dude's old, blacklisted, can't write, can't get a gig. He's –

ALVARO: Rich

VALERIE: Relevance?

JAVIER: *Filthy* rich —

ALVARO: *Blanco*

JAVIER: *Blanco* ... right. More important he's washed up.
   He's a has-been who never really *was*.

HERMAN: In all fairness, he did write that play —

NERO: Which play?

HERMAN: *Winter Soldiers. Best Plays 1942.*

JAVIER: I read that shit, only proves my point.
   Dude's gotta find something to do with his time.
   Pulls up in Lincoln Heights
   In his convertible Caddy ...
   Meets a bunch of Chicanos
   Feels an affinity,
   Feels like he's *home*
   Picks up the language,
   Mannerisms, stories ...
   Over the years they crystallize
   Into this kid — Chato

   Chato starts talking

   You've felt it, Alvaro
   Voice in your head?
   That keeps talking, talking, talking?
   You don't ignore it
   You write down what it *says* ...

   If you're Daniel James?
   Masochist who's been making dents in his forehead
   Getting nowhere at a typewriter for *fifty. years?*
   and suddenly? A *real* voice pops in your head?
   You write down what it says, no matter
   how big a price you'll pay ...
   Especially if you've been *silenced.*

HERMAN: Exactly what Valerie and I are trying to say.

JAVIER: Just shut up, will you?

> So this voice, this monster comes out
> voice more real than anything he wrote for fifty years.
> are you gonna get tangled in some useless ethical dilemma,
> cause the voice is a barely literate kid, while you studied classics at Yale?
> NO …You justify, you say, I put my time in,
> helped those people, broke bread in their homes, loaned them money
> got drunk with the men, played stickball with the kids, prayed at their funerals …
> I *earned* the right to write about it – who cares if real Chicanos get escorted out the
> lobby of Simon & Schuster … I tapped *my* inner Chicano, I don't owe them shit …

HERMAN: Exactly what I am trying to say –

JAVIER: NO, you fucking knucklehead, I'm not DONE.

Silence.

JAVIER: Key is … if we're gonna do this …

> We have no access.

HERMAN: *Do. what?*

VALERIE: Yeah, do what?

JAVIER: *Be* him.

ALVARO: Huh?

JAVIER: *Be* him.

VALERIE: You mean …

JAVIER: *Be. Him.*

Silence.

ALVARO: I have no idea what you mean?

> But I can tell you, my brother,
> I have
> ZERO interest

312

in *"Being"*

that vampire-mother//fucker.

HERMAN: Why not?

ALVARO: I don't have to explain it to you.

HERMAN: I think you do.

ALVARO: Do *you* know what he means by "being" him

HERMAN: No, but …

ALVARO: Then you can't be ask//ing me –

HERMAN: Just your
    Vehemence –
    NO, your total inflexibility
    to even consider what Javi's propos//ing

ALVARO: Well, *Herman*
    I'm a little skeptical of you and *Valerie's* willingness
    to accept whatever he's say//ing

HERMAN: I'm not accepting any//thing –

ALVARO: You are // you are

HERMAN: No no no // NO

VALERIE: *Boys*.

The room stops.

VALERIE: Javi: Do you mean a forgery.

JAVIER: Huh?

A pause. Valerie stares at Javier.

VALERIE: A forgery. That's what you mean, isn't it? Javi?

Silence.

HERMAN: That's brilliant. That's genius.

NERO: What?

ALVARO: What do you mean forgery?

Javier seizes the moment, though it is offset by the fact he's in boxers and t-shirt and unclean.

JAVIER: We're gonna *be* him.

> We're gonna *write like him* —
> we're gonna write *his* story,
> story that ain't ours to tell,
> story we got no *right* to tell
> cause we're not white.
> we're not rich.   NERO: I'm white
> we're not ex-Communists.
> we never been blacklisted
> never hobnobbed with Charlie Chaplin
> broke bread with John Steinbeck.
> We're not seventy-two
> and none of us has ever set foot in a mansion in Carmel.
> But we're gonna tell it.
> Make everyone think he wrote that shit —
> last will and testament.
> Never seen by human eyes.
> Written by *you. Me.*

ALVARO: We could rip that motherfucking straitjacket off once and for all …

JAVIER: Joe Papp only calls once, *muthafukka*

Silence.

NERO: Look, this conversation …

> Call me when you have some material … ?
> I'd be happy to swing by and read —
> I have to go, I've got //aud—

HERMAN: Auditions. First thing. Right …

Nero downs the remainder of his beer.

NERO: LINA! Let's go!

VALERIE: Would you shush?! Lila ...

Lina comes out of the bathroom. She's seething. They exit.

ALVARO: Why does she put up with him?

VALERIE: You shouldn't have said – chasing co-eds?

ALVARO: You think she don't know?

VALERIE: She didn't need a reminder. From you. In front of everyone.

ALVARO: Just keeping it real ...

The child in the next room begins to cry. Valerie sighs.

VALERIE: Great. See what you jerks did? You woke Lila

Neither she nor Javier move. The child continues to cry.

HERMAN: Anyone um

    going to ...
    get that?

No one moves. Alvaro gets up, heads to the room.

VALERIE: No, Alvaro I –

ALVARO: I *got* it.

He disappears into the room. Silence.

HERMAN: This mean we're done for the evening?

No answer.

HERMAN: Okay ... I uhhh ...

    should head out.

VALERIE: Let me show you to the door.

In the threshold they hug – long enough to make one wonder ...

HERMAN: Night, Valerie ...

    Javi ... ?

Javier responds with a vague nod. Herman exits.

JAVIER: You fucking him?

VALERIE: Don't be ridiculous.

She starts cleaning up the mess. Silence. Javier watches her.

JAVIER: What do you think?
  Should we do this?

VALERIE: Not for me to decide.

JAVIER: I'd like your opinion.

VALERIE: Oh, you would?

JAVIER: Yes.

VALERIE: If you're gonna do it, start writing it already.
  I'm sick of talking about it.

JAVIER: That's not what I –

VALERIE: Any case, seems to me you've already // decided.

JAVIER: Talk to me, please.
  I want to know what you're thinking. Really thinking.

Valerie stops cleaning.

VALERIE: I think you're afraid.

JAVIER: Oh yeah? What am I afraid of?

VALERIE: That bringing this old, sad, empty, *forgotten* man to life –
  a man you think is so far outside of yourself –
  white, patrician, a mediocre writer …
  You might realize? Him? You? No difference.

Javier smiles. She's nailed him.

JAVIER: I fucking love you.

VALERIE: Stop it.

He slowly moves to her.

JAVIER: I fucking *love* you …

VALERIE: Javier ... no ... I'm cleaning

He gets behind her, presses against her, kisses her neck. Doesn't take her long to get into it. They're all over each other. Alvaro re-enters, closing the door to the child's room. He watches as Javier lifts Valerie onto the kitchen counter and hikes up her skirt. They're in their own world. Alvaro gathers his things. He stands in the threshold watching as Javier undoes his belt. He exits. As Javier and Valerie begin having sex, Lila's cries emerge from the next room. They continue, letting the child cry it out. The child's cries intensify as we reach the —

End of Act One

ACT TWO. Puerto Angel

1. JESSE JAMES

Courtyard of a small hotel in Puerto Angel, a small fishing village on the Pacific coast of Mexico.

It's an open space with patio style furnishings, filled with sunlight. The place is a bit shabby, decorated with kitschy tropical motifs. Along the upstage wall a series of numbered doors – guest rooms. Alvaro, Javier, Herman and Valerie arrange the furniture, creating an impromptu rehearsal space. They set up a table, complete with scripts, highlighters, water and a large sketch pad which Valerie will use later. A low table and two chairs serve as a "set." On the table, a large box – perhaps the discarded packaging of a children's toy.

Valerie wears a sarong and a wide-brimmed hat. Alvaro, a tank top and cut-off jeans. Herman sports a pink golf shirt with light khakis. Javier wears a faded Pink Floyd Dark Side of the Moon t-shirt and jeans.

JAVIER: I went down there with Pablo to teach him how to make paper airplanes, and this guy was running around naked, looked like he hadn't showered in a week.

VALERIE: Guidebook said that stretch of beach is crawling with German tourists.

JAVIER: Pablo was like, "Papi? Why's that man running around with his pi pi flapping around?"

HERMAN: Where was this?

JAVIER: Mile up the road –

HERMAN: Is it a town?

JAVIER: Just a stretch of beach with some shacks.
People rent hammocks, stay out in the open air …
Dude and his crew had dreadlocks, skin all red …

HERMAN: They were all Germans?

JAVIER: Every last one.
I told him – look, I don't mind you running around butt naked?
But I got my son here? You mind not having sex with your girl out in the open like that?

VALERIE: They were having sex?

JAVIER: Know what he says to me?

    "Look meestah … Ve're in nayychah …

    Ve're ze speereechual descendantz of ze Mayan race."

Alvaro cracks up.

ALVARO: For real? He said that? What'd you say?

JAVIER: I walked away – how do you respond to something like that?

HERMAN: Where are the kids?

VALERIE: The guy who runs this place introduced us to a little old *abuelita*

    that lives down the road. They're spending the afternoon there.

ALVARO: And you trust her?

VALERIE: What's not to trust?

A guest room door opens. Lina appears in a bikini. Nero follows, dressed rather bizarrely in Western gear: cowboy boots, tight jeans, wide belt with an enormous ornate buckle, Western shirt, brown leather vest, red scarf around his neck. Only thing missing: cowboy hat. He holds a stack of paper rolled into a scroll. Everyone notices his peculiar appearance. Nero unrolls the pages, reads them, mouths the words to himself. He makes gestures punctuating words we can't hear.

Lina sits on a chair and rubs sunblock on her body.

HERMAN: Warm enough for you, Nero?

Nero stares at him for a beat, goes back to the script. The furniture by this point has been rearranged.

JAVIER: Okay …

    so you know,

    I'm not married to any of this –

    more a

    first stab. Not sure if it comes at the beginning, middle –

VALERIE: Could come at the end –

HERMAN: How so?

VALERIE: A kind of Rosebud moment?

That puts everything else into perspective?

HERMAN: It's too long for that kind of // thing

JAVIER: It's a first stab –

ALVARO: Let's just do it

NERO: Let's do it!

Points to the toy box.

That's the present?

VALERIE: Yes.

NERO: Anything inside?

VALERIE: It's a surprise …

ALVARO: Look, we're not staging it, we're just messing a//round

NERO: Alright! Let's do it!

The men get into position. Nero sits in one of the chairs. He covers one eye with his fist as if he's holding an ice pack. Javier hovers over him. While they play the scene, Valerie makes sketches of what she's seeing in a large drawing pad. Alvaro reads the stage directions:

ALVARO: Scene. D.L.'s study at *Seaward*. 1934. D.L., fifty-something stands over Daniel James, 23 who has an ice pack over his eye. The men are dressed casually – but expensively, as if they've just come from the Country Club. A low table sits between them, on top of which rests a large wrapped gift box.

VALERIE: What's Nero wearing?

HERMAN: He's "lobbying."

VALERIE: Lobbying? For what?

LINA: *Shhhhhhhh.*

The men begin. They are skilled actors, but being a first read, their performances are slightly stilted. Even so, they are very committed to the scene's stakes.

D.L. (JAVIER): *(Hint of an accent – Javier's idea of what a Missourian from the '30s might sound like.)* How's the face?

DANIEL JAMES (NERO): *(Similar accent that doesn't fit quite comfortably yet.)* Aches.

D.L.: Got you good in the eye, huh?

DANIEL: Should have seen the
Rageful look on that copper's face.

Herman makes a note. Javier senses it, but continues.

DANIEL: Like he wanted it to hurt.

D.L.: Billy club grand slam home run to your head.

DANIEL: Protest started out peaceful, Dad – police came in?
Turned it into a war zone …

D.L.: Be thankful it wasn't worse, Dan.
Could've lost an eye …

DANIEL: Plenty of others got it worse than me.

ALVARO: *(Making a note on the script.)* Hm.

D.L.: Anyhow …
you're here now, safe – take your time to recuperate.

DANIEL: I'm thinking of going up to San Francisco

D.L.: Dan …

DANIEL: Tension's been building for months …
ILA's gaining the upper hand, Longshoremen
are gonna strike any day …
They got the backing of the seamen
They need support

Valerie whispers something in Herman's ear. He chuckles. Everyone notices, but pretends to ignore.

D.L.: You have no business trucking with them.

Herman makes a note in his script.

DANIEL: It *should* be everyone's business. Should be the whole *world's* business.

D.L.: Dan. No.

DANIEL: (*Pointing to the box on the table.*) What's in the box?

D.L.: All in good time.

Son ... you realize there are many ways to
make a meaningful contribution to the betterment of this world

DANIEL: Advancing the strikers' cause is one of them

D.L.: Perhaps

DANIEL: Hawking Limo-jes china to —

HERMAN: *Limoges*

DANIEL: *Limoges* — Hawking *Limoges* china to starving Okies is *not*.

D.L.: Wasn't for you — I understand.
Dan, I'm proud of you.
I've watched you since graduating Yale

Herman makes a note in his script. Sensed by everyone. Javier stops, turns to him.

JAVIER: Something you wanna say?

HERMAN: No ... // no.

JAVIER: I keep hearing that pencil of yours scratching away

HERMAN: Just sounds ...

Exposition-y?
Continue.

NERO: Where do you want to go from?

D.L.: Dan, I'm proud of you.
I've watched you since graduating Yale
trying on different suits for size —
discarding ones that don't fit,
retailoring ones that sort of fit
not being satisfied til you find the one that fits you like a glove.

I admire that … I know your mother may not approve, but

you and me? We're kindred spirits

cut from a more complex cloth

than other members of this family.

You, me, we want more, we *need* more.

DANIEL: We have more than plenty. That's the problem —

D.L.: I don't mean *things,* Dan.

I mean more in the sense of *purpose.*

Hawking Limoges china door to door,

Not your idea of purpose, // I —

DANIEL: I felt like a darn fool, knocking on doors?

Half-starved people with their sallow, hungry faces

Should have seen the *looks* they gave me —

"What is this *boy* doing here?

Does he have any idea we're in the middle of a Depression?

I'm not in the market for *Limoges.*"

D.L.: Awkward times to sell luxury items.

Herman chuckles.

DANIEL: Awkward? It was *horrible.*

Ended up giving them my samples

So *they* could sell them ten cents a pop,

Put some food on their tables.

D.L.: You root for the underdog.

Long history of that in this family, Dan.

Proud you've inherited it.

Pause. Nero breaks character.

NERO: I have a thought …

HERMAN: Let's hold thoughts for the end?

JAVIER: No, no — I wanna hear what you gotta say.

NERO: I was thinking,

> This might be the right point to … ?
> You know
> *Introduce?* Jesse James?

HERMAN: Huh?

NERO: They're talking about family … inheritance …

VALERIE: May not be a bad // idea –

NERO: His grandfather was Jesse James' first cousin, for // God's sake

JAVIER: Let's just get through it –

NERO: Cool … I'm just saying – from?

ALVARO: "underdog"

D.L.: You root for the underdog –

> Long history of that *in the James* family,
> Proud that you inherited it.
>
> That said –
> All that fine china? Built *this*.

He gestures to indicate the surroundings.

DANIEL: I'm aware of that, and I'm not ungrateful.

D.L.: China salesman suit doesn't fit.

> I understand.
> You wanted something more,
> Learn what it feels like to make a living –
> Fantastic.
> What do I do?
> I make some calls. Land you work in the oil fields.

DANIEL: *Dad –*

D.L.: Again, I'm proud of you.

> While your fellow Elis were off

on their post-graduation Grand Tours of Europe
You busted your rear-end in Oklahoma. Takes balls, Dan.

DANIEL: It was hard work.

D.L.: When I was your age?
Sure as hell wouldn't've got me
Working as a *swamper*.

ALVARO: What's a swamper?

HERMAN: Oil trucker's assistant

ALVARO: Bitch was slummin' it

HERMAN: "trucking" with the "truckers"

LINA: *Shhhhhhh*

D.L.: When I was your age?
Sure as hell wouldn't have gotten me
Working as a *swamper*.

Valerie cracks up.

VALERIE: Sorry …

DANIEL: I learned more in those six months
Than I ever did at Yale.

D.L.: Don't doubt it.
But I'd venture to guess *one* thing you learned:
it's next to impossible for a man to reinvent himself *down*.

DANIEL: What do you mean?

Javier rises as D.L. He seizes the moment for the forthcoming monologue.

D.L.: Whole country's founded on the idea, son
That a man can *reinvent* himself
Start with a pile of straw? Spin it into gold

ALVARO: Psss.

D.L.: Abe Lincoln. Poor kid from the Kentucky backwoods.

Reinvents himself? Becomes President.

Alvaro shakes his head through the rest.

My buddy Chaplin?
Orphan straight out of a Dickensian nightmare.
Crosses the Atlantic? Invents a new self?
He's the most famous man on earth.

Story never goes the opposite direction.
Never hear the likes of Rockefeller
Reinventing himself as a *swamper*.

Once you've got the Yale in you,
Can't ever rub it out.

VALERIE: *(To Herman.)* I love that line …

DANIEL: I know I can't ever *be* one of them.
But I can organize, educate, stand in solidarity —

D.L.: Get your face cracked open by a cop.

DANIEL: This is going nowhere —

He gets up.

D.L.: Dan, you are not excused. Sit down.

I recognize your passion.
But there are lines, Daniel.
Cross them? There's no going back.
Work in an oil field? Carmel's here for you
when you've had enough.

But jail. That's a no-no.

DANIEL: I'm sorry you had to bail me out.

D.L.: Part of me was envious. Takes balls to get yourself arrested.

Herman makes a note in the script. Mouths the words "takes balls" to Valerie, gestures "twice" with his fingers. Valerie cracks up.

D.L.: But you understand …

　　Arrest … the implications …

　　To this family …

NERO: See here it is again – opportunity …

　　Jesse James.

HERMAN: Jesus …

NERO: It's like the whole reason he has to *become* Danny Santiago
　　is cause Jesse James.

HERMAN: That's an interesting … *leap.*　　　ALVARO: Say what?

NERO: What leap? There's no leap.

　　Next speech:

　　"Half the family's changed their name.

　　They would get a transfusion if they could –

　　Rid themselves of that TAINTED blood.

　　Though some of us, myself included, ARE GLAD TO HAVE THAT BLOOD RUNNINNG
　　THROUGH OUR VEINS. I THINK YOU ARE ONE OF US."

　　And I love the next part – let's read it:

D.L.: Don't think I didn't notice the games you played when you were a child.

DANIEL: What games?

D.L.: Re-enactments?

　　Of certain criminal acts?

　　Committed by those Sibling-Relations-Whose-Names-Must-Go-Unspoken?

NERO: Why do those names have to go unspoken?

HERMAN: Because they both know who they're talking about?

　　If they say it, it'll sound exposition-y…

NERO: That would be a great opening scene,

　　Little Danny – reenacting the Daviess County bank robbery.

ALVARO: I like that –　　　　　　　　　　　HERMAN: That was the first one—//

　　　　　　　　　　　　　　　　　　　　　　right

Nero's struck by an idea.

NERO: Whoa.

JAVIER: What?

NERO: Did Jesse ever hide out in Mexico?

LINA: They used to do that, right? Outlaws hiding out in Mexico?

NERO: You could have this little kid,
> playing bank robber?
> And like a light could come up …
> There's Jesse
> behind a scrim
> wearing a sombrero —

ALVARO: Yeah, he could be like —
> *(In an over the top "Mexican" accent — purposefully offensive.)*
> "Oye, muchacho … der r too kines uff pee-pel een dees worl:
> Mejicanos an doz dat weesh
> Dey wer Mejicanos."

Javier cracks up.

HERMAN: Could we just please finish the scene —

NERO: Okay … I'm just saying. Jesse James.

Pause.

D.L.: Don't think I didn't notice the games you played when you were a child.

DANIEL: What games?

D.L.: The re-enactments?
> Certain criminal acts?
> Committed by those *Sibling-Relations-Whose-Names-Must-Go-Unspoken?*
>
> You were always a rebel.
> For family decorum sake,
> I kept you in check. But in my heart
> I wanted you to doubt.

To question. To see that
every coin?
Has two faces.

You can do more with what you *have*
than what you can do if you
let them take it all away from you.
Because they can. *They will.*

HERMAN: *(Whispering to Valerie.)* Who's they?

Valerie giggles. Alvaro crumples up a piece of paper, throws it at her.

DANIEL: What do you propose I do?

ALVARO: D.L. points to the gift on the table.

Javier does this as Alvaro reads — eye contact: "I'm doing it, why are you reading that?"

D.L.: Open it.

Daniel unwraps the box, revealing a 1934 Remington Noiseless Portable typewriter.

D.L.: She's a beauty, idd't she?

DANIEL: What's this for?

D.L.: Want to be useful?
You can go to San Francisco, get your head knocked in.
OR
you can bring San Francisco to the *world*. With *this*.

DANIEL: You've got to be kidding me.

D.L.: Why do you think I write plays?

DANIEL: Uhhh ... to kill time?

Alvaro cracks up.

JAVIER: What?

ALVARO: Line's hilarious

D.L.: To change the world, transform the way people think

Alvaro can't help but crack up. He covers his mouth and tries to make a "serious" face.

DANIEL: Dad, your plays have never seen the light of day —

D.L.: One I'm working on will … *(whispers)* … It's about "the brothers"

DANIEL: You serious …

D.L.: Show the world who they *really* were. Don't tell your Mother …
    she's sensitive about that …
    episode …
    in the family's history …

DANIEL: How close are you to finishing?

D.L.: Got act one sewed up …
    Just gotta sort out acts two three four and five …

He smiles. Daniel smiles.

D.L.: It's Shakespearean in scope.

They both laugh. A warm moment between father and son.

D.L.: Look: I'm just a dabbler.
    I love the company I built,
    feel of china on my fingers
    rush you feel when you close a deal …
    I love knowing I can dream up a house like this,
    build it to my specifications —
    My play's never seen the light of day
    but the hole that leaves in me?
    Iddn't big enough that I need to fill it.

    But you son —
    you got fire,
    sense of mission,
    resources —
    talent —
    and you've got that thing

most men at the end of their lives realize they've squandered:
Time.

VALERIE: Love that …

DANIEL: I don't know the first thing about writing plays.

D.L.: I'll help you, Dan.

D.L.: You. Me. Twins. Co-writers.

DANIEL: You want to collaborate on a play.

D.L.: Everything that's happening in San Francisco
    we'll capture right here – show the world what must be done.

DANIEL: I'm not sure I'm comfortable inheriting –

D.L.: Indulge your old man?
    Who bailed you out of jail?

ALVARO: D.L. smiles his most disarming smile. Daniel lets out a deep exhale.

D.L.: That's my boy.

DANIEL: So when do we start?

D.L.: Tomorrow.

DANIEL: Tomorrow …

D.L.: "To-morrow, and to-morrow, and to-morrow,
    Creeps in this petty pace from day to day,
    To the last syllable of recorded time … "

    Tomorrow. We'll start first thing.

Daniel gets up to go.

D.L.: I got us a good title.

DANIEL: Oh yeah?

D.L.: *Pier 17.*
    Like the sound of it.
    Muscular. Gritty.

DANIEL: Tomorrow.

   Dad?

D.L.: Yes, Dan?

DANIEL: Thanks.

D.L.: You bet, son.

Alvaro can't help himself from groaning. Daniel starts to leave.

D.L.: One more thing …

   Steinbeck's swinging by for drinks tonight.

   Might be a good idea if you joined us.

ALVARO: Daniel nods, exits. Lights fade. Sounds of the Pacific Ocean crashing against
   the bluff. Blackout.

Half enthusiastic applause.

VALERIE: Beautiful … really good start …

   Right, Herman?

HERMAN: It's something. …

*Javier has curled up into a ball under a table. Nero goes straight to Lina where he gets the
approval he needs.*

VALERIE: Javi … you okay, baby?

Dying animal groan from Javier.

ALVARO: Wanna know what I think?

Javier lowers his arms slightly — he wants to pay attention to this.

ALVARO: It's a little Hallmark for my tastes, bro.

NERO: You kidding me? That's primo father-son shit.

Javier sits up, focuses on Alvaro. This is painful for him, but his opinion matters.

VALERIE: Alvaro — why are you so mean —

ALVARO: I seen that a million times.

   Tired, pseudo-Freudian *mierda*.

"Son, I want you to be like me"

"Daddy! I don't want to be like you"

"Look, we're just like each other!"

"Thanks, son!"

"Thank *you,* Dad."

Cue the violins.

Cause the rich also cry, right?

Puro Hallmark.

HERMAN: It might actually make sense ... I mean

    If it's supposed to be a forgery of a lost Daniel James play

    Most of what he wrote *was* crap —

Angry dying animal sound from Javi.

VALERIE: What do you want it to do, Javi?

Javi forces himself off the floor.

JAVIER: It's about inheriting something

    That's gonna ruin your life ...

ALVARO: Reads like they're gonna go play catch in the backyard

JAVIER: No. NononononononoNO.

    What I'm trying to get across —

    He never wanted to be a writer,

    But his father laid down this burden —

    If he doesn't give in

    Would he have inherited the house?

    His father's desire to write?

    His father's *failure* as a writer?

    Would he have written *Famous All Over Town*?

    It's like he sees his own future and all he can do

    Is sigh ... Sigh like he's

    sighing out his soul —

NERO: Comes across to me ...

ALVARO: Okay, Jesse James …

JAVIER: FUCK!
FUCKFUCKFUCKMEIRDACOÑOFUCKSHITPUTACOÑOMADRE!

The outburst stuns everyone. Silence.

NERO: I really think there's gotta be a scene with Jesse James.

Javier goes up to Alvaro — confrontational, nose to nose. Neither man is used to this.

JAVIER: You got something to show?

ALVARO: You getting up in my face?

JAVIER: You talk shit,
You got something to show?

ALVARO: Yeah, I got something to show.
Step back.

Javier holds his ground for a spell, steps back and sits. Alvaro distributes pages from a folder to everyone except for Javier.

ALVARO: Herman?
Stage directions?

HERMAN: Sure …

ALVARO: Lina?

She looks up from her magazine.

ALVARO: You're Anna Maria.

HERMAN: Who's Anna Maria?

ALVARO: Listen and learn.
Nero?

NERO: Yo.

ALVARO: Daniel James.

VALERIE: Who's playing Danny Santiago?

Alvaro and Javier make eye contact.

ALVARO: Me.

    Ready?

HERMAN: Scene One. 1984. Light up on Anna Maria, a woman in her 30s, surrounded
    by piles and piles of open letters.

*Lina, sits on the ground. Her performance is simple, focused and heartfelt. During the scene,
the visual landscape transforms slowly — as if the courtyard has become a theatre where the
play is being performed. This transformation is not a literal shift in time and space — rather
it's an imaginative leap the characters are taking — what they see in their mind's eye, like
the material is casting a spell on them.*

ANNA MARIA: I woke that Tuesday morning
    Had no idea I'd end the week with a shattered heart.

    Letter came in the mail.
    Familiar envelope
    paper, typeface …
    Familiar smell of sea salt and pine …

Javier tilts his head back and closes his eyes.

ANNA MARIA: I'd received dozens of letters from him
    Over thirteen years.
    Each one
    lit up a familiar
    giddiness inside me —
    reawakened a long lost teenage girl
    who finds a note
    from a secret admirer …
    Heartbeat quickens
    Skin tingles …
    Each letter
    I re-lived that first moment
    you entertain the thought,
    "maybe I am special … "

HERMAN: Anna Maria picks up a letter.

ANNA MARIA: The letter that came on Tuesday had its

    familiar envelope,

    paper and typeface …

    sea salt and pine …

    But the familiar music of his voice …

    Absent.

HERMAN: A Young Man appears behind Anna Maria. She senses his presence. It is Danny Santiago. She opens the letter and reads.

Javier sighs. He's not liking this one bit.

DANNY SANTIAGO: Dearest Anna Maria.

    I want you to read this letter

    while the seas are still calm.

    In a few days time

    the surface will roil

    awakening a long dormant monster

ANNA MARIA: Danny always opened his letters with

    a little flirtation –

    He was so *bad*.

    First sentence …

    Something was wrong.

DANNY SANTIAGO: On the 16th, I ask you to purchase

    The New York Review of Books.

    In its pages you'll find an article by John Gregory Dunne –

    a biography. Of me.

    Or at least someone that bears a resemblance.

    Unearths all the secrets I kept from you all these years.

ANNA MARIA: "Unearths"

    Thirteen years

    Danny never used that word.

    "Secrets" – yes, there were secrets –

    Not mine –

When I open my heart?
It's wide open ...
But he had secrets:
where he lived, where he was from,
what he did when he wasn't writing ...
if he had a girl, a family, a life ...

Never bothered me —
every man's got a whole world of secrets inside him,
no one's allowed to see.

DANNY SANTIAGO: Make sure you're sitting when you read it.
It will shock you. Shocks me.
Shock you feel when you sense a stranger
staring at you through a window at night
only to see
it's just a hazy reflection of yourself ...

Javier looks up, glares at Alvaro.

JAVIER: Plagiarist ...

Everyone is into the scene, so no one pays attention.

ANNA MARIA: For a long time
I figured
he was in jail ...
or he was married ...

But secrets so big?
They'd write an article in
The New York Review of Books?
Would it be something I couldn't stomach?
Did he kill someone?
Rape someone? Hurt a child?

I prayed to God ...
Don't let that be his secret.

HERMAN: Daniel James appears behind Danny. Danny is aware of him, but not Anna Maria.

Nero follows the stage direction. At this point the world of the hotel courtyard has fully transformed into the imagined stage world of the scene.

DANNY SANTIAGO: I hope learning the truth

DANNY SANTIAGO/DANIEL JAMES: About the man typing these words,

DANIEL JAMES: You can still see me as I see you … as whole …

ANNA MARIA: Yours, Danny …

HERMAN: She folds the letter and presses it against her heart.

ANNA MARIA: What do I do with this feeling
that's grown inside me for thirteen years …
Do I have to hate a man I've grown to love?

HERMAN: Shift in time and place – thirteen years earlier, 1971. An imaginary landscape, somewhere between the world of *Famous All Over Town*, Daniel James' imagination, and bleak reality.

JAVIER: Ha! What does that mean?

VALERIE & HERMAN: Shhhh

HERMAN: Ruined street in East Los Angeles, outside the Aztec Club, a dive bar that's boarded up. Mounds of garbage – detritus from destroyed homes. Prominent in the pile: a red dress and crayons scattered, flecks of color in the dreariness –

JAVIER: You puto thief –

No one pays attention. Nero enacts the following.

HERMAN: An old man, Daniel James, appears, towing a red child's wagon piled with artifacts he's collected from the ruins. He's tall, gangly, dressed like a longshoreman from the '40s –

He finds a red crayon on the pile. On the boarded window he writes in big, curvy letters: Chato de Shamrock.

Nero, finding a marker on the table writes this on the wall.

JAVIER: Thief …

Alvaro stares at him.

HERMAN: Danny Santiago appears in jeans and a clean white t-shirt. Daniel James finds a broken picture frame – a family photo. He's a about to hang it when Danny makes the shape of a gun with his hand, points it at the old man.

DANNY SANTIAGO: BANG!

That's how your ancestor got it, right?

Jesse James?

Nero breaks character for a second and gives thumbs up to Alvaro.

DANIEL JAMES: Yeah, though …

St. Joseph, Missouri's a tad bit more bucolic than this place.

DANNY SANTIAGO: Why you always comin down here to steal shit, old man?

DANIEL JAMES: Can't call it stealing if it's just lying around discarded.

DANNY SANTIAGO: People might come back,

reclaim what they left behind.

DANIEL JAMES: Doubtful.

DANNY SANTIAGO: What are you gonna do with all of it?

DANIEL JAMES: I don't know …

recycle it, turn it into a book …

DANNY SANTIAGO: Know what I did today?

DANIEL JAMES: Lemme guess … jacked a car? Went for a joyride?

DANNY SANTIAGO: Yeah, you'd think that …

No, man … I went down to the PO Box

DANIEL JAMES: More rejection letters?

DANNY SANTIAGO: Fan letter.

DANIEL JAMES: Really …

DANNY SANTIAGO: From a woman

DANIEL JAMES: *Woman*

DANNY SANTIAGO: She musta sprayed perfume all over the pages –
   made me cross-eyed …

DANIEL JAMES: Lemme see it.

DANNY SANTIAGO: No, bro … letter's for my eyes only.

DANIEL JAMES: Who is this fan letter writing woman?

DANNY SANTIAGO: School teacher.
   Teaches ninth grade English at Garfield.
   Crazy shit? She's a sister, man
   from the *barrio*

   Feel sorry for her …

DANIEL JAMES: Why's that?

DANNY SANTIAGO: Freshman English at Garfield?
   Bet they talked in British accents where you went –
   Teachers quoting Shakespeare?
   Garfield? Man, b.s. they make you read,
   room full a kids that don't give a shit.

DANIEL JAMES: Hope she's not good-looking.

DANNY SANTIAGO: Why would you hope that?

DANIEL JAMES: Teenage boys –
   spend the whole class making movies in their heads
   about getting in her pants – so much for David Copperfield

DANNY SANTIAGO: More like David Cop a Feel

Daniel laughs.

DANIEL JAMES: I've seen teachers like that –
   watch too many Hollywood movies
   come in all idealistic, think that just by
   being there they'll make a difference

DANNY SANTIAGO: Cynical … She's gonna be different

DANIEL JAMES: How so?

DANNY SANTIAGO: She's a sister.

She's got taste.

DANIEL JAMES: How do you know she has taste?

DANNY SANTIAGO: She wrote me.

She reads that ladies' magazine

DANIEL JAMES: *Redbook?*

She read the story?

DANNY SANTIAGO: Mmm hmmm …

DANIEL JAMES: Lemme see that letter.

DANNY SANTIAGO: Nah, man. So you could stick it in your wagon with your other
piles a stolen shit?

DANIEL JAMES: I'm not gonna do that

Read it to me at least … ?

HERMAN: Danny Santiago is struck by Daniel James's sudden vulnerability. He takes
the letter from his pocket and opens it.

ANNA MARIA: I came across your story "The Somebody" in *Redbook.*

I am very impressed by its vivid portrayal
of *barrio* life through the eyes of a teen. This kind of material is
painfully absent from the curriculum.

I copied the story to share with my students – they loved it.
It's a miracle – like they finally see themselves in what they read.
Chato's become a hero to them

DANNY SANTIAGO: Think she's blowing smoke up my ass?

DANIEL JAMES: Sounds like the genuine article to me …

ANNA MARIA: For at least a few class sessions, your story rescued me
from the dreaded non-response

a teacher always fears from her students …

They want more stories.

I want more —

Are there further Chato adventures you'd be willing to share?

Gratefully Yours …

DANNY SANTIAGO: Anna Maria Mayorga
    English Department
    Garfield High

Danny laughs. He's very proud of this achievement.

Putty. In My. *Hands.*

DANIEL JAMES: That's quite a letter …

DANNY SANTIAGO: Bet you never got one like that …

DANIEL JAMES: It's impolite to gloat.

DANNY SANTIAGO: I rescued her … I can gloat all I want.

DANIEL JAMES: You going to write her back?

DANNY SANTIAGO: Yeah …
    I got a classroom full of fans.

DANIEL JAMES: What are you gonna tell her?

DANNY SANTIAGO: My mouth's gonna jump out the envelope,
    kiss her right on the lips …

DANIEL JAMES: She'll ask you questions …

DANNY SANTIAGO: She can ask me anything she likes …

DANIEL JAMES: What'll you say if she asks where you live?

Pause.

    If she asks for your phone number?

Pause.

    What'll you say if she wants to meet you?

DANNY SANTIAGO: Enough, man

    I got answers …

    I got ways of keeping things mysterious …

    Women like that, right?

DANIEL JAMES: What about stories? You have more stories you can send her?

Danny Santiago looks at Daniel James seriously, vaguely threatening.

DANNY SANTIAGO: Yeah, I got stories,

    What? You don't think I got stories?

HERMAN: Daniel James goes to the pile, finds a half busted 1930s typewriter.

DANIEL JAMES: You'll need this.

HERMAN: He blows dust off it. Danny Santiago reaches for it, lights abruptly shift —

The group applauds, except Javier. "Nice work," "Not bad." etc. The world restores to the "normal" courtyard. After the collective congrats, everyone notices Javier's silence. They turn to him and await his reaction.

JAVIER: He wouldn't write like that.

VALERIE: Javi, don't be a prick —

JAVIER: It's confusing …

    Like watching one of those multiple personality movies —

    Three Faces of Eve? Sybil?

    Whatchya gonna call it —

    Three Faces of Daniel James?

HERMAN: I thought it played pretty good.

JAVIER: Only good stuff in there? You stole from me.

    He wouldn't write it like that.

Javi gets up, kicks over his chair, goes to one of the rooms. Door slam. Silence. Valerie looks at her watch.

VALERIE: Well … guess I should go pick up Pablo and Lila …

2. TESTIMONY

Kurtz's apartment. Kurtz and Alex on the couch. Alex sits with her legs folded under her, shoes off. Kurtz tries to manipulate an iPad he's using as a remote control to operate an unseen television. Take-out food containers, notebooks, library books, two bottles of wine (one empty, one half full). Cozy informality with more than a hint of flirtation.

ALEX: Index cards?

KURTZ: Thousands – I tried to get him to digitize but he was an old school technophobe.

ALEX: And the cards documented the lives of playwrights?

KURTZ: Playwrights no one's ever heard of.
    Slowik called them the "Ugh-Known Vitals."
    You must understand:
    Slowik never doubted the importance
    of O'Neill, Miller, Williams, Albee, Shepard, et cetera –
    But he set out to prove
    they owed their existence to playwrights
    written out of the "official" history

ALEX: Sounds like he was being ironic –

KURTZ: When you are shot down behind enemy lines
    and spend more than half the War in a
    Nazi prison camp … you rarely have time for irony.

    In any case,
    I did his research, dug up lost manuscripts,
    located ruined men, peeled them off bar stools to interview them …
    Most of the plays were garbage, BUT
    every now and then … gold.

ALEX: Like who?

KURTZ: Esther Fox?

ALEX: Never heard of her …

KURTZ: Serena Lowman, August Phelps, Henry Butterfield Ryan

ALEX: They don't ring a bell.

KURTZ: What about Alvaro Mendez? No? Javier C.? You've never heard of *Javier C.?*

Alex shrugs in non-recognition.

KURTZ: So sad …

ALEX: But all that work – that's how you …

KURTZ: Built my formidable reputation?

ALEX: Unearthing gold from the garbage …

KURTZ: In a sense …

ALEX: And he just … gave them to you?

KURTZ: Not exactly. We were preparing a book.
     The accident happened. He didn't make it.
     No one besides me was willing to carry on his work.

ALEX: And Daniel James was …

KURTZ: One of them, yes.
     But the last notation on his card
     was made in Slowik's hand in 1952.
     Just one play to go on:
     Winter Soldiers, Best Plays of 1942.

ALEX: Is it gold or garbage?

KURTZ: Unwashed recycling.

ALEX: Okay, then why the obsession with him?

KURTZ: I have reason to believe Daniel James wrote more –

ALEX: So is this the big, secret, mysterious project you want me to assist you on?

KURTZ: Not exactly.

ALEX: Or did you make that up to get me to come to your apartment?

KURTZ: Do you have any idea how to use this thing?

She takes the iPad away from him. She gets it working.

KURTZ: Ah! Watch:

Sounds from the television set. Low fidelity — a document from the 1950s.

CONGRESSMAN'S RECORDED VOICE: Mr. Daniel James?
Will you raise your right hand and be sworn?

Shift. While Kurtz and Alex watch, the world of the motel courtyard appears. The group reenacts the testimony. They're focused, committed to the material. Javier plays the Congressman, Nero plays Daniel James.

CONGRESSMAN: Do you solemnly swear to tell the truth and nothing but the truth, so help you God?

DANIEL JAMES: I do.

CONGRESSMAN: Mr. James, when and where were you born?

DANIEL JAMES: Kansas City, Missouri. January 1911.

CONGRESSMAN: What is your profession?

DANIEL JAMES: I'm a freelance writer.

CONGRESSMAN: What has been your record of employment?

DANIEL JAMES: First years out of Yale I was a traveling salesman, which I hope isn't too incriminating. I began writing in 1935. '38 I came to Hollywood, was employed in an independent studio as a sort of junior writer-assistant to a producer.

Kurtz laughs, pauses the video.

KURTZ: I love that. "Independent studio/junior writer-assistant to a producer."

ALEX: I don't get it …

KURTZ: Who refers to United Artists and Charlie Chaplin that way?

He clicks play.

DANIEL JAMES: '42 I wrote a play, *Winter Soldiers*, which was produced in New York. I did a screenplay on it but it was shelved. I then worked with my wife on what turned out to be a Broadway musical. Since that period my
fortunes
have been rather bad.
Wrote a novel, couple of plays … none were published or produced.

CONGRESSMAN: Mr. James, have you at any time been a member of the Communist Party?

DANIEL JAMES: I would like to answer that by saying

I am not a member of the Communist Party.

However, as to the second part of your question

I will stand on the fifth amendment and refuse to answer.

ALEX: Huh?

KURTZ: Right?

CONGRESSMAN: I asked you only one question, Mr. James.

When did you withdraw from the Communist Party?

DANIEL JAMES: I would have to decline, sir, on the same ground.

CONGRESSMAN: What ground?

DANIEL JAMES: That an American citizen, as I understand it, is not compelled to testify against himself in such a way as to be incriminated, prosecuted in – something. I am not a lawyer, sir. I think that should be sufficient.

ALEX: Awkward ...

KURTZ: He's bombing ...

CONGRESSMAN: Have you ever been a member of any Communist front organizations –

DANIEL JAMES: To the best of my knowledge, I am not. Nor am I sympathetic to communism. At the same time, I must decline to answer the question on the grounds stated.

CONGRESSMAN: Well, that's a strange answer.

You heard me ask witnesses whether or not they believe this committee serves an important function. What is your answer to that same question?

DANIEL JAMES: I think it is necessary for there to be an investigation of subversive organizations. At the same time, I am not sympathetic to communism nor am I sympathetic to this investigation.

In addition – this takes a considerable amount of courage,
though I expect no applause either from this committee,

nor from *The Daily Worker*.

This is a lonely position.

I assure you:

When I say I am not a Communist,

I am meaning it.

KURTZ: Watch: this is the kicker ...

Daniel James reaches into his pocket, removes an antique, small brown volume. He's hoping to make this a "moment."

DANIEL JAMES: I have in my pocket this little brown book. If you gentlemen would
like to see it.

It's in French. First edition.

CONGRESSMAN: May I —

ALEX: What is he doing?

KURTZ: Watch ... Congressman takes the book ...

Looks at it ...

Congressman looks over the book, unmoved by the possibility of what's coming.

KURTZ: Hands it right back

Congressman hands the book back.

CONGRESSMAN: I realize you've come prepared to make a "speech,"

But I want to ask you, again —

ALEX: Wait. Pause that. What was that about?

Kurtz pauses it.

KURTZ: Brought a first edition
of Voltaire's *Candide*.

Borrowed from his father's library ...

ALEX: What? Why?

KURTZ: Voltaire published it under a pseudonym.

"Monsieur Le Docteur Ralph" —

Wanted to show if the Committee got its way

American writers would be forced to hide behind false names …

James' way of going for the jugular …

ALEX: What a kick in the gut …

KURTZ: He was no Dalton Trumbo …

Alex's phone goes off. Incoming text. She reads it. Frustration.

KURTZ: What is it?

ALEX: I have to go.

KURTZ: So soon?

ALEX: Trish. My roommate. Locked herself out of the apartment.

KURTZ: One more, before you go … ?

He pours her a glass of wine.

ALEX: Sure.

KURTZ: Watch … end the evening on a comic note.

He clicks play. As before, what begins as a recording becomes a full blown re-enactment in the motel. Valerie plays Lilith.

CONGRESSMAN'S RECORDED VOICE: Will you state that again?

LILITH'S RECORDED VOICE: Lilith James. —

In the courtyard.

CONGRESSMAN: In what profession are you engaged?

LILITH: I am a writer-housewife.

CONGRESSMAN: How long have you been writing?

LILITH: My first writing was on a Broadway musical, *Bloomer Girl*, in 1944.

CONGRESSMAN: Are there some …

little Jameses?

LILITH: There is a little James and a big James.

CONGRESSMAN: I take it then you are not writing much now …

LILITH: I still write.

CONGRESSMAN: Have you ever been a member of the Communist Party?

LILITH: I am not a Communist, but I decline to answer your questions on Fifth Amendment grounds.

CONGRESSMAN: When did you leave the Communist Party?

LILITH: I never said I was a Communist.

CONGRESSMAN: Were you a member of the Communist Party before these hearings began? Say, this past Sunday?

LILITH: I decline on the same grounds.

CONGRESSMAN: On Monday? Tuesday?

LILITH: I decline —

CONGRESSMAN: What about when you entered this room today?

LILITH: No I was not.

CONGRESSMAN: I have no further questions.

Kurtz clicks the recording off. Alex is strangely affected by it.

KURTZ: What's the matter?

ALEX: I really have to go …

She gathers her things. As she moves to exit, Kurtz removes a large cardboard box from behind the couch, puts it on the coffee table. The sound stops Alex. She turns.

ALEX: What's that?

KURTZ: Open it.

ALEX: Does it have to do with the big, mysterious project you keep dangling like a carrot?

Kurtz shrugs. Alex moves to the box. She's about to open it, Kurtz touches her hand.

KURTZ: So it's clear: you open the box, there's no closing it.

She moves his hand away and opens the box. She removes a couple of old manuscripts.

ALEX: *Death of a Liberal* by Javier C.? *The Rich Also Cry.* Javier C.

She looks at him puzzled. She removes another item from the box — a rolled up poster of Charlie Chaplin's The Great Dictator. *Another puzzled look. She removes what appears to be a full head mask of a Godzilla-like creature. More puzzlement. Last, she pulls out an identical typewriter to the one D.L. gifted Daniel James.*

ALEX: What is all this?

KURTZ: Don't you have to go rescue your friend — Trish? Is that her name?

ALEX: Trish can wait …

KURTZ: Will you help me?

They stare at each other for a long time. Kurtz puts on the Godzilla-like mask. Unclear who initiates it, but the two fall into a sexual embrace.

3. MONTAGE

Hotel courtyard. The group is spread out across two tables. Javier, Herman and Alvaro are at one table combing over stacks of paper trying to determine a scene order.

The other table is covered in different colored fabrics, drawings and a sewing machine. Lina stands wearing a Gorgo costume, while Valerie makes adjustments to the fabric.

Nero sits sunbathing in his underwear. Valerie eats a nacho dipped in salsa.

VALERIE: Awesome sauce.

HERMAN: —beginning's always a
    good place to start

JAVIER: But what beginning –
    We got like seventy-two years of
    Beginnings—not to mention
    Beginnings, like *deep* beginnings

NERO: What about that massacre?
    What was it? Centralia Massacre?

ALVARO: Enough with Jesse James!

HERMAN: HUAC's as good a place as
    any to start –

Javier throws his pencil down.

JAVIER: NO!

HERMAN: Why not? It's inherently dramatic
    We don't even have to write anything
    Type up the transcript
    Presto, a first act

JAVIER: Boring!

VALERIE: You look fantastic.

LINA: I don't look ridiculous?

VALERIE: You look *amazing.* Is it too
tight around the neck?

LINA: No, it's fine.

Valerie steps back.

VALERIE: Wave your arms around like
    you're on the rampage.

Lina does so, making Gorgo-like sounds.

VALERIE: Feel like you can move?

LINA: Perfect.

HERMAN: Total destruction of lives?

    Friendships? Careers?

    Explain how that's boring ...

JAVIER: Too obvious!

Herman throws a pile of papers in the air.

VALERIE: Fantastic ...

    I'm gonna take some photos

    Maybe you can strike some poses ...

Valerie finds a camera. Lina puts on Gorgo's head and goes to Nero—stalking him like a monster, growling. He laughs. She straddles him. They kiss. Valerie snaps a photo.

Throughout the following "photo shoot," Lina strikes poses for Valerie. Some are "monster-like," while others mock "sexy." The women and Nero enjoy this immensely.

ALVARO: Might give it, you know, a sense of

    scope? World-historic importance?

JAVIER: Why do you have to say shit like that?

ALVARO: What'd I say? I'm making a // sugg

JAVIER: Like you think I'm some pompous ass

    who thinks about shit like "world-historical // imp —

ALVARO: You do think about shit like that, and, yeah, Javi, you are a pompous ass

Javier flips. He lunges over the table and physically attacks Alvaro. Neither is a skilled fighter — more elementary school playground fisticuffs than anything. They roll on the ground punching, wrestling each other.

HERMAN: Whoa! Whoa whoa // whoa whoa ...

VALERIE: Javi!   NERO: Jesus.

Lina cracks up, while everyone tries to peel the men apart. Lina pretends she's Gorgo, knocking furniture over, throwing paper, empty drink bottles, fabric around. She roars wildly, having a grand old time. The fight between the men, and the struggle to peel them apart ... well ... just kind of fizzles out. They all notice Lina going nuts as Gorgo — at first they're puzzled, but then they start cracking up. The laughter becomes maniacal — some of them are literally rolling on the floor.

Lights shift, and suddenly, as before, we are inside the world of their play. We will stay in this world through the end — as we go deeper into it, the performers become so engrossed in the story that we, the audience, forget we're watching a play-within-a-play.

VALERIE: *(Reading stage direction.)* Sound of ocean waves transitions us to:

Office of a Theatrical Producer in New York City, 1936. Daniel James, 25, sits across from a no-nonsense man in his 60s.

Nero, as Daniel, and Herman, as producer, perform the scene. Nero/Daniel wears a wool red and black plaid hunting jacket. He wears it through the remaining scenes. They do not have scripts this time — they are fully committed to the performance.

PRODUCER: Who's your father?

DANIEL: D.L. James.

PRODUCER: D.L.? That stand for —? Any//thing?

DANIEL: Funny story actually ...

His parents gave him initials when he was born

Thinking when he was old enough

He'd choose his own name

D.L. just kind of stuck ...

PRODUCER: What's he written?

DANIEL: Plays, mostly

West coast productions, Midwest

Hasn't really

Broken

In New York ...

He's working on a play about Jesse James

PRODUCER: You don't say

DANIEL: It's quite the epic.

Kind of an

American *Macbeth*

Grapples with whether Jesse

Was a sinner or sinned against.

PRODUCER: Man was a racist, cold-blooded killer.

DANIEL JAMES: We're related to him …

Awkward pause.

DANIEL JAMES: So have you … ?

PRODUCER: Yes. *Pier 17.*
Which you and your father

DANIEL JAMES: Co-authored, yes.
We wanted to uhhh
Render *dramatically* the
Human cost of the labor struggle
On a *working* family, working *immigrant* family

PRODUCER: Yes, I got that –

DANIEL JAMES: Based on a true story –
San Francisco longshoremen's strike couple of years back

PRODUCER: Eight-year-old kid got shot by the National Guard?

DANIEL JAMES: Not exactly – uhhh – dramatic license, sharpen the uh
Impact

PRODUCER: Dead kid's'll do that …

Awkward pause.

PRODUCER: How much of this play is yours, how much your father's?
Ballpark.

DANIEL JAMES: 70 percent mine? 20 percent his? Other 10 … ?
We were made to understand you're one of the
Producers in town who
Believes in using the stage
To
Wrestle
With the great issues of our time.

PRODUCER: I'm all for "issues."

    But.

    Reality is ...

    A theater is a very large room.

    Filled with empty seats.

    Facing a big, empty platform.

    It's basically a useless piece of architecture

    Sitting on squandered real estate –

    Unless there are human *buttocks*

    in those seats.

    Now: it's more sorcery than science,

    But to get butts *in* those seats

    You gotta figure out

    What to put on that empty platform.

    If that something has redeeming social value,

    Icing on the cake.

    But when you've done this as long as I have –

    You know what NOT to put up there.

DANIEL JAMES: Does that mean ... ?

PRODUCER: Look:

    You seem like a really nice kid.

    But this writing business?

    Not for everyone.

    You're lucky. You're young.

    You have what most men at the end of their lives realize they've squandered ...

    Time.

    Do something else with your life ...

ALVARO: Shift in time and space: 1948, the Brentwood, Los Angeles home of Daniel James and his wife, Lilith.

Nero as Daniel, and Lilith, played by Valerie.

LILITH: They're coming from New York?

DANIEL JAMES: That's right.

LILITH: They want to do it *here?* In our *house?*
  Tell them NO.

DANIEL JAMES: Can't say no to them.

LILITH: Why not? You want that on your head?
  Watch the Comintern hang Maltz by his toes.
  In our *living room*.

DANIEL JAMES: He's the best writer in the Party.
  They can't afford to hang him.

LILITH: You read *The Daily Worker* rebuttal to his editorial —
  They're out for blood.

DANIEL JAMES: They just want to sit him down, have a conversation —

LILITH: This isn't going to be a conversation, Dan.
  It's going to be a lynching. Make him
  An example to anyone who doesn't toe the Party line —
  We're opening our home to facilitate that?

DANIEL JAMES: That upsets you

LILITH: Of course it upsets me — it doesn't upset you?

DANIEL JAMES: He'll recant, the whole thing'll blow over.

LILITH: Is that what you think he ought to do? Recant?

DANIEL JAMES: It's not what I think, what the Party thinks is what matters

LILITH: You. What do *you*. Think.

DANIEL JAMES: Maltz is a good man.
  But repudiating the idea
  That art is a weapon
  In the cause —

LILITH: That's *not* what he said —

DANIEL JAMES: Lilith —

LILITH: No! No. He said

> We've been straitjacketed into believing
> That serving the cause is art's *sole* purpose.
> With every contradictory directive
> Sent down from the Party heads,
> It's impossible to finish *anything* –
> It's impossible to write anything true ...

DANIEL JAMES: I know what he said, Lilith.

LILITH: Then where's your outrage?

> Why won't you stand up, say NO!
> You may not stage a lynching in my home.

DANIEL JAMES: You're saying I'm in a straitjacket –

LILITH: Yes. And you know it's true.

Pause.

DANIEL JAMES: Yes, Lilith. We're all wearing straitjackets.

> BUT. If everyone took Maltz's position ...

Pause.

LILITH: I'm waiting, Dan.

DANIEL JAMES: It'd be every man for himself.

> That would be the end of the Party.
> End of the whole movement.

LILITH: You actually believe that horseshit.

DANIEL JAMES: Lilith ... I can't not believe it. Without it, what do I have?

> I have NOTHING. I *am* nothing.

LILITH: They didn't put you in a straitjacket.

> Straitjacket *you're* wearing is entirely of your own creation.
> You love it. Because it gives you the perfect excuse to do nothing.

HERMAN: *(Performing text of stage direction.)* Shift ... 1971. Danny Santiago replies to Anna Maria's first letter.

Shift. Danny Santiago. Daniel James hovers behind him.

DANNY SANTIAGO: Dear Anna Maria —

> My agent forwarded me your letter
> Was like an early Christmas present …

> You'll be happy to know
> I got lots of Chato stories …
> Even playing with stringing them together
> Some day make a novel out of them … .
> Knowing I got a school teacher
> Plus a class full of fans
> Might motivate me to put em down.

> I'm sending you skeletons of a few chapters
> Maybe you'll write me back … ?
> Tell me what you think?
> Maybe share them with the kids
> Tell me what *they think* … ?

ANNA MARIA: Dear Danny —

> I love the chapters you sent —
> Hope it's not too forward of me, but
> I'm sending you notes —
> Places where we could fix the grammar
> Clarify the storytelling —

DANNY SANTIAGO: Listen to you, Miss English Teacher

ANNA MARIA: Am I crossing a line?

DANNY SANTIAGO: No … I like having you as my teacher.
> What did the kids think?

ANNA MARIA: They went crazy for them … said it was like looking in a mirror
> They had lots of ideas, suggestions, which I'm also forwarding …

DANNY SANTIAGO: How'd I get so lucky to find a little angel like you?

ANNA MARIA: So … you're up in Salinas? You ever get to LA?

    My students would get a kick out of meeting a real life author …

    So might a certain English teacher –

DANNY SANTIAGO: I'm always on the move, maybe some day

ANNA MARIA: I'm enclosing a few of the "must-read" books I wrote you about

    Melville, Virginia Woolf, Steinbeck … inspiration for the inspired.

VALERIE: Sound of ocean waves crashing against a bluff transitions us to: 1983.

HERMAN: Night. *Seaward*. Daniel James' study – the room where many years earlier

    Daniel inherited his father's typewriter.

VALERIE: Daniel James, now 73, chats with his friend John Gregory Dunne, 52.

Nero as Daniel James and John Gregory Dunne, played by Javier.

DANIEL JAMES: They need a bio, John.

DUNNE: Who needs a bio?

DANIEL JAMES: The committee.

DUNNE: What committee is that, Dan?

DANIEL JAMES: THE committee. *Pulitzer* committee.

DUNNE: Fuck.

    Schuster's submitting it?

DANIEL JAMES: They need a bio and a *photograph*.

    Otherwise they won't consider it.

DUNNE: Well there's your answer …

    Shame on the one hand, but

    Take it as vindication.

DANIEL JAMES: How's Joan?

DUNNE: She's well –

DANIEL JAMES: And Quintana Roo? She must be quite the young lady now …

DUNNE: Dan, you're not thinking …

DANIEL JAMES: Course it's impossible – but amusing isn't it?

> To entertain all kinds of hypotheticals?
>
> Hypothetically, a bio could … *surface*

DUNNE: Why do I get the feeling this

> "hypothetical" bio's already been written?

DANIEL JAMES: It's the photograph that's the pain in the ass –

DUNNE: Why don't you get one of your

> Charity youth club kids
>
> To loan you one?

DANIEL JAMES: Not a bad idea …

DUNNE: I'm joking. That was a joke, Dan.

DANIEL JAMES: Oh, I'm *teasing* John.

> Indulge a crotchety old man.
>
> If you lived my history,
>
> I'd forgive you entertaining multiple "what ifs" …
>
> Might make for a nice third act twist to a pretty glum movie.

DUNNE: I'm appalled.

DANIEL JAMES: You weren't appalled when you sent Danny's first story to Carl.

DUNNE: I never thought –

DANIEL JAMES: They were publishable?

DUNNE: I never would have sent them to Carl if I didn't think they were good.

> Look, I told you I was uncomfortable about the pseudonym business *then* –

DANIEL JAMES: Then why'd you do it?

DUNNE: One, I thought the stories had a chance.

> Two? When Joan and me were starting out? You were good to us.
>
> At that point I was in a position I could return your kindness.

DANIEL JAMES: Hm. But the possibility of a Pulitzer makes you uncomfortable.

> I respect your discomfort, John.
>
> If I were in your shoes, I might feel a little on edge …

DUNNE: What are you getting at?

DANIEL JAMES: You wrote under a pseudonym yourself // so you

DUNNE: *Once.*

DANIEL JAMES: Kill a man once, you're always a killer.

DUNNE: Look: you're not gonna win.

DANIEL JAMES: Ouch.

DUNNE: There might exist an alternate universe where you DO win –
You realize how fucked you'd be?

DANIEL JAMES: Jack Kennedy won the Pulitzer.

DUNNE: What does that have to do with anything?

DANIEL JAMES: He didn't write a word of that book.

DUNNE: Look: they want to submit it.
Isn't that vindication enough?

DANIEL JAMES: I suppose in the way that
Seeing your hazy reflection in a window
Is vindication that you exist in the world ...

DUNNE: Promise me you won't do this –

DANIEL JAMES: Don't worry, Johnny-boy, I won't.
Relieved?

Pause.

Wouldn't that be something?
To have that? Relief?

Silence.

Maybe in the next life.

VALERIE: Shift. Danny and Anna Maria, Late 1970s.

HERMAN: A decade into their correspondence. Yet, they have never met in person.
However, their intimacy has deepened to the point they inhabit the same space.

Shift. Danny and Anna Maria.

DANNY SANTIAGO: Five, six, seven, eight rejection letters …

ANNA MARIA: I am *so* sorry Danny

DANNY SANTIAGO: Should have known no one would care –
  Story of my life –

ANNA MARIA: I care. My students care.

DANNY SANTIAGO: I feel like I disappointed you –
  All that time you put in? Helping me finish?

ANNA MARIA: Disappointed?
  Danny: I'm *proud* of you …
  It's a beautiful book. Some day
  Every publisher will realize the mistake they made
  It's going to happen, Danny.
  You deserve it.

HERMAN: Shift. Outside the Aztec Club – the ruins of Chato's neighborhood. 1983.

VALERIE: Danny Santiago throws rocks at the wall. Daniel James appears reading a
  newspaper.

DANIEL JAMES: Ouch.

DANNY SANTIAGO: What?

DANIEL JAMES: *San Francisco Chronicle*.
  " … Santiago's novel will seem just a gallery of stereotypical Mexican characters –

DANNY SANTIAGO: Whoa …

DANIEL JAMES: "The drunken Mexican macho father who beats up
  his wife and abandons his family –

DANNY SANTIAGO: That shit happens.

DANIEL JAMES: "The ever suffering wife who returns to Mexico with her youngest
  child;

DANNY SANTIAGO: Again, known to happen.

DANIEL JAMES: "The perplexed son who becomes a gang member to feel wanted … "

DANNY SANTIAGO: We should find him. Beat his ass.

What does he know …

DANIEL JAMES: Name's worrisome.

Arturo Islas.

DANNY SANTIAGO: He's probably Cuban.

DANIEL JAMES: He's Chicano.

Says here in his bio.

Stanford University. "First Chicano in the US to earn a PhD in English Lit."

DANNY SANTIAGO: He's one of *those* Chicanos.

DANIEL JAMES: What do you mean?

DANNY SANTIAGO: All uppity cause he got fancy degrees.

DANIEL JAMES: All the other reviews have been good –

Bad review in the *Chronicle* won't do much damage.

DANNY SANTIAGO: It's the principle …

Where does he get off

Taking another brother down?

DANIEL JAMES: Best to leave it.

DANNY SANTIAGO: How can you say that?

That's your problem –

You let the world walk all over you

Fifty years a that shit,

Ain't you sick of it?

Silence.

DANNY SANTIAGO: Fine. Sit there

Like a dog used to getting his ass beat –

But not me, nah uh.

Danny finds the typewriter.

DANIEL JAMES: What are you doing?

DANNY SANTIAGO: "Dear Mr. Arturo 'Uppity PhD' Islas –
    I would love for you to come up here
    say the shit you wrote in your so called 'review' to my // face –

DANIEL JAMES: Danny …

DANNY SANTIAGO: What?!?!

DANIEL JAMES: Reason. *Eloquence.*
    Harsh language – will only blow up in your face.

DANNY SANTIAGO: This dude is blowing up in my face.

DANIEL JAMES: Some people's agendas are for
    Things to be "uplifting" at all costs

DANNY SANTIAGO: So if I lied, said his Papa
    Was a CPA instead of a mean drunk?
    Think he'd be cool with that?

DANIEL JAMES: Why don't you ask him?

DANNY SANTIAGO: Alright …
    "Dear Mr. Islas,
    I read your review of my book, and it pissed me off –

DANIEL JAMES: How about …
    "Dear Mr. Islas,
    It was with considerable puzzlement and dismay that I read your review" –

DANNY SANTIAGO: "Puzzlement," "dismay" – I like that

DANIEL JAMES: "Why do I take the trouble to write to you?
    Not because yours is the only truly negative review –
    My beef is against the 'stereotypical' way certain people
    Insist Mexicans should only be shown as
    Dentists and CPAs."

DANNY SANTIAGO: That don't sound like me.

DANIEL JAMES: You gotta show you can match wits with him.

DANNY SANTIAGO: Okay – I got it:

"You will be surprised to see what happens in the sequels."

Daniel turns inward.

DANNY SANTIAGO: "There will be five novels in all –

That's a project no writer would undertake

If he has only a bunch of 'pathetic figures' –

As you say in your review –

To write about."

Danny notices Daniel looking morose.

DANNY SANTIAGO: What's the matter?

We got sequels planned, right? *Right?*

DANIEL JAMES: Right.

DANNY SANTIAGO: *(Typing.)* "Saludos,

Danny Santiago."

Danny takes the paper out of the spool, folds it, and puts it in an envelope.

DANIEL JAMES: May not be the best idea to send that.

DANNY SANTIAGO: I'm sending it.

LINA: Sounds of waves crashing transition us to: Seaward, 1984.

HERMAN: Night. Daniel James' study.

LINA: Daniel James, his wife Lilith and John Gregory Dunne, six months later ...

DUNNE: *New York Review of Books* asked me to review it.

DANIEL JAMES: Talk about serendipity. Surprised it got their attention.

DUNNE: After the Rosenthal Prize fiasco

DANIEL JAMES: Wasn't the first time

Writer doesn't show to

Pick up an award.

DUNNE: It's raised ... doubt. In certain circles.

> You understand the pickle I'm in ...

DANIEL JAMES: What are you asking

DUNNE: I could turn them down.

> I could review it as I'd review any other book ...
> Or I could tell the truth.

LILITH: Tell the "truth"

> Funny that's an option unto itself.

DUNNE: What are you getting at?

LILITH: Would there be no truth in turning it down?

> Reviewing it as you would any other book?

DUNNE: I'm not here to play rhetorical games.

LILITH: Neither am I.

DANIEL JAMES: You're your own man.

> You're faced with a crisis.
> Decision is yours and only yours to make.

DUNNE: Are you just saying that?

DANIEL JAMES: It's not an abstraction to me, John.

> You know, once upon a time
> I picked up my daughter
> From a friend's house.
> Girl's father was also a writer.
> Named names. Made some pretty good pictures.
> On the way home
> She ranted and raved, what an awful man he was.
> Called him a rat.
> Hearing this sweet kid say that ...
> Last person on earth
> Who deserved to inherit grudges from the past ...

I pulled the car over,

Told her, "Sweetie …

We have no right to judge someone

Forced into a tougher decision than we had to make."

DUNNE: This is a chance to set the record straight.

Tell the whole story —

LILITH JAMES: Including your participation in it.

DUNNE: Including my participation.

DANIEL JAMES: Why the crisis of conscience now?

DUNNE: The Rosenthal Award bothers me, Dan.

If all this comes out in an uncontrolled way

They're gonna come after you.

You think you've been living in a grave all these years?

They will dig you out of that one, Dan

Just so they can bury you in another one.

They won't give a shit

You got a nice review in the *Times*.

DANIEL JAMES: Nice? I'd say it was a / / rave

DUNNE: Look:

Hundreds of novels come out each year

Most collect dust on bookstore shelves

None of those books

Get the attention of

The Academy of Arts and Letters.

It's a *major.* Award.

People that dole out those sorts of things

Live inside very exclusive rooms.

They protect

Who they let in, keep out.

Danny Santiago?

They've gone out on a limb

To admit someone of *dubious* pedigree.

They expect him to *thank* them on his knees.

When he doesn't show?

"How dare a half-literate *cockroach*

snub us."

Daniel laughs.

DANIEL JAMES: I didn't need the five grand —

DUNNE: You didn't show because you're ashamed.

LILITH: How dare you?

We put years of our time serving those people.

They welcomed us, made us part of their community.

Dan had every right to write about it.

Show him the letters.

DANIEL JAMES: Lilith …

LILITH: Show him, Dan.

Daniel rises and retrieves a thick bundle of letters. He drops it on Dunne's lap.

DUNNE: What's this.

DANIEL JAMES: Letters. Thirteen years of them.

First one? 1971.

Twenty-two-year-old schoolteacher in East L.A.

Writes to *thank* me.

For telling a story her kids could relate to.

Kids that see only three future options —

Getting mowed down on the mean streets,

Getting mowed down in Vietnam,

Getting mowed down in prison.

Kids that have no idea

Their miserable lives are worthy of being chronicled anywhere

Let alone in the pages of a book

That *thing* happens, John.
Interest. Possibility.
For a moment
Class becomes a class,
Teacher *teaches,*
Students *learn.*

DUNNE: She wrote you for thirteen years?

DANIEL JAMES: That's right.

DUNNE: You wrote to her as Danny … ?
Lilith, you knew … ?
Wow. That's fucked.

DANIEL JAMES: Sometimes you have to deceive a little to serve a more essential truth.

DUNNE: "Essential truth … "
Didn't know "truth" needed any adjectives to make it more of what it is.

Silence.

DUNNE: You know what, Dan? Lilith?
I don't give a shit about truth.
If you're honest with yourself, Dan,
Neither do you.

What we *do* care about
Is a good story.
We're the same that way.
Good story trumps everything.
Friends, spouses, family, country.
Mexican women who write you fan letters.
Your own damned *self.*

We're writers.
Not every day a story this good falls in your lap.

I can do it with or without your cooperation.
Either way it's good.

But it could be a knockout if you help me.

Get the whole picture right.

DANIEL JAMES: By "whole picture" you mean ...

DUNNE: Everything.

Danny.

East L.A.

Monster movies.

HUAC.

The Party.

Chaplin.

This house.

Your father.

Jesse James.

School teacher groupies –

DANIEL JAMES: You leave her name out of this.

DUNNE: Okay ...

This is an American story, Dan.

DANIEL JAMES: Call it *Citizen Santiago*.

LILIITH: It's taken years to put it all behind us.

You want to destroy us all over again?

You want our permission to name our names?

DUNNE: I'm not HUAC, Lilith.

DANIEL JAMES: Fifty years, John.

Couldn't find an honest word.

Danny shows up,

Stranger peering through a window at night.

He gives me honest words.

I'm more *me,* more *free* as him

Than I ever was writing as myself.

DUNNE: Everyone's looking for some whiz kid to throw accolades at

While you're alone up here, in the house your father built?

You can finally get the recognition I know you crave in your heart.

DANIEL JAMES: It's gonna kill him.

DUNNE: You don't have to stop writing as him.

DANIEL JAMES: It's gonna kill him.

DUNNE: He's not real.

DANIEL JAMES: It's gonna kill him.

VALERIE: Shift. 1984. Sounds of a monster from a 1950s B Movie. Danny Santiago, Daniel James, Anna Maria.

DANNY SANTIAGO: I ask that you purchase a copy of *The New York Review of Books*.

ANNA MARIA: Every man's got a whole world of secrets inside him – no one's allowed to see

DANNY SANTIAGO/DANIEL JAMES: It will shock you.

ANNA MARIA: Did he kill someone? Hurt a child?

Don't let that be his secret.

VALEIRE: Shift. 1985. Living room of Anna Maria's modest Los Angeles home.

HERMAN: Daniel James face to face with Anna Maria for the first and only time.

Danny Santiago hovers in the background, silenced.

DANIEL JAMES: Am I anything like you expected?

ANNA MARIA: No. Am I?

DANIEL JAMES: Pictured you different. But now I see you …

Danny was right to feel what he felt for you.

ANNA MARIA: I sent you books by Steinbeck. You broke bread with him.

DANIEL JAMES: Ironic, isn't it.

Can you forgive me?

ANNA MARIA: My mother always told me forgiveness is everything.

I think you belong in my "Men Behaving Badly" file …

VALERIE: Shift. May 18, 1988. The Death of Daniel James.

HERMAN: Ruined Street in East L.A. Old Daniel James writes in crayon on the wall: "Chato de Shamrock". He finds a family photo, tries to hang it on the wall. Danny Santiago appears, carrying a gun. Points it at the Old Man.

JAVIER: Wait …

Nero, can I have a crack at this?

Nero turns, looks at Javier, puzzled.

JAVIER: Just this one time, Nero … I promise.

Nero removes the wool hunting jacket and exchanges it with Javier. Nero steps away, Javier puts on the jacket, assuming the role of Daniel James. He and Alvaro stare at each other.

DANNY SANTIAGO: BANG!

That how it went down? With your famous ancestor?

DANIEL JAMES: Yep. Though St. Joseph, Missouri's

Tad bit more bucolic than this place.

DANNY SANTIAGO: Hear he's got a plaque there.

Think they'll hang a plaque for you on this wall?

DANIEL JAMES: Nah.

Taking a stroll down memory lane?

DANNY SANTIAGO: Not much left to remember

They murdered this place.

DANIEL JAMES: How's your mother?

DANNY SANTIAGO: Back in Mexico. With the baby.

DANIEL JAMES: Your sister?

DANNY SANTIAGO: Married that Mexican Romeo.

She put on the inevitable few pounds.

He's growing the inevitable bald spot.

DANIEL JAMES: Your father?

DANNY SANTIAGO: Who?

DANIEL JAMES: That bad, huh?

DANNY SANTIAGO: Don't care where he is.

Got stuck in his own straitjacket …

DANIEL JAMES: What about you?

DANNY SANTIAGO: Between places …

Waiting. For the next chapter.

Got all this anticipation built up …

For the next chapter.

They stare at each other.

DANIEL JAMES: I know …

DANNY SANTIAGO: That something you gonna help me out with?

DANIEL JAMES: Can't.

DANNY SANTIAGO: But I heard you got *Famous All Over Town*.

DANIEL JAMES: I knew a man once.

Was accused of a crime.

He knew it was his right to say nothing.

Still, judge found him guilty. Sentence?

Took half the alphabet from him for 20 years

DANNY SANTIAGO: That's cruel and unusual

DANIEL JAMES: Worst part, he only got one vowel. A "u."

Even the word "I" was off limits to him.

Twenty years trying to put words together,

Could only make growling sounds,

Like some monster under the sea.

Twenty years later,

He got all his letters back.

DANNY SANTIAGO: What'd he do with them?

DANIEL JAMES: Like you said. He got famous.

> But the price ...

> Had to give up the whole alphabet.

DANNY SANTIAGO: Sad story.

DANIEL JAMES: Would you really pull that trigger?

DANNY SANTIAGO: Maybe.

> Would you kill me if you could?

DANIEL JAMES: I'd give up everything to keep you alive.

DANNY SANTIAGO: Yeah?

DANIEL JAMES: That's not up to me anymore.

> Man only gets a finite number of names in his life.

> Once they're used up, poof ...

> I don't have any names left.

DANNY SANTIAGO: What about me? Don't I got names left?

Daniel James shrugs, he turns to go.

DANNY SANTIAGO: What about *me?* You listening old man?

> *How many names do I got left?!?!?*

DANIEL JAMES: Take care of yourself, Danny. Was good while it lasted ...

Daniel James walks away.

DANNY SANTIAGO: Back to your castle, huh?

> Back to your fortress by the sea?!

> Back to starin out that window?

> At the waves? At your reflection?!?!

Daniel James is gone.

DANNY SANTIAGO: You know there's a monster under that sea!!!!

> BIG MOTHERFUCKING GODZILLA MONSTER!!!!

> UNDER THAT SEA! Waiting to come up ...

Danny goes to the "Chato de Shamrock" tag on the wall. He picks up a black crayon, and scribbles thick lines obliterating the name. Slow fade. Just before blackout, the world of the courtyard pops up. It's night. Nero pops open a bottle of champagne. Celebration. The group exchanges hugs, high fives, etc. They cheer, pour drinks — it gets raucous quickly. Herman and Valerie embrace. A kiss to the cheek turns sexual instantly. Nero lifts and spins Lina. They're all over each other. Javier and Alvaro embrace. A brotherly kiss becomes a sensual exchange.

Suddenly one of the motel room doors opens — blast of light and the frightened, terrifying cry of a toddler silences the group. They all freeze in their respective embraces looking at the door. They watch in fear — no one dares to step forward. Alvaro finally moves towards the door. He looks in. By his reaction at the threshold, something has gone dreadfully wrong. He enters the room. No one moves. He returns carrying Lila, who screams.

VALERIE: Alvaro ... what is it ... ?

ALVARO: Pablo's gone.

Valerie and Javier rush to the threshold to look inside the room. They hold that position through the end of the play —

World shift. Kurtz's apartment. Clothes strewn on the floor, take out food cartons, empty liquor bottles, a beat up video camera on a tripod, stacks of pages, post-its, index cards. Images are pasted to the wall — Daniel James, Chaplin, Seaward, Jesse James, posters for Gorgo, Behemoth, Great Dictator, black and whites of HUAC hearing rooms, etc.

On the coffee table the same typewriter D.L. gave to Daniel James. Kurtz is on the couch furiously typing. He's in his boxers and a dirty t-shirt. Next to the typewriter a neatly stacked manuscript.

Sound of a toilet flushing. Alex appears wearing a green slip. She's a wreck. She stumbles to Kurtz, kisses him. She's drunk and distraught.

ALEX: No. Not Pablo. He's just a little boy, you can't do that to a little boy ...

KURTZ: Hush.

ALEX: You can't do that to them!
    They finished their play. They're going to make their deadline —
    it's supposed to be a happy ending.
    You *can't* make Pablo disappear —

KURTZ: They weren't paying attention. They deserve it.

ALEX: No one. No one deserves to lose their child.

    You *can't. do* that to them.

Kurtz types a few more strokes. Stops. He removes the page from the scroll, places it on the completed manuscript.

KURTZ: It's done.

End of play

AFTERWORD: THE MYSTIQUE OF FAILURE

by Dr. Alexandra Tanner

The following is an unedited, partial transcript of a talk given by Alexandra Tanner, PhD at the Modern Languages Association conference in Chicago in January 2014. Due to technical difficulties with the recording device, no documentation exists of the complete talk. The transcript marks points in the talk when the recording device ceases to function properly.

> "To each eye, perhaps, the outlines of a great civilization present a different picture. In the wide ocean upon which we venture, the possible ways and directions are many; the same studies that have served for my work might easily, in other hands, not only receive a wholly different treatment and application, but lead to essentially different conclusions."
>
> — *Jacob Burckhardt, from* The Civilization of the Renaissance in Italy

A thousand years from now, if the only cultural artifacts to survive an American apocalypse were the output of its dramatists, what picture would future cultural historians paint of the civilization that produced them? Would they deem America a latter day ancient Greece, a Renaissance Italy, an Elizabethan England? Would judgment of its surviving plays relegate America to the pantheon of enigmatic lost civilizations like the Harappa of the Indus Valley, or the pre-Inca Puma Punku in South America, Baalbek hidden beneath the ruins of ancient Heliopolis in Lebanon or Göbekli Tepe in eastern Turkey? Or would America remain as illegible, inscrutable and inaccessible as the Asmat of southwestern New Guinea?

If cultural artifacts, as art historian Jacob Burckhardt posits, provide essential clues to understanding the ethos of a civilization, what do the plays by the Colombian-born, American playwright Javier C. reveal about the late 20th-century landscape of the American theater and, in a larger sense, the America, in which they were written? Further, what will they make of the unlikely resurrection, reconsideration and renaissance (yes, admittedly a minor one at that) of his work in the second decade of the 21st century?

Our internet era has spawned a phenomenon described by the late cultural historian Emiliano Kurtz as "resurrection fever," a term he coined in the introduction of his seminal *The Mystique of Failure: A Reconsideration of Modern American Drama Through its Lost Plays and Playwrights* (Northwestern University Press, 2007). Kurtz argues that the information superhighway has been clogged by a virtual bumper-to-bumper traffic jam of historians, critics, museum curators, documentarians and bloggers bent on digging into the shadowy recesses of the past to resurrect works of artists, writers and musicians that have long languished in obscurity. Their aim is fourfold: 1) to rewrite accepted art-historical trajectories; 2) to create new markets for artifacts that history originally

deemed marginal; 3) to mark their territory as vital contributing authors of the never-ending narrative of cultural development; and 4) to feed the public with the comforting myth that resurrection is not just the stuff of biblical fairy tale, but a fact of contemporary life.

In the visual art world, the trend of resurrecting obscure 20th-century artists (Konrad Lueg, Germaine Richier, Esteban Gutierrez y Palma, Julije Knifer and Richard Van Buren, to name a few) is as much about creating new and lucrative market opportunities as it is about filling gaps in (if not entirely redefining) the trajectory of modern art. A recent example of artistic exhumation and reanimation centers on the work of Vivian Maier, Chicago's reclusive "North Shore nanny-slash-street photographer," chronicled by her "discoverer" John Maloof in the forthcoming film *Finding Vivian Maier* (IFC, 2014).

[Editor's note: The film had an official release date of March 2014 — Dr. Tanner apparently saw an early cut of the film in a private screening she attended in December 2013. For an alternative documentary treatment of the subject, see Jill Nichols' The Vivian Maier Mystery *(FilmBuff, 2013).]*

Maloof, a former product design student at Columbia College in Chicago and "a top real estate agent for Century 21" ("Accidental Archivist," *Demo: The Alumni Magazine of Columbia College Chicago*, Issue 20) stumbled on a treasure trove of Maier's photographs and personal artifacts at an auction in 2007. Maier, living out her last remaining months penniless in a Rogers Park one-room apartment at the time, had neglected to pay the rent on her storage unit, relegating her personal effects and life's work to the highest bidder, as it were.

Initially unaware of what he stumbled on, Maloof did what any directionless post-collegiate 20-something would do — he uploaded the images to his blog. Only after reading enthusiastic responses in the comments section, and quickly turning a tidy profit on a handful of prints he sold on eBay, did Maloof realize that the mountain of discarded images he was sitting on was a potential money printing machine, initiating his journey from real estate whiz kid to art world mogul. Maloof claims to have attempted locating Maier — eerily, in the two years between the "discovery" in 2007 and the online publication of her obituary in April 2009, Maloof could discern no footprint of Maier's on the Internet. Maloof's unleashing of the deceased Maier's work on the public raises numerous controversies, the most obvious being the fact that thousands of rolls of Maier's film remained undeveloped decades after they were exposed, and that in her lifetime she never sought attention for her work. Would she have consented to having her photographs seen by, let alone sold to, the public, or would she have preferred they disappear into obscurity, mirroring her own destiny? Maier's photographs are indeed striking — at least the ones made available to the public by Maloof, who, as the self-appointed gatekeeper of her estate, deems what is and isn't worthy of public consumption.

[Editor's note: In 2014, lawsuits filed in Cook County Court over the ownership of the images have relegated them to legal limbo for the foreseeable future.]

All this would be troubling enough. More disturbing, Maloof has fueled "Maier-Fever" through his fixation with uncovering her strange biography, placing a fetishistic

emphasis on her peculiarities, suggesting her eccentricities were a sign of deep mental instability (crazy artists sell, the crazier the better, let's face it), his necrophiliac inclusion of Maier's personal effects alongside prints of Maier's photographs in gallery exhibitions of her work, conflating the personality of the creator with the work itself – a curatorial strategy that on the one hand sells lots of prints, but on the other, poisons any clear-eyed assessment of her work's value on its own terms. In the film, she's described as a missing link between Henri Cartier-Bresson and Diane Arbus. Maier undoubtedly was aware of the output of these giants of photography. Equally certain, these masters knew nothing of the anonymous chronicler of Chicago's gritty street life in the 1950s. Which raises the question: Is it even possible to label an artist a "missing link" when no one on either end of the chain knew of her work or that she even existed? Undoubtedly –

[Ed. note: Here, the technical difficulties in the recording begin. A full 2 minutes and 47 seconds of silence pass before sound resumes.]

– same "resurrection fever" phenomenon perpetuated by the music industry, not coincidentally at a time when the Internet has brought that Goliath industry to its knees. A cursory glance at Elijah Wald's provocative reassessment of 20th-century popular music, *How The Beatles Destroyed Rock 'n' Roll: An Alternative History of American Popular Music* (Oxford University Press, 2011), reveals with high-definition clarity our culture's deep hunger for art-historical revisionism. Also, one only has to consider the recent explosion of documentary films chronicling and reassessing obscure rock musicians that were overlooked in their day: *Big Star: Nothing Can Hurt Me* (Ardent Studios, 2012), *A Band Called Death* (Drafthouse Films, 2012), and my own forthcoming film *This Record Will Kill You: The Life and Times of Gummy Rickett* (Subterranean Films, 2015). Of course, the gold standard of the rock-n-roll-resurrection-fable genre was set by the popular Oscar-winning 2012 documentary-slash-bedtime story *Searching for Sugarman*. In *Sugarman*, our contemporary Lazarus, the "lost" musician Sixto Rodriguez, is depicted as an unheard "voice of his generation" comparable to Bob Dylan.

By summoning an artist of incomparable stature, Dylan, as a point of comparison with the "unknown" Sixto, the filmmaker employs a tried and true narrative deception – similar to Maloof's comparison of Maier with Cartier-Bresson and Arbus. Juxtaposing an unknown with an icon in the context of a film lends such pronouncements an authority that has little basis in objective reality. Context here is everything: if I made

such pronouncements after putting back five Cosmopolitans at a bar, you might forgive my overzealousness as a consequence of my alcohol-fueled state – but if I stare into a camera, sober, with my credentials neatly summarized in a tasteful subtitle, the statement becomes magically endowed with weight and authority. Add to all this the fact that the filmmaker goes out of his way to paint a picture of Sixto's hopeless reclusiveness contrary to conveniently omitted facts – for example, the film omits the minor detail that Sixto Rodriguez staged at least two successful concert tours of Australia at the peak of his "obscurity."

Entombed as a working stiff and activist in inner-city Detroit, Sixto Rodriguez, our Lazarus, is raised from the dead by Jesus-in-the-guise-of-first-time-Swedish-filmmaker Malik Bendjelloul.

[Ed. note: At this point on the recording, we here stirring and muttering in the audience. The first walkout happens here.]

Bendjelloul grants Rodriguez that rare second act in American life, providing audiences with a true-life triumph-of-the-human-spirit narrative that trumps any fictional concoction Hollywood could ever dream up – precisely because it is "real." Contrast Sixto Rodriguez with the protagonist of another, albeit fictional, triumph-of-the-human-spirit film, Rocky Balboa. *Rocky* (and its sequels, though to an exponentially lesser degree) uplifts our spirits, spinning for us the comforting tale that even the most wretched and forgotten figures can earn their 45 minutes in the ring – and find true love in the process. But we know in the darkest corners of our hearts that Rocky is *not* real, and therefore his promise to us must be counterfeit. Whereas, "Sugarman" is "real," so the promise he makes us by being called forth from his tomb in Detroit and thrust into the glaring lights of Hollywood celebrity must be the genuine article.

But is it "real," especially when considering the many well-documented omissions in the film?

Both the Maier and Rodriguez films satisfy all the criteria of the "resurrection fever" phenomenon: 1) history is rewritten by inserting previously marginal figures into an accepted sweeping art-historical narrative; 2) the once bear markets for the work of Maier and Rodriguez become bullish overnight; 3) Maloof and Bendjelloul, stumbling on hidden tombs containing riches, become latter-day Howard Carters *[Ed. note: Howard Carter, British archaeologist, "discovered" the tomb of King Tut in 1922. Questions remain to this day whether or not Carter stole artifacts from the tomb and smuggled them back to England prior to its "official" opening. See: Crossland, David. "Howard Carter 'stole from the tomb of Tutankhamen.'" The National. January 21, 2010]*; and 4) both tales are ominously successful in casting the resurrection narrative spell on audiences.

It is this fourth impulse – crafting the contemporary resurrection narrative – that is the chief preoccupation of this talk and its aim to illuminate the plays of Javier C. Before addressing the plays in question, it's worth taking a moment to revisit the West's original resurrection narrative – Jesus' restoration of life to the dead Lazarus – as told in Chapter 11 in the Gospel of John.

[Ed. note: At this point in the recording, audible groans and mutterings are heard coming from the audience. More walkouts.]

Jesus arrives to Bethany four days after the death of Lazarus. Mary and Martha, Lazarus' sisters, mourn his death and tell Jesus, "Lord, if you had been here my brother would not have died." Jesus weeps, and asks the women to lead him to Lazarus' burial place. At first Martha resists Jesus' request that they remove the stone ("Lord, by now there will be a stench; he has been dead for four days!") to which Jesus responds: "Did I not tell you that if you believe you will see the glory of God?" After removing the stone, uttering a prayer, and calling out to the dead man, Lazarus emerges confused, bleary eyed, perhaps a little cross from having been stirred from eternal sleep, but alive, nonetheless. This climactic action provides definitive proof that Jesus is Messiah, adding an army of former doubters and haters to the ranks of his small following of true believers. The act also serves as the straw that broke the camel's back: learning of

this deed and the popularity it yielded for Jesus, the Pharisees conclude that the vagabond teacher and rabble rouser must be rubbed out, precipitating –

[Ed. note: Here, the technical difficulties interrupt the recording. A full three minutes and seventeen seconds of silence pass before it resumes.]

– contours and meaning of this narrative in a contemporary context, it is not enough only to consider the story's actual content, it is essential to undertake a rigorous analysis of what is *missing* from it. The central narrative abyss lies in the question: Who is Lazarus? Aside from the fact that Lazarus and his sisters loved Jesus and were devoted acolytes to his mission, why is *he*, of all the Israelites who died that week, chosen for resurrection? Remember: this is not just any run-of-the-mill miracle – it's THE miracle that precipitates the Passion. It is the key to both Jesus' and, paradoxically, Lazarus', attainment of immortality. Lazarus' name resonates through the ages, yet you would be hard pressed to find a more passive protagonist in all of literature – there is no indication that he did anything remarkable to deserve this distinction. For the narrative to have meaning in a contemporary cultural-historical context, this omission must be corrected. In other words, the contemporary Lazarus must possess some cultural worth to justify the act of resurrection. In Vivian Maier's case, her cultural worth lay in the 100,000 plus negatives she left behind. In the case of Sixto Rodriguez, he owes his cultural currency to his two albums, *Cold Fact* (1970) and *After the Fact* (1971). Though largely ignored at the time of their creation, both artists' creative output served as the equivalent of a small sum of money deposited in a long-term, high-interest IRA. But what did Lazarus ever produce?

And what of Jesus? How does the modern cultural historian transpose His through-line as described in John to fit the contemporary resurrection narrative? First, Jesus' motives in John must be scrutinized carefully, and second, those motives must find distinct, convincing and concrete contemporary parallels in order for them to be of any use in this present inquiry. Even the most cursory reading of John begs the question: if Jesus has demonstrated his healing abilities *prior* to the death of Lazarus, why does he show up four days *after* his death, as opposed to appearing sooner? Clearly Jesus had a masterfully intuitive – albeit primitive – understanding of the high-impact, well-timed media event. Yes, he could have shown up in Bethany and healed Lazarus as he writhed in agony on his deathbed. But that would have downgraded the healing to lesser miracle status, when circumstances necessitated a more decisive –

[Ed. note: Here, the technical difficulties interrupt the recording again, this time for 37 seconds.]

– crucifixion became the endgame. To connect this to contemporary manifestations of "resurrection fever" one might scoff – Maloof and Bendjelloul were hardly crucified for resurrecting Vivian Maier and Sixto Rodriguez – it would be the apex of absurdity to equate receiving an Oscar with the physical agony of crucifixion. However, both Oscar victory and crucifixion assure the recipients a measure of immortality, the difference being only with regard to scale. *[Ed. note: This speech was delivered five months prior to Bendjelloul's suicide in May, 2014, and a year prior to Maloof's Oscar nomination for his Maier documentary.]* Filling in the omissions of Lazarus as recounted in John, the contemporary resurrection narrative takes on the contours and simplicity of a folk tale, but promises near endless malleability depending on whose hands the story is in.

The narrative goes something like this:

1. Artist creates remarkable work.

2. Artist launches remarkable work into marketplace.

3. Marketplace responds to remarkable work with indifference.

4. Inconclusive speculation by artist: marketplace indifference stems from a) work being ahead of its time; b) poor marketing strategy on part of those responsible for disseminating work to public; c) ignorance/complacency/conservatism/insider-y-ness of cultural industry and audience it claims to serve; d) plain, old-fashioned rotten luck. Lurking in the shadows, a hidden "e," which artist only entertains during darkest hours, usually under influence of alcohol or narcotics: work was not remarkable to begin with.

5. Artist makes attempt at second go-round believing market will get it right this time. In doing so, not only will they gain recognition for new work, original work will be rediscovered and recognized as remarkable.

6. Repeat steps 2, 3 and 4. Add to step 4: f) God hates them.

7. Artist concludes world conspiracy against them. They either: a) continue to make work which, to inflict punishment to an indifferent world, tends towards aggressive, alienating and/or hostile to public, therefore unmarketable (see my forthcoming documentary film on Gummy Rickett's post-"She's Like Jesus" work); b) abandon art-making activities to join labor force, often pursuing employment some would consider "degrading" or "beneath them"; c) commit suicide (either literally or figuratively).

8. Artist and work languish for years in obscurity.

9. After lengthy period of time – often a generation or two – work rediscovered.

10. Discoverer(s) shocked that work of such quality failed to reach large audience.

11. Discoverer becomes evangelist for work.

12. Discoverer crafts formulation: SRLA=ARA–CPA–UM x MTCWUO. (Translation: Successfully Resurrected Lost Artist equals Accomplished Revered Artist minus Critical and Popular Acclaim minus Units Moved multiplied by Mystique That Comes With Unjust Obscurity.)

13. Acolytes of new church search for creator of work, often forced to untangle myths of artist's death/suicide on stage, and bear witness to artist's unjust relegation to economic situation far beneath perceived worth of artist.

14. Acolytes' plan to exhume artist and work meets with initial reluctance on artist's part (they had a rough time the first go round, they're not keen on reopening old wounds).

15. Acolytes overcome artist's resistance with delivery of concrete evidence of success of work (reviews, unpaid royalties, Google search hits).

16. Artist emerging from private Dark Age into public Renaissance experiences initial trauma – similar to Lazarus' eyes burned by sunlight when emerging from the lightless tomb – that people actually care.

17. Audience clamors for piece of artist.

18. Unspoken question hovers: is newfound interest result of genuine recognition of high quality art that slipped through the cracks? Or does interest stem from resurrection mythology surrounding artist and artist's contemporary discoverer's marketing skill.

19. Artist becomes force in marketplace for period of time. Reputation grows or wanes depending on generosity of time, fickleness of marketplace and ability to create new work matching or superseding quality of original.

20. Time determines whether artist and work earns permanent place in accepted historical trajectory of form.

Which brings us to the curious case of the Colombian-born, American playwright Javier C. *[Ed. note – at this point on the tape we hear a heckler utter "finally" loud enough to be picked up by Dr. Tanner's microphone.]* Who is this would-be Lazarus of the American Theater?

Little is known about Javier C. The first attempt to chronicle his work and life appears in the aforementioned *The Mystique of Failure: A Reconsideration of Modern American Drama Through its Lost Plays and Playwrights* by my mentor, the late Dr. Emiliano Kurtz. For those not familiar with Kurtz's monumental work, it is the outcome of a two-decade study. Having served as Kurtz's graduate assistant during the writing of his magnum opus, I can personally attest to the rigor, intensity and obsessiveness he brought to the project. Most analogous studies of the field measuring the health of the American Theater focus on widely produced, critically acclaimed and otherwise successful plays and playwrights. Kurtz's innovation was to dive head first into the immense body of American dramatic literature that never saw the light of day, believing those neglected works – or what Kurtz called "The Shadow Cannon" or, jokingly, "The Theater That Never Was" – would reveal the true state of American playwriting, and, borrowing from Burckhardt, "lead to essentially different conclusions" than more traditional studies. Kurtz's work was painstaking: from 1985 to his death in 2008, he amassed and catalogued 270,000 plus unproduced manuscripts written by American playwrights, wrote brief but penetrating critical analyses for thousands of works, capsule biographies on as many authors as he could find, and a sobering statistical analysis that concluded that a mere .063% of plays written each year in the period of the study were ever seen by the public on any meaningful scale.

Like most of the dramatists chronicled in *Mystique*, Javier C. left virtually no imprint on the American theater during his lifetime, let alone a footprint on the civilization that spawned him. Having read and re-read the entire body of Javier C.'s extant work over the years, it remains unclear to me why Javier C. became Kurtz's White Whale. Unlocking the source of Kurtz's fixation still escapes me. The entry in the book reads:

"Little is known about the Colombian born, American playwright Javier C. Born in Bogota in 1958, he emigrated with his mother to the United States in 1958 following the murder of his father during the waning days of *La Violencia*, the political civil war in Colombia that claimed 200,000 lives between 1948 and 1958. Settling in Jackson –

[Ed. note: Here, more technical difficulties interrupt the recording. Two minutes and forty nine seconds of silence pass before it resumes.]

– dropped out of NYU, forming a collective with fellow students that staged two of his plays for a total of six performances in 1981 at Club 57 on St. Mark's Place – (where

I'm told he frequently attended on Monster Movie Tuesdays and Model World of Glue Nights, when patrons would build plastic model airplanes, set them on fire and get high off the burning glue).

During that time, he married visual artist and theatrical designer Valerie Marcks. According to several people who knew them, they had two children, although others insist they only had one.

"Documentation exists in the archives of The Public Theatre that the collective was commissioned by Joseph Papp in 1988 to write a play. According to the commission contract, the play would 'explore appropriation of Latino culture in the US through the lens of exiles at the margins of the culture.' No evidence exists that they ever completed the commission.

"From 1988 through 2007, details of Javier C.'s life remain sketchy. It can be inferred that he moved around quite a bit, spending stints in NY, Chicago, Chippewa Falls, Wisconsin, Mexico City, and finally Gallup, New Mexico where he spent the final year of his life.

"Body of work includes: 3 full length —

[Ed. note: Technical difficulties. Seven minutes and four seconds of silence pass before it resumes. From here to the end of the recording, the device captures only fragments of the remainder of the talk. Brackets and ellipses ([. . .]) indicate where the recording ceases.]

— it is likely apocryphal."

Of all [....] —rgotten American Dramati [...], why has this man's work [....] been tapped for resurrection? [...] —pecially when none of his work meets [...] the four criteria I outlined before?

[Ed. note: Here the recording goes silent for three minutes and twenty-seven seconds.]

Who owns the legacy [...] of Javier and his work? [...] Despite dubious claims to his discovery by Professor Carlo—

[Ed. note: Here the recording goes silent for two minutes and eleven seconds.]

— so-called "Dramatic Reconstructions," [...] so called [...] really amount to nothing more than forgeries and [...] file cabinet? An intern named "Nicole"? Really? [....] owes his resurrection not to [...] but to [...] painstaking work of the late [...] sexual exploitation [...] which I would categorically de— [...] unfounded accusations [...] devoted the last two [...] of his caree —

[Ed. note: Here the recording goes silent for four minutes and twenty-three seconds.]

Murillo's [...] vampiric, fetishistic [....]

— appropriation and fascists —

[....]

— genuine artistic preoccupations or masturb—

[...]

—that pale in comparison to —

[...]

— grandiosity, delusion —

[...]

— like flogging dead horses —

[...]

— exhume and fuck a corpse because all that he —

[...]

—f can do nothing [...] abou—

[...]

—in the end twice — or perhaps thrice — buried.

[Ed. note: At this point the recording device ceases to function.]

379 Jacob Burckhardt (1818-1897) on his way to a lecture at the University of Basel, 1890. Burckhardt, regarded as a pioneer in the discipline of cultural history, is best known for *The Civilization of the Renaissance in Italy* (1860).

380 Illustration depicting the murder of Ingram Frazer by Elizabethan playwright Christopher Marlowe - a bold example of historical revisionism given Frazer murdered Marlowe. The illustration appears in the 1895 novel *It Was Marlowe* by W.G. Ziegler, which makes the case that Marlowe faked his death in order to write under the pseudonym "William Shakespeare." Image in the Public Domain.

The Temple of Baalbeck in present-day Lebanon. Romans worshipped the Gods Jupiter, Venus and Bacchus at this site. In their own act of revisionism, they superimposed these Romn deities onto existing iconography depicting indigenous deities Hadad and Atargatis.

Asmat ancestor skull from the De Young Museum in San Francisco. The Asmat people of southwestern New Guinea preserve and worship the skulls of deceased ancestors, decorating them with feathers, seeds and carved sea shell rings. Image in the Public Domain.

381 April 22, 1955, Central Park, a vintage color transparency of a portrait of Vivian Maier from the Ron Slattery Collection. Pamela Bannos, artist, researcher, Maier scholar and professor at Northwestern University originally shot this image in color, noting, "It's quite extraordinary that Maier, most well known for her black and white work, was shooting this color transparency film at that time." Courtesy Pamela Bannos.

"Finding Vivian Maier: Chicago Street Photographer" exhibition in Chicago, 2011.

382 Apartment building in Rogers Park neighborhood where Vivian Maier lived in the final years of her life. Photo by Carlos Murillo

Park bench in Rogers Park Beach where Vivian Maier was known to sit afternoons. Photo by Carlos Murillo.

383 Sixto Rodriguez live in concert in 2014.

384 Harry Burton's legendary photo of Howard Carter (kneeling), an unknown Egyptian worker and Arthur Callender before the entrance to the burial shrine of Tutankhamen's tomb. The photo, taken on January 24, 1924, is almost definitely a recreation/staging of the actual opening of the shrine which, according to Carter's diary, took place the day before. Public Domain, New York Times Archive.

385 Etching of Christ raising Lazarus from his tomb by Friedrich August Ludy (1823-1866) from a painting by Johann Friedrich Overbeck (1789-1869). From Wellcome Images.

389 A legendary nightclub located on St. Mark's Place in NY City, Club 57 was a hub for performance and visual artists, musicians and punk scenesters from it's origins in the mid-70s to it's demise in 1983. Gary Winter archive.

Valerie Marcks, theatrical designer and sculptor, who was married to Javier C. in 1982 and divorced in 1990. Photo Courtesy Amanda Powell.

ACKNOWLEDGEMENTS AND CREDITS

Over the last eight years, *The Javier Plays* has occupied a significant part, if not the bulk, of my creative life. In that time, I have accumulated significant debts to many family members, friends, collaborators, organizations and funders who helped me along the way. My gratitude runs deep.

First and foremost, I want to express my deepest thanks to my wife, Lisa Portes, and our two children, Eva Rose and Carlitos. Without their love, encouragement, sense of humor and support, these plays would not exist. They've patiently endured numerous periods of absence (and absent mindedness), but embrace me with warmth and kindness when I return. They provide inspiration, respite, reality checks and soft landings when I am in the thick of my work. Scary to imagine what my life would be without them. I love and cherish them dearly.

In 2007, I was granted the gift of a seven-year residency at New Dramatists in New York City – *The Javier Plays* were born and raised there. My residency kicked off with a reading of the ten-page *Fragment of a Paper Airplane* at the Class of 2014 Welcome Celebration, and culminated three months prior to graduation with a weeklong Creativity Fund workshop presentation of the entire 350 page trilogy. In between, the plays were conceived and nurtured, grew up and found their legs through The Creativity Fund, PlayTime, and many conversations with the extraordinary resident playwrights, staff and extended artistic family of the organization. I want to name names: Todd London for keeping true to his mensch-y promise on day one that New Dramatists was our artistic home and that it existed so we could pursue even our wildest ideas; Emily Morse, for her tireless support, dramaturgical insight, genius for connecting artists with the right collaborators and her artistry in creating spaces in which artists can do their best work; John Steber, a true alchemist who innately senses the heartbeat of a character on the page and unfailingly finds the actor whose heartbeat matches that rhythm – even when, astonishingly, the character has yet to be written; Joel Ruark, who always welcomes you home with an embrace, a fantastic story and, from time to time, a glass of the best Kentucky bourbon; and everyone on the New Dramatists staff past and present: Morgan Allen, Tiffany Kleeman Baran, Christie Brown, Erin Detrick, Jennie Greer,

Rachel Hutt, Ron Riley, the Board of Directors and the dozens of interns that cycle in and out – each individual at New Dramatists plays a vital role in making the church a true sanctuary for American playwrights. I also want to thank my peer playwrights in the Class of 2014 – Eugenie Chan, Sarah Hammond, Taylor Mac, Julie Marie Myatt, J.T. Rogers, Deborah Stein, and John Walch – their singular and inspired voices, their generosity and humanity, made me a better person and writer for having walked alongside them over seven years.

I've been blessed to have my friend and agent Antje Oegel in my corner for almost a decade. Our paths crossed at a static point in my professional life – her infectious positive energy, passion for the work, her honesty, collaborative spirit and kindness reenergized me then, and still does to this day. When I approached Antje with the idea of doing a book that wasn't a typical three-play anthology, but a hybrid work containing drama, autobiography, literary criticism, memoir, fiction, and a load of images, she understood it, embraced it and set the wheels in motion to make it happen. The form of this book and its publication stems directly from Antje's out-of-the-box thinking and visionary approach to disseminating her writers' work.

I am extremely grateful for Karinne Keithley Syers, who performed heroic work in editing and designing this volume. Her attention to detail, patience and artistry are evident on every page. It was a long process piecing the world of this book together, and I couldn't have asked for a more generous and tireless collaborator.

My colleagues and students at The Theatre School of DePaul University, especially Dean John Culbert, Associate Dean, Dean Corrin, and Chair of Theatre Studies, Barry Brunetti, have been a strong supporters and champions not only my work within the school, but my creative endeavors outside of it. On numerous occasions, *The Javier Plays* took me away for extended stretches of time from my day-to-day duties at The Theatre School – they've often bent over backwards to accommodate, and always have been nothing but generous and kind about it. I'm grateful for my students, who keep me honest – I feel strongly that if I'm not in the thick of my own writing while guiding them through their own processes, I really have no business being there. They challenge me and I learn as much from them as they learn from me.

I try to impart to my students the idea that each play they write is a unique organism with its own origin story, DNA, life support system, nervous system, chemical and psychological makeup. Being distinct organisms, each play follows a very specific journey through its life cycle. This applies to all three of the plays that make up *The*

Javier Plays – each one had its own unique travelogue from their origins to landing in the pages of this book.

The Goodman Theatre provided instrumental early support when they awarded me The Ofner Commission in 2007 to write *Diagram of a Paper Airplane*. I am especially grateful to Tanya Palmer, the Goodman's Director of New Play Development, who championed my work to Artistic Director Bob Falls. Sarah Jane DeHoff and William DeHoff provided valuable writing time on *Diagram* when they hosted a retreat for New Dramatists Playwrights at their beautiful camp near Lake Placid, NY in 2008. Philip Himberg and Christopher Hibma provided invaluable support when they selected *Diagram* as a project of the Sundance Theatre Lab in 2009. They assembled a remarkable team of collaborators to explore the play in the majestic setting of the Sundance Resort: director Eric Rosen, who wowed me with the razor sharp intelligence he brought to the room, Mame Hunt, a dramaturg of tremendous insight, a fierce cast that included Giancarlo Esposito, Laura Innes, Maximilian Osinski, Larry Pine and Maria Thayer. A number of other institutions supported *Diagram* over the years: The William Inge Theatre Festival, the Playwrights Realm in NYC, Forum Theatre in DC, the Kennedy Center's Page-to-Stage Festival, Chicago Dramatists and the National New Play Network. There's a long list of actors and directors to thank: Raphael Baez, David Greenspan, Elizabeth Morton, Mary Shultz, Liam Torres, Larry Neumann Jr., Lisa Tejero, Henry Godinez, Mando Alvarado, Michael Cumpsty, Teresa Avia Lim, Joyce O'Connor, Janet Ulrich Brooks, Ian Paul Custer, Ricardo Gutierrez, Kay Kron, Rick Foucheux, Juan Villa, T.Ryder Smith, Betty Gilpin, Lou Moreno, Joe Tippett, Lori Wilner, Jerry Ruiz, Shade Murray, Jenny McConnell Frederick and Kip Fagan.

A Thick Description of Harry Smith was originally commissioned by Berkeley Repertory Theatre in 2008 thanks to the advocacy of Madeleine Oldham, their Director of New Play Development. I am deeply indebted to two organizations for subsequent support: New Dramatists, which presented two Creativity Fund workshops of the play in 2009 and again in 2014, and Page 73 Productions, which produced a workshop production at The Culture Project in New York City in July 2012. The folks at P73, Liz Jones, Michael Walkup and Asher Richelli, are fantastic producers, genuine advocates for adventurous new work and kind spirits – I'm grateful for the leap they took to make this project a reality. The brilliant Kip Fagan has been a key collaborator, having helmed all three of these incarnations of the piece. The play is so much better for all his insight, imagination, humor and the effortless way he handles a room full of larger than life personalities. I'm also grateful for the crack design team Kip assembled for the P73 version: Seth Reiser (sets and lights), Jessica Pabst (costumes) and Daniel Kluger (sound) fashioned a rich, immersive world that transformed the basement space at The Culture Project into the Medicine Show-Fantasia that lives inside Harry's mind. The extraordinary actor and musician Lucas Papaelias has been an indispensible force in the life of this play through all its incarnations. He brings his heart and soul into playing the role of Marlowe – to the point where I can't make the distinction between their voices. Lucas crafted explosive arrangements for the music, making old folk songs sound like they were written yesterday, and led the band with ferocity and passion. I'm especially in awe of him for putting 100 percent of himself into the P73 version, when he was simultaneously putting 100 percent into performing *Once* eight times a week on Broadway. The play has been blessed to have amazing actors and musicians breathe life into it from the beginning: David Patrick Kelly, Larry Neumann, Jr., Sean Patrick Reilly, T. Ryder Smith, Birgit Huppuch, Kate Ferber, Joe Jung, Joe Tippett, Chris Sullivan, Paul Whitty, Ray Rizzo, Matthew Stadelmann, Kellie Overbey, Alfredo Narciso, Gabe Ruiz, Andrew Gallant, Stephanie Chavara, Sandra Delgado and Aaron Rustebakke. I also wish to thank Peter Taub, the Director of Performance Programs at Chicago's Museum of Contemporary Art, and Anthony Moseley, artistic director of Chicago's Collaboraction Theatre, for co-presenting a concert version of *Harry Smith* in the summer of 2011, directed by that force of nature, Michael John Garcés. Lastly, many thanks to The Watermill Center and the NYC Summer Play Festival for providing me with a two-week residency in winter 2011 to finish the play.

I thank the brilliant Polly Carl, former Director of New Play Development at Steppenwolf Theatre in Chicago, for bringing my work to the attention of Artistic Director Martha Lavey, which lead to a commission to write *Your Name Will Follow You Home*. In December 2012, I arrived at New Dramatists for their annual Playtime Festival with a thick folder containing the gigantic, incoherent, unfinished mess I'd been making over the previous year. I left the building two weeks later with the complete version of the play thanks to the collaborative brilliance and generosity of Kip Fagan, Raúl Castillo, Christy Escobar, Polly Lee, Greg McFadden, Hanna Moon, Bobby Plasencia and Michael Tisdale. Steppenwolf held two workshops of the play in 2013, culminating in a performance at the First Look Festival of New Work, directed by Dexter Bullard and featuring a superb cast including Cliff Chamberlain, Sandra Delgado, Yasen Peyankov, Adam Poss, Amanda Powell, Sarah Price and Juan Villa. I also want to thank Jaime Castaneda for including the play in Atlantic Theatre Company's Latino Mix Fest in 2013. *Your Name* received the 2013 MetLife Nuestros Voces Award from the legendary Repertorio Español in NYC, Robert Federico, Executive Producer. In November 2014, the play received its Spanish language world premiere off-Broadway at Repertorio, translated by Caridad Svich and directed by Jose Zayas. The excellent cast included

David Crommet, Luis Carlos de La Lombana, Ana Grosse, Gerardo Gudiño, Soraya Padrao, Bobby Plasencia, Thallis Santesteban González and Jerry Soto, with scenic, costume and projection design by Leni Méndez, lights by Eduardo Navas and sound by David Margolin Lawson.

I wish to acknowledge several folks who were instrumental in researching the real life backstory of *Your Name*.

Alicia Hernández, Emeritus Professor of English at Rio Hondo College in California, was immensely helpful in bringing this play to life. I came into contact with her when I stumbled on a riveting short memoir she wrote chronicling her 13 year correspondence with Danny Santiago in a hard-to-find collection of essays, *Life Writing / Writing Lives* (Bette H. Kirschtein, Ed., Malabar, FL: Krieger, 2001.) Alicia provided me with a rich account of their correspondence, as well as examples of letters exchanged, photos, newspaper articles, and a wealth of stories about her life and relationship to Danny. Over time we've developed a rewarding friendship stemming from our own regular correspondence through snail and e-mail. I was deeply moved when she traveled from California to Chicago to see the Steppenwolf reading, and again when she brought a huge contingent of family and friends to a staged reading of the play at Pasadena's Theatre @ Boston Court in November 2014. She is currently writing a book-length memoir of her friendship with Danny Santiago / Daniel James – I can't wait to read it.

I nod to Eric F. James, a family relation of Jesse James, who I met via his blog "Leaves of Gas." Eric is the author of *Jesse James: Soul Liberty*, a multi-volume saga chronicling the James Family. Volume I of the history, *Behind the Family Wall of Stigma & Silence*, includes a highly informative chapter detailing the life and times of Daniel Lewis James. Eric James was generous enough to share his work with me prior to the book's publication, as well as valuable insights into the James family history. In our conversations, we discovered common ground: Eric grew up in the south side of Chicago, a few addresses away on the same street where I live in the Bridgeport neighborhood with my wife and children.

A word of appreciation for journalist Jonah Raskin, who provided me with the raw transcript of an interview he conducted with Daniel James after his "outing" in 1984, as well as a few examples of their correspondence. The resulting article, "The Man Who Would be Danny Santiago" appeared in the *San Francisco Bay Guardian* in 1984. A hand-written postcard he included in the package he sent to me read: "Facts are all well and good, but whatever happened to imagination?" Vital words when I needed them most.

There are a bunch of folks who have, more generally, in both past and present, and in both large and small ways, kept me afloat in my life and work: my father Francisco Murillo, my late mother Minerva Murillo, my siblings Frank Murillo, Mario Murillo and Susan O'Brien, my in-laws Nancy and Doug Kuhnel, Alejandro Portes and Patricia Fernandez-Kelly, Mark Sanders, Andrew Dausch, Brian Lennon, Todd Lauterbach, Robert Steel, Tamsen Wolff, Lisa D'Amour, Jennifer Rudin, Bonnie Metzgar, Stuart Flack, Morgan Jenness, Robert Woodruff, Maria Irene Fornes, Paul Rivadue, Dr. Clayton, Ms. Jural, and David Bowie.

Finally – Robert Panico, a kid I went to middle and high school with and barely knew. I have not seen you since graduation in 1989. I have no idea where you are or who you have become. For reasons unknown to me, you randomly popped in my head summer of 2007, and in doing so you set this whole beast in motion. Thanks, man. I hope it got better.

—Carlos Murillo, Chicago, June 2015

CARLOS MURILLO is the recipient of a 2015 Doris Duke Impact Award in performing arts. His most recent work, *Killing of a Gentleman Defender*, was commissioned by The Goodman Theatre in Chicago, where he was a member of the 2014-15 Playwrights Unit. His work has been seen widely throughout the US and Europe. Plays include: *The Javier Plays, dark play or stories for boys, Augusta and Noble, Mayday Mayday Tuesday, Unfinished American Highwayyscape #9 & 32, Mimesophobia, A Human Interest Story or The Gory Details and All, Offspring of the Cold War, Schadenfreude, The Patron Saint of the Nameless Dead, Near Death Experiences with Leni Riefenstahl, Never Whistle While You're Pissing* and *Subterraneans*. They have been seen at venues throughout the US and in Europe, including Theatre der Stadt Aalen in Germany, the Vigszinhaz in Budapest, Hungary, The State Youth Theatre in Vilnius, Lithuania, Actors Theatre of Louisville, NYC Summer Play Festival, P73, En Garde Arts, Soho Rep, Repertorio Español, Salt Lake Acting Company, Adventure Stage in Chicago, Collaboraction, Walkabout Theatre, Theatre @ Boston Court, Circle X, Son of Semele, the University of Iowa International Writers Program, the Hangar Theatre Lab, The Group in Seattle, Red Eye in Minneapolis, the Sundance Theatre Lab, The Playwrights' Center and others. His plays have been commissioned by The Goodman, The Public, Berkeley Rep, Playwrights Horizons and South Coast Rep, and published by Dramatists Play Service, Playscripts, Smith & Kraus and Broadway Play Publishing. Awards include The Frederick Loewe Award from New Dramatists, the MetLife Nuestros Voces Award from Repetrorio Español, the Ofner Prize from The Goodman Theatre, the Otis Guernsey Award from the William Inge Theatre Festival, two National Latino Playwriting Awards from Arizona Theatre Company and a Jerome Fellowship from The Playwrights' Center. Carlos was a resident playwright at New Dramatists from 2007-14, and currently is an Associate Professor and Head of Playwriting at The Theatre School of DePaul University. He lives in south side of Chicago with his wife, the director Lisa Portes, and their two children Eva Rose and Carlos Pablo.

Titles from 53rd State Press 2007-2016

The Book of the Dog // Karinne Keithley

Joyce Cho Plays // Joyce Cho

No Dice // Nature Theater of Oklahoma

Rambo Solo // Nature Theater of Oklahoma

When You Rise Up // Miguel Gutierrez

Montgomery Park, or Opulence // Karinne Keithley

Crime or Emergency // Sibyl Kempson

Off the Hozzle // Rob Erickson

A Map of Virtue and Black Cat Lost // Erin Courtney

Pig Iron: Three Plays // Pig Iron Theatre Company

The Mayor of Baltimore and Anthem // Kristen Kosmas

Ich, KürbisGeist and The Secret Death of Puppets // Sibyl Kempson

Soulographie: Our Genocides // Erik Ehn

Life and Times: Episode 1 // Nature Theater of Oklahoma

Life and Times: Episode 2 // Nature Theater of Oklahoma

Life and Times: Episodes 3 &4 // Nature Theater of Oklahoma

The 53rd State Occasional No. 1 // Ed. Paul Lazar

Seagull (Thinking of you) // Tina Satter

There There // Kristen Kosmas

Another Telepathic Thing // Big Dance Theater

Another Tree Dance // Karinne Keithley Syers

Let Us Now Praise Susan Sontag // Sibyl Kempson

Pop Star Series // Neal Medlyn

The Javier Plays // Carlos Murillo

Dance Pamphlet No. 1: Self Made Man Man Made Land // Ursula Eagly

Dance Pamphlet No. 2: Dance by Letter // Annie-B Parson

53rdstatepress.org

PORTUGUESE
TRAVELMATE

compiled by
LEXUS

with
Mike Harland
and
Alberto Luis de Moura Rodrigues

Chambers

First published 1982
by Richard Drew Publishing Ltd
Reprinted 1982, 1984
Second edition 1986
Third edition 1988
Reprinted 1989, 1990

This edition published 1991 by W & R Chambers Ltd,
43–45 Annandale Street, Edinburgh EH7 4AZ

**British Library Cataloguing in
Publication Data**

A catalogue record for this book is
available from the British Library

ISBN 0-550-22005-4

Printed and bound in Great Britain by
Cox & Wyman Ltd

YOUR TRAVELMATE
gives you one single easy-to-use list of useful
words and phrases to help you communicate in
Portuguese.

Built into this list are:
– Travel Tips with facts and figures which provide
 valuable information.
– Portuguese words you'll see on signs and notices
– typical replies to some of the things you might
 want to say.

There is a menu reader on pages 70–71 and
numbers and the Portuguese alphabet are given
on pages 127–128.

Your TRAVELMATE also tells you how to
pronounce Portuguese. Just read the
pronunciations as though they were English and
you will communicate – although you might not
sound like a native speaker.

One special sound:
j is like the second consonant in 'measure' or
'seizure'.
And uh should be pronounced as in English 'a' or
the 'u' in 'butter'.
Vowels given in italics show which part of a word
to stress.

Where two translations are given the second is
the feminine form.

a, an um, uma [oom, *oo*muh]
    200 escudos a litre du*z*entos escudos o litro
    [doo*z*entoosh shk*oo*d*oo*z' oo leetroo]
abdomen o abdómen [ab*d*omeng]
aberto open
aboard a bordo [bordoo]
about: is he about? está aqui? [shtah ak*ee*]
    about 15 cerca de quinze [s*ai*r-kuh duh k*ee*nz]
    about 2 o'clock por volta das duas [poor
    v*o*ltuh dush d*oo*-ush]
above em cima [eng s*ee*muh]
    above that em cima disso [. . . d*ee*soo]
abroad no estrangeiro [noo shtranj*a*yroo]
absolutely! com certeza! [kong serteh-zuh]
accelerator o acelerador [assu*l*luh-ruh-d*o*r]
accept aceitar [assay-t*a*r]
accident um acidente [asseed*e*nt]
    there's been an accident houve um acidente
    [ove oom asseedent]
» *TRAVEL TIP: EEC reciprocal health agreement*
    applies; see **hospital**
accommodation o alojamento [alojuh-mentoo]
    we need accommodation for three
    queríamos alojamento para três pessoas [kree-
    amooz alojuh-mentoo para tresh pessoh-ush]
» *TRAVEL TIP: apart from hotels, there is also a*
    cheaper category called 'pensão' which is quite
    adequate and provides meals
accurate certo [s*ai*rtoo]
acenda as luzes headlights on
ache uma dor [dor]
    my back aches tenho dor nas costas [t*e*nyoo
    dor nush k*o*shtush]

....

A.C.P. = Automóvel Clube de Portugal *like AA or RAC*

across através de [atraveh duh]
    how do we get across? como atravessamos? [komoo atravsuh-moosh]

adaptor um adaptador [adaptuh-dor]

address o endereço [endereh-soo]
    will you give me your address? quer dar-me o seu endereço? [kair darmuh oo seh-oo . . .]

admission a entrada [entrah-duh]

advance: can we book in advance? podemos marcar lugar antecipadamente? [poodeh-moosh merkar loogar antusseepah-duh-ment]

advert o anúncio [anoons-yoo]

afraid: I'm afraid I don't know lamento, mas não sei [lamentoo, mush nowng say]
    I'm afraid so lamento que sim [kuh seeng]
    I'm afraid not lamento que não

after: after you você primeiro [vosseh preemayroo]
    after 2 o'clock depois das duas [depoish dush doo-ush]

afternoon a tarde [tard]
    this afternoon esta tarde [eshtuh . . .]
    in the afternoon à tarde [ah tard]
    good afternoon boa tarde [bo-uh tard]

aftershave aftershave

again outra vez [oh-truh vesh]

against contra [kontruh]

age a idade [eedahd]
    under age menor [muh-nor]
    it takes ages leva muito tempo [levvuh mweentoo tempoo]

ago: a week ago há uma semana [ah oomuh suh-mah-nuh]
    it wasn't long ago não foi há muito tempo [nowng foy ah mweentoo-tempoo]
    how long ago was that? há quanto tempo aconteceu? [ah kwantoo tempoo . . .]

agree: I agree concordo [kong-kordoo]

it doesn't agree with me faz-me mal [fash–]
água potável *drinking water*
air o ar [ahr]
  by air de avião [davvee-*o*wng]
  by airmail por avião
  air conditioning ar condicionado [ar
  kondeess-yoon*a*h-doo]
airport o aeroporto [a-*a*irooportoo]
alarm o alarme [al*a*hrm]
  alarm clock o despertador [dushpairtuh-d*o*r]
alcohol o álcool [*a*lkwol]
  is it alcoholic? tem álcool [teng . . .]
Alfândega *Customs*
alive vivo [*vee*voo]
  is he still alive? ainda está vivo? [a-*ee*nduh
  shtah *vee*voo]
all todo [*toh*-doo]
  all night toda a noite [t*o*h-dah noyt]
  that's all wrong está tudo errado [shtah
  t*oo*doo err*a*h-doo]
  all right muito bem [mw*ee*ntoo beng]
  that's all é tudo [eh t*oo*doo]
  thank you – not at all obrigado – não tem de
  quê [oh-brig*a*h-doo – nowng teng duh keh]
allergic: I'm allergic to sou alérgico a [soh
  al*ai*rjikoo . . .]
allowed permitido [permeet*ee*doo]
  is it allowed? é permitido? [eh . . .]
  allow me permita-me [perm*ee*ta-muh]
almost quase [kw*a*hz]
alone só
  did you come here alone? veio só?
  [v*a*yoo . . .]
  leave me alone deixe-me em paz [d*a*ysh-muh
  eng pash]
already já
also também [tambeng]
alternator o alternador [altair-nad*o*r]
although embora [emb*o*r-uh]
alto *halt*

altogether totalmente [tootalment]
    what does that make altogether? a quanto
    monta tudo isso? [uh kwantoo montuh toodoo
    ee-soo]
aluga-se to let
always sempre [sempruh]
a.m. da manhã [duh munyang]
    » *TRAVEL TIP: official times are usually expressed
    by 24 hour system*
ambassador o embaixador [embye-shuh-dor]
ambulance ambulância [amboolanss-ya]
    get an ambulance! chame uma ambulância!
    [shahm oomuh . . .]
    » *TRAVEL TIP: dial 115; often quicker and cheaper
    by taxi*
America a América do Norte [. . . doo nort]
American norte-americano [nortee-amerikah-
    noo]
among entre [entruh]
amps amperes [ampeh-rush]
    15 amp fuse um fusível de quinze amperes
    [foozeevel duh keenz . . .]
anchor a âncora [ankooruh]
and e [ee]
angry zangado [zangah-doo]
    I'm very angry estou muito zangado [shtoh
    mweentoo zangah-doo]
    please don't get angry por favor, não se irrite
    [poor fuh-vor, nowng seerreet]
animal o animal [aneemal]
ankle o tornozelo [toornoozelloo]
anniversary: it's our anniversary é o nosso
    aniversário [eh oo nosso aneeversahr-yoo]
annoy: he's annoying me está a chatear-me
    [shtah uh shut-yar-muh]
    it's very annoying que maçada! [kuh
    mussah-duh]
another: can we have another room?
    podemos ter um outro quarto? [poodeh-
    moosh tair oom oh-troo kwartoo]

another beer, please mais uma cerveja, se faz favor [myze oomuh serveh-juh, suh fash fuh-vor]

answer: what was his answer? o que respondeu? [oo kuh reshpondeh-oo]

there was no answer não houve resposta [nowng ove reshposhtuh]

antifreeze o anticongelante [anteekonjuh-lant]

any: have you got any bananas/butter? tem bananas/manteiga [teng banahnush/mantayguh]

I haven't got any não tenho [nowng tenyoo]

anybody qualquer pessoa [kwalkair pessoh-uh]

can anybody help? alguém pode ajudar? [algaing pod ajoodar]

anything qualquer coisa [kwalkair koy-zuh]

I don't want anything não quero nada [nowng kairoo nah-duh]

aperitif um aperitivo [apurreeteevoo]

apology: please accept my apologies por favor, peço-lhe desculpa [poor fuh-vor, pessoo-lyuh deshkoolpuh]

I want an apology peço uma satisfação [pessoo oomuh sateesh-fassowng]

appendicitis a apendicite [apendeeseet]

appetite o apetite [uh-peteet]

I've lost my appetite perdi o apetite [perdee oo . . .]

apple a maçã [masang]

application form uma folha de inscrição [fol-yuh deenshkree-sowng]

apricot o damasco [damashkoo]

April Abril [abreel]

aqualung garrafas de oxigénio [garrah-fush doxi-jenn-yoo]

area a zona [zoh-nuh]

arm o braço [brah-soo]

around see **about**

arrange: will you arrange a taxi/a table/ tickets? pode conseguir-me um táxi/uma

....

mesa/um bilhete [pod konsugg*ee*r-muh oom
taxi/oom m*e*h-zuh/oom beel-yet]
it's all arranged está tudo tratado [shtah
t*oo*doo tratah-doo]
arrest prender [prend*air*]
he's been arrested foi preso [foy preh-zoo]
arrival a chegada [shuh-g*a*h-duh]
arrive chegar [shuh-g*a*r]
we only arrived yesterday chegámos ontem
mesmo [shuh-g*a*mmooz *o*nteng m*e*j-moo]
art a arte [art]
art gallery a galeria de arte [gall*e*r*ee*-uh dart]
arthritis a artrite [artr*ee*t]
artificial artificial [artif*ee*ss-y*a*l]
artist o pintor [peent*o*r]
as: as quickly as you can tão depressa quanto
puder [towng duh-pressuh kw*a*ntoo pood*ai*r]
as much as you can tanto quanto puder
[t*a*ntoo kw*a*ntoo pood*ai*r]
do as I do faça como eu faço [f*a*ssuh koh- moo
eh-oo f*a*ssoo]
as you like como quiser [koh-moo keez*ai*r]
ashore: to go ashore desembarcar
[dezembark*a*r]
ashtray o cinzeiro [seenz*a*yroo]
ask: could you ask him to . . . podia pedir-lhe
para . . . [pood*ee*-uh ped*ee*r-lyuh para . . .]
I didn't ask for that não pedi isso [nowng
ped*ee* *ee*-soo]
asleep: he's still asleep está ainda a dormir
[shta uh-*ee*ndah doo-rm*ee*r]
asparagus o espargo [shp*a*rgoo]
aspirin a aspirina [ushpeer*ee*nuh]
assistant *(shop)* o empregado [empruh-g*a*h-doo]
asthma asma [*a*jma]
at: at the café no café [noo kuff*e*h]
at my hotel no meu hotel [noo m*e*h-oo o-t*e*l]
at one o'clock à uma [ah *oo*muh]
atmosphere a atmosfera
[atmoosh-f*ai*ruh]

attitude a atitude [ateet*oo*d]
attractive tentador [tent-a-d*o*r]
  I think you're very attractive penso que és
  muito atraente [pensoo kee esh mw*ee*ntoo
  atrah-ent]
aubergine a beringela [bereenjelluh]
August Agosto [ag*o*shtoo]
aunt: my aunt minha tia [m*ee*n-yuh t*ee*-uh]
Australia Austrália [owsh-tr*a*h-lee-uh]
Australian australiano [owsh-tralee-*a*h-noo]
authorities as autoridades [uz ow-toorid*a*h-
  dush]
autocarro bus (stop)
automatic *(car)* automático [ow-toom*a*tikoo]
autumn Outono [o-t*o*h-noo]
away: is it far away from here? é longe daqui?
  [eh lonj dak*ee*]
  go away! vai-te embora! [vye-tuh emb*o*ruh]
awful horrível [orr*ee*vel]
axle o eixo [*a*y-shoo]
baby o bebé [beb*e*h]
  we'd like a baby-sitter gostávamos de
  arranjar uma baby-sitter [goosht*a*h-vamoosh
  darranjar oomuh . . .]
back: I've got a bad back tenho uma dor nas
  costas [ten-yoo oomuh dor nush k*o*sh-tush]
  I'll be back soon estou de volta em breve
  [shtoh duh v*o*ltuh aim brev]
  can I have my money back? posso reaver o
  meu dinheiro? [possoo re-av*ai*r oo m*e*h-oo
  din-y*a*y-roo]
  come back! venha cá! [ven-yuh kah]
  I go back tomorrow regresso amanhã
  [regr*e*ssoo uh-man-y*a*ng]
  at the back atrás [atr*a*sh]
bacon o 'bacon'
  bacon and eggs ovos com bacon [*o*vvoosh . . .]
bad mau/má [m*a*h-oo/mah]
  it's not bad não é mau [nown*g* eh m*a*h-oo]
  too bad! que pena! [kuh peh-nuh]

....

bag um saco [sackoo]
　　(handbag) uma mala de mão [oomuh mah-luh
　　duh mowng]
　　(suitcase) uma mala de viagem [oomuh
　　mah-luh duh vee-ah-jeng]
baggage a bagagem [bagah-jeng]
baker's a padaria [padduh-ree-uh]
balcony a varanda
　　a room with a balcony um quarto com
　　varanda [oom kwartoo kong . . .]
ball uma bola [bolluh]
ball-point pen uma esferográfica
　　[shferoografikuh]
banana uma banana [banah-nuh]
band a orquestra [orkesh-truh]
bandage uma ligadura [leeguh-doo-ruh]
　　could you change the bandage? pode mudar
　　a ligadura? [pod moodar uh . . .]
bank o banco [oo bankoo]
　» *TRAVEL TIP: banking hours: 8.30 to 12.00 and*
　　1.00 to 2.30 Mon–Fri. Closed Sat & Sun: in
　　Lisbon try airport; bank holidays see **public**
bar um bar [bar]
　　when does the bar open? a que horas abre o
　　bar? [uh kee-oruz abroo bar]
barber's a barbearia [barbee-aree-uh]
bargain: it's a real bargain é uma pechincha
　　[eh oomuh pusheenshuh]
barmaid a empregada de balcão
　　[empruh-gah-duh duh bal-cowng]
barman o barman
basket um cesto [seshtoo]
bath um banho [ban-yoo]
　　can I have a bath? posso tomar um banho?
　　[possoo toomar . . .]
　　could you give me a bath towel? pode
　　dar-me uma toalha de banho? [pod dar-muh
　　oomuh too-al-yuh duh ban-yoo]
bathing costume um fato de banho [fah-too duh
　　ban-yoo]

bathroom a casa de banho [kah-zuh duh
ban-yoo]
   **we want a room with a private
bathroom** queremos um quarto com casa de
banho [kreh-mooz oom kwartoo kong . . .]
   can I use your bathroom? posso ir à casa de
banho? [possoo eer ah . . .]
battery a bateria [battuh-ree-uh]
be ser [sair]
beach a praia [prah-yuh]
beans *(green)* feijão [fay-jowng]
   (broad) favas [fah-vush]
beautiful lindo [leendoo]
   that was a beautiful meal foi uma refeição
óptima [foy oomuh ruh-fay-sowng ottimuh]
because porque [poor-kuh]
   because of the bad weather por causa do
mau tempo [poor cow-zuh doo mah-oo tempoo]
beco sem saída cul-de-sac
bed a cama [kah-muh]
   single/double bed cama individual/cama de
casal [kah-muh eendiveedoo-al/. . . duh kazal]
   you haven't changed my bed não mudou a
roupa da minha cama [nowng moo-doh uh
roh-puh duh meen-yuh kah-muh]
   bed and breakfast dormida e pequeno almoço
[doo-rmeeduh ee pekeh-noo al-mo-soo]
bedroom o quarto de dormir [kwartoo duh
doo-rmeer]
bee uma abelha [abell-yuh]
beef a carne de vaca [karn duh vah-kuh]
beer a cerveja [ser-veh-juh]
   two beers, please duas cervejas, por favor
[doo-ush ser-veh-jush poor fuh-vor]
» *TRAVEL TIP:* 'cerveja' *implies a lager-type beer,
usually the only type available*
before: before breakfast antes do pequeno
almoço [antsh doo pekeh-noo al-mo-soo]
   before we leave antes de partirmos [antsh
duh perteermoosh]

....

I haven't been here before nunca aqui estive
[noonkuh akee shteev]

begin: when does it begin? quando começa?
[kwandoo koomessuh]

behind atrás de [atrash duh]

the car behind me o carro atrás de mim [oo
karroo atrash duh meeng]

believe: I don't believe you não o acredito
[nowng oo akredeetoo]

I believe you acredito

bell a campainha [kampuh-eenyuh]

belong: that belongs to me isso é meu [eessoo
eh meh-oo]

who does this belong to? a quem pertence
isto? [uh keng pertenss eeshtoo]

below em baixo [embye-shoo]

below that debaixo disso [duh-bye-shoo
deesoo]

belt um cinto [seentoo]

berries bagas [bah-gush]

berth (on ship) um beliche [beleesh]

beside junto a [joontoo uh]

best o melhor [mul-yor]

it's the best holiday I've ever had foram as
melhores férias que já tive [for-owng ush
mul-yorush fair-yush kuh jah teev]

better melhor

haven't you got anything better? não tem
nada melhor? [nowng teng nah-duh mul-yor]

are you feeling better? sente-se melhor?
[sent-suh mul-yor]

I'm feeling a lot better sinto-me muito
melhor [seentoo-muh mweentoo mul-yor]

between entre [entr]

beyond além de [a-leng duh]

beyond the mountains para além das
montanhas [prah leng dush montahn-yush]

bicycle uma bicicleta [bee-see-kletta]

can we hire bicycles here? alugam-se aqui
bicicletas? [aloo-gowng-suh akee-klettush]

big grande [grand]
   a big one um maior [oom muh-yor]
   that's too big é grande demais [eh grand duh-my-sh]
   it's not big enough é pequeno
   have you got a bigger one? tem um maior?
bikini um bikíni
bilheteira ticket office
bill a conta [kontuh]
   could I have the bill, please? a conta, por favor [uh kontuh, poor fuh-vor]
bird um pássaro [passuh-roo]
birthday o dia de anos [dee-uh dah-noosh]
   happy birthday feliz aniversário [feleez anneeversar-yoo]
biscuit uma bolacha [boolashuh]
bit: just a little bit só um bocadinho [so oom bookadeen-yoo]
   that's a bit too expensive é um bocado caro
   a bit of that cake uma fatia daquele bolo [oomuh fatee-uh dakehl bo-loo]
bite uma mordedura [moordadooruh]
   I've been bitten fui mordido [fwee moordeedoo]
bitter amargo [amargoo]
black preto [preh-too]
   he's had a blackout teve um desmaio [tev oom dush-my-oo]
bland brando [brandoo]
blanket um cobertor [koobertor]
   I'd like another blanket queria mais um cobertor [kree-uh myz oom koobertor]
bleach lixívia [leesheev-yuh]
bleed sangrar
   he's bleeding está a sangrar [shtah sangrar]
bless you *(after sneeze)* santinho [santeen-yoo]
blind cego [seh-goo]
blister uma borbulha [boorbool-yuh]
blonde uma loira [loy-ruh]
blood o sangue [oo sanguh]

....

his blood group is . . . o grupo sanguíneo dele
é . . . [oo gro*o*poo sangw*i*n-yoo dehl eh]
I've got high blood pressure a minha tensão
é alta [uh m*ee*nyuh ten-s*o*wng eh *a*ltuh]
he needs a blood transfusion precisa duma
transfusão de sangue [pres*ee*zuh d*oo*muh
tranjfoo-z*o*wng duh sanguh]
blouse uma blusa [bl*oo*zuh]
blue azul [az*oo*l]
board: full board pensão completa [pen-s*o*wng
kompl*e*ttuh]
half board meia pensão [m*a*yuh pen-s*o*wng]
boarding pass o cartão de embarque [oo
kar-t*o*wng demb*a*rk]
boat um barco [b*a*rkoo]
body o corpo [oo kore-poo]
(dead body) um cadáver [kad*a*ver]
boil ferver [furv*ai*r]
(med) um furúnculo [foor*oo*nkooloo]
do we have to boil the water? é preciso
ferver a água? [eh pruh-s*ee*zoo furv*ai*r uh
*a*gwuh]
boiled egg um ovo cozido [*o*-voo kooz*ee*doo]
bone o osso [*o*-soo]
bonnet *(car)* a capota [kap*o*ttuh]
book um livro [l*ee*vroo]
booking office a bilheteira [beel-yuh-t*a*yruh]
can I book a seat for . . . posso reservar um
bilhete para . . .? [p*o*ssoo rezerv*a*r oom beel-y*e*t
para]
I'd like to book a table for four queria
reservar uma mesa para quatro pessoas
[kr*ee*-uh rezerv*a*r *oo*muh m*e*h-zuh para kw*a*troo
puss*o*h-ush]
bookshop a livraria [leevruh-r*ee*-uh]
boot uma bota [b*o*ttuh]
(car) a mala [m*a*h-luh]
booze: I had too much booze last night ontem
à noite apanhei uma grande bebedeira [onteng
ah noyt apan-y*a*y*oo*muh grand bubba-d*a*y-ruh]

border a fronteira [front*a*yruh]
bored: I'm bored estou chateado [shtoh shutty-*a*h-doo]
boring maçador [massuh-d*o*r]
born: I was born in . . . nasci em . . . [nash-s*ee*]
boss o patrão [patr*o*wng]
both os dois [oosh d*o*ysh]
  I'll take both of them levo os dois [l*e*vvoo oosh doysh]
bottle uma garrafa [garr*a*h-fuh]
  bottle-opener um saca-rolhas [oom sackuh-r*o*l-yush]
bottom: at the bottom of the hill no sopé do monte [noo soop*e*h doo mont]
box uma caixa [k*y*-shuh]
boy um rapaz [rap*a*sh]
boyfriend namorado [namoor*a*h-doo]
bra um soutien [sooty*a*ng]
bracelet uma pulseira [pools*a*y-ruh]
brake *(noun)* o travão [trav*o*wng]
  could you check the brakes? pode ver-me os travões? [pod v*a*ir-muh oosh trav-*o*ingsh]
  I had to brake suddenly tive de travar de repente [teev duh trav*a*r duh rep*e*nt]
  he didn't brake não travou [nowng tra-v*o*h]
brandy um brandy
bread pão [powng]
  could we have some bread and butter? traga pão e manteiga, se faz favor [tr*a*h-ga powng ee mant*a*y-ga suh fash fuh-v*o*r]
  some more bread, please mais pão, por favor [m*y*-sh powng poor fuh-v*o*r]
break partir [pert*ee*r]
breakable frágil [fr*a*jeel]
breakdown uma avaria [avuh-r*ee*-uh]
  I've had a breakdown tive uma avaria [teev oomuh avuh-r*ee*-uh]
  nervous breakdown esgotamento nervoso [eejgotuh-m*e*ntoo nerv*o*zoo]
» *TRAVEL TIP: breakdown services: nearest garage!*

breakfast o pequeno almoço [pek*e*h-noo alm*o*-soo]

breast o peito [p*a*y-too]

breath a respiração [rushpeera-s*o*wng]

breathe respirar [rushpeer*a*r]
  I can't breathe não posso respirar [n*o*wng p*o*sso . . .]

bridge a ponte [pont]

briefcase a pasta [p*a*shtuh]

brighten up: do you think it'll brighten up later? pensa que o tempo ainda melhora? [pensuh kee-*o*o temp*o*o a-*ee*nduh mel-y*o*ruh]

brilliant brilhante [breel-y*a*nt]

bring trazer [tra*z*air]

Britain Grã-Bretanha [grambret*a*hn-yuh]

British britânico [breet*a*h-nikoo]

brochure um folheto [fol-y*e*ttoo]
  have you got any brochures about . . .? tem alguns folhetos sobre . . .? [teng alg*oo*ngsh fol-yettoosh s*o*h-bruh]

broken partido [pert*ee*doo]
  you've broken it partiu-o [pert-y*oo*-oo]
  it's broken está partido [sht*a*h pert*ee*doo]
  my room/car has been broken into o meu quarto foi remexido [*oo*meh-oo kw*a*rtoo foy remush*ee*doo]/o meu carro foi assaltado [oo m*e*h-oo k*a*rroo foy assal-t*a*h-doo]

brooch um alfinete de peito [al-f*ee*net duh p*a*y-too]

brother: my brother meu irmão [m*e*h-oo eer-m*o*wng]

brown castanho [kasht*a*hn-yoo]
  (tanned) bronzeado [bronzee-*a*h-doo]
  brown paper papel de embrulho [puh-p*e*l dembro*o*lyoo]

browse: can I just browse around? posso dar uma vista de olhos por aí? [p*o*ssoo dar *oo*muh v*ee*shtuh d*o*l-yoosh poor a-*ee*]

bruise uma contusão [kontoo-z*o*wng]

brunette *(noun)* uma morena [moor*e*h-nuh]

brush *(noun)* uma escova [shkovvuh]
(artist's) um pincel [peensell]
Brussels sprouts couve de Bruxelas [kove duh brooshellush]
bucket um balde [bal-duh]
buffet o bufete [boofet]
building o edifício [eedifeess-yoo]
bulb uma lâmpada [lampa-duh]
the bulb's gone a lâmpada fundiu-se [uh lampa-duh foond-yoo-suh]
bull um touro [toh-roo]; **bullfight** uma tourada *in Portugal the bull is not killed*
bump: he's had a bump on the head ele bateu com a cabeça [ehl bateh-oo kong uh kabeh-suh]
bumper o pára-choques [para-shocksh]
bunch: a bunch of flowers um ramo de flores [rah-moo duh florush]
bunk um beliche [beleesh]
buoy a bóia [boh-yuh]
burglar um ladrão [lad-rowng]
they've taken all my money roubaram-me todo o meu dinheiro [roh-barowng-muh toh-doo oo meh-oo dunyay-roo]
burnt: this meat is burnt esta carne está esturricada [eshtuh karn shtah shtoorikah-duh]
my arms are burnt queimei os braços [kay-may oosh bra-soosh]
can you give me something for these burns? pode receitar-me alguma coisa para estas queimaduras? [pod russay-tar-muh al-goomuh koy-zuh para eshtush kay-madoorush]
bus um autocarro [owtoo-karroo]
bus stop uma paragem de autocarro [oomuh parah-jeng dowtoo-karroo]
could you tell me when we get there? podia dizer-me onde é que devo sair? [podee-uh deezair-muh onduh eh kuh devvoo suh-eer]
business um negócio [negoss-yoo]

....

I'm here on business estou aqui em negócios
[shtoh ak*ee* eng nego*ss*-yoosh]
    business trip uma viagem de negócios [oomuh
vee-*a*h-jeng . . .]
    none of your business isso não é contigo
[*ee*ssoo nowng eh kont*ee*goo]
bust o peito [p*a*y-too]
» *TRAVEL TIP: bust measurements*
  UK   32 34 36 38   40
  Portugal 80 87 91 97 102
busy ocupado [o-koop*a*h-doo]
    (telephone) impedido [eemped*ee*doo]
but mas [mush]
butcher's o talho [t*a*l-yoo]
butter a manteiga [mant*a*y-guh]
button um botão [boot*o*wng]
buy: I'll buy it levo este [l*e*vvoo ehsht]
    where can I buy . . .? onde posso comprar . . .?
[*o*nduh p*o*ssoo kompr*a*r]
by: I'm here by myself estou aqui sozinho
[shtoh ak*ee* soz*ee*n-yoo]
    are you by yourself? estás sozinha? [shtash
soz*ee*n-yuh]
    can you do it by tomorrow? pode fazê-lo para
amanhã? [pod f*a*zeh-loo prah man-y*a*ng]
    by train/car/plane de comboio/carro/avião
[duh k*o*mb*o*yoo/k*a*rroo/av-y*o*wng]
I parked by the trees estacionei o carro
debaixo das árvores [shtass-yoon*a*y oo k*a*rroo
de-b*y*-shoo duz*a*rvoorush]
    who's it made by? quem é que o fez? [keng eh
kee-*oo* fesh]
cabaret um cabaré [kabar*eh*]
cabbage uma couve [k*o*ve]
cabin *(on ship)* um camarote [kama-rot]
café um café [kuff*eh*]
» *TRAVEL TIP: most cafés and bars provide both
non-alcoholic and alcoholic drinks as well as
snacks; a 'pastelaria' sells cakes and also serves
coffee, tea etc*

cais *platform*
caixa *cash desk*
cake um bolo [bo-loo]
  a piece of cake uma fatia de bolo [fatee-uh duh bo-loo]
calculator uma máquina de calcular [macky-nuh duh kalkoolar]
call: will you call the manager? chame o gerente [sham oo juh-rent]
  what are you called? como se chama? [ko-moo suh shah-muh]
  what is this called? como se chama isto? [. . . eesh-too]
  call box uma cabine telefónica [oomuh kabeen tul-fonnickuh]
calm *(sea)* calmo [kal-moo]
  calm down! calma! [kal-muh]
câmbio *foreign exchange*
camera uma máquina fotográfica [macky-nuh footoo-grafickuh]
camp: is there somewhere we can camp? há lá algum sítio para acampar? [ah lah algoom seet-yoo para akampar]
  can we camp here? pode-se acampar aqui? [pod-suh akampar akee]
  campsite o parque de campismo [oo park duh kampeejmoo]
» TRAVEL TIP: *international campers' card sometimes necessary; most sites are along the coast.*
can¹: a can of beer uma cerveja em lata [ser-veh-juh eng lah-tuh]
  can-opener um abre-latas [ah-bruh lah-tush]
can²: can I have . . .? queria . . . [kree-uh]
  can you show me . . .? pode mostrar-me . . .? [pod moosh-trar muh]
  I can't . . . não posso . . . [nowng possoo]
  he can't . . . não pode . . . [. . . pod]
  we can't . . . não podemos . . . [. . . poodeh-moosh]

Canada Canadá [kan-adah]
Canadian canadiano [kanadee-ah-noo]
cancel: I want to cancel my booking quero cancelar a minha marcação [kairoo kanselar uh meen-yuh markuh-sowng]
can we cancel dinner for tonight? podemos desmarcar o jantar de hoje à noite? [poodeh-moosh dushmarkar oo jantar doje ah noyt]
candle uma vela [velluh]
by candlelight à luz da vela [ah loosh . . .]
capsize soçobrar [soo-soobrar]
car o carro [karroo]
by car de carro [duh . . .]
carafe um jarro [jarroo]
cáravan uma roulotte [roo-lot]
carburettor o carburador [karbooruh-dor]
cards cartas [kar-tush]
do you play cards? sabe jogar às cartas? [sab joo-gar ash kar-tush]
care: goodbye, take care adeus, tome cuidado [a-deh-oosh, tom kweedah-doo]
will you take care of this for me? toma-me conta disto, por favor? [tomuh-muh kontuh deeshtoo, poor fuh-vor]
careful: be careful tenha cuidado [ten-yuh kweedah-doo]
car ferry o 'ferry boat'
car park o estacionamento [shtass-yoonuh-mentoo]
carpet o tapete [tuh-pet]
carrots cenouras [sun-o-rush]
carry: will you carry this for me? leve-me isto, por favor [lev-muh eeshtoo, poor fuh-vor]
carry cot um carrinho de bebé [kareen-yoo duh bebeh]
carving uma obra de talha [obruh duh tal-yuh]
casa de banho bathroom
case *(suitcase)* a mala [mah-luh]
cash dinheiro [din-yay-roo]

I haven't got any cash estou sem dinheiro [shtoh seng . . .]
to pay in cash pagar à vista [ah veesh-tuh]
cash desk a caixa [uh kye-shuh]
will you cash a cheque for me? troca-me este cheque? [trocka-muh eh-sht sheck]
casino o casino [kazeenoo]
cassette uma cassette
castle o castelo [kashtelloo]
cat o gato [gah-too]
catch: **where do we catch the bus?** onde se apanha o autocarro? [onduh see apan-yuh oo ow-too-karroo]
he's caught a bug apanhou uma infecção [apan-yoh oomuh eemfessowng]
cave basement
cathedral a catedral [kuttadral]
cauliflower uma couve-flor [kove-flor]
cave uma caverna [kavairnuh]
ceiling o tecto [tettoo]
celery aipo [eye-poo]
cellophane celofane [seloofan]
centigrade centígrado [senteegradoo]
» *TRAVEL TIP: to convert C to F:* $\frac{C}{5} \times 9 + 32 = F$

| centigrade | −5 | 0 | 10 | 15 | 21 | 30 | 36.9 |
| Fahrenheit | 23 | 32 | 50 | 59 | 70 | 86 | 98.4 |

centimetre centímetro [senteemetroo]
» *TRAVEL TIP: 1 cm = 0.39 inches*
central central [sentral]
with central heating com aquecimento central [kong akussy-mentoo sentral]
centre o centro [sentroo]
how do we get to the centre? como se vai para o centro, por favor? [ko-moo suh vye proh sentroo, poor fuh-vor]
certain certo [sair-too]
are you certain? tem a certeza? [teng uh ser-teh-zuh]
certificate a certidão [ser-tee-downg]

chain uma cadeia [kaday-uh]

chair uma cadeira [kaday-ruh]

chambermaid a criada de quarto [kree-ah-duh duh kwar-too]

champagne champanhe [sham-pan-yuh]

change: could you change this into escudos? pode trocar isto por escudos? [pod trookar eeshtoo poor shkoodoosh]

I haven't any change não tenho troco [nowng ten-yoo troh-koo]

do we have to change trains? temos de mudar de comboio? [teh-moosh duh moodar duh komboyyoo]

I'd like to change my booking queria mudar a minha reserva [kree-uh moodar uh meen-yuh rezairvuh]

I'll just get changed vou mudar de roupa [voh moodar duh roh-puh]

» *TRAVEL TIP: changing money: look for sign 'câmbio' in banks or hotels; take your passport with you; most banks accept cheques with banker's card.*

channel: the Channel o Canal da Mancha [kanal da man-shuh]

charge: what will you charge? quanto vai pedir? [kwantoo vye pedeer]

who's in charge? quem é o responsável? [keng eh oo rushponsah-vel]

chart *(sea)* uma carta [kar-tuh]

cheap barato [barah-too]

cheaper mais barato [my-sh . . .]

cheat: I've been cheated fui enganado [fwee enganah-doo]

check: will you check? pode verificá-lo? [pod verifeekah-loo]

I'm sure, I've checked tenho a certeza, porque eu próprio verifiquei [ten-yoo uh ser-teh-zuh, poor-kee eh-oo propree-oo verifeekay]

will you check the total? quer conferir a

conta? [kair konfuh-*reer* uh k*o*n-tuh]
cheek a face [uh fass]
cheeky descarado [dushkar*a*h-doo]
cheerio até à vista [at*e*h ah v*ee*sh-tuh]
  (toast) saúde [suh-*oo*d]
cheers! *(toast)* saúde [suh-*oo*d]
  (thank you) obrigadinho [o-brigad*ee*n-yoo]
cheese queijo [k*a*y-joo]
  say cheese! sorria! [soo-rr*ee*-uh]
chef o cozinheiro [oo koozeen-y*a*y-roo]
chegadas *arrivals*
chemist's a farmácia [fur-m*a*ss-yuh]
  » *TRAVEL TIP: a chemist can advise on minor*
    ailments; the duty chemist rota, with addresses,
    is to be found on the door (or in local press)
cheque um cheque [sheck]
  will you take a cheque? aceita um cheque?
    [a-s*a*ytuh oom sheck]
  cheque book o livro de cheques [*lee*vroo duh
    sh*e*cksh]
  cheque card o cartão bancário [kar-t*o*wng
    ban-k*a*r-yoo]
  » *TRAVEL TIP: see* **change**
chest o peito [p*a*y-too]
  » *TRAVEL TIP: chest measurements*

UK	34	36	38	40	42	44	46
Portugal	87	91	97	102	107	112	117

chewing gum pastilha elástica [pash-t*ee*l-yuh
  ee*la*sh-tickuh]
chicken *(food)* frango [fr*a*n-goo]
chickenpox a varicela [varee-s*e*lluh]
child uma criança [kree-*a*n-suh]
  my children os meus filhos [oosh m*e*h-oosh
    f*ee*l-yoosh]
  children's portion meia dose [m*a*y-uh doze]
chin o queixo [k*a*y-shoo]
china a porcelana [poor-sull*a*h-nuh]
chips batatas fritas [bat*a*h-tush fr*ee*tush]
  (casino) fichas [f*ee*shush]
chocolate chocolate [shookool*a*t]

a box of chocolates uma caixa de bombons [oomuh kye-shuh duh bombonsh]
hot chocolate um chocolate quente [oom shookoolat kent]
choke *(car)* o ar [ar]
chop *(noun)* uma costeleta [kooshtelettuh]
Christian name nome (de baptismo) [nom duh bateejmoo]
Christmas o Natal [nuh-tal]
Happy Christmas! Feliz Natal! [feleesh . . .]
church a igreja [eegreh-juh]
where is the Protestant/Catholic church? onde é a Igreja Protestante/Católica? [ondee eh uh eegreh-juh proot-shtant/katollikuh]
cider cidra [see-druh]
cigar um charuto [sharootoo]
cigarette um cigarro [see-garroo]
would you like a cigarette? quer um cigarro? [kair oom . . .]
tipped/plain cigarettes . . . com/sem filtro [kong/saim feeltroo]
cine-camera uma câmara de filmar [kammeruh duh feelmar]
cinema o cinema [seeneh-muh]
circle um círculo [seer-kooloo]
(cinema) balcão [bal-cowng]
city a cidade [see-dahd]
clarify clarificar [klarry-feekar]
clean *(adjective)* limpo [leem-poo]
can I have some clean sheets? mude-me os lençóis, por favor [mood-muh oosh len-soysh, poor fuh-vor]
my room hasn't been cleaned today hoje o meu quarto não foi arrumado [oje oo meh-oo kwar-too nowng foy aroomah-doo]
it's not clean não está limpo [nowng shtah leempoo]
cleansing cream creme de limpeza [crem duh leempeh-zuh]

clear: I'm not clear about it estou com dúvidas
    acerca disso [shtoh kong *doo*vy-dush as*sair*-kuh
    d*ee*-soo]
clever esperto [shp*air*-too]
climate o clima [kl*ee*muh]
cloakroom o vestiário [vushty-*ar*-yoo]
    (W.C.) os lavabos [oosh lav*ah*-boosh]
clock um relógio [reloj-yoo]
close[1] perto [p*air*-too]
    (weather) abafado [abaf*ah*-doo]
close[2]**: when do you close?** a que horas fecha?
    [a kee *o*rush f*e*shuh]
closed encerrado [enser*rah*-doo]
cloth pano [p*ah*-noo]; *(rag)* um trapo [tr*a*ppoo]
clothes a roupa [roh-puh]
cloud uma nuvem [n*oo*veng]
clutch a embraiagem [emb-rye-*ah*-jeng]
    the clutch is slipping a embraiagem patina
coach a camioneta [kamee-oo-n*e*tta]
    coach party um grupo de excursão [oom
    gr*oo*poo dush-koor-s*o*wng]
coast a costa [k*o*shtuh]
    coastguard a guarda costeira [gw*a*rduh
    koosh-t*a*y-ruh]
coat um casaco [kaz*ah*-koo]
cockroach uma barata [bar*ah*-tuh]
coffee café [kuff*e*h]
    white coffee/black coffee um garoto/uma
    bica [oom gar*oh*-too/oomuh b*e*ekuh]
coin uma moeda [moo-*e*h-duh]
cold frio [fr*ee*-oo]
    I'm cold tenho frio [t*e*n-yoo . . .]
    I've got a cold apanhei uma constipação
    [apan-y*a*y oomuh k*o*nshteepa-s*o*wng]
collapse: he's collapsed desmaiou
    [dushma-y*oh*]
collar a colarinho [koolar*ee*n-yoo]
» *TRAVEL TIP: collar sizes*
    (old) UK: 14 14½ 15 15½ 16 16½ 17
    continental: 36 37 38 39 41 42 43

collarbone a clavícula [klav*ee*-kooluh]
collect: I want to collect . . . venho buscar . . .
[v*e*n-yoo booshk*a*r]
colour a cor [kohr]
have you any other colours? tem doutras
cores? [teng d*o*h-trush k*o*hrush]
comb um pente [pent]
come vir [veer]
I come from London sou de Londres [soh duh
l*o*n-drush]
we came here yesterday chegámos cá ontem
[shug*a*mmoosh kah *o*n-teng]
come on! despache-se! [dush-p*a*shuh-suh]
come with me venha comigo [v*e*n-yuh
koo-m*ee*goo]
comfortable confortável [komfoort*a*h-vel]
it's not very comfortable não é muito
confortável [nowng eh mw*ee*ntoo . . .]
Common Market o Mercado Comum
[merk*a*h-doo koom*oo*ng]
communication cord o alarme [alarm]
company uma companhia [kompan-y*ee*-uh]
you're good company és um tipo bestial [ez
oom t*ee*poo bushtee-*a*l]
compartment *(train)* o compartimento
[komparteem*e*ntoo]
compass uma bússola [b*oo*sooluh]
compensation indemnização
[eendemneezuh-s*o*wng]
I demand compensation exijo uma
indemnização [eez*ee*-joo oomuh . . .]
complain queixar-se [kay-sh*a*r-suh]
I want to complain about my room/the
waiter quero queixar-me do quarto/do
empregado [k*ai*roo kay-sh*a*r-muh doo
kw*a*rtoo/doo empruh-g*a*h-doo]
have you got a complaints book? tem um
livro de reclamações? [teng oom l*ee*vroo duh
recklamuh-s*oi*ngsh]
completely completamente [komplettuh-m*e*nt]

completo full up

complicated: it's very complicated é muito complicado [eh mweentoo komplikah-doo]

compliment: my compliments to the chef transmita ao cozinheiro que tudo estava muito bom [tranj-meetuh ow koozeen-yay-roo kuh toodoo shtah-vuh mweentoo bong]

concert um concerto [konsairtoo]

concussion traumatismo [trowma-teej-moo]

condition a condição [kondee-sowng]

it's not in very good condition não está em muito boas condições [nowng shtah eng mweentoo bo-ush kondee-soingsh]

conference a conferência [konferen-see-uh]

confession a confissão [konfeessowng]

confirm confirmar [konfeermar]

confuse: you're confusing me está a confundir-me [shtah uh konfoondeer-muh]

congratulations parabéns [para-bengsh]

conjunctivitis a conjuntivite [konjoontiveet]

con-man um vigarista [veega-reesh-tuh]

connection (travel) a ligação [leega-sowng]

connoisseur um conhecedor [koonyuh-sedor]

conscious consciente [konsh-see-ent]

consciousness: he's lost consciousness ele desmaiou [ehl dush-ma-yoh]

constipation prisão de ventre [preezowng duh ventr]

consul o cônsul [konsool]

consulate o consulado [konsoolah-doo]

contact: how can I contact...? como posso contactar...? [ko-moo possoo kontactar]

contact lenses lentes de contacto [lentsh duh kontaktoo]

contraceptive um contraceptivo [–septeevoo]

convenient conveniente [konven-yent]

cook: it's not cooked não está bem cozinhado [nowng shtah beng koozeenyah-doo]

it's beautifully cooked está muito bem feito [shtah mweentoo beng fay-too]

....

you're a good cook é boa cozinheira [eh bo-uh koozeen-yay-ruh]
  cooker o fogão [foogowng]
cool fresco [freshkoo]
corkscrew um saca-rolhas [sacka-rol-yush]
corn *(foot)* um calo [kah-loo]
corner: on the corner na esquina [nuh shkeenuh]
  in a corner num canto [noom kantoo]
  can we have a corner table? podemos ficar naquela mesa do canto? [poodeh-moosh feekar nakelluh meh-zuh doo kantoo]
cornflakes 'cornflakes'
correct exacto [eezattoo]
Correio Post Office
cosmetics cosméticos [koojmettikoosh]
cost: what does it cost? quanto custa? [kwantoo kooshtuh]
  that's too much é muito caro [eh mweentoo kah-roo]
  I'll take it levo isso [levvoo ee-soo]
cotton algodão [al-goo-downg]
  cotton wool algodão
couchette beliche [beleesh]
cough *(noun)* tosse [tohss]
  cough drops rebuçados para a tosse [reboosah-doosh prah tohss]
could: could you please . . .? pode . . . por favor? [pod . . . poor fuh-vor]
  could I have . . .? pode dar-me . . .? [pod dar-muh]
country o país [pa-eesh]
  in the country no campo [noo kampoo]
couple: a couple of . . . um par de . . .
courier o guia turístico [ghee-uh tooreeshtikoo]
course *(of meal)* prato [prah-too]
  of course! claro! [klah-roo]
court: I'll take you to court vou processá-lo [voh proo-sessah-loo]

cousin: my cousin o meu primo [oo meh-oo preemoo]
cover: keep him covered tapem-no [tapeng-noo]
cover charge imposto adicional [eemposhtoo adeess-yoo-nal]
cow uma vaca [vah-kuh]
crab um caranguejo [karangheh-joo]
craft shop uma loja de artigos regionais [lojjuh darteegoosh rej-yoon-eye-sh]
crash: there's been a crash houve um desastre [ove oom dezash-truh]
crash helmet um capacete [kap-a-set]
crazy: you're crazy tu és doido [too esh doy-doo]
cream creme [crem]
creche uma 'creche'
credit card um cartão de crédito [kartowng duh kreditoo]
crisis uma crise [kreez]
crisps batatinhas [batateen-yush]
crossroads um cruzamento [kroozuh-mentoo]
crowded apinhado [apeen-yah-doo]
cruise um cruzeiro [kroozay-roo]
crutch uma muleta [moolettuh]
(of body) as ilhargas [uz eel-yar-gush]
cry chorar [shorar]
don't cry não chore [nowng shore]
cuidado caution
cup uma chávena [shavven-uh]
a cup of coffee um café [oom kuffeh]
cupboard um armário [armar-yoo]
curry caril [kareel]
curtains cortinas [koorteenush]
cushion uma almofada [oomuh almoofah-duh]
Customs Alfândega [al-fan-dugguh]
cut: I've cut myself cortei-me [koor-tay-muh]
cycle: can we cycle there? podemos ir até lá de bicicleta [poodeh-mooz eer ateh lah duh bee-see-klettuh]

....

cylinder o cilindro [see-*lee*n-droo]
  cylinder-head gasket junta para cabeça de
  cilindro [*joo*ntuh para kab*eh*-suh duh . . .]
dad(dy) paizinho [pye-z*ee*n-yoo]
damage: I'll pay for the damage pago os
  estragos [p*ah*-goo oosh shtr*ah*-goosh]
  it's damaged está amachucado [sht*ah*
  amash*oo*k*ah*-doo]
damn! raios me partam! [rye-oosh muh
  p*a*rtowng]
damp húmido [*oo*midoo]
dance: is there a dance on? vai haver baile?
  [vye av*ai*r byle]
  would you like to dance? quer dançar? [kair
  dans*a*r]
dangerous perigoso [pereeg*oh*-zoo]
dark escuro [shk*oo*roo]
  dark blue azul-marinho [az*oo*l-mar*ee*n-yoo]
  when does it get dark? a que horas anoitece?
  [a kee *or*-uz a-noy-t*e*ss]
darling querido [ker*ee*doo]
  (to woman) querida [ker*ee*duh]
dashboard o painel [pye-n*e*l]
date: what's the date? a quantos estamos hoje?
  [uh kw*a*ntoosh sht*ah*-mooz ohj]
  it's the 6th of May é seis de Maio [eh s*a*ysh
  duh m*ah*-yoo]
  in 1982 em mil novecentos e oitenta e dois [eng
  meel nov-s*e*ntooz ee oy-t*e*ntee doysh]
  can we make a date? podemos
  encontrarmo-nos outra vez? [pood*eh*-mooz
  enkontr*a*rmoo-nooz *o*h-truh vesh]
  (fruit) tâmaras [t*a*mma-rush]
  » *TRAVEL TIP: to say the date in Portuguese just use
  the ordinary number; see page 127 for a list of
  numbers*
daughter: my daughter minha filha
  [m*ee*n-yuh f*ee*l-yuh]
day o dia [d*ee*-uh]
dazzle: his lights were dazzling me as luzes

dele encandearam-me [ush looozush dehl
enkandy-ah-rowng-muh]
dead morto [mor-too]
deaf surdo [soor-doo]
   deaf-aid um aparelho para a surdez [oom
aparel-yoo prah soordesh]
deal um negócio [negoss-yoo]
   it's a deal negócio fechado [. . . feshah-doo]
   will you deal with it? quer tratar disso? [kair
tratar dee-soo]
dear *(expensive)* caro [kah-roo]
   Dear Sir Exmo. Senhor
   Dear Madam Exma. Senhora
   Dear Francisco querido Francisco; *(written
by man)* caro Francisco
December Dezembro [dezembroo]
deck o convés [konvesh]
   deckchair uma cadeira de lona [kaday-ruh
duh lonnuh]
declare: I have nothing to declare não tenho
nada a declarar [nowng ten-yoo nah-duh uh
duh-klarar]
deep fundo [foondoo]
   is it deep? é fundo? [eh . . .]
defendant o réu [reh-oo]
delay: the flight was delayed o voo foi
atrasado [oo voh-oo foy atrazah-doo]
deliberately de propósito [duh proopozitoo]
delicate *(person)* débil [debeel]
delicatessen charcutaria [sharkoota-ree-uh]
delicious delicioso [deleess-yoh-zoo]
delivery a distribuição
   is there another mail delivery? há alguma
outra distribuição de correio? [ah algoomuh
oh-truh dush-treeb-wee-sowng duh koo-rayoo]
de luxe de luxo [duh loo-shoo]
democratic democrático [duh-mookrattikoo]
dent uma amolgadela [amolga-delluh]
   you've dented my car amolgou-me o carro
[amolgoh-muh oo karroo]

....

dentist o dentista [dent*ee*shtuh]
> YOU MAY THEN HEAR . . .
> abra a boca [*ah*-brah uh boh-kuh] *open wide*
> bocheche, por favor [boo-sh*e*sh, poor fuh-vor]
> *rinse, please*

dentures a dentadura postiça [dentad*oo*ruh
poosht*ee*-suh]
deny: I deny it nego isso [n*e*ggoo *ee*-soo]
deodorant um desodorizante
[dez*o*h-dooreez*a*nt]
departure a partida [part*ee*-duh]
depend: it depends (on . . .) depende (de)
[duh-p*e*nd duh]
deport deportar [duh-poort*ar*]
deposit um depósito [duh-p*o*zzeetoo]
> **do I have to leave a deposit?** tenho de deixar
> algum depósito? [t*e*n-yoo duh day-sh*ar* . . .]

depressed deprimido [duh-preem*ee*doo]
depth a profundidade [proofoondid*a*hd]
desperate: I'm desperate for a drink
apetece-me imenso beber qualquer coisa
[upt*e*ss-muh eem*e*nsoo buh-b*air* kwalk*air*
koy-zuh]
depósito de bagagem *left luggage*
dessert a sobremesa [soh-bruh-m*e*h-zuh]
destination o destino [dusht*ee*noo]
desvio *diversion*
detergent um detergente [duh-terj*e*nt]
detour um detour [dujv*ee*oo]
devagar *slow*
devalued desvalorizado [dujvaloreez*ah*-doo]
develop: could you develop these? pode
revelar-mas? [pod ruh-vel*ar*-mush]
diabetic diabético [dee-ab*e*ttikoo]
dialling code o código [k*o*ddy-goo]
diamond um diamante [dee-am*a*nt]
diarrhoea a diarreia [dee-ar*a*yuh]
> **have you got something for diarrhoea?** tem
> algum anti-laxante? [teng alg*oo*m
> anti-lash*a*nt]

diary uma agenda [a*j*enduh]
dictionary um dicionário [d*ee*-see-oon*a*ree-oo]
die morrer [moo-r*ai*r]
  he's dying está a morrer [shtah . . .]
diesel *(fuel)* gasóleo [gaz*o*ll-yoo]
diet dieta [dee-*e*ttuh]
  I'm on a diet estou a fazer dieta [shtoh uh
  fuh-z*ai*r . . .]
different: they are different são diferentes
  [sowng deef-r*e*ntsh]
  can I have a different room? posso ter um
  outro quarto? [p*o*ssoo tair oom *o*h-troo
  kw*a*r-too]
  is there a different route? há alguma outra
  estrada?
  [ah alg*oo*muh *o*h-truh shtr*a*h-duh]
difficult difícil [dif*ee*-seel]
digestion a digestão [dee-jush-t*o*wng]
dinghy um bote [bot]
dining room a sala de jantar
dinner o jantar [j*a*ntar]
  dinner jacket um 'smoking'
dipped headlights faróis médios [far*o*ysh
  m*e*d-yoosh]
direct direito
  does it go direct? vai direito? [vy*e* deer*a*y-too]
dirty sujo [s*oo*-joo]
disabled deficiente [duh-feess-y*e*nt]
disappear desaparecer [duzza-par-s*ai*r]
  it's just disappeared desapareceu mesmo
  [duzza-par-s*e*h-oo m*e*j-moo]
disappointing: it was disappointing foi uma
  desilusão [foy *oo*muh duzzee-looz*o*wng]
disco uma boîte [bwat]
  see you in the disco encontramo-nos mais
  tarde na boîte [encontr*a*h-moo-noosh my-sh
  tard nuh bwat]
discount um desconto [dush-k*o*ntoo]
disgusting nojento [noo-j*e*ntoo]
dish o prato [pr*a*h-too]

....

dishonest desonesto [duz-oh-n*e*shtoo]
disinfectant desinfectante [duzzeenfect*a*nt]
dispensing chemist uma farmácia
  [farm*a*ss-yuh]
» *TRAVEL TIP: see* **chemist**
distance: in the distance à distância [ah
  deesh-t*a*nss-yuh]
distress signal um envio de S.O.S. [emv*ee*-oo
  duh . . .]
distributor *(car)* o distribuidor
  [dushtree-bwee-d*o*r]
disturb: the noise is disturbing us o barulho
  perturba-nos [oo bar*oo*l-yoo pert*oo*rbuh-noosh]
divorced divorciado [dee-voor-see-*a*h-doo]
do: how do you do? muito prazer [mw*ee*ntoo
  praz*ai*r]
  what are you doing tonight? o que fazes esta
  noite? [oo kuh f*a*h-zush *e*sh-tuh noyt]
  how do you do it? como é que faz isso?
  [k*o*-moo eh kuh faz *ee*-soo]
  will you do it for me? faz isso por mim? [faz
  ee-soo poor meeng]
  I've never done it before nunca fiz isso antes
  [nunca feez *ee*-soo antsh]
  I was doing 60 kph ia a sessenta quilómetros
  por hora [*ee*-uh uh sess*e*ntuh keel*o*mmetroosh
  poor *o*r-uh]
  he did it fê-lo [f*e*h-loo]
doctor o médico [m*e*ddikoo]
  I need a doctor preciso dum médico
  [pres*ee*-zoo doom m*e*ddikoo]
» *TRAVEL TIP: look under 'médicos' in the yellow
  pages (páginas am*a*relas); see* **hospital**
  YOU MAY HEAR . . .
  já sofreu disto alguma vez? *have you had this
  before?*
  onde é que dói? *where does it hurt?*
  já está a tomar qualquer medicamento? *are you
  taking any drugs?*
  tome um/dois destes: de três em três horas/todos

os dias/duas vezes ao dia *take one/two of these:
every three hours/every day/twice a day*
document um documento [dookoomentoo]
dog um cão [kowng]
don't não faças isso [nowng fass-uz ee-soo]
see **not**
door a porta [por-tuh]
dosage a dosagem [doo-zah-jeng]
double: double room um quarto duplo
[kwartoo doo-ploo]
   double whisky um whisky duplo
down: get down baixar [by-shar]
   downstairs em baixo [em by-shoo]
drain o cano de esgoto [kah-noo deej-goh-too]
drawing pin um pionés [pee-oonesh]
dress um vestido [veshteedoo]
» *TRAVEL TIP: dress sizes*

UK	10	12	14	16	18	20
Portugal	38	40	42	44	46	48

dressing gown um roupão [roh-powng]
drink *(verb)* beber [bebair]
   (alcoholic) um copo [oom koppoo]
   would you like a drink? deseja tomar
   alguma bebida? [dezeh-juh toomar algoomuh
   bubeeduh]
   I don't drink não bebo [nowng beboo]
   is the water drinkable? a água é potável? [uh
   ah-gwuh eh pootah-vel]
drive guiar [ghee-ar]
   I've been driving all day tenho guiado todo o
   dia [ten-yoo ghee-ah-doo toh-doo dee-uh]
driver o condutor [kondootor]
driving licence a carta de condução [kartuh duh
   kondoo-sowng]
» *TRAVEL TIP: driving in Portugal: always carry
   your licence and registration papers; seat belts
   are compulsory once out of town*
drown: he's drowning está a afogar-se [shtah
   afoogar-suh]
drug um medicamento [meddikamentoo]

....

drunk bêbedo [b*e*bdoo]
dry seco [s*e*h-koo]
  dry-clean limpar a seco [leemp*a*r uh s*e*h-koo]
duche *shower*
due: when is the bus due? a que horas chega o
  autocarro? [uh kee *o*r-ush sheguh oo
  ow-too-k*a*rroo]
during durante [door*a*nt]
dust o pó [poh]
duty-free *(shop)* a 'free-shop'
dynamo o dínamo [d*ee*na-moo]
e/esq. = *left*
each: can we have one each? pode ser um para
  cada um de nós? [pod sair oom para k*a*h-duh
  oom duh nosh]
  how much are they each? quanto é cada um?
  [kw*a*ntoo eh k*a*h-duh oom]
ear a orelha [or*e*l-yuh]
  I have earache tenho dor de ouvidos [t*e*n-yoo
  dor doh-v*ee*doosh]
early cedo [s*e*h-doo]
  we want to leave a day earlier queremos
  partir um dia antes [kr*e*h-moosh pert*ee*r oom
  d*ee*-uh antsh]
earrings brincos [br*ee*nkoosh]
east este [esht]
easy fácil [f*a*h-seel]
Easter a Páscoa [p*a*sh-kwuh]
eat comer [koo-m*a*ir]
  something to eat alguma coisa para comer
  [alg*oo*muh koy-zuh para koo-m*a*ir]
egg um ovo [oh-voo]
Eire a República do Eire [rep*oo*blikuh doo ayr]
either: either . . . or . . . ou . . . ou . . . [oh . . .
  oh]
  I don't like either não gosto de nenhum
  [nowng g*o*sh-too duh nun-y*oo*m]
elastic elástico [eel*a*shtikoo]
  elastic band uma fita elástica [f*ee*tuh
  eel*a*shtikkuh]

elbow o cotovelo [ko-toovelloo]
electric eléctrico [eeletrikoo]
  electric blanket um cobertor eléctrico [oom koobertor . . .]
  electric fire um aquecedor eléctrico [oom akussdor . . .]
electrician um electricista [eeletree-seeshtuh]
electricity a electricidade [eeletree-seedahd]
elegant elegante [eelagant]
elevador lift
else: something else uma outra coisa [oomuh oh-truh koy-zuh]
  somewhere else noutra parte [noh-truh part]
  let's go somewhere else vamos a qualquer outro sítio [vah-mooz uh kwalkair oh-troo seet-yoo]
  or else ou senão [oh sunnowng]
embarrassing embaraçoso [embarra-soh-zoo]
embarrassed aflito [afleetoo]
embassy a embaixada [em-by-shah-duh]
emergency uma emergência [ee-mer-jensee-uh]
empty vazio [vazee-oo]
empurre push
encerrado closed
enclose: I enclose . . . incluo . . . [eenkloo-oo]
encomendas parcels
end o fim [oo feeng]
  when does it end? quando termina? [kwandoo termeenuh]
engaged *(telephone, toilet)* ocupado [oh-koopah-doo]
  (person) noivo [noy-voo]
engagement ring o anel de noivado [anel duh noy-vah-doo]
engine o motor [mootor]
  engine trouble um problema no motor [oom prooblemmuh noo . . .]
England Inglaterra [eenglaterruh]

....

English inglês [eenglesh]
enjoy: I enjoyed it very much gostei imenso
[goosht*ay* ee-m*e*n-soo]
enlargement *(photo)* uma ampliação
[amplee-uss*o*wng]
enormous enorme [ee-n*o*rm]
enough: thank you, that's enough chega,
obrigado [sh*e*gguh, oh-bree-g*ah*-doo]
entertainment divertimentos
[deevertee-m*e*ntoosh]
entrada entrance
entrada proibida no entry
entrance a entrada [entr*ah*-duh]
entry a entrada [*e*ntr*ah*-duh]
envelope um envelope [emvel*o*p]
equipment material [maturry-*a*l]
error um erro [*e*rroo]
esc. = escudos
escalator escadas rolantes [shk*ah*-dush
roo-l*a*ntsh]
especially especialmente [eesh-puss-yal-m*e*nt]
essential essencial [eesenss-y*a*l]
it is essential that . . . é essencial que . . .
[eh . . . kuh]
estacionamento proibido no parking
Europe a Europa [eh-ooroh-puh]
evacuate abandonar [abandoon*a*r]
even: even the British até os Britânicos [at*e*h
oosh breet*ah*-nikoosh]
evening a tarde [tard]
in the evening à tarde [ah tard]
this evening esta tarde [*e*shtuh . . .]
good evening boa tarde [bo-uh . . .]
evening dress traje de noite [trahj duh noyt]
ever: have you ever been to . . .? já alguma
vez esteve em . . .? [jah alg*oo*muh vesh shtev
eng]
every: every day todos os dias [t*o*h-dooz oosh
d*ee*-ush]
everyone toda a gente [t*o*h-dah jent]

everything tudo [toodoo]
everywhere em toda a parte [eng . . .]
evidence provas [provvush]
exact exacto [eezattoo]
example um exemplo [eezemploo]
  for example por exemplo [poor . . .]
excellent excelente [eesh-selent]
except: except me salvo eu [salvoo eh-oo]
excess o excesso [eesh-sessoo]
  excess baggage um excesso de bagagem
exchange (money) kâmbio [kamb-yoo]
  (telephone) a central telefónica [sentral
  tull-fonnikuh]
exciting emocionante [ee-mooss-yoonant]
excursion uma excursão [eesh-koor-sowng]
excuse: excuse me (to get past, etc.) com licença
  [kong leesensuh]
  (to get attention) se faz favor [suh fash fuh-vor]
  (apology) desculpe [dush-koolp]
exhaust (car) o escape [shcap]
exhausted cansado [kansah-doo]
exhibition uma exposição [eesh-poozee-sowng]
exhibitor o expositor [eesh-poozitor]
exit a saída [suh-eeduh]
expect: she's expecting está à espera de bebé
  [shtah ash-pair-uh duh bebeh]
expenses: it's on expenses vou com ajudas de
  custo [voh kong ajoodush duh kooshtoo]
expensive caro [kah-roo]
expert um perito [pereetoo]
explain explicar [shpleekar]
  would you explain that slowly? pode
  explicá-lo mais devagar? [pod shpleekah-loo
  my-sh duh-vagar]
export (noun) a exportação [eesh-poorta-sowng]
exposure meter um fotómetro [footometroo]
extra: an extra glass/day mais um copo/dia
  [myze oom koppoo/dee-uh]
  is that extra? isso é um extra? [ee-soo eh oom
  eshtruh]

....

extremely extremamente [eesh-tremma-ment]
eye o olho [ohl-yoo]
  eyebrow sobrancelha [soh-bran-sell-yuh]
  eyeshadow sombra
  eye witness uma testemunha ocular
  [tushtamoon-yuh oh-koolar]
face a cara [kah-ruh]
fact o facto [factoo]
factory uma fábrica [fabrikkuh]
Fahrenheit Fahrenheit

» *TRAVEL TIP: to convert F to C: $F - 32 \times \dfrac{5}{9} = C$*

| *Fahrenheit* | 23 | 32 | 50 | 59 | 70 | 86 | 98.4 |
| *centigrade* | −5 | 0 | 10 | 15 | 21 | 30 | 36.9 |

faint: she's fainted desmaiou [dushma-yoh]
fair *(fun)* a feira [fay-ruh]
  (commercial) a feira
  that's not fair não é justo [nowng eh jooshtoo]
faithfully: yours faithfully com os melhores
  cumprimentos
fake *(noun)* uma falsificação
  [fal-seefeeka-sowng]
fall: he's fallen caiu [kuh-yoo]
false falso [fal-soo]
  false teeth a dentadura postiça [dentadoo-ruh
  poosh-tee-suh]
family a família [fameel-yuh]
fan *(mechanical)* uma ventoinha
  [ventoo-een-yuh]
  (hand held) um leque [leck]
  (football) entusiasta [entoozee-ashtuh]
  fan belt a correia da ventoinha [koo-rayuh
  duh ventoo-eenyuh]
far longe [lonj]
  is it far? é longe? [eh lonj]
  how far is it? qual é a distância? [kwal eh uh
  deesh-tanss-yuh]
fare *(travel)* o bilhete [beelyet]
farm a quinta [keentuh]
farther mais longe [my-sh lonj]

fashion a moda [m*o*dduh]
fast rápido [r*a*peedoo]
   don't speak so fast não fale tão depressa
   [nowng fal towng duh-pressuh]
fat *(adjective)* gordo [gor-doo]
   (on meat) gordura [goord*oo*ruh]
fatal mortal [moor-t*a*l]
father: my father meu pai [m*e*h-oo pye]
fathom uma braça [br*a*h-suh]
fault *(defect)* um defeito [duff*a*y-too]
   it's not my fault a culpa não é minha [uh
   k*oo*lpuh nowng eh m*ee*n-yuh]
favourite *(adjective)* favorito [favoor*ee*too]
February Fevereiro [fuvr*a*y-roo]
fechado closed
fed up: I'm fed up estou farto [shtoh f*a*rtoo]
feel: I feel cold/hot estou com frio/calor [shtoh
   kong fr*ee*-oo/kuh-l*o*r]
   I feel sad estou triste [shtoh tr*ee*sht]
   I feel like ... apetece-me ... [upt*e*ss-muh]
ferry o barco de passageiros [b*a*rkoo duh
   passuh-j*a*y-roosh]
fetch: will you come and fetch me? vem
   buscar-me? [veng booshk*a*r-muh]
fever febre [f*e*bruh]
few: only a few só uns poucos [so oonsh
   p*o*h-koosh]
   a few days só uns dias [so oonsh d*ee*-ush]
fiancé/e noivo/a [n*o*y-voo/-vuh]
fiddle: it's a fiddle é uma vigarice [eh oomuh
   veegar*ee*ss]
field um campo [k*a*mpoo]
fifty-fifty a meias [uh m*e*yyush]
figs figos [f*ee*goosh]
figure a figura [feeg*oo*ruh]
   (number) o algarismo [algar*ee*j-moo]
   I'm watching my figure olho para a minha
   figura [ol-yoo prah m*ee*n-yuh ...]
fill: fill her up encha o depósito, por favor
   [*e*nshuh oo duh-p*o*zitoo poor fuh-v*o*r]

....

to fill in a form preencher um impresso [pree-ensh*air* oom eempre*ss*oo]

fillet um filete [feel*et*]

filling *(tooth)* uma obturação [obt*oo*ruh-sowng]

film um filme [feelm]
  do you have this type of film? tem este tipo de película? [teng *e*h-shtuh t*ee*poo duh pel*ee*kooluh]

filter filtro [f*ee*ltroo]
  filter or non-filter? com filtro ou sem filtro? [kong f*ee*ltroo oh saim f*ee*ltroo]

find encontr*a*r
  if you find it se o encontrar [see oo . . .]
  I've found a . . . encontrei um . . . [enkontr*a*y . . .]

fine *(weather)* bom [bong]
  a 500 escudos fine uma multa de quinhentos escudos [*oo*muh m*oo*ltuh duh keen-y*e*ntoosh shk*oo*doosh]
  OK, that's fine está bem [shtah beng]

finger um dedo [d*e*h-doo]
  fingernail a unha [*oo*n-yuh]

finish: I haven't finished não terminei [nowng termeen*a*y]

fire! fogo! [f*oh*-goo]
  can we light a fire here? podemos fazer aqui uma fogueira? [pood*e*h-moosh faz*a*ir ak*ee* *oo*muh foo-g*a*y-ruh]
  it's not firing *(car)* a corrente não chega às velas [uh k*oo*rent nowng sheg ash v*e*llush]
  fire brigade os bombeiros [oosh bomb*a*y-roosh]
  fire extinguisher um extintor [shteent*o*r]

» *TRAVEL TIP:* dial 32 22 22

first primeiro [pree-m*a*y-roo]
  I was first eu cheguei primeiro [*e*h-oo shugg*a*y . . .]
  first aid primeiros socorros [pree-m*a*y-roosh sook*o*rroosh]

first aid kit a caixa de primeiros socorros [uh
kye-shuh duh . . .]
first class primeira classe
first name nome de baptismo [nom duh
bat*ee*j-moo]
the first of . . . um de . . . [oom duh]
fish peixe [paysh]
    fishing rod/tackle cana/apetrechos de pesca
    [k*a*h-nuh/uptr*e*shoosh duh p*e*sh-kuh]
five cinco [s*ee*nkoo]
fix: can you fix it? *(arrange, repair)* pode
arranjá-lo? [pod arranj*a*h-loo]
fizzy espumoso [shpoom*o*h-zoo]
flag a bandeira [band*ay*-ruh]
flash *(photo)* um flash
flat plano [pl*a*h-noo]; *(apartment)* um
apartamento [apartam*e*ntoo]
    this drink is flat esta bebida está morta
    [*e*shtuh beb*ee*duh shtah m*o*r-tuh]
    I've got a flat *(tyre)* tenho um pneu furado
    [t*e*n-yoo oom pn*e*h-oo foor*a*h-doo]
flavour o sabor
flea uma pulga [p*oo*lguh]
flight o voo [v*o*h-oo]
flirt *(verb)* namoriscar [namooreeshk*a*r]
float *(verb)* boiar [b*o*yar]
floor o chão [sh*o*wng]
    on the second floor no segundo andar [noo
    seg*oo*ndoo and*a*r]
    on the floor no chão [noo sh*o*wng]
flower uma flor
flu uma gripe [*oo*muh greep]
fly *(insect)* uma mosca [m*o*shkuh]
foggy enevoado [eenev-w*a*h-doo]
follow seguir [sugg*ee*r]
food a comida [koom*ee*duh]
    food poisoning envenenamento alimentar
    [envenenna-m*e*ntoo aleement*a*r]
    see pages 70–71
fool tolo [t*o*h-loo]

....

foot o pé [peh]; **football** o futebol
[foo-tbol]; *(ball)* uma bola [bolluh]
» *TRAVEL TIP: 1 foot = 30.1 cm = 0.3 metres*
for para
forbidden proibido [proo-eebeedoo]
foreign: foreign exchange câmbio estrangeiro
[kamb-yoo shtran-jay-roo]
  foreigner um estrangeiro [shtran-jay-roo]
forest a floresta [floreshtuh]
forget esquecer-se [shkuh-sair-suh]
  I forget, I've forgotten não me lembro
  [nowng muh lembroo]
  don't forget não se esqueça [nowng
  sushkessuh]
  I'll never forget you nunca te esquecerei
  [noonkuh tushkussa-ray]
fork um garfo [garfoo]
form *(document)* um impresso [eempressoo]
formal *(person)* cerimonioso
  [surry-moon-yoh-zoo]
  (dress) de noite [duh noyt]
fortnight uma quinzena [keen-zennuh]
forward *(adverb)* para a frente [prah frent]
  forwarding address futuro endereço
  [footooroo enderessoo]
  could you please forward my mail? pode
  enviar-me o correio posteriormente? [pod
  emvee-ar-muh oo koo-rayoo
  poosh-turry-or-ment]
foundation cream creme de base [krem duh
  bahz]
fracture uma fractura [fractooruh]
fragile frágil [frah-jeel]
France França [fransuh]
fraud a fraude [frowd]
free livre [leevruh]
  admission free entrada gratuita [entrah-duh
  grat-weet-uh]
freight mercadorias [merkadoo-ree-yush]
French francês [fransesh]

Friday sexta-feira [seshtuh fay-ruh]
fridge um frigorífico [freegooreefikkoo]
fried egg um ovo estrelado [oh-voo shtrelah-doo]
friend um amigo [ameegoo]
friendly simpático [seempattikoo]
frio cold
from de [duh]
  where is it from? donde é? [dondy-eh]
front a frente [frent]
  in front of you em frente de si [aim frent duh see]
  at the front à frente [ah . . .]
frost a geada [jee-ah-duh]
frozen gelado [jelah-doo]
fruit fruta [frootuh]
  fruit salad uma salada de frutas [salah-duh duh frootush]
fry fritar [freetar]
  nothing fried nada frito [nah-duh freetoo]
  frying pan uma frigideira [freejeeday-ruh]
full cheio [shayoo]
fumadores smokers
fun: it's fun é divertido [eh deeverteedoo]
funny *(strange)* estranho [shtran-yoo]
  (comical) engraçado [engrassah-doo]
furniture os móveis [oosh movvaysh]
further mais longe [my-sh lonj]
fuse um fusível [foozeevel]
future futuro [footooroo]
  in future no futuro [noo . . .]
gale uma rajada [rajah-duh]
gallon um galão [galowng]
» *TRAVEL TIP: 1 gallon = 4.55 litres*
gallstone um cálculo biliar [kalkooloo beel-yar]
gamble jogar [joogar]
gammon fiambre [fee-ambruh]
garage *(repair)* uma garagem [garah-jeng]
  (petrol) uma bomba de gasolina [bombuh duh gazooleenuh]; *(parking)* um estacionamento [ishtuss-yoona-mentoo]

....

» *TRAVEL TIP: petrol stations do not usually have any mechanics, so look for nearest general garage or 'garagem de serviço'*

garden o jardim [jardeeng]

garlic o alho [al-yoo]

gas gás [gash]
 (petrol) gasolina [gazooleenuh]
 gas cooker um fogão a gás [foogowng uh gash]
 gas cylinder uma bilha de gás [beel-yuh duh gash]

gasket uma junta [joontuh]

gay *(homosexual)* uma bicha [beesh-uh]

gear *(car)* a mudança de velocidades [moodan-suh duh veloosidah-dush]
 (equipment) o equipamento [eekeep-amentoo]
 gearbox trouble um problema na caixa de velocidades [proobleh-muh nuh kye-shuh duh veloosidah-dush]
 gear lever a alavanca das mudanças [alavankuh dush moodan-sush]
 I can't get it into gear não posso meter a mudança [nowng possoo metair uh moodan-suh]

gelo *ice*

gents Homens [ommengsh]

gesture um gesto [jeshtoo]

get: will you get me a . . .? traga-me um . . . [trah-guh muh . . .]
 how do I get to . . .? como vou para . . .? [ko-moo voh para]
 where can I get a bus for . . .? onde posso apanhar um autocarro para . . .? [onduh possoo apanyar oom owtoo-karroo para]
 when can I get it back? quando me devolvem isso? [kwandoo muh duh-volveng ee-soo]
 when do we get back? a que horas voltamos? [uh kee or-ush voltah-moosh]
 where do I get off? onde é que saio? [ondy eh kuh sa-yoo]

gin um gin

gin and tonic um gin-tónico [jin-t*o*nnikoo]
girl uma rapariga [ruppar*ee*guh]
   my girlfriend a minha namorada [uh
   m*ee*n-yuh namoor*a*h-duh]
give dar
   will you give me ...? dá-me ...? [d*a*h-muh]
   I gave it to him dei-lho [d*a*y-l-yoo]
glad satisfeito [sateesh-f*a*y-too]
gland a glândula [gl*a*ndooluh]
   glandular fever febre glandular [f*e*bruh
   glandool*a*r]
glass vidro [v*ee*droo]
   (drinking) um copo [k*o*ppoo]
   a glass of water um copo de água [oom k*o*ppoo
   d*a*h-gwuh]
glasses óculos [*o*ckooloosh]
gloves luvas [l*oo*vush]
glue cola [k*o*lluh]
go: can I have a go? posso tentar também?
   [p*o*ssoo tent*a*r tamb*e*ng]
   where are you going? aonde vai?
   [uh-*o*nduh vye]
   my car won't go o meu carro não anda [oo
   m*e*h-oo k*a*rroo nowng *a*nduh]
   when does the bus go? a que horas parte o
   autocarro? [uh kee *o*rush part oo ow-took*a*rroo]
   go on! vai, continua! [vye kontin*oo*-uh]
   the bus has gone o autocarro já partiu [oo
   ow-took*a*rroo jah pert-y*oo*]
   he's gone foi-se embora [foy-suh embor-uh]
goal um golo [g*o*-loo]
goat uma cabra [k*a*h-bruh]
   goat's cheese queijo de cabra [k*a*y-joo ...]
god deus [d*e*h-oosh]
gold ouro [*o*h-roo]
golf o golf
good bom/boa [bong/b*o*-uh]
   good! bom!
goodbye adeus [a-d*e*h-oosh]
gooseberry uva-espim [*oo*vuh shpeeng]

....

got: have you got . . .? tem . . .? [taing . . .]

GNR = *National Guard (provincial police)*

gramme uma grama [gr*a*h-muh]

» *TRAVEL TIP: 100 grammes = approx 3½ oz*

grand: grandfather o avô [avoh]
   grandmother a avó [avo]
   grandson o neto [n*e*ttoo]
   grand-daughter a neta [n*e*ttuh]

grapefruit toranja [toor*a*njuh]
   grapefruit juice sumo de toranja [soomoo . . .]

grapes uvas [oovush]

grass a relva [r*e*lvuh]

grateful grato [gr*a*h-too]
   I'm very grateful to you estou-lhe muito
   agradecido [sht*o*hl-yuh mw*ee*ntoo
   agrud-s*ee*doo]

gratitude a gratidão [grateed*o*wng]
   as a sign of our gratitude como sinal da nossa
   estima [ko-moo seen*a*l duh n*o*ssuh sht*ee*muh]

gravy molho [m*o*le-yoo]

grease gordura [goord*oo*ruh]

greasy gorduroso [goord*oo*roh-zoo]

great grande [grand]
   great! porreiro! [poorr*a*y-roo]

greedy avaro [av*a*h-roo]
   (for food) guloso [gool*o*h-zoo]

green verde [vaird]
   greengrocer's o lugar [loog*a*r]
   green card carta verde [k*a*rtuh vaird]

grey cinzento [seenz*e*ntoo]

gristle cartilagem [karteel*a*h-jeng]

grocer's a mercearia [mersee-ar*ee*-uh]

ground o chão [showng]
   on the ground no chão [noo . . .]
   on the ground floor no rés do chão [noo resh
   doo showng]

group grupo [gr*oo*poo]
   our group leader o chefe do nosso grupo [oo
   shef doo n*o*ssoo gr*oo*poo]
   I'm with the English group estou com o

grupo inglês [shtoh kong oo groopoo eenglesh]
guarantee uma garantia [garahn-tee-uh]
  is there a guarantee? tem garantia?
  [taing . . .]
guest um convidado [konveedah-doo]
  guesthouse hospedaria [oshpud-aree-uh]
guide um guia [ghee-uh]
guilty culpado [koolpah-doo]
guitar uma viola [vee-olluh]
gum *(mouth)* a gengiva [jenjeevuh]
gun uma pistola [peeshtolluh]
gynaecologist um ginecologista
  [jeenuh-kooloojeeshtuh]
hair o cabelo [kabeh-loo]
  hairbrush uma escova de cabelo [shkovvuh
  duh . . .]
  where can I get a haircut? onde posso cortar
  o cabelo? [onduh possoo koortar . . .]
  is there a hairdresser's here? há, aqui,
  algum cabeleireiro? [ah akee algoom
  kubbalay-ray-roo]
half a metade [meetahd]
  a half portion meia dose [meyyuh doze]
  half an hour meia hora [meyyuh or-uh]
ham presunto [prezoontoo]
  hamburger um hamburger [amboorguh]
hammer um martelo [martelloo]
hand a mão [mowng]
  handbag uma mala de senhora [mah-luh duh
  sun-yoruh]
  handbrake o travão de mão [travowng duh
  mowng]
handkerchief um lenço [lensoo]
handle *(door)* o fecho [feh-shoo]
  (cup) a asa [ah-zuh]
hand luggage bagagem de mão [bagah-jeng duh
  mowng]
handmade feito à mão [fay-too ah mowng]
handsome bonito [booneetoo]
hanger um cabide [kabeed]

....

hangover uma ressaca [ressah-kuh]
 my head is killing me a minha cabeça parece
 que estoira [uh meen-yuh kabeh-suh paress kuh
 shtoy-ruh]
happen acontecer [akontussair]
 I don't know how it happened não sei como
 aconteceu [nowng say ko-moo akontusseh-oo]
 what's happening/happened? o que está a
 acontecer/aconteceu? [oo kuh shtah uh . . .]
happy contente [kontent]
harbour o porto [portoo]
hard duro [dooroo]
 (difficult) difícil [deefeeseel]
 hard-boiled egg um ovo duro [oh-voo dooroo]
 push hard empurre com força [empoorr kong
 forsuh]
harm *(noun)* mal
hat um chapéu [shapeh-oo]
hate: I hate . . . detesto . . . [duh-teshtoo]
have ter [tair]
 I have no time não tenho tempo [nowng
 ten-yoo tempoo]
 do you have any cigars/a map? tem
 charutos/um mapa? [teng sharootoosh/oom
 mah-puh]
 can I have some water/some more? pode
 trazer-me um copo de água/mais? [pod
 trazair-muh oom koppoo dahg-wuh/my-sh]
 I have to leave tomorrow amanhã tenho de
 partir [aman-yang ten-yoo duh perteer]
hay fever febre dos fenos [februh doosh
 feh-noosh]
he ele [ehl]
 does he live here? mora aqui? [mor-uh akee]
 he is my friend é o meu amigo [eh oo meh-oo
 ameegoo]
 he is ill está doente [shtah doo-ent]
head a cabeça [kabeh-suh]
 headache uma dor de cabeça
 headlight o farol

head waiter o chefe de mesa [shef duh meh-zuh]
head wind vento de proa [ventoo duh proh-uh]
health a saúde [sa-ood]
  your health! à sua saúde! [ah soo-uh sa-ood]
healthy saudável [sowdah-vel]
hear: I can't hear não ouço [nowng oh-soo]
  hearing aid um aparelho para a surdez [oom aparel-yoo prah soordesh]
heart o coração [kooruh-sowng]
  heart attack um enfarte [aim-fart]
heat o calor
  heat stroke uma insolação [oomuh eensooluh-sowng]
heating o aquecimento [akussy-mentoo]
heavy pesado [puzzah-doo]
heel *(body)* o calcanhar [kalkan-yar]
  (shoe) o salto [saltoo]
  could you put new heels on these? pode pôr-me uns saltos novos? [pod por-muh oonsh saltoosh novvoosh]
height a altura [altooruh]
hello olá [o-lah]
help ajuda [ajooduh]
  can you help me? pode ajudar-me? [pod ajoodar-muh]
  help! socorro! [sookorroo]
her: I know her conheço-a [koon-yessoo-uh]
  will you give it to her? quer dar-lho [kair darl-yoo]
  it's her é ela [eh elluh]
  it's her bag, it's hers é o saco dela, é dela [eh oo sakoo delluh]
here aqui [akee]
  come here venha cá [ven-yuh ka]
high alto [altoo]
hill a colina [kooleenuh]
  up/down the hill para cima/baixo [para seemuh/by-shoo]
him: I know him conheço-o [koon-yessoo-oo]

will you give it to him? quer dar-lho? [kair darl-yoo]

it's him é ele [eh ehl]

hire *see* **rent**

his: it's his drink, it's his é a bebida dele, é dele [eh uh bebeeduh dehl, eh dehl]

hit: he hit me bateu-me [bateh-oo-muh]

hitch-hike andar à boleia [. . . ah boolayuh]

hold *(verb)* segurar [suggoorar]

hole um buraco [boorah-koo]

holiday férias [fairy-ush]

I'm on holiday estou em férias [shtoh . . .]

home casa [kah-zuh]

I want to go home quero ir para casa [kairoo eer . . .]

at home em casa [eng . . .]

I'm homesick estou com saudades de casa [shtoh kong sowdahdj duh . . .]

Homens Gents

honest honesto [onneshtoo]

honestly? de verdade? [duh verdahd]

honey o mel

honeymoon a lua-de-mel [loo-uh-duh-mel]

hope *(noun)* esperança [shperansuh]

I hope that . . . espero que [shperoo kuh]

I hope so/not espero que sim/não [. . . seeng/nowng]

horizon o horizonte [o-reezont]

horn *(car)* a buzina [boozeenuh]

horrible horrível [orreevel]

hors d'oeuvre a entrada [entrah-duh]

horse um cavalo [kavah-loo]

hospital um hospital [o-shpeetal]

» *TRAVEL TIP: EEC reciprocal health agreement; get form E111 from Post Office before you go—it gives full details of medical services available*

host o anfitrião [amfeetree-owng]

hostess a anfitriã [amfeetree-ang]

(air) a hospedeira [o-shpeday-ruh]

hot quente [kent]; *(spiced)* picante [peekant]

hotel um hotel [o-*te*l]
hotplate chapa eléctrica [sh*a*h-puh eel*e*trikuh]
hot water bottle um saco de água quente
  [s*a*h-koo d*a*h-gwuh kent]
hour a hora [or-uh]
house a casa [k*a*h-zuh]
  housewife a dona de casa [uh d*o*nnuh . . .]
how como [k*o*-moo]
  how many quantos [kw*a*ntoosh]
  how much quanto
  how often quantas vezes [kw*a*ntush veh-zush]
  how long does it take? quanto tempo leva
  isso? [kw*a*ntoo t*e*mpoo l*e*vvuh *ee*-soo]
  how long have you been here? há quanto
  tempo está aqui? [ah kw*a*ntoo t*e*mpoo shtah
  ak*ee*]
  how are you? como está? [k*o*-moo shtah]
hull o casco [k*a*shkoo]
humid húmido [*oo*midoo]
humour humor [oom*o*r]
  haven't you got a sense of humour? não tem
  sentido do humor? [nowng teng sent*ee*doo doo
  oom*o*r]
hundred cem [seng]
  hundredweight quintal inglês [keent*a*l
  eengl*e*sh]
» *TRAVEL TIP: 1 cwt = 50.8 kilos*
hungry: I'm hungry/not hungry tenho/não
  tenho fome [t*e*n-yoo/nowng t*e*n-yoo fom]
hurry: I'm in a hurry estou com pressa [shtoh
  kom pr*e*ssuh]
  please hurry! despache-se, por favor!
  [dushp*a*sh-suh, poor fuh-v*o*r]
hurt: it hurts dói-me [d*o*y-muh]
  my leg hurts dói-me a perna [. . . uh p*ai*rnuh]
  YOU MAY THEN HEAR . . .
  é uma dor aguda? [eh *oo*muh dor ag*oo*duh] *is it a*
  sharp pain?
husband: my husband o meu marido [oo
  m*e*h-oo mar*ee*doo]

I eu [eh-oo]
   I am a doctor sou médico [soh meddikoo]
   I am tired estou cansado [shtoh . . .]
   I live in London vivo em Londres [veevoo eng
   londrush]
ice gelo [jeh-loo]
   ice-cream um gelado [jelah-doo]
   iced coffee um café gelado [kuffeh . . .]
   with lots of ice com muito gelo [kong
   mweentoo . . .]
identity papers o bilhete de identidade [beel-yet
   deedenty-dad]
idiot idiota [eed-yottuh]
if se [suh]
ignition a ignição [eegnee-sowng]
ill doente [doo-ent]
   I feel ill sinto-me doente [seentoo-muh . . .]
illegal ilegal [eeluh-gal]
illegible ilegível [eeluh-jeevel]
illness a doença [doo-ensuh]
immediately imediatamente
   [eemuddy-ahtuh-ment]
import *(verb)* importar [eempoortar]
important importante [eempoortant]
   it's very important é muito importante [eh
   mweentoo . . .]
import duty direitos de importação
   [deeray-toosh deempoortuh-sowng]
impossible impossível [eempoo-seevel]
impressive impressionante [eempress-yoonant]
improve melhorar [mulyoorar]
   I want to improve my . . . quero melhorar o
   meu . . . [kairoo mul-yoorar oo meh-oo]
in em [eng]
inch uma polegada [pole-gah-duh]
   » *TRAVEL TIP: 1 inch = 2.54 cm*
include incluir [eenklweer]
   does that include breakfast? o pequeno
   almoço está incluído? [oo pickeh-noo almoh-soo
   shtah eenklweedoo]

inclusive inclusíve [eenkloozeev]
incompetent incompetente [eenkompuh-tent]
inconsiderate mal-educado [maleedookah-doo]
incredible incrível [eenkreevel]
indecent indecente [eenduh-sent]
independent independente [eenduh-pendent]
India Índia [eendee-uh]
Indian Indiano [eendee-ah-noo]
indicator indicador [eendeekador]
indigestion indigestão [eendeejesh-towng]
indoors dentro de casa [dentroo duh kah-zuh]
industry a indústria [eendooshtree-uh]
inexpensive barato [barah-too]
infant uma criança [oomuh kree-ansuh]
infection uma infecção [eemfessowng]
infectious infeccioso [eemfess-yoh-zoo]
inflation a inflação [eemflassowng]
informações Information
informal informal [eemfoormal]
(person) natural [natooral]
information informação [eemfoorma-sowng]
  do you have any information in English about . . .? tem algum folheto em inglês sobre . . .? [teng algoom fool-yettoo eng eenglesh so-bruh]
  is there an information office? há algum centro de turismo? [ah algoom sentroo duh tooreejmoo]
inhabitant habitante [abeetant]
injection uma injecção [eenjessowng]
injured ferido [fereedoo]
  he's been injured foi ferido [foy . . .]
injury ferimento [furry-mentoo]
innocent inocente [eenoosent]
insect um insecto [eensettoo]
inside dentro de [dentroo duh]
insist: I insist (on it) insisto [eenseeshtoo]
insomnia a insónia [eenson-yuh]
instant coffee café instantâneo [kuffeh eenshtantahn-yoo]

....

instead no seu lugar [noo seh-oo loogar]
   instead of ... em vez de ... [eng vesh duh]
insulating tape fita isoladora [feetuh
   eezooluh-doruh]
insulation o isolamento [eezoolamentoo]
insult um insulto [eensooltoo]
insurance o seguro [suggooroo]
intelligent inteligente [eentully-jent]
interesting interessante [eenteressant]
international internacional
   [eenternuss-yoonal]
interpret interpretar
   would you interpret for us? quer ser o nosso
   intérprete? [kair sair oo nossoo eentair-pret]
into para [paruh]
introduce: can I introduce ...? posso
   apresentar ...? [possoo apruh-zentar]
invalid (noun) um inválido [eenvalidoo]
   invalid chair uma cadeira de rodas [oomuh
   kaday-ruh duh roddush]
invitation um convite [konveet]
   thank you for the invitation obrigado pelo
   convite [o-breegah-doo peloo ...]
invite: can I invite you out? quer ir sair
   comigo? [kair eer suh-eer koo-meegoo]
invoice a factura [fattooruh]
Ireland Irlanda [eerlanduh]
Irish irlandês [eerlandesh]
iron (noun: clothes) um ferro [ferroo]
   will you iron these for me? passa-me isto a
   ferro? [pah-suh-muh eeshtoo uh ferroo]
ironmonger's a loja de ferragens [lojjuh duh
   ferah-jengsh]
is é/está [eh/shtah]
island uma ilha [eel-yuh]
it: I see it vejo-o [veh-joo-oo]
   it's not working não funciona [nowng
   foonss-yonnuh]
   give me it dê-mo [deh-moo]
   is it ...? é ...?/está ...? [eh/shtah]

itch comichão [koomee-sho*w*ng]
  it itches faz comichão [fash . . .]
itemize: would you itemize it for me? pode
  discriminar-me isto? [pod
  deesh-kreemin*a*r-muh *ee*shtoo]
jack um macaco [mak*a*h-koo]
jacket um casaco [kaz*a*h-koo]
jam compota [komp*o*ttuh]
  traffic jam um engarrafamento
  [engarr*a*h-famentoo]
January Janeiro [jan*a*yroo]
jaw a maxila [uh maks*ee*luh]
jealous ciumento [s-yoomentoo]
jeans 'jeans'
jellyfish uma alforreca [alfoor*e*ckuh]
jetty o cais [kye-sh]
jeweller's/jewellery a joalharia
  [joo-al-yer*ee*-uh]
jib a bujarrona [boojarr*o*nnuh]
job um emprego [empr*e*h-goo]
  just the job óptimo [*o*ttimoo]
joke *(noun)* uma piada [pee-*a*h-duh]
  you must be joking está a brincar [shtah
  breenk*a*r]
journey uma viagem [vee-*a*h-jeng]
  have a good journey boa viagem [b*o*-uh . . .]
July Julho [j*o*ol-yoo]
jumper uma camisola [kameez*o*lluh]
junction um cruzamento [kroozamentoo]
June Junho [j*o*on-yoo]
junk velharias [vel-yuh-r*ee*-ush]
just: just two apenas dois [ap*e*h-nush doysh]
  just a little só um pouco [so oom p*o*h-koo]
  just there ali mesmo [al*ee* m*e*jmoo]
  not just now agora não [ag*o*ruh nowng]
  that's just right é isso mesmo [eh *ee*-soo
  m*e*jmoo]
  he was here just now há pouco esteve aqui
  [ah p*o*-koo shtev ak*ee*]
keen entusiástico [entoozee-*a*shtickoo]

I'm not keen não estou muito inclinado [nowng shtoh mweentoo eenkleenah-doo]
keep: can I keep it? posso ficar com isto? [possoo feekar kong eeshtoo]
    you keep it fique com isso [feek kong ee-soo]
    keep the change guarde o troco [gward oo tro-koo]
    you didn't keep your promise não cumpriu a palavra [nowng koompree-oo uh palahv-ruh]
    it keeps on breaking está sempre a partir-se [shtah semprah perteer-suh]
kettle uma chaleira [shalay-ruh]
key a chave [shahv]
kidney o rim [reeng]
kill matar
kilo um quilo [keeloo]
» TRAVEL TIP: conversion: $\dfrac{kilos}{5} \times 11 = pounds$

kilos	1	1½	5	6	7	8	9
pounds	2.2	3.3	11	13.2	15.4	17.6	19.8

kilometre um quilómetro [keelommetroo]
» TRAVEL TIP: conversion: $\dfrac{kilometres}{8} \times 5 = miles$

kilometres	1	5	10	20	50	100
miles	0.62	3.11	6.2	12.4	31	62

kind: that's very kind of you é muito amável da sua parte [eh mweentoo amah-vel duh soo-uh part]
kiss um beijo [bay-joo]
kitchen a cozinha [koozeen-yuh]
knee o joelho [joo-el-yoo]
knickers cuecas [kweckush]
knife uma faca [fah-kuh]
knock bater à porta [batair ah portuh]
    there's a knocking noise from the engine o motor tem uma batida [oo mootor teng oomuh bateeduh]
know saber [sabair]
    (be acquainted with) conhecer [koon-yussair]
    I don't know the area não conheço esta

região [nowng koon-yessoo eshtuh rej-yowng]
   I don't know não sei [nowng say]
label um rótulo [rottooloo]
laces (shoe) atacadores [–rush]
lacquer laca [lah-kuh]
ladies senhoras [sun-yorush]
lady a senhora [sun-yoruh]
lager uma Sagres [sahg-rush]
   lager and lime Sagres com lima [. . . kong leemuh]
» *TRAVEL TIP: not generally available*
lamb (meat) cordeiro [kor-day-roo]
lamp uma lanterna [lantair-nuh]
   lampshade um quebra-luz [kebruh loosh]
   lamp-post um candeeiro [kandy-ay-roo]
land (noun) terra [terruh]
lane (car) a via [vee-uh]
language a língua [leeng-wuh]
large grande [grand]
laryngitis a laringite [larinjeet]
last último [ooltimoo]
   last year/week o ano passado/a semana passada [oo ah-noo passah-doo/uh semah-nuh passah-duh]
   last night ontem à noite [onteng ah noyt]
   at last! finalmente [feenalment]
late: sorry I'm late desculpe o atraso [dushcoolp oo atrah-zoo]
   it's a bit late já é um bocado tarde [jah eh oom bookah-doo tard]
   please hurry, I'm late despache-se, por favor, já estou atrasado [dushpash-suh poor fuh-vor, jah shtoh atra-zah-doo]
   at the latest o mais tardar [oo my-sh tardar]
   later mais tarde
   I'll come back later volto mais tarde
   see you later até logo [ateh loggoo]
laugh (verb) rir-se [reer-suh]
launderette uma lavandaria automática [lavanduh-ree-uh ow-too-mattikuh]

....

lavabos toilets
lavatory o lavabo [lav*a*h-boo]
law a lei [lay]
lawyer um advogado [oom advoog*a*h-doo]
laxative um laxativo [lashat*ee*voo]
lazy preguiçoso [pruggy-s*o*zoo]
leaf uma folha [*fo*al-yuh]
leak uma fuga de água [*fo*oguh d*a*h-gwuh]
   there's a leak in my ceiling cai água do tecto
   [kye *a*hg-wuh doo t*e*ttoo]
   it leaks há uma fuga [ah *oo*muh f*oo*guh]
learn: I want to learn . . . quero aprender . . .
   [k*a*iroo aprend*a*ir]
lease *(verb)* arrendar [arrend*a*r]
least: not in the least de modo algum [duh
   m*o*-doo al-g*oo*m]
   at least pelo menos [peloo m*e*h-noosh]
leather couro [k*o*h-roo]
   this meat's like leather esta carne é dura
   como pedra [*e*shtuh karn eh d*o*oruh ko-moo
   p*e*druh]
leave: we're leaving tomorrow vamos partir
   amanhã [v*a*moosh per-t*ee*r a-man-y*a*ng]
   when does the bus leave? a que horas parte o
   autocarro? [uh kee *o*r-ush part oo
   ow-too-k*a*rroo]
   I left two shirts in my room deixei duas
   camisas no meu quarto [day-sh*a*y d*o*o-ush
   kam*ee*zush noo m*e*h-oo kw*a*rtoo]
   can I leave this here? posso deixar isto aqui?
   [possoo day-sh*a*r *ee*shtoo ak*ee*]
left esquerdo [shk*a*ir-doo]
   on the left à esquerda [ah shk*a*ir-duh]
   left-handed canhoto [kan-yot-oo]
left luggage (office) o depósito de bagagem
   [dep*o*zitoo duh bag*a*h-jeng]
leg a perna [p*a*ir-nuh]
legal legal [legg*a*l]
lemon um limão [leem*o*wng]
lemonade uma limonada [leemoon*a*h-duh]

lend: will you lend me your . . .? quer
emprestar-me o seu . . .? [kair empresht*a*r-muh
oo s*e*h-oo]
lengthen along*a*r
lens *(photography)* a objectiva
[objet*ee*vuh]
Lent a quaresma [uh kwer*e*j-muh]
less menos [m*e*h-noosh]
  less than three menos de três [. . . tresh]
  less than that menos do que isso [. . . doo kee
ee-soo]
let: let me help deixe-me ajudar [d*a*ysh-muh
ajood*a*r]
  let me go! deixe-me ir! [d*a*ysh-muh eer]
  will you let me off here? deixe-me sair aqui
[. . . suh-*ee*r ak*ee*]
  let's go! vamos! [v*a*moosh]
letter uma carta [k*a*rtuh]
  are there any letters for me? há correio para
mim? [ah koor*a*yoo para meeng]
  letterbox um marco de correio [oom m*a*rkoo
duh koo-r*a*yoo]
lettuce alface [al-f*a*ss]
level crossing passagem de nível [passah-jeng
duh n*ee*-vel]
liable responsável [rushpons*a*h-vel]
library a biblioteca [beebleeoo-t*e*ckuh]
licence uma licença [lees*e*nsuh]
lid a tampa [t*a*mpuh]
lie *(noun)* mentira [ment*ee*ruh]
  can he lie down for a bit? pode deitar-se um
momento? [pod dayt*a*r-suh oom moom*e*ntoo]
life a vida [v*ee*duh]
  life assurance seguro de vida [seg*oo*roo duh
v*ee*duh]
  lifebelt o cinto de salvação [s*ee*ntoo duh
salva-s*o*wng]
  life-jacket o colete de salvação [kool*e*t duh . . .]
  lifeboat o barco salva-vidas [b*a*rkoo
salva-v*ee*dush]

....

lifeguard o salva-vidas [salva-*vee*dush]
lift: do you want a lift? quer uma boleia? [kair
  oomuh bool*ay*-uh]
  could you give me a lift? pode dar-me uma
  boleia? [pod d*a*r-muh . . .]
  the lift isn't working o ascensor não anda [oo
  ash-sen*sor* nowng *a*nduh]
light: the lights aren't working *(car)* as luzes
  não funcionam [ush l*oo*zush nowng
  foons-yon-owng]
  have you got a light? tem lume, por favor?
  [teng loom poor fuh-*vor*]
  when it gets light quando amanhecer
  [kw*a*ndoo aman-yess*air*]
  light bulb uma lâmpada [oomuh l*a*mpa-duh]
  light meter um fotómetro [foot*o*mmuh-troo]
  (not heavy) ligeiro [leej*ay*-roo]
like: would you like . . .? gostaria de . . .?
  [gooshtar*ee*-uh duh]
  I'd like a . . ./I'd like to . . . queria [kr*ee*-uh]
  I like it/you gosto disso /de ti [g*o*shtoo
  dee-soo/duh tee]
  I don't like it não gosto disso [nowng g*o*shtoo
  dee-soo]
  what's it like? como é? [k*o*-moo eh]
  one like this um como este
  [oom k*o*-moo ehsht]
  do it like this faça-o assim [f*a*ssuh-oo ass*ee*ng]
lime lima [*lee*muh]
line uma linha [l*ee*n-yuh]
lip o lábio [l*a*hb-yoo]
  lipstick o baton [b*a*h-tong]
  lip salve manteiga de cacau [mant*a*y-guh duh
  kak*o*w]
liqueur licor [leek*o*r]
 » *TRAVEL TIP:* 'ginginha' = a cherry liqueur;
  'amêndoa amarga' = almond flavour; 'licor
  beirão' & 'tríplice' = local blends
Lisbon Lisboa [leej-boh-uh]
list *(noun)* uma lista [*lee*shtuh]

listen escutar [shkoot*a*r]
litre um litro [l*ee*troo]
» *TRAVEL TIP: 1 litre* = $1\frac{3}{4}$ *pints* = *0.22 gals*
little pequeno [pick*eh*-noo]
   a little ice um pouco de gelo [oom po-koo duh jeh-loo]
   a little more um bocado mais [oom book*a*h-doo my-sh]
   just a little só um bocadinho [so oom bookad*ee*n-yoo]
live viver [veev*a*ir]
   I live in . . . moro em . . . [m*o*roo eng]
   where do you live? onde mora? [onduh m*o*r-uh]
liver fígado [f*ee*guh-doo]
livre vacant
lizard um lagarto [lag*a*rtoo]
loaf um pão [powng]
lobster lagosta [lag*o*shtuh]
local: could we try a local wine? podemos provar um vinho da região? [pood*eh*-moosh proov*a*r oom v*ee*n-yoo duh rej-y*o*wng]
   a local restaurant um restaurante local [oom reshtowr*a*nt look*a*l]
   is it made locally? é feito na região [eh f*a*y-too nuh rej-y*o*wng]
lock: the lock's broken a fechadura está partida [uh feshad*oo*ruh shtah purt*ee*duh]
   I've locked myself out fechei o quarto com a chave lá dentro [fush*a*y oo kw*a*rtoo kong uh shahv lah d*e*ntroo]
London Londres [l*o*ndrush]
lonely solitário [sooleet*a*r-yoo]
long comprido [kompr*ee*doo]
   we'd like to stay longer queremos fi*c*ar mais tempo
   [kr*eh*-moosh feek*a*r my-sh t*e*mpoo]
   that was long ago isso aconteceu há muito tempo [*ee*-soo akont-s*eh*-oo ah mw*ee*ntoo t*e*mpoo]

....

loo: where's the loo? onde é a casa de banho?
[ondy eh uh kah-zuh duh bahn-yoo]

look: you look tired tens um ar cansado [tainz
oom ar kansah-doo]

I'm looking forward to ... estou desejoso
de ... [shtoh duzza-joh-zoo duh]

look at that olhe para isso [ol-yuh paree-soo]

I'm just looking estou a ver [shtoh uh vair]

I'm looking for ... procuro ... [prookooroo]

look out! tem cuidado! [teng kweedah-doo]

loose solto [sole-too]

lorry um camião [kamee-owng]

lorry driver um camionista
[kamee-ooneeshtuh]

lose perder [perdair]

I've lost my ... perdi o meu ... [perdee oo
meh-oo]

excuse me, I'm lost desculpe, estou perdido
[dushkoolp, shtoh perdeedoo]

lost property (office) depósito de objectos
achados [depozitoo dobjettooz ashah-doosh]

lot: a lot/not a lot muito/não muito
[mweentoo/nowng ...]

a lot of chips/wine muitas batatas
fritas/muito vinho [mweentush batah-tush
freetush/mweentoo veen-yoo]

a lot more expensive muito mais caro
[mweentoo my-sh kah-roo]

lots muito

lotação esgotada all tickets sold

lotion uma loção [loo-sowng]

loud ruidoso [rweedoh-zoo]

louder mais forte [my-sh fort]

love: I love you gosto de ti [goshtoo duh tee]

do you love me? gostas de mim? [goshtush
duh meeng]

he's in love está apaixonado [shtah
apye-shoonah-doo]

I love this wine gosto imenso deste vinho
[goshto eemensoo deh-sht veen-yoo]

lovely encantador
  we had a lovely time foi muito agradável [foy mweentoo agradah-vel]
low baixo [by-shoo]
luck a sorte [sort]
  good luck! boa sorte [bo-uh sort]
lucky afortunado [afortoonah-doo]
  you're lucky está com sorte [shtah kong . . .]
  that's lucky que sorte! [kuh sort]
luggage a bagagem [bagah-jeng]
lumbago lumbago [loombah-goo]
lump um inchaço [oom een-shah-soo]
lunch o almoço [al-mo-soo]
lungs os pulmões [oosh poolmoingsh]
luxurious sumptuoso [soomp-too-ozoo]
luxury o luxo [looshoo]
  a luxury hotel um hotel de luxo [oom o-tel duh looshoo]
luzes *headlights (on)*
Lx.a = Lisboa *Lisbon*
mad doido [doy-doo]
madam minha senhora [meen-yuh sun-yoruh]
Madeira Madeira [maday-ruh]
made-to-measure feito por medida [fay-too poor medeeduh]
magazine uma revista [reveeshtuh]
magnificent esplêndido [shplendidoo]
maiden name nome de solteira [nom duh soltay-ruh]
mail correio [koorayoo]
  is there any mail for me? há correio para mim? [ah koorayoo para meeng]
mainland continente [konteenent]
main road a rua principal [roo-uh preen-sipal]
  (country) a estrada principal [shtrah-duh . . .]
make *(verb)* fazer [fazair]; *(type)* a marca
  will we make it in time? vamos chegar a tempo? [vah-moosh shegar uh tempoo]
  make-up a maquillage [uh makee-yaj]
man um homem [ommeng]

manager o gerente [jerent]
  can I see the manager? pode chamar o
  gerente, por favor? [pod shamar oo jerent, poor
  fuh-vor]
manicure a manicura [manikooruh]
manners boa educação
  [bo-uh eedooka-sowng]
  haven't you got any manners? você não tem
  maneiras! [vosseh nowng teng manay-rush]
many muitos/as [mweentoosh/tush]
map um mapa [mah-puh]
  a map of ... um mapa de ... [... duh]
March Março [marsoo]
margarine a margarina [margareenuh]
marina uma marina [mareenuh]
mark: there's a mark on it tem uma mancha
  [teng oomuh manshuh]
market mercado [merkah-doo]
  marketplace a praça [prah-suh]
marmalade doce de laranja [dose duh laranjuh]
married casado [kazah-doo]
marry: will you marry me? queres casar
  comigo? [kairush kazar koomeegoo]
marvellous maravilhoso [maraveel-yo-zoo]
mascara rímel [reemel]
mashed potatoes puré de batatas [pooreh duh
  batah-tush]
massage massagem [massah-jeng]
mast o mastro [mashtroo]
mat um capacho [kapah-shoo]
match: a box of matches uma caixa de fósforos
  [kye-shuh duh fosh-fooroosh]
  football match um desafio de futebol
  [duzza-fee-oo duh foot-boll]
material material [maturry-al]
  (cloth) tecido [tesseedoo]
matter: it doesn't matter não faz mal [nowng
  fash mal]
  what's the matter? o que há? [oo kee ah]
mattress um colchão [kol-showng]

mature *(wine)* velho [vel-yoo]
maximum máximo [massimoo]
May Maio [my-oo]
may: may I have ...? pode dar-me ...? [pod darr-muh]
maybe talvez [tal-vesh]
mayonnaise maionese [ma-yoo-nez]
me me [muh]
   for me para mim [para meeng]
   with me comigo [koomeegoo]
   it's me sou eu [so eh-oo]
meal uma refeição [refay-sowng]
mean: what does this mean? o que significa isto? [oo kuh seegnifeekuh eeshtoo]
measles sarampo [sarampoo]
   German measles rubéola [roobeh-ooluh]
meat carne [karn]
mechanic: is there a mechanic here? há algum mecânico aqui? [ah algoom mekah-nikoo akee]
medicine a medicina [mud-see-nuh]
meet: when shall we meet? quando nos reunimos? [kwandoo noosh ree-oonee-moosh]
   I met him in the street encontrei-o na rua [enkontray-oo nuh roo-uh]
   pleased to meet you muito prazer em conhecê-lo/la [mweentoo prazair eng koon-yuh-seh-loo/luh]
meeting uma reunião [ree-oon-yowng]
melon um melão [melowng]
member um membro [membroo]
   how do I become a member? como é que me torno sócio? [... tornoo soss-yoo]
mend: can you mend this? pode consertar isto? [pod konsertar eeshtoo]
mention: don't mention it não tem de quê [nowng teng duh keh]
menu a ementa [eementuh]; **can I have the menu, please?** pode dar-me a ementa, por favor?

Menu Ementa
ENTRADAS: Starters
cocktail de gambas *prawn cocktail*
salada de atum *tuna salad*
melão *melon*
sumo de laranja/tomate *orange/tomato juice*
chouriço *smoked pork sausage*
ovos à Minhota *baked eggs, tomato, onions*
omeleta de marisco/presunto/cogumelos
   shellfish/cured ham/mushroom omelette

SOPA: Soup
açorda de alho *bread soup, garlic, herbs*
canja *chicken broth + rice*
caldo verde *potato broth, shredded cabbage*
gaspacho *refreshing cold soup: tomatoes, green*
   peppers and cucumber

PEIXE: Fish dishes
amêijoas *clams*
gambas *scampi*
santola *crab*
sardinhas assadas *charcoal-grilled sardines*
salmão grelhado *grilled salmon*
bacalhau à Gomes de Sá *cod baked with parsley,*
   potatoes, onion, olives, etc
chocos *cuttlefish*
lulas/calamares *squid*
lampreia *lamprey*
caldeirada *mixed fish in onions, potato*

CARNE: Meat dishes
carne de vaca (assada) *(roast) beef*
borrego *lamb*
porco *pork*
frango *chicken*
vitela *veal*
um bife de . . . a . . . *steak*
costeleta *cutlet/chop*
leitão *suckling pig*
cordorniz *quail*

faisão *pheasant*
peru *turkey*
cozido à portuguesa *boiled beef, gammon, smoked sausage, rice and veg*
arroz de frango *fried chicken in wine, ham and rice casserole*
frango na púcara *chicken stewed in Port and brandy, fried with almonds*
almôndegas *meatballs*
espetada mista *shish-kebab*
feijoada *pigs feet, sausage, white beans and cabbage*

SOBREMESA: Dessert
Fruit: ananás *pineapple*
melancia *watermelon*
cerejas *cherries*
ameixas *plums*
morangos *strawberries*
Sweets: salada de frutas *fruit cocktail*
pudim flã *creme caramel*
pudim molotov *eggwhite mousse, caramel*
arroz doce *rice pudding*
farófias *eggwhite beaten with milk, egg custard and cinnamon*
gelado *ice cream*
Cheese: queijo de Elvas *mild white*
queijo de azeitão *matured in oil*
queijo fresco *very bland goat's milk cheese*
COFFEE: *most Portuguese have a small strong black coffee after a meal called 'uma bica'* [beekuh]; *if you prefer it weaker, ask for a 'carioca'; the equivalent to our white coffee is a 'galão'* [galowng]
Brandy, etc: *if you like an after-meal drink, try a Carvalho Ribeiro e Ferreira brandy or Aguardente de Medronho*

....

message: are there any messages for me? há
algum recado para mim? [ah algoom rekah-doo
para meeng]
   can I leave a message for . . .? posso deixar
um recado para . . .? [possoo day-shar oom
rekah-doo para]
metre um metro [metroo]
  » *TRAVEL TIP: 1 metre = 39.37 ins = 1.09 yds*
metro underground
  » *TRAVEL TIP: flat rate fare; cheaper to buy a book of
tickets, 'caderneta', or a 7 day 'passe'*
midday meio-dia [mayoo-dee-uh]
middle o centro [sentroo]
  in the middle no centro [noo sentroo]
  in the middle of the road no meio da rua [noo
mayoo duh roo-uh]
midnight meia-noite [mayuh noyt]
might: I might be late sou capaz de chegar
tarde [soh kapash duh shuggar tard]
  he might have gone ele já pode ter-se ido
embora [ehl jah pod tair-suh eedoo emboruh]
migraine a enxaqueca [enshackeckuh]
mild suave [swahv]
mile uma milha [meel-yuh]
  » *TRAVEL TIP: conversion:* $\frac{miles}{5} \times 8 = kilometres$

miles	$\frac{1}{2}$	1	3	5	10	50	100
kilometres	0.8	1.6	4.8	8	16	80	160

milk o leite [layt]
  a glass of milk um copo de leite [oom koppoo
duh layt]
  milkshake um batido [oom bateedoo]
millimetre um milímetro [meeleemitroo]
milometer a conta-quilómetros
[kontuh-keelometroosh]
minced meat carne picada [karn peekah-duh]
mind: I've change my mind mudei de opinião
[mooday doh-peen-yowng]
  I don't mind não me importo [nowng muh
eemportoo]

do you mind if I . . .? importa-se que . . .?
[eemportuh-suh kuh]
never mind não faz mal [nowng fash mal]
mine meu/minha [meh-oo/meen-yuh]
it's mine é meu/minha [eh . . .]
mineral water água mineral [ahg-wuh
meen-ral]
minimum mínimo [meeny-moo]
minus menos [meh-noosh]
minus 3 degrees três graus abaixo de zero
[tresh growz abye-shoo duh zairoo]
minute um minuto [meenootoo]
in a minute dentro dum momento [dentroo
doom moomentoo]
just a minute só um minuto
mirror um espelho [shpel-yoo]
Miss a Menina [uh meneenuh]
miss: I miss you tenho saudades tuas [ten-yoo
sow-dahdush too-ush]
he's missing está perdido [shtah perdeedoo]
there is a . . . missing falta um/uma . . .
[faltuh oom/oomuh . . .]
mist a névoa [uh nev-wuh]
mistake um erro [erroo]
I think you've made a mistake acho que se
enganou [ashoo kuh see enganoh]
misunderstanding um mal-entendido
[mal-entendeedoo]
modern moderno [moodairnoo]
Monday segunda-feira [segoonduh fay-ruh]
money dinheiro [din-yay-roo]
I've lost my money perdi o meu dinheiro
[perdee oo meh-oo . . .]
I've no money não tenho dinheiro [nowng
ten-yoo . . .]
» *TRAVEL TIP: the Portuguese dollar sign is placed
after the 'escudos', so that 10$50 means 10
escudos and 50 centavos*
month o mês [mesh]
moon a lua [loo-uh]

....

moorings o ancoradouro [ankooruh-doh-roo]
moped um ciclomotor [seekloo-mootor]
more mais [my-sh]
  can I have some more? posso repetir? [possoo
  repuh-teer]
  more wine, please um pouco mais de vinho,
  por favor [oom po-koo my-sh duh veen-yoo . . .]
  no more mais nada [my-sh nah-duh]
  more comfortable mais confortável [my-sh
  komfoortah-vel]
  more than three mais de três [my-sh duh
  tresh]
  more than that mais do que isso [my-sh doo
  kee ee-soo]
morning a manhã [man-yang]
  good morning bom dia [bong dee-uh]
  this morning esta manhã [eshtuh . . .]
  in the morning de manhã [duh man-yang]
most: I like it/you the most é do que/és de
  quem: gosto mais [eh doo kuh/esh duh keng
  goshtoomy-sh]
  most of the time/the people a maior parte do
  tempo/das pessoas [uh muh-yor part doo
  tempoo/dush pussoh-ush]
motel um motel
mother: my mother minha mãe [meen-yuh
  my-ng]
motor o motor [mootor]
motorbike uma mota [mottuh]
motorboat um barco a motor [barkoo uh mootor]
motorcyclist um motociclista
  [mottoo-seekleeshtuh]
motorist o motorista [mootooreeshtuh]
motorway a auto-estrada [owtoo-shtrah-duh]
mountain uma montanha [montahn-yuh]
mouse um rato [rah-too]
moustache o bigode [beegod]
mouth a boca [boh-kuh]
move: don't move não se mexa [nowng suh
  meshuh]

could you move your car? não se importa de
chegar o carro para o lado? [nowng seemportuh
duh shuggar oo karroo proh lah-doo]
Mr o Senhor [oo sun-yor]
Mrs a Senhora [uh sun-yoruh]
Ms *no equivalent in Portuguese*
much muito [mweentoo]
   much better/much more muito
   melhor/muito mais [. . . mel-yor/. . . my-sh]
   not much não muito [nowng . . .]
mug: I've been mugged atacaram-me
   [atakah-rowng-muh]
mum mamã [mumang]
muscle um músculo [mooshkooloo]
museum o museu [moozeh-oo]
mushrooms cogumelos [koogoomelloosh]
music a música [moozickuh]
must: I must have a . . . tenho de tomar
   um/uma . . . [ten-yoo duh toomar oom/oomuh]
   I must not eat . . . não devo comer . . . [nowng
   devvoo koomair]
   you must (do it) tem de fazê-lo [teng duh
   fazeh-loo]
   must I . . .? tenho de . . .? [ten-yoo duh . . .]
mustard a mostarda [mooshtarduh]
my o meu/a minha [oo meh-oo/uh meen-yuh]
nail *(finger)* a unha [oon-yuh]
   (wood) um cravo [krah-voo]
   nailclippers alicate de unhas [aleekat
   doon-yush]
   nailfile uma lima de unhas [leemuh . . .]
   nail polish verniz de unhas [verneesh . . .]
   nail scissors tesoura de unhas [tezoh-ruh . . .]
naked nu [noo]; nua [noo-uh]
name o nome [nom]
   my name is chamo-me [shah-moo-muh]
   what's your name? como se chama? [ko-moo
   suh shah-muh]
não potável *not for drinking*
napkin um guardanapo [gwarduh-nappoo]

....

nappy uma fralda [fr*a*lduh]
   disposable nappies fraldas de papel
   [fr*a*ldush duh pap*e*ll]
narrow estreito [shtr*a*y-too]
national nacional [nuss-yoon*a*l]
nationality a nacionalidade [nuss-yoonalid*a*hd]
natural natural [natoor*a*l]
naughty: don't be naughty não sejas mau
   [nowng sejjush m*a*h-oo]
near: is it near? fica perto? [f*ee*kuh p*a*irtoo]
   near here aqui perto [ak*ee* . . .]
   do you go near . . .? passa perto de . . .?
   [p*a*ssuh p*a*irtoo duh]
   where's the nearest . . .? onde é o/a . . . mais
   próximo? [ondee eh . . . my-sh pr*o*ssimoo]
nearly quase [kw*a*hz]
neat *(drink)* puro [p*o*oroo]
necessary necessário [nussuss*a*ree-oo]
   it's not necessary não é necessário [nowng
   eh . . .]
neck o pescoço [push-k*o*-soo]
   necklace um colar [k*o*olar]
need: I need . . . preciso de . . . [pruss*ee*zoo duh]
needle uma agulha [ag*o*ol-yuh]
negotiation a negociação [negoossee-uss*o*wng]
neighbour o vizinho [viz*ee*n-yoo]
neither: neither of them nenhum deles
   [nun-y*oo*m deh-lush]
   neither . . . nor . . . nem . . . nem . . . [neng]
   neither do I eu também não [eh-oo tambeng
   nowng]
nephew: my nephew o meu sobrinho [oo
   m*e*h-oo soobr*ee*nyoo]
nervous nervoso [nerv*o*h-zoo]
net uma rede [red]
   net price o preço fixo [pr*e*h-soo f*ee*xoo]
never nunca [n*o*onkuh]
   well, I never! nunca ouvi tal coisa [n*o*onkuh
   o-vee tal k*o*y-zuh]
new novo/nova [n*o*-voo/n*o*vvuh]

New Year Ano Novo [ah-noo novoo]
New Year's Eve a véspera do Ano Novo [uh veshperuh doo . . .]
Happy New Year Feliz Ano Novo [feleez ah-noo no-voo]
news as notícias [ush nooteess-yush]
newsagent vendedor de jornais [venduh-dor duh joor-nye-sh]
newspaper um jornal [joornal]
do you have any English newspapers? tem jornais ingleses? [teng joor-nye-zeen-glezush]
New Zealand Nova Zelândia [novvuh-zelahndee-uh]
New Zealander Neo-Zelandês [nee-o zelandesh]
next próximo [prossimoo]
sit next to me sente-se a meu lado [sent-suh uh meh-oo lah-doo]
please stop at the next corner pare na próxima esquina, por favor [par nuh prossimuh shkeenuh, poor fuh-vor]
see you next year até ao ano que vem [a-teh ow ah-noo kuh veng]
next week/next Tuesday na próxima semana/terça-feira [nuh prossimuh semah-nuh/tairsuh-fay-ruh]
nice agradável [agradah-vel]
niece: my niece a minha sobrinha [uh meen-yuh soobreen-yuh]
night a noite [noyt]
good night boa noite [bo-uh noyt]
at night à noite [ah noyt]
is there a good nightclub here? pode indicar-me um bom 'nightclub'? [pod eendikar-muh . . .]
night-life a vida nocturna [veeduh noktoor-nuh]
night porter o porteiro de noite [poortay-roo duh noyt]
no não [nowng]
there's no . . . não há [nowng ah . . .]

....

no way! nem pensar [neng pen*sar*]
I've no money não tenho dinheiro [nowng
te*n*-yoo din-*yay*-roo]
nobody ninguém [neen-ga*yng*]
nobody saw it ninguém o viu [neen-ga*yng* oo
vee-*oo*]
noisy barulhento [barool-*yentoo*]
our room is too noisy o nosso quarto é muito
barulhento [oo n*ossoo* kw*artoo* eh mw*eentoo*
barool-*yentoo*]
none nenhum [nun-*yoom*]/nenhuma
none of them nenhum deles [nun-*yoom*
d*eh*-lush]
nonsense disparate [deeshper*at*]
normal normal [n*oormal*]
north o norte [nort]
Northern Ireland Irlanda do Norte [eerl*anduh*
doo nort]
nose o nariz [na*reesh*]
I've a nosebleed estou a deitar sangue do
nariz [shtoh uh day-t*ar* s*anguh* doo na*reesh*]
not não [nowng]
not that one esse não [*ehss* nowng]
not me eu não [*eh*-oo nowng]
I don't understand não percebo [nowng
pers*ebboo*]
he didn't tell me não mo disse [nowng moo
deess]
note *(banknote)* uma nota [n*ottuh*]
nothing nada [n*ah*-duh]
November Novembro [noov*embroo*]
now agora [a-g*oruh*]
nowhere em parte nenhuma [eng part
nun-*yoo*muh]
nudist um nudista [nood*eeshtuh*]
nudist beach uma praia de nudistas [pry-uh
duh nood*eeshtush*]
nuisance: it's a nuisance é muito chato [eh
mw*eentoo* sh*attoo*]
this man's being a nuisance este homem

está a ser um chato [ehsht *o*mmeng shtah sair oom sh*a*ttoo]

numb entorpecido [entorpuh-s*ee*doo]

number o número [n*oo*meroo]
see pages 127–128

  number plate a chapa da matrícula [sh*a*h-puh duh matr*ee*kooluh]

nurse a enfermeira [emferm*a*y-ruh]

nut uma noz [nosh]
  (for bolt) uma porca [p*o*rkuh]

oar um remo [r*eh*-moo]

obligatory obrigatório [o-brigat*o*r-yoo]

obras *road works*

obviously obviamente [obvee-am*e*nt]

occasionally de vez em quando [duh vehz eng kw*a*ndoo]

occupied ocupado [okoo-p*a*h-doo]

o'clock *see* time

October Outubro [o-t*oo*-broo]

octopus polvo [p*o*le-voo]

ocupado *engaged*

odd *(number)* ímpar [*ee*mpar]
  (strange) estranho [shtr*a*hn-yoo]

of de [duh]

off: the milk/meat is off o leite está estragado/a carne está estragada [oo layt/uh karn shtah shtrag-*a*h-doo/duh]
  it just came off soltou-se mesmo [sole-t*o*h-suh m*e*jmoo]
  10% off dez por cento de desconto [desh poor s*e*ntoo duh dush-k*o*ntoo]

offence uma injúria [eenj*oo*ree-uh]
  (legal) uma infracção [eemfrass*ow*ng]

office o escritório [shkreet*o*r-yoo]

officer *(to policeman)* Senhor Guarda [sun-y*o*r gw*a*r-duh]

official *(noun)* um funcionário [foons-yoon*a*r-yoo]

often muitas vezes [mw*ee*ntush v*e*h-zush]

oil óleo [*o*llee-oo]

....

I'm losing oil está a perder óleo [shtah perd*air* *o*llee-oo]
   will you change the oil? pode mudar o óleo? [pod mood*ar* . . .]
ointment uma pomada [poom*ah*-duh]
OK O.K.
old velho [v*e*l-yoo]
   how old are you? que idade tem? [kuh eed*ah*d t*ai*ng]
olive uma azeitona [azay-t*o*nnuh]
   olive oil azeite [az*a*yt]
omelette uma omeleta [ommuh-l*e*t]
on em [eng]
   I haven't got it on me não o tenho comigo [nowng oo t*e*n-yoo koom*ee*goo]
   on Friday na sexta-feira [nuh s*e*shtuh f*a*y-ruh]
   on television na televisão [nuh tulluh-veez*o*wng]
once uma vez [oomuh vesh]
   at once imediatamente [eemuddy-aht-m*e*nt]
one um/uma [oom/*oo*muh]
   the red one o vermelho [oo verm*e*l-yoo]
onion uma cebola [sub*o*lluh]
only *(adjective)* único [*oo*nikoo]
   only one só um/uma [so oom/*oo*muh]
   only once só uma vez [so oomuh vesh]
open *(adjective)* aberto [a-b*ai*r-too]
   I can't open it não o posso abrir [nowng oo possoo abr*eer*]
   when do you open? quando abre? [kw*a*ndoo *a*bruh]
opera a ópera [*o*pperuh]
operation uma operação [o-peruh-s*o*wng]
   will I need an operation? tenho de ser operado? [t*e*n-yoo duh sair o-per*ah*-doo]
operator *(tel)* a telefonista [tulluh-foon*ee*shtuh]
opposite: opposite the hotel em frente do hotel [aim frent doo o-t*e*l]
optician's o oculista [ockool*ee*shtuh]

....

or ou [oh]
orange laranja [lar*a*hn-juh]
   orange juice sumo de laranja [s*oo*-moo
   duh . . .]
order: could we order now? podemos escolher
   agora? [pood*e*h-moosh shkool-y*ai*r ag*o*ruh]
   thank you, we've already ordered obrigado,
   já pedimos [o-breeg*a*h-doo jah ped*ee*moosh]
other: the other one o outro [oo oh-troo]
   do you have any others? tem mais? [teng
   my-sh]
   (different ones) tem outros? [. . . o-troosh]
otherwise doutro modo [d*o*h-troo m*o*ddoo]
ought: I ought to go devo de ir [d*e*vvoo duh eer]
ounce uma onça [*o*nsuh]
» *TRAVEL TIP: 1 ounce = 28.35 grammes*
our nosso [n*o*ssoo]/nossa [n*o*ssuh]
   that's ours isso é nosso [ee-soo eh n*o*ssoo]
out: we're out of petrol ficámos sem gasolina
   [feek*a*mmoosh seng gazool*ee*nuh]
   get out! rua! [r*o*o-uh]
outboard *(motor)* fora de bordo [f*o*ruh duh
   bordoo]
outdoors fora de casa [f*o*ruh duh k*a*h-zuh]
outside: can we sit outside? podemos
   sentar-nos lá fora? [pood*e*h-moosh sent*a*r-noosh
   lah f*o*ruh]
over: over here/there cá/lá [kah/lah]
   over 40 mais de quarenta [my-sh duh
   kwar*e*ntuh]
   it's all over acabou-se [akab*o*h-suh]
overboard: man overboard! homem ao mar!
   [*o*mmeng ow mar]
overcharge: you've overcharged me você
   vendeu-me mais caro [voss*e*h vend*e*h-oo-muh
   my-sh k*a*h-roo]
overcooked esturrado [shtoorr*a*h-doo]
overexposed *(phot)* demasiado clara
   [demuzzy-*a*h-doo kl*a*h-ruh]
overnight *(travel)* de noite [duh noyt]

oversleep dormir de mais [doo-rm*eer* duh-my-sh]
  I overslept acordei tarde [a-koor-d*a*y]
overtake ultrapassar [ooltruh-pass*a*r]
owe: what do I owe you? quanto lhe devo? [kw*a*ntool-yuh d*e*vvoo]
own: my own . . . o meu próprio . . . /a minha própria . . . [oo m*e*h-oo propree-oo/uh m*e*en-yuh propree-uh]
  I'm on my own estou sòzinho [shtoh sozz*ee*n-yoo]
owner o dono [d*o*h-noo]
oyster uma ostra [*o*shtruh]
P. = Praça *Square*
pack: can I have a packed lunch? pode dar-me umas sandes em vez do almoço? [pod d*a*r-muh *oo*mush sandsh eng vesh doo al-m*o*-soo]
  I haven't packed yet ainda não fiz as malas [uh-*ee*nduh nowng feez ush m*a*h-lush]
package tour uma excursão organiz*a*da [shkoor-s*o*wng]
page *(of book)* a página [p*a*h-jinnuh]
  could you page him? pode chamá-lo? [pod sham*a*h-loo]
pain uma dor
  I've got a pain in my . . . tenho uma dor de . . . [t*e*n-yoo *oo*muh dor duh]
  painkillers calmantes [kalm*a*ntsh]
painting uma pintura [peent*oo*ruh]
Pakistan Paquistão [pakisht*o*wng]
Pakistani Paquistanês [pakishtan*e*sh]
pale pálido [p*a*llidoo]
pancake um crepe [krep]
panties um par de cuecas [par duh kw*e*ckush]
pants calças [k*a*lsush]
  (underpants) uns slips [oonsh sl*ee*psh]
paper papel [p*u*pp*e*l]
  (newspaper) o jornal [joorn*a*l]
para alugar to let
paragem stop (bus, tram, etc)

parcel um embrulho [embrool-yoo]
pardon *(didn't understand)* como disse? [ko-moo
    deess]; **I beg your pardon** *(sorry)* desculpe
    [dush-koolp]
pare stop
parents: my parents os meus pais [oosh
    meh-oosh pye-sh]
park o parque [park]
    where can I park my car? onde posso
    estacionar o meu carro? [onduh possoo
    shtass-yoonar oo meh-oo karroo]
part uma parte [part]
partidas departures
partner *(dance, game)* parceiro [persay-roo]
    (social) companheira [kompan-yay-ruh]
party *(group)* o grupo [groopoo]
    (celebration) uma festa [feshtuh]
    I'm with the ... party estou com o grupo
    ... [shtoh kong oo groopoo]
pass *(mountain)* um desfiladeiro
    [dushfeeladay-roo]
    he's passed out desmaiou [duj-my-oh]
passable *(road)* transitável [tranzitah-vel]
passagem de nível level crossing
passagem subterrânea subway
passe cross now
passenger um passageiro [passajay-roo]
passer-by um transeunte [tranz-yoont]
passport o passaporte [pass-port]
past: in the past no passado [noo passah-doo]
    see **time**
pastry massa folhada [massuh fol-yah-duh]
    (cake) um bolo [bo-loo]
path um caminho [kameen-yoo]
patient: be patient tenha paciência [ten-yuh
    pass-yenss-yuh]
pattern *(print)* desenho [dezen-yoo]
pavement o passeio [passayoo]
pay *(verb)* pagar; **can I pay, please** por favor,
    queria pagar [poor fuh-vor, kree-uh pagar]

....

peace a paz [pash]
peach um pêssego [pehss-goo]
peanuts amendoins [amend-weensh]
pear uma pêra [peh-ruh]
peas ervilhas [air-veel-yush]
pebble um seixo [say-shoo]
pedal (noun) o pedal [puh-dal]
pedestrian um peão [pee-owng]
   pedestrian crossing uma passadeira
   [passuh-day-ruh]
peg uma estaca [shtah-kuh]
pelvis a pélvis [pelveesh]
pen uma caneta [kanettuh]
   have you got a pen? tem uma caneta?
pencil um lápis [lah-peesh]
penfriend um correspondente
   [koorush-pondent]
penicillin a penicilina [punny-sileenuh]
penknife um canivete [kaneevet]
pensioner um reformado [refoormah-doo]
people a gente [jent]
   the Portuguese people os Portugueses [oosh
   poortoo-geh-zush]
pepper pimenta [peementuh]
peppermint hortelã-pimenta
   [ortelang-peementuh]
per: per night/week/person por
   noite/semana/pessoa [poor
   noyt/semah-nuh/pussoh-uh]
per cent por cento [poor sentoo]
perdidos e achados lost property
perfect perfeito [perfaytoo]
   the perfect holiday as férias ideais [ush
   fairy-ush eedee-eye-sh]
perfume o perfume [perfoom]
perhaps talvez [talvesh]
perigo danger
period (also med) o período [peree-oodoo]
perm uma permanente [permanent]
permit (noun) uma licença [leesensuh]

person uma pessoa [puss*o*h-uh]
  in person em pessoa
pessoal *staff only*
petrol a gasolina [gazool*ee*nuh]
  petrol station uma bomba de gasolina
  [bombuh duh . . .]
» *TRAVEL TIP:* '*super*' *is equivalent to 3 star,*
'normal' to 2 star
phone *see* **telephone**
photograph uma fotografia [footoograf*ee*-uh]
  would you take a photograph of us? quer
  tirar-nos uma fotografia?
  [kair teer*a*r-nooz . . .]
piano um piano [pee-*a*h-noo]
pickpocket um carteirista [kurtay-r*ee*shtuh]
picture um quadro [kw*a*droo]
pie *(meat)* um pastel [pasht*e*l]
  (fruit) uma torta [t*o*rtuh]
piece um pedaço [ped*a*h-soo]
  a piece of . . . um bocado de . . . [oom
  book*a*h-doo duh]
pig um porco [p*o*rkoo]
pigeon um pombo [p*o*mboo]
pile-up um acidente múltiplo [asseed*e*nt
  m*oo*ltiploo]
pill uma pílula [p*ee*looluh]
  do you take the pill? está a tomar a pílula?
  [shtah toom*a*r uh . . .]
pillion *(passenger)* o pendura [pend*oo*ruh]
  on the pillion no assento de trás [noo ass*e*ntoo
  duh trash]
pillow uma almofada [almoof*a*h-duh]
pin um alfinete [alf*ee*net]
pineapple ananás [anan*a*sh]
pink rosa [r*o*zzuh]
pint: a pint of beer uma caneca de cerveja
  [kan*e*ckuh duh serv*e*h-juh]
» *TRAVEL TIP: 1 pint = 0.57 litres*
pipe um cachimbo [kash*ee*mboo]
  (sink) o cano [k*a*h-noo]

....

pipe tobacco tabaco de cachimbo
[tab*a*h-koo . . .]
piston o êmbolo [embooloo]
pity: it's a pity é uma pena [eh *oo*muh p*e*h-nuh]
place um lugar [loog*a*r]
  is this place taken? este lugar está ocupado?
  [ehsht loog*a*r shtah o-koop*a*h-doo]
  do you know any good places to go?
  conhece algum sítio bom onde se possa ir?
  [koon-y*e*ss alg*oo*m s*ee*t-yoo bong *o*nduh suh
  p*o*ssuh eer]
plain *(food)* simples [s*ee*mplush]
  (not patterned) liso [l*ee*zoo]
plane um avião [uh-vee-*o*wng]
  by plane de avião [davvy-*o*wng]
plant uma planta [pl*a*ntuh]
plaster *(med)* um emplastro [empl*a*shtroo]
  see **sticking**
plastic plástico [pl*a*shtickoo]
plate um prato [pr*a*h-too]
platform o cais [kye-sh]
  which platform, please? qual é o cais, por
  favor? [kwal eh oo kye-sh, poor fuh-v*o*r]
play: somewhere for the children to
  play algum sítio onde as crianças possam
  brincar [alg*oo*m s*ee*t-yoo *o*nduh ush
  kree-*a*n-sush p*o*ssowng breenk*a*r]
pleasant agradável [agrad*a*h-vel]
please: could you please . . .? por favor,
  pode . . .? [poor fuh-v*o*r, pod . . .]
  (yes) please (sim) por favor [seeng . . .]
pleasure o prazer [praz*ai*r]
  my pleasure não tem de quê [nowng teng duh
  keh]
plenty: plenty of . . . muito [mw*ee*ntoo]
  thank you, that's plenty chega, obrigado
  [sh*e*gguh, o-breeg*a*h-doo]
pliers um alicate [aleek*a*t]
plimsolls sapatos de ténis [sap*a*h-toosh . . .]
plonk vinho [v*ee*n-yoo]

plug *(elec)* uma ficha [feeshash]
  (car) uma vela [velluh]
  (bath) a tampa do ralo [tampuh doo rah-loo]
» *TRAVEL TIP: sockets are two-pin in Portugal*
plum uma ameixa [amay-shuh]
plumber o canalizador [kanaleezador]
plus mais [my-sh]
p.m. da tarde [duh tard]*official times are usually expressed by 24 hour system*
pneumonia a pneumonia [pneh-oo-moonee-uh]
poached egg um ovo escalfado [o-voo shkalfah-doo]
pocket o bolso [oo bole-soo]
point: could you point to it? pode indicar-mo? [pod eendikar-moo]; **four point six** quatro vírgula seis [kwatroo veergooluh saysh]
points *(car)* os platinados [plateenah-doosh]
police a polícia [pooleess-yuh]
  get the police chame a polícia [shahm . . .]
  policeman um polícia
  police station o Posto da Polícia [poshtoo]
» *TRAVEL TIP: grey uniform; phone number in front of phone book*
polish *(noun)* graxa [grashuh]; **will you polish my shoes?** pode engraxar-me os sapatos? [pod engrashar-muh oosh sapah-toosh]
polite bem-educado [beng eedookah-doo]
politics a política [pooleetickuh]
polluted contaminado [kontameenah-doo]
polythene bag um saco de plástico
pool *(swimming)* uma piscina [peesh-seenuh]
poor: poor quality de má qualidade [duh mah kwaleedad]; **I'm very poor** sou muito pobre [soh mweentoo pobruh]
popular popular [poopoolar]
population a população [poop-luh-sowng]
pork carne de porco [karn duh pore-koo]
port um porto [portoo]
  (drink) vinho do Porto [veen-yoo doo . . .]
  (opp. starboard) bombordo [–doo]

....

portagem *toll*
porteiro *porter (janitor)*
porter *(station)* um carregador [kargad*o*r]
    (hotel) um rapaz [rap*a*sh]
portrait um retrato [ruh-tr*a*h-too]
Portugal Portugal [poortoog*a*l]
Portuguese português [poortoog*e*sh]
    a Portuguese woman uma portuguesa
    the Portuguese os Portugueses [–gh*e*h-zush]
    I don't speak Portuguese não falo português
    [nowng f*a*h-loo . . .]
posh *(place)* de luxo [duh l*o*o-shoo]
    (person) elegante [eeleg*a*nt]
possible possível [poo-s*ee*vel]; **could you
    possibly?** era-lhe possível [*e*rrul-yuh . . .]
post o correio [koor*a*yoo]
    postcard um postal [poosht*a*l]
    post office o correio
» *TRAVEL TIP: look for sign 'Correios' or CTT on
    blue sign*
poste restante a posta restante [p*o*shtuh
    resht*a*nt]
posto de socorros *first aid post*
potatoes batatas [bat*a*h-tush]
pottery louça [l*o*h-suh]
pound uma libra [l*ee*bruh]
» *TRAVEL TIP: conversion:* $\dfrac{pounds}{11} \times 5 = kilos$

pounds	1	3	5	6	7	8	9
kilos	0.45	1.4	2.3	2.7	3.2	3.6	4.1

pour: it's pouring está a chover a cântaros
    [sht*a*h shoov*ai*r uh k*a*ntuh-roosh]
powder pó
power cut um corte de energia [kort
    deenerj*ee*-uh]
power point uma tomada [toom*a*h-duh]
prawns gambas [g*a*mbash]
    prawn cocktail cocktail de gambas
prefer: I prefer this one prefiro isto [pref*ee*roo
    *ee*shtoo]

pregnant grávida

pré-pagamento *pay and get your receipt before being served*

prescription uma receita [russay-tuh]

present: at present agora
  here's a present for you tens aqui um presente [tainz akee oom prezent]

president o presidente [pruzzy-dent]

press: could you press these? pode passar-me estas [pod passar-muh eshtush]

pretty bonito [booneetoo]
  it's pretty good é bastante bom [eh bashtant bong]

price o preço [preh-soo]

priest um padre [oom pahd-ruh]

printed matter impressos [eempressoosh]

prison a cadeia [kadayyuh]

private privado [preevah-doo]

probably provavelmente [proovah-velment]

problem um problema [proobleh-muh]

product um produto [proodootoo]

profit lucro [lookroo]

proibido: – fumar *no smoking;* **– acampar** *no camping;* **– a ultrapassagem** *no overtaking;* **– a entrada** *no entry*

promise: do you promise? promete? [proomet]
  I promise prometo [proomettoo]

pronounce: how do you pronounce it? como se pronuncia? [ko-moo suh proonoon-see-uh]

propeller uma hélice [elleess]

properly correctamente [koorettament]

property a propriedade [proopree-uh-dahd]

prostitute a prostituta [prooshteetootuh]

protect proteger [prootuh-jair]

Protestant protestante [prootushtant]

proud orgulhoso [orgool-yo-zoo]

public: the public o público [pooblikoo]
  public convenience casas-de-banho públicas [kah-zush duh bahn-yoo pooblikush]
  see **toilet**

....

» *TRAVEL TIP: public holidays:*
Jan 1 Ano Novo *New Years Day*
     Sexta-feira Santa *Good Friday*
April 25 Vinte e cinco de Abril *Day of the*
     Revolution
May 1 Dia do Trabalho *Labour Day*
     Corpo de Deus *Corpus Christi*
Jun 10 Dia de Portugal *National Holiday*
Aug 15 Assunção *Assumption Day*
Oct 5 Dia da República *Day of the Republic*
Nov 1 Todos os Santos *All Saints*
Dec 1 Primeiro de Dezembro *Restoration of*
     Independence
Dec 8 Imaculada Conceição *Immaculate*
     Conception
Dec 25 Natal *Christmas Day*

pull *(verb)* puxar [pooshar]
  he pulled out in front of me pôs-se à minha
  frente [posh-suh ah meen-yuh frent]
pump uma bomba [bombuh]
punctual pontual [pontoo-al]
puncture um furo [fooroo]
pure puro [pooroo]
purple cor de púrpura [kor duh poorpooruh]
purse uma bolsa [bole-suh]
push *(verb)* empurrar [empoorrar]
  push-chair um carrinho de bebé [kareen-yoo
  duh bebeh]
put: where can I put . . .? onde posso
  colocar . . .? [onduh possoo koolookar]
puxe pull
pyjamas um pijama [peejah-muh]
quality a qualidade [kwallidahd]
quarantine a quarentena [kwaraintennuh]
quarter a quarta parte [kwartuh part]
  a quarter of an hour um quarto de hora [oom
  kwartoo dee or-uh]
quay o cais [kye-sh]
quente hot
question uma pergunta [pergoontuh]

queue *(noun)* uma bicha [b*ee*shuh]
quick rápido [r*a*pidoo]
  that was quick! que rápido que foi! [kuh
  r*a*pidoo kuh foy]
quiet tranquilo [tran-kw*ee*loo]
  be quiet! cale-se! [k*a*l-suh]
quite *(fairly)* bastante [busht*a*nt]
  (very) absolutamente [absoolootuh-m*e*nt]
  quite a lot bastante
R. = *Rua* street
radiator um radiador [rad-yuh-d*o*r]
radio um rádio [r*a*hd-yoo]
rail: by rail por caminho-de-ferro [poor
  kam*ee*nyoo duh f*e*rroo]
rain a chuva [sh*oo*vuh]
  it's raining está a chover [shtah shoov*ai*r]
  raincoat um impermeável
  [eempermee-*ah*-vel]
rally *(car)* um rally
rape a violação [vee-ooluh-s*o*wng]
rare *(steak)* em sangue [em s*a*nguh]
raspberry framboesa [frambweh-zuh]
rat uma ratazana [rattuh-z*ah*-nuh]
rather: I'd rather sit here prefiro sentar-me
  aqui [pref*ee*roo sent*a*r-muh ak*ee*]
  I'd rather not prefiro que não [pref*ee*roo kuh
  nowng]; **it's rather hot** está muito calor
  [shtah mw*ee*ntoo k*a*lor]
raw cru/crua [kroo/kroo-uh]
razor uma máquina de barbear [m*a*cky-nuh duh
  berbee-*a*r]; **razor blades** lâminas para
  barbear [l*a*minush para berbee-*a*r]
r/c = *rés-do-chão* ground floor
read: you read it leia-o [l*a*yuh-oo]
  something to read alguma coisa para ler
  [alg*oo*muh k*o*y-zuh para lair]
ready: when will it be ready? quando está
  pronto? [kw*a*ndoo shtah pront]
  I'm not ready yet ainda não estou pronto
  [uh-*ee*nduh nowng shtoh pront]

....

real verdadeiro [verdad*ay*-roo]

really realmente [ree-alm*e*nt]

rear-view mirror o espelho retrovisor
[sh*p*ell-yoo retroo-veez*o*r]

reasonable razoável [razw*ah*-vel]

receipt um recibo [res*ee*boo]
    can I have a receipt, please? pode dar-me um
    recibo, por favor? [pod d*a*r-muh . . .]

recently há pouco [ah p*o*-koo]

reception *(hotel)* a recepção [resep-s*o*wng]

receptionist a recepcionista
[reseps-yoo-n*ee*shtuh]

recipe uma receita [res*ay*tuh]

recommend: can you recommend . . .? pode
    aconselhar-me . . .? [pod akonsul-y*a*rmuh]

record *(music)* um disco [d*ee*shkoo]

red vermelho [verm*e*l-yoo]

reduction *(in price)* um desconto [dushk*o*ntoo]

refuse: I refuse recuso-me [rek*oo*zoo-muh]

region a região [rej-y*o*wng]
    in this region nesta região [n*e*shtuh . . .]

registered letter uma carta registada [kartuh
    rejeesht*a*h-duh]

regret: I have no regrets não tenho pena
    nenhuma [nowng t*e*n-yoo p*e*nnuh
    nun-y*oo*-muh]

relax: I just want to relax só quero descansar
    [so k*a*iroo dush-kans*a*r]
    relax! calma! [k*a*lmuh]

remember: don't you remember? não se
    lembra? [nowng suh l*e*mbruh]
    I'll always remember lembrar-me-ei sempre
    [lembrar-mee-*a*y s*e*mpruh]
    something to remember you by uma coisa
    para me lembrar de ti [k*o*y-zuh para muh
    lembr*a*r duh tee]

rent: can I rent a car/boat/bicycle? posso
    alugar um carro/um barco/uma bicicleta?
    [p*o*ssoo aloog*a*r oom k*a*rroo/oom b*a*rkoo/oomuh
    beeseekl*e*ttuh]

repair: can you repair it? pode consertá-lo [pod konsert*ah*-loo]

repeat: could you repeat that? pode repeti-lo? [pod repet*ee*-loo]

reputation a reputação [repootuh-s*ow*ng]

rés-do-chão *ground floor*

rescue *(verb)* salv*a*r

reservas *reservations*

reservation uma reserva [rez*ai*rvuh]
  I want to make a reservation for ... quero fazer uma reserva para ... [*kai*roo faz*ai*r *oo*muh rez*ai*rvuh para]

reserve: can I reserve a seat? posso reservar um lugar? [p*o*ssoo rezerv*a*r oom loog*a*r]

responsible responsável [rushpons*ah*-vel]

rest: I've come here for a rest estou aqui para descansar [shtoh ak*ee* para dushkans*a*r]
  you keep the rest fique com o resto [feek kong oo r*e*shtoo]

restaurant um restaurante [rushtoh-r*a*nt]

retired reformado [ruh-foorm*ah*-doo]

return: a return/two returns to .. uma ida e volta/duas idas e voltas para ... [*oo*muh *ee*duh ee v*o*ltuh/doo-uz *ee*duz ee v*o*ltush para]

reverse gear a marcha atrás [m*a*rshuh atr*a*sh]

rheumatism o reumatismo [reh-oomat*eej*-moo]

rib uma costela [koosht*e*lluh]

rice arroz [ar*o*sh]

rich rico [r*ee*koo] *(food)* forte [fort]

ridiculous ridículo [rid*ee*kooloo]

right: that's right está certo [shtah s*ai*rtoo]
  you're right tem razão [teng raz*o*wng]
  on the right à direita [ah deer*ay*tuh]
  right here aqui mesmo [ak*ee* m*e*j-moo]
  right-hand drive de volante à direita [duh vool*a*nt ah deer*ay*tuh]

ring *(on finger)* um an*e*l

ripe maduro [mad*oo*roo]

rip-off: it's a rip-off isso é um roubo [*ee*soo eh oom r*o*-boo]

....

river um rio [*ree*-oo]
road a estrada [sht*ra*h-duh]
    which is the road to . . .? qual é a estrada
    para . . .? [kwal eh uh sht*ra*h-duh para]
    roadhog um pé [oom peh]
rob: I've been robbed roubaram-me
    [roh-b*a*rowng-muh]
rock *(noun)* uma rocha [*ro*shuh]
    whisky on the rocks whisky com gelo [. . .
    kong j*e*h-loo]
roll *(bread)* um papo-sêco [p*a*poo s*e*h-koo]
Roman Catholic católico romano [kat*o*llikoo
    room*a*h-noo]
romantic romântico [room*a*ntikoo]
roof o telhado [tul-y*a*h-doo]
room um quarto [kw*a*rtoo]
    have you got a (single/double) room? tem
    um quarto (individual/de casal)? [teng oom
    kw*a*rtoo (eendivid-w*a*l/duh kaz*a*l)]
    for one night/three nights para uma noite/
    três noites [para *oo*muh noyt/tresh noytsh]
    YOU MAY THEN HEAR . . .
    desculpe, estamos cheios *sorry, we're full*
    com ou sem banho? *with or without bath?*
room service serviço de quartos [serv*ee*so duh
    kw*a*rtoosh]
rope uma corda [k*o*rduh]
rose uma rosa [r*o*zzuh]
rosé rosé [*ro*o-zeh]
rough *(sea, weather)* tempestuoso
    [tempesht-w*o*-zoo]
roughly *(approximately)* aproximadamente
    [aproossim*a*h-dam*e*nt]
roulette a roleta [rool*e*ttuh]
round *(circular)* redondo [red*o*ndoo]
roundabout uma rotunda [rot*oo*nduh]
route a estrada [sht*ra*h-duh]
    which is the prettiest/fastest route? qual é a
    estrada mais bonita/mais rápida? [kwal eh uh
    sht*ra*h-duh my-sh boon*ee*tuh/my-sh r*a*piduh]

rowing boat um barco a remos [b*a*rkoo uh reh-moosh]
rubber borracha [boor*a*shuh]
  rubberband uma fita elástica [*f*eetuh el*a*shtikuh]
rubbish o lixo [*l*eeshoo]
  rubbish! que disparate! kuh deeshpar*a*t]
rucksack uma mochila [moosh*ee*luh]
rudder o leme [lem]
rude grosseiro [groos*a*yroo]
  (indecent) indecente [eendes*e*nt]
ruins as ruínas [ush roo-*ee*nush]
rum rum [roong]; **rum and coke** uma cuba livre [*k*oobuh leevruh]
run: hurry, run! corra, depressa!
  I've run out of petrol/money acabou-se-me a gasolina/o dinheiro [akabohss-muh uh gazool*ee*nuh/oo din-y*a*y-roo]
sad triste [treesht]
safe seguro [seg*oo*roo]
  will it be safe here? está seguro aqui? [shtah seg*oo*roo ak*ee*]
  is it safe to swim here? pode-se nad*a*r aqui sem perigo? [pod-suh nad*a*r ak*ee* saim per*ee*goo]
safety a segurança [segoor*a*n-suh]
  safety pin um alfinete de segurança [alfy-n*e*t duh . . .]
saída exit — *de emergência* emergency exit
sail *(noun)* uma vela [*v*elluh]
  can we go sailing? podemos ir fazer vela? [poodeh-mooz eer faz*a*ir *v*elluh]
sailor um marinheiro [mareen-y*a*yroo]
sala de espera waiting room
salad uma salada [sal*a*h-duh]
salami salame [sal*a*m]
saldos sales
sale: is it for sale? está à venda? [shtah ah *v*enduh]
salmon salmão [salm*o*wng]
salt o sal [sal]

....

same mesmo [m*e*jmoo]
   the same again, please o mesmo, por favor
   the same to you igualmente [eeg-wal-m*e*nt]
sand areia [ar*e*yyuh]
sandals umas sandálias [*oo*mush sand*a*hl-yush]
sandwich uma sandes [sandsh]
sanitary towels toalhas higiénicas [tw*a*l-yuz
   eej-y*e*nnikush]
satisfactory satisfatório [s*a*teesh-fat*o*r-yoo]
Saturday sábado [s*a*b-doo]
sauce molho [m*o*le-yoo]
   saucepan uma caçarola [kassar*o*lluh]
saucer um pires [p*ee*rush]
sauna uma sauna [s*o*w-nuh]
sausage salsicha [sals*ee*shuh]
save *(life)* salv*a*r
say: how do you say . . . in Portuguese? como
   se diz . . . em português? [k*o*-moo suh deesh
   . . . eng poortoo-gh*e*sh]
   what did he say? o que é que ele disse? [oo kee
   eh kehl deess]
scarf um lenço de pescoço [lensoo duh
   pushk*o*-soo] *(headscarf)* um lenço de cabeça
   [. . . kabeh-suh]
scenery a paisagem [pye-z*a*h-jeng]
schedule o programa [proogr*a*h-muh]
   on/behind schedule a horas/com atraso [uh
   *o*rush/kong atr*a*h-zoo]
   scheduled flight um voo regular [v*o*-oo
   regool*a*r]
school uma escola [shk*o*lluh]
scissors: a pair of scissors uma tesoura
   [tez*o*h-ruh]
scooter uma motoreta [mootoor*e*ttuh]
Scotland Escócia [shk*o*ss-yuh]
Scottish escocês [shk*o*oss*e*sh]
scrambled eggs ovos mexidos [*o*vvoosh
   mesh*ee*doosh]
scratch *(verb) (self)* coçar-se [koos*a*r-suh]
   (car) riscar [reeshk*a*r]

scream (noun) um grito [greetoo]
screw (noun) um parafuso [parafoozoo]
   screwdriver uma chave de fendas [shahv duh
   fendush]
sea o mar
   by the sea à beira-mar [ah bay-ruh mar]
seafood mariscos [mareeshkoosh]
search (verb) procurar [prookoorar]
   search party uma expedição de socorro
   [oomuh shpedeesowng duh sookorroo]
seasick: I feel seasick estou enjoado [shtoh
   enj-wah-doo]
   I get seasick enjoo sempre [enjoh-oo sempruh]
seaside a praia [pry-uh]
   let's go to the seaside vamos para a praia
   [vamoosh prah pry-uh]
season a época [eppokuh]
   the high/low season a estação alta/baixa
   [shtassowng altuh/by-shuh]
seasoning condimento [condeementoo]
seat um assento [assentoo]
   is this somebody's seat? este lugar está
   ocupado? [ehsht loogar shtah o-koopah-doo]
   seat belt o cinto de segurança [seentoo duh
   suggoo-ran-suh]
sea-urchin ouriço-do-mar [oh-ree-soo doo mar]
seaweed a alga
second segundo [segoondoo]
   just a second espera um momento [shpairuh
   oom moomentoo]
   second hand em segunda mão [eng
   segoonduh mowng]
see ver [vair]
   oh, I see já percebo [jah persebboo]
   have you seen ...? viu ...? [vee-oo]
   can I see the room? posso ver o quarto?
   [possoo vair oo kwartoo]
seem parecer [purruh-sair]
   it seems so assim parece
   [asseeng paress]

....

seldom raras vezes [rah-rush veh-zush]
sell vender [vendair]
selos stamps
semáforos traffic lights
send mandar
senhoras Ladies
sensitive sensível [senseevel]
sentido único one-way street
sentimental sentimental
separate *(adjective)* separado [supperah-doo]
  I'm separated estou separado [shtoh . . .]
  can we pay separately? podemos pagar cada
  um separadamente? [poodeh-moosh pagar
  kah-duh oom supperah-duh-ment]
September Setembro [suttembroo]
serious sério [sair-yoo]
  I'm serious estou a falar a sério [shtoh uh
  falahr uh sair-yoo]
  is it serious, doctor? é grave, Sr. doutor? [eh
  grav sun-yor doh-tor]
service: the service was excellent/poor o
  serviço foi óptimo/mau [ooh servee-soo foy
  ottimoo/mah-oo]
  service station uma estação de serviço
  [shtassowng duh servee-soo]
serviette um guardanapo [gwarduh-nappoo]
sexy sexy
shade: in the shade à sombra [ah sombruh]
shake sacudir [sakoodeer]
  to shake hands apertar a mão [apertar uh
  mowng]
» TRAVEL TIP: *always shake hands with people
  when you meet or are introduced*
shallow pouco profundo [po-koo proofoondoo]
shame: what a shame! que pena!
  [kuh pennuh]
shampoo *(noun)* um champô [shampoh]
  shampoo and set lavagem e mise [lavah-jeng
  ee meez]

shandy uma cerveja com limonada [serv*eh*-juh kong leemoon*ah*-duh] *no real equivalent*

share *(room, table)* partilhar [perteel-y*ar*]

shark um tubarão [toobarowng]

sharp afiado [afee-*ah*-doo]

shave fazer a barba [fa*za*ir uh b*a*rbuh]
    shaver uma máquina de barbear [oomuh m*a*ckinuh duh berbee-*ar*]
    shaving foam espuma para a barba [shp*oo*muh prah . . .]
    shaving point a tomada para a máquina de barbear [t*oo*mah-duh prah]

she ela [*ell*uh]
    she is my friend é minha amiga [eh m*ee*n-yuh am*ee*guh]
    she is tired está cansada [shtah kans*ah*-duh]

sheep uma ovelha [o-v*el*-yuh]

sheet um lençol [len-s*ol*]

shelf uma prateleira [prut-l*ay*-ruh]

shell uma concha [k*o*nshuh]
    shellfish mariscos [mar*ee*shkoosh]

shelter *(noun)* um abrigo [abreeg*oo*]
    can we shelter here? podemos abrigar-nos aqui? [pood*eh*-mooz abreeg*a*r-nooz ak*ee*]

sherry Xerez [shurr*esh*]

ship um barco [b*a*rkoo]

shirt uma camisa [kam*ee*zuh]

shock *(noun: surprise)* um choque [shock]
    I got an electric shock from the . . . apanhei um choque eléctrico de . . . [apan-y*ay* oom shock eel*e*trikoo duh]
    shock-absorber o amortecedor [amort-suh-d*or*]

shoe um sapato [sap*a*h-too]

» *TRAVEL TIP: shoe sizes*

UK	4	5	6	7	8	9	10	11
Portugal	37	38	39	41	42	43	44	46

shop uma loja [l*o*jjuh]; **I've some shopping to do** tenho de fazer umas compras [t*e*n-yoo duh fa*za*ir *oo*mush k*o*mprush]

....

shore a praia [pry-uh]
short *(height)* baixo [by-shoo] *(dress)* curto
[koortoo]
   I'm four short faltam-me quatro
[faltowng-muh kwatroo]
   short cut um atalho [atal-yoo]
shorts calções [kal-soyngsh]
shoulder o ombro [ombroo]
shout gritar [greetar]
show: please show me pode mostrar-me, por
favor? [pod moosh-trar-muh, poor fuh-vor]
shower: with shower com duche [kong doosh]
shrimps camarões [kamaroyngsh]
shrink: it's shrunk está encolhido [shtah
enkool-yeedoo]
shut *(verb)* fechar [fushar]
   when do you shut? a que horas fecha? [uh kee
orush feshuh]
   shut up! cale-se! [kal-suh]
shy tímido [teemidoo]
sick doente [doo-ent]
   I feel sick sinto-me enjoado [seentoo-muh
enj-wah-doo]
   he's been sick vomitou [voomitoh]
side o lado [lah-doo]
   side lights *(car)* as luzes de presença [ush
loozush duh prezen-suh]
   side road rua lateral [roo-uh lateral]
   by the side of the road na berma da estrada
[nuh bairmuh duh shtrah-duh]
sight: out of sight longe da vista [lonj duh
veeshtuh]
   the sights of . . . os centros de interesse de . . .
[oosh sentroosh deenteress duh]
   sightseeing tour um circuito turístico
[seer-kweetoo tooreeshtikoo]
sign *(road)* sinal *(notice)* o letreiro [letray-roo]
signal: he didn't signal ele não fez sinal [ehl
nowng fesh seenal]
signature a assinatura [asseena-tooruh]

silence *(noun)* o silêncio [seelenss-yoo]
silencer a panela de escape [panelluh duh shkap]
silk a seda [sedduh]
silly tolo [toh-loo]
silver prata [prah-tuh]
similar semelhante [summel-yant]
since: since last week desde a semana passada [dej-duh semah-nuh pussah-duh]
since we arrived desde que chegámos [dej-duh kuh shuggammoosh]
(because) como [ko-moo]
sincere sincero [seen-sairoo]; **yours sincerely** com os meus cumprimentos
sing cantar
single: single room um quarto individual [kwartoo eendiveed-wal]
I'm single sou solteiro [sohsoltay-roo]
a single to ... uma ida para ... [oomuh eeduh para]
sink: it sank afundou-se [afoondoh-suh]
sir senhor [sun-yor]
sister: my sister minha irmã [meen-yuh eer-mang]
sit: can I sit here? posso sentar-me aqui? [possoo sentar-muh akee]
size o tamanho [tamahn-yoo]
skid *(verb)* patinar [pateenar]
skin a pele [pell]
skin-diving mergulhar [mergool-yar]
skirt uma saia [sa-yuh]
sky o céu [seh-oo]
sleep: I can't sleep não posso dormir [nowng possoo doo-rmeer]; **sleeper** *(rail)* a carruagem-cama [kar-wah-jeng kah-muh]
sleeping bag um saco de dormir [sah-koo duh doo-rmeer]; **sleeping pill** um comprimido para dormir [kompreemeedoo para doormeer]
YOU MAY HEAR ...
dormiu bem? *did you sleep well?*

sleeve a manga [manguh]
slide *(phot)* um diapositivo [dee-uh-poozi*tee*voo]
slow lento [*len*too]
  could you speak a little slower? pode falar
  mais devagar? [pod fal*ar* my-sh duvvag*ar*]
small pequeno [puh-k*eh*-noo]
  small change trocos [*trock*oosh]
smallpox varíola [var*ee*-ooluh]
smell: there's a funny smell há um cheiro
  desagradável [ah oom sh*ay*-roo
  duzza-grad*ah*-vel]
  it smells cheira mal [sh*ay*-ruh mal]
smile *(verb)* sorrir [soo-r *eer*]
smoke *(noun)* o fumo [*foo*moo]
  do you smoke? fuma? [*foo*muh]
  can I smoke? posso fumar? [*possoo* foom*ar*]
» *TRAVEL TIP: no smoking in cinemas, theatres*
smooth liso [*lee*zoo]
snack: can we just have a snack? só
  queríamos uma refeição ligeira [so
  kr*ee*-uh-mooz *oo*muh refay-s*o*wng lee-j*a*y-ruh]
snorkel o tubo de respiração [*too*boo duh
  rushp*ee*eras*o*wng]
snow a neve [nev]
so: it's so hot está tanto calor [sht*a*h t*a*ntoo
  kal*or*]; **not so much** não tanto
  so-so assim, assim [ass*ee*ng . . .]
soap o sabonete [saboon*et*]
  soap powder detergente [deter-j*ent*]
sober sóbrio [*sobree*-oo]
socks as peúgas [ush pee-*oo*gush]
soda (water) soda [*sodd*uh]
soft drink bebida não alcoólica [beb*ee*duh nowng
  alk-w*olli*kuh]
sole *(shoe)* a sola [*soll*uh]
  could you put new soles on these? pode
  pôr-lhes solas novas? [pod p*ore*-l-yush *soll*ush
  *no*vvush]
  YOU MAY THEN HEAR . . .
  de borracha ou sola? *rubber or leather?*

some: some people algumas pessoas
[al*goo*mush pussoh-ush]
**can I have some grapes/some
bread?** queria uvas/um pouco de pão [kr*ee*-uh
*oo*vush/oom po-koo duh powng]
can I have some more? posso repetir? [possoo
ruh-pet*ee*r]
somebody alguém [al-gh*eng*]
something alguma coisa [al*goo*muh k*o*y-zuh]
sometimes às vezes [ash veh-zush]
somewhere nalguma parte [nal*goo*muh part]
son: my son meu filho [m*eh*-oo f*ee*l-yoo]
song uma canção [kan-s*o*wng]
soon cedo [s*eh*-doo]
sooner mais cedo [my-sh s*eh*-doo]
as soon as possible o mais cedo possível [oo
my-sh s*eh*-doo poo-s*ee*-vel]
sore: it's sore dói-me [d*o*y-muh]
sore throat uma dor de garganta
sorry: (I'm) sorry desculpe [dushk*oo*lp]
sort: this sort este género [ehshtuh j*en*-roo]
what sort of . . .? que tipo de . . .? [kuh t*ee*poo
duh]
will you sort it out? pode resolvê-lo? [pod
rezolv*ai*r-loo]
soup uma sopa [s*o*-puh]
sour azedo [az*eh*-doo]
south sul [sool]
South Africa África do Sul [*a*frikuh doo sool]
South African sul-africano [sool-afrik*ah*-noo]
souvenir uma lembrança [lembr*an*-suh]
spade uma enxada [ensh*ah*-duh]
spaghetti esparguete [shpar-g*et*]
Spain Espanha [shp*ah*n-yuh]
Spanish espanhol [shpan-y*ol*]
spanner a chave de porcas [sh*ah*v duh p*o*rkush]
spare: spare part uma peça sobresselente
[p*e*ssuh sobruh-sel*en*t]
spare wheel roda sobresselente
[r*o*dduh . . .]

....

spark(ing) plug uma vela [velluh]
speak: do you speak English? fala inglês?
  [fah-luh eenglesh]
  I don't speak ... não falo ...
  [nowng fah-loo]
special especial [eshpuss-yal]
specialist um especialista
  [eshpuss-yaleeshtuh]
specially especialmente [eshpuss-yal-ment]
spectacles óculos [ockooloosh]
speed a velocidade [veloossy-dahd]
  speed limit o limite de velocidade [leemeet
  duh veloosy-dahd]
  he was speeding excedia o limite de
  velocidade [eesh-sedee-uh ...]
  speedometer o conta-quilómetros
  [kontuh-keelommetroosh]
» *TRAVEL TIP: the limit in built-up areas is 60 kph
  (37 mph)*
spend *(money)* gastar [gashtar]
spice especiaria [shpess-yaree-uh]
  is it spicy? é picante? [eh peekant]
  it's too spicy é demasiado picante [eh
  damuzzy-ah-doo peekant]
spider uma aranha [arahn-yuh]
spirits bebidas alcoólicas [bebeeduz
  alk-wolly-kush]
spoon uma colher [kool-yair]
sprain: I've sprained my ... torci o/a ...
  [toorsee]
spring uma mola [molluh]
  (season) Primavera [preemuh-verruh]
square *(in town)* uma praça [prah-suh]
  2 square metres dois metros quadrados
  [doysh metroosh kwadrah-doosh]
stairs a escada [shkah-duh]
stale *(bread)* duro [dooroo]
stall: it keeps stalling está a falhar [shtah uh
  fal-yar]
stalls plateia [platayyuh]

....

stamp um selo [*se*lloo]
   two stamps for England dois selos para
   Inglaterra [doysh *se*lloosh para eenglat*e*rruh]
stand *(verb)* estar de pé [shtar duh peh]
standard *(adjective)* normal [noorm*a*l]
star uma estrela [sht*re*lluh]
starboard estibordo [shteeb*o*rdoo]
start o começo [koom*e*ssoo]
   my car won't start o motor não pega [oo
   m*oo*tor nowng p*e*gguh]
   when does it start? a que horas começa? [uh
   kee *o*rush koom*e*ssuh]
starter *(car)* o motor de arranque [m*oo*tor
   darr*a*nk]
starving: I'm starving estou morto de fome
   [shtoh mort duh fom]
station a estação [shtass*o*wng]
statue uma estátua [sht*a*t-wuh]
stay: we enjoyed our stay gostámos imenso da
   nossa estadia [goosh-*ta*mmooz eem*e*nsoo duh
   n*o*ssuh shtad*ee*-uh]
   stay there pare aí [par a-*ee*]
   I'm staying at . . . estou hospedado em . . .
   [astoh oshped*a*h-doo eng . . .]
steak um bife [beef]
   YOU MAY THEN HEAR . . .
   bem passado [beng pass*a*h-doo] *well done*
   normal [noorm*a*l] *medium*
   em sangue [eng s*a*nguh] *rare*
steep íngreme [*ee*ngrem]
steering *(car)* a direção [deeress*o*wng]
steering wheel o volante [vool*a*nt]
step *(noun)* um degrau [d*u*grow]
stereo estereofónico [sht*e*rry-oo-f*o*nnikoo]
sterling esterlina [shterl*ee*nuh]
stewardess a hospedeira [o-shped*a*y-ruh]
sticking plaster um adesivo [ad-z*ee*voo]
sticky pegajoso [pugguh-jo-zoo]
stiff *(door etc)* duro [d*oo*roo]
still: keep still fique quieto [f*ee*kuh kee-*e*ttoo]

....

I'm still here ainda estou aqui [uh-*ee*nduh shtoh ak*ee*]

stink *(noun)* um mau cheiro [m*a*h-oo sh*a*yroo]

stolen: my wallet's been stolen roubaram-me a carteira [ro-b*a*rowng-muh uh kart*a*yruh]

stomach o estômago [shtoh-magoo]

I've got stomach-ache estou com dores de estômago [shtoh kong d*o*rush duh sht*o*h-magoo]

have you got something for an upset stomach? tem alguma coisa para as dores de estômago? [teng alg*oo*muh k*o*y-zuh para ush d*o*rush dush-t*o*h-magoo]

stone uma pedra [p*e*druh]

» *TRAVEL TIP: 1 stone = 6.35 kilos*

stop: stop! pare! [par]

a stop-over escala [shk*a*h-luh]

do you stop near . . .? pára perto de . . .? [p*a*h-ruh p*a*irtoo duh]

storm uma tempestade [tempesh-t*a*hd]

straight direito [deer*a*ytoo]

go straight on vá a direito [vah uh deer*a*ytoo]

straight away imediatamente [eemuddy-*a*htuh-m*e*nt]

straight whisky um whisky puro [p*oo*roo]

strange estranho [shtr*a*hn-yoo]

stranger um estranho [shtr*a*hn-yoo]

I'm a stranger here sou de fora [soh . . .]

strawberries morangos [moor*a*ngoosh]

street a rua [r*oo*-uh]

string: have you got any string? tem cordel? [teng koord*e*l]

stroke: he's had a stroke teve um ataque cardíaco [tev oom at*a*ck kerd*ee*-uh-koo]

strong forte [fort]

student um estudante [shtood*a*nt]

stung: I've been stung (by a jelly fish) picou-me (uma alforreca) [peek*o*h-muh *oo*muh alfoor*e*ckuh]

stupid estúpido [sht*oo*piddoo]

such: such a lot tanto [t*a*ntoo]

suddenly subitamente [soobittuh-ment]
sugar açúcar [assookar]
suit um fato [fah-too]
  suitcase uma mala [mah-luh]
suitable adequado [adduh-kwah-doo]
summer Verão [verowng]
sun o sol
  in the sun ao sol [ow . . .]
  out of the sun à sombra [ah sombruh]
  sunbathe tomar banhos de sol [bahn-yoosh]
  sunburn queimadura de sol
    [kay-madooruh . . .]
  sunglasses óculos de sol [okkooloosh . . .]
  sunstroke uma insolação [eensooluh-sowng]
  suntan um bronzeado [bronzee-ah-doo]
  suntan oil óleo para bronzear [ollee-oo . . .]
Sunday domingo [doomeengoo]
supermarket um supermercado
  [sooper-merkah-doo]
supper o jantar
sure: I'm not sure não tenho a certeza [nowng
  ten-yoo uh serteh-zuh]
  sure! claro! [klah-roo]
  are you sure? tem a certeza? [teng . . .]
surfboard uma prancha [pranshuh]
surfing: to go surfing fazer surf [fazair . . .]
surname o apelido [uppel-eedoo]
swearword uma praga [prah-guh]
sweat (verb) suar [soo-ar]
sweet doce [dose]
  (dessert) uma sobremesa [sobruh-meh-zuh]
  sweets rebuçados [reboosah-doosh]
swerve: I had to swerve tive de guinar para o
  lado [teev duh gheenar proh lah-doo]
swim: I'm going for a swim vou tomar banho
  [voh toomar bahn-yoo]
  let's go for a swim vamos tomar banho
  [vah-moosh . . .]
  swimming costume um fato de banho
  [fah-too . . .] .

....

swimming pool a piscina [peesh-*see*nuh]
switch *(noun)* o interruptor [eenter*oop*tor]
   to switch something on/off ligar/desligar
   [leeg*ar*/dushleeg*ar*]
table uma mesa [*meh*-zuh]
   a table for 4 uma mesa para quatro pessoas
   [*meh*-zuh para kw*a*troo pus*soh*-ush]
   table wine vinho de mesa [*veen*-yoo . . .]
take tomar [toom*ar*]
   can I take this with me? posso levar isto
   comigo? [p*o*ssoo luvv*ar* *ee*shtoo koom*ee*goo]
   will you take me to the airport? quer
   levar-me ao aeroporto? [kair luvv*ar*-muh ow
   uh-airoo-p*or*too]
   how long will it take? quanto tempo vai
   levar? [kw*a*ntoo t*e*mpoo vye luvv*ar*]
   somebody has taken my bags roubaram-me
   as malas [ro-b*a*rowng-muh ush m*a*h-lush]
   can I take you out tonight? posso convidá-la
   a sair comigo esta noite? [p*o*ssoo konveed*a*h-luh
   uh suh-*eer* koom*ee*goo *e*shtuh noyt]
   is this seat taken? está ocupado este lugar
   [shtah okoop*a*h-doo ehsht loog*ar*]
talcum powder pó de talco [poh duh t*a*l-koo]
talk *(verb)* falar
tall alto [*a*ltoo]
tampons tampax
tan um bronzeado [bronzee-*a*h-doo]
tank *(of car)* o depósito [dep*o*zzitoo]
tap a torneira [toorn*a*yruh]
tape uma fita [*fee*tuh]
tape-recorder um gravador [gruvvad*o*r]
tariff a tarifa [tar*ee*fuh]
taste *(noun)* o sabor
   can I taste it? posso prová-lo? [p*o*ssoo
   proov*a*h-loo]
   it tastes horrible/very nice sabe muito
   mal/bem [sahb mw*ee*ntoo mal/beng]
taxi um táxi
   will you get me a taxi? pode chamar-me um

....

táxi? [pod shamar-muh . . .]
where can I get a taxi? onde posso encontrar
um táxi? [onduh possoo enkontrar . . .]
taxi-driver o pracista [prasseeshtuh]
tea chá [sha]
could I have a cup of tea? queria um chá
[kree-uh oom sha]
YOU MAY THEN HEAR . . .
com leite? [kong layt] *with milk*
com limão? [kong leemowng] *with lemon?*
» *TRAVEL TIP: tea is normally served without milk*
teach: could you teach me? pode ensinar-me?
[pod enseenar-muh]
could you teach me Portuguese? pode
ensinar-me português? [. . . poortoo-gesh]
teacher o professor [proof-sor]
telegram um telegrama [tulluh-grah-muh]
I want to send a telegram quero enviar um
telegrama [kairoo envee-ar . . .]
telephone *(noun)* o telefone [tulluh-fon]
can I make a phone-call? posso usar o
telefone? [possoo oo-zar . . .]
can I speak to . . .? posso falar com . . .
could you get the number for me? *(dial)*
podia marcar-me, por favor? [poodee-uh
markar-muh, poor fuh-vor]
telephone directory a lista telefónica [uh
leeshtuh tulfonnikuh]
» *TRAVEL TIP: two types of phone: normal one, you
dial then feed when you get an answer; red one in
cafés, feed first then dial*
television a televisão [tulluh-veezowng]
I'd like to watch television queria ver a
televisão [kree-uh vair . . .]
tell: could you tell me where . . .? pode
dizer-me onde . . .? [pod deezair-muh onduh]
temperature *(weather etc)* a temperatura
[temperuh-tooruh]
he's got a temperature tem febre [taim
februh]

....

tennis ténis
   tennis court o campo de ténis [kampoo . . .]
   tennis racket a raquete de ténis [rakett . . .]
   tennis ball a bola de ténis [bolluh . . .]
tent uma tenda [tenduh]
terminus o terminal [termeenal]
terrible terrível [terreevel]
terrific porreiro [poorayroo]
than do que [doo kuh]
   bigger/older than . . . maior/mais velho do
   que . . . [muh-yor/my-sh vel-yoo doo kuh]
thanks, thank you obrigado/a
   [o-breegah-doo/duh]
   thank you very much muito obrigado
   no thank you não obrigado/a [nowng . . .]
   thank you for your help agradeço-lhe muito
   a sua ajuda [agradessool-yuh mweentoo uh
   soo-uh ajooduh]
   YOU MAY THEN HEAR . . .
   não tem de quê *you're welcome*
that: that man/that table/that esse
   homem/essa mesa/isso [ehss ommeng/essuh
   meh-zuh/ee-soo]
   I would like that one queria esse mesmo
   [kree-uh ehss mej-moo]
   how do you say that? como se diz isso?
   [ko-moo suh deez ee-soo]
   I think that . . . acho que . . . [ah-shoo kuh]
the o/a/os/as **the book(s)** o(s) livro(s) [oo(sh)
   leevroo(sh)]
   the table(s) a(s) mesa(s) [uh(sh) meh-zuh(sh)]
theatre o teatro [tee-ah-troo]
their o/a/os/as deles [oo/uh/oosh/ush deh-lush]
   it's their bag/it's theirs é a mala/é deles [eh
   uh mah-luh/eh deh-lush]
them os [oosh]; as [ush]
   for them para eles [par eh-lush]
   who? – them quem? – eles [kaing – eh-lush]
then então [entowng]
there ali [alee]

how do I get there? como é que chego lá?
[komoo eh kuh sheggoo lah]
there is/there are há [ah]
is there . . .?/are there . . .? há . . .?
there you are *(giving something)* tome lá [tom lah]
these estes/estas [eh-shtush/eshtush]
they eles/elas [eh-lush/ellush]
they are são [sowng]; estão [shtowng]
thick espesso [shpessoo]
(stupid) estúpido [shtoopidoo]
thief um ladrão [ladrowng]
thigh a coxa [koshuh]
thin magro [magroo]
thing uma coisa [koy-zuh]
all my things todas as minhas coisas [toh-duz ush meen-yush koy-zush]
think pensar
I'll think it over pensarei nisso [pensaray neesoo]
I think so/I don't think so acho que sim/não [ah-shoo kuh seeng/nowng]
third *(adjective)* terceiro [ter-say-roo]
thirsty: I'm thirsty tenho sede [tenyoo sed]
this: this hotel/this street/this este hotel/esta rua/isto [ehsht o-tel/eshtuh roo-uh/eeshtoo]
can I have this one? posso levar este? [possoo luvvar ehsht]
this is my wife/this is Mr . . . esta é a minha mulher/este é o Sr . . . [eshtuh eh uh meenyuh mool-yair/ehsht eh oo sun-yor]
is this . . .? é isto . . .? [eh eeshtoo]
those esses/essas [eh-sush/essush]
thread *(noun)* fio [fee-oo]
throat a garganta
throttle *(motorbike, boat)* o acelerador [asulleruh-dor]
through através de [atravesh duh]
throw *(verb)* atirar [uh-teerar]
thumb o polegar

thunder *(noun)* o trovão [troovowng]
  thunderstorm a trovoada [troov-*wah*-duh]
Thursday quinta-feira [*kee*ntuh f*a*yruh]
ticket *(train, bus, plane, boat, cinema)* um bilhete
  [oom beel-yet]
  (cloakroom) a senha [uh s*e*nyuh]
tie *(necktie)* uma gravata
tight *(clothes)* apertado [apert*a*h-doo]
  they're too tight apertam-me muito
  [ap*a*ir-towng-muh mw*ee*ntoo]
tights uns collants [oonsh koll*a*ntsh]
time tempo [t*e*mpoo]
  what's the time? que horas são? [kee *o*rush
  sowng]
  I haven't got time não tenho tempo [nowng
  t*e*nyoo t*e*mpoo]
  for the time being por enquanto [poor
  enkw*a*ntoo]
  this time/last time/next time esta vez/a
  última vez/a próxima vez [*e*shtuh vesh/uh
  *oo*ltimuh vesh/uh pr*o*ssimuh vesh]
  3 times três vezes [tresh v*e*h-zush]
  have a good time! divirta-se!
  [deev*ee*rtuh-suh]
  timetable o horário [oo or*a*r-yoo]
» *TRAVEL TIP: how to tell the time*
  it's one o'clock é uma hora [eh *oo*muh *o*ruh]
  it's two/three/four o'clock são
  duas/três/quatro horas [sowng
  d*oo*-ush/tresh/kw*a*troo *o*rush]
  it's 5/10/20/25 past seven são sete e
  cinco/dez/vinte/vinte e cinco [sowng set ee
  s*ee*nkoo/desh/veent/veent-ee-s*ee*nkoo]
  it's quarter past eight/eight fifteen são oito
  e um quarto [sowng *o*y-too ee oom kw*a*rtoo]
  it's half past nine/nine thirty são nove e meia
  [sowng nov ee m*a*yuh]
  it's 25/20/10/5 to ten são dez menos vinte e
  cinco/vinte/dez/cinco [sowng desh
  m*e*h-noosh . . .]

it's quarter to eleven/10.45 são onze menos
um quarto
it's twelve o'clock (midday/p.m.) é meio-
dia [eh mayoo-*dee*-uh]
it's twelve o'clock (midnight/a.m.) é
meia-noite [eh mayuh-*noyt*]
it's 12.10 p.m. é meio-dia e dez [eh
mayoo-*dee*-uh ee desh]
at one à uma [ah *oo*muh]
at two/three/etc às duas/três/etc [ash
doo-ush . . .]
tin *(can)* uma lata
tin-opener um abre-latas [*a*h-bruh-l*a*tush]
tip *(noun)* uma gorjeta [goor-j*e*ttuh]
is the tip included? está incluído o serviço?
[shtah eenkl*wee*doo oo serv*ee*-soo]
» *TRAVEL TIP: a 10% tip would be normal*
(restaurant, hotel, bar, porter, taxi); don't forget
a tip for the cinema usher
tired cansado [kans*a*h-doo]
I'm tired estou cansado [shtoh . . .]
tissues lenços de papel [l*e*nsoosh duh pupp*e*ll]
to: **to Lisbon/England** a Lisboa/para
Inglaterra [uh leej-b*o*-uh/para eengluh-t*e*rruh]
toast uma torrada [toor*a*h-duh]
(drinking) um brinde [breend]
tobacco tabaco [tab*a*h-koo]
tobacconist's a tabacaria [tabakker*ee*-uh]
today hoje [oje]
toe um dedo do pé [d*e*h-doo doo peh]
together junto [j*oo*ntoo]
we're together viemos juntos [vee-
*e*mmoosh . . .]
can we pay all together? podemos pagar tudo
junto? [pood*e*h-moosh pag*a*r t*oo*doo . . .]
toilet o quarto de banho [kw*a*rtoo duh b*a*hn-yoo]
where are the toilets? onde ficam os lavabos?
[*o*nduh f*ee*kowng oosh lav*a*h-boosh]
I have to go to the toilet tenho de ir ao quarto
de banho [t*e*n-yoo duh eer ow . . .]

....

there's no toilet paper não há papel higiénico
[nowng ah puppell eej-yennikoo]
» *TRAVEL TIP: not many public conveniences; but*
you can use a bar or cafe instead
tomato tomate [toomat]
   tomato ketchup ketchup
   tomato juice um sumo de tomate [oom soomoo
   duh . . .]
tomorrow amanhã [aman-yang]
   tomorrow morning/afternoon/evening
   amanhã de manhã/à tarde/à noite [. . . duh
   man-yang/. . . ah tard/. . . ah noyt]
   the day after tomorrow depois de amanhã
   [duh-poysh daman-yang]
   see you tomorrow até amanhã [ateh . . .]
ton tonelada [toonelah-duh]
» *TRAVEL TIP: 1 ton = 1,016 kilos*
tongue a língua [leen-gwuh]
tonic *(water)* água tónica [ahg-wuh tonnikuh]
tonight esta noite [eshtuh noyt]
tonne uma tonelada (métrica) [toonelah-duh
   metrikuh]
» *TRAVEL TIP: 1 tonne = 1000 kilos = metric ton*
tonsils as amígdalas [uz ameegdalush]
tonsilitis amigdalite [ameegdaleet]
too demasiado [demuz-yah-doo]
   (also) também [tambeng]
   that's too much é demasiado [eh . . .]
tool uma ferramenta [furruh-mentuh]
tooth um dente [dent]
   I've got toothache tenho uma dor de dentes
   [ten-yoo oomuh dor duh dentsh]
   toothbrush escova de dentes [shkovvuh . . .]
   toothpaste pasta de dentes [pashtuh . . .]
top: on top of . . . em cima de . . . [eng seemuh
   duh]
   on the top floor no último andar [noo
   ooltimmoo andar]
   at the top no alto [noo altoo]
torch uma lanterna [lantairnuh]

total *(noun)* o total [tootɑl]

tough *(meat)* dura [dooruh]

tour *(noun)* uma excursão [shkoorsɔwng]

    we'd like to go on a tour of . . . gostaríamos de ir fazer uma viagem por . . . [gooshtaree-amoosh deer fazair oomuh vee-ɑh-jeng poor]

    we're touring around estamos a fazer turismo [shtɑh-mooz uh fazair tooreej-moo]

tourist um turista [tooreeshtuh]

    I'm a tourist sou turista [so . . .]

    tourist office o turismo [tooreej-moo]

tow *(verb)* rebocar [rebookɑr]

    can you give me a tow? pode rebocar o meu carro? [pod rebookɑr oo mɛh-oo kɑrroo]

    towrope o cabo de reboque [kɑh-boo duh rebɔck]

towards para [para]

    he was coming straight towards me vinha direito a mim [veen-yuh deerɑytoo uh meeng]

towel uma toalha [too-ɑl-yuh]

town uma cidade [seedɑhd] *(small)* uma vila [veeluh]

    in town na cidade [nuh seedɑd]

    would you take me into the town? pode levar-me para o centro? [pod luvvɑr-muh proh sɛntroo]

traditional tradicional [tradeess-yoonɑl]

    a traditional Portuguese meal uma refeição tradicional portuguesa [refay-sowng tradeess-yoonɑl poortoo-ghɛh-zuh]

traffic o trânsito [oo trɑnzitoo]

    traffic lights os semáforos [oosh semɑffooroosh]

train o comboio [kombɔyyoo]

    » *TRAVEL TIP: often crowded; wise to book in advance*

tranquillizers tranquilizantes [trankweeleezɑntsh]

translate traduzir [tradoozeer]

would you translate that for me? pode traduzir-me isso? [pod tradoozeer-muh eesoo]

transmission *(car)* a transmissão [tranjmeesowng]

travel agent's a agência de viagens [ajenss-yuh duh vee-ah-jensh]

traveller's cheque um travel-cheque [travel-sheck]

tree uma árvore [arvoor]

tremendous bestial [bushtee-al]

trim: just a trim please um pequeno corte, por favor [oom pekeh-noo kort, poor fuh-vor]

trip *(noun)* uma excursão [shkoor-sowng]

we want to go on a trip to . . . queremos fazer uma excursão a . . . [kreh-moosh fazair oomuh shkoor-sowng uh]

trouble *(noun)* problemas [proobleh-mush]

I'm having trouble with . . . tenho tido problemas com . . . [ten-yoo teedoo . . .]

trousers as calças [ush kal-sush]

true verdadeiro [verdaday-roo]

it's not true não é verdade [nowng eh verdad]

trunks *(swimming)* um fato de banho (para homens) [fah-too duh bahn-yoo para ommengsh]

trust: I trust you confio em você [komfee-oo aim vo-seh]

try *(verb)* tentar

please try tente, por favor [tent poor fuh-vor]

can I try it on? posso prová-lo? [possoo proovah-loo]

T-shirt uma 'T-shirt'

Tuesday terça-feira [tersuh-fayruh]

tunnel um túnel [toonell]

turn: where do we turn off? onde é que viramos? [ondee-eh kuh veerah-moosh]

he turned without indicating virou sem fazer sinal [veeroh seng fazair seenal]

twice duas vezes [doo-ush veh-zush]

twice as much o dobro [oo doh-broo]

twin beds duas camas separadas [d*oo*-ush k*a*h-mush seper*a*h-dush]

two dois [doysh]; duas [d*oo*-ush]

typewriter uma máquina de escrever [m*a*cky-nuh duh shkruvv*a*ir]

typical típico [t*ee*pikoo]

tyre um pneu [p-n*e*h-oo]
   I need a new tyre preciso dum pneu novo [pres*ee*zoo doom p-n*e*h-oo n*o*-voo]
   » *TRAVEL TIP: tyre pressures*

lb/sq in	18	20	22	24	26	28	30
kg/sq cm	1.3	1.4	1.5	1.7	1.8	2	2.1

ugly feio [fayyoo]

ulcer uma úlcera [*oo*lseruh]

Ulster Ulster [*oo*lstair]

umbrella um guarda-chuva [gw*a*rduh-sh*oo*vuh]

uncle: my uncle o meu tio [oo m*e*h-oo t*ee*-oo]

uncomfortable incómodo [eenkommoodoo]

unconscious inconsciente [eenkonsh-see-*e*nt]

under debaixo de [duh-by-shoo duh]

underdone mal passado [pass*a*h-doo]

underground (*rail*) o metro [m*e*troo]; see **metro**

understand: I understand já percebi [jah perseb*ee*]
   I don't understand não percebo [nowng pers*e*bboo]
   do you understand? está a compreender? [shtah uh kompree-end*a*ir]

undo desfazer [dush-fuzz*a*ir]

unfriendly antipático [anteep*a*ttikoo]

unhappy infeliz [eemfel*ee*sh]

United States Estados Unidos [shtah-dooz-oon*ee*doosh]

unleaded sem chumbo [saing sh*oo*mbo]

unlock abrir [abr*ee*r]

until até a [at*e*h uh]
   until next year até ao ano que vem [at*e*h ow *a*h-noo kuh veng]

unusual pouco vulgar [pokoo voolg*a*r]

up: up there lá em cima [lah eng s*ee*muh]

he's not up yet ainda não está levantado [uh-*ee*nduh nowng shtah levant*ah*-doo]

what's up? o que aconteceu? [oo kee akontuss*eh*-oo]

upside-down de pernas para o ar [duh p*ai*rnush proh ar]

upstairs em cima [eng s*ee*muh]

urgent urgente [oor-jent]

us nos [noosh]

    for us para nós [para nosh]

    with us connosco [kon*o*shkoo]

use: can I use ...? posso usar ...? [possoo oo*za*r]

useful útil [*oo*teel]

uso externo for external use only

usual usual [ooz-w*al*]; **as usual** como de costume [k*o*-moo duh koosht*oo*m]

usually usualmente [ooz-wal-ment]

U-turn inversão de marcha [eemver-s*o*wng duh m*a*rshuh]

vacancy: do you have any vacancies? tem quartos livres? [teng kw*a*rtoosh l*ee*vrush]

vacate *(room)* desocupar [duzzoh-koop*a*r]

vaccination a vacinação [vasseena-s*o*wng]

vacuum flask um termo [t*ai*rmoo]

valid válido [v*a*llidoo]

    how long is it valid for? é válido para quanto tempo? [eh v*a*llidoo para kw*a*ntoo t*e*mpoo]

valley um vale [oom val]

valuable valioso [valee-*o*-zoo]

    will you look after my valuables? pode guardar-me os meus objectos? [pod gward*a*r-muh oosh m*eh*-ooz objettoosh]

value *(noun)* o valor

valve uma válvula [v*a*lvooluh]

van um furgão [foorg*o*wng]

vanilla baunilha [bow-n*ee*l-yuh]

varicose veins varizes [var*ee*zush]

veal vitela [veet*e*lluh]

vedado ao trânsito road closed

vegetables legumes [leg*oo*msh]
vegetarian vegetariano [vejeturry-*a*h-noo]
vende-se for sale
veneno poison
ventilator o exaustor [eezowsh-t*o*r]
very muito [m*wee*ntoo]
   very much imenso [eem*e*nsoo]
via via [vee-uh]
village uma aldeia [al-d*a*y-uh]
vine uma videira [vee-d*a*y-ruh]
vinegar vinagre [veen*a*h-gruh]
vineyard uma vinha [v*ee*n-yuh]
vintage *(noun)* a colheita [kool-y*a*y-tuh]
   (adjective) velho [v*e*l-yo]
violent violento [vee-ool*e*ntoo]
visibility a visibilidade [veezeebeeleed*a*d]
visit *(verb)* visitar [veezeet*a*r]
vódka vodka
voice a voz [vosh]
voltage a voltagem [volt*a*h-jeng]
waist a cintura [seent*oo*ruh]
  » *TRAVEL TIP: waist measurements*

UK	24	26	28	30	32	34	36	38
Portugal	61	66	71	76	80	87	91	97

wait: will we have to wait long? temos de
esperar muito tempo ainda? [t*e*h-moosh duh
shper*a*r mw*ee*ntoo t*e*mpoo uh-*ee*nduh]
   wait for me espere por mim [shpair poor
meeng]
   I'm waiting for a friend/my wife estou à
espera dum amigo/da minha mulher [shtoh ah
shp*ai*ruh doom am*ee*goo/duh m*ee*n-yuh
mool-y*ai*r]
waiter o empregado [empreg*a*h-doo]
   waiter! se faz favor! [suh fash fuh-v*o*r]
waitress a empregada [empreg*a*h-duh]
   waitress! se faz favor! [suh fash fuh-v*o*r]
wake: will you wake me up at 7.30? pode
acordar-me às sete e meia? [pod akoord*a*r-muh
ash set ee m*a*yyuh]

Wales País de Gales [pa-*ee*sh duh g*ah*-lush]
walk: can we walk there? podemos ir até lá a
pé? [pood*e*h-mooz eer at*e*h lah uh peh]
   are there any good walks around here? há
   alguns passeios bonitos por aqui? [ah alg*oo*nsh
   pass*a*yyoosh boon*ee*toosh poor ak*ee*]
   walking shoes sapatos leves [sap*ah*-toosh
   levsh]
   walking stick uma bengala [beng*ah*-luh]
wall a parede [par*e*d]
wallet uma carteira [kart*a*yruh]
want: I want a . . . queria um . . . [k*ree*-uh oom]
   I want to talk to . . . quero falar com . . .
   [k*ai*roo fal*a*r kong]
   what do you want? o que deseja? [oo kuh
   duzz*e*jjuh]
   I don't want to não quero [nowng k*ai*roo]
   he wants to . . . quer . . . [kair]
warm quente [kent]
   it's rather warm está calor [sht*a*h kal*o*r]
   I'm very warm estou com muito calor [sht*o*h
   kong mweent kal*o*r]
warning um aviso [av*ee*zoo]
was: I was/he was (eu) era; estava (ele) era;
   estava
   it was era; estava [*e*rruh; sht*a*h-vuh]
wash: can you wash these for me? pode
   lavar-me isto? [pod lavv*a*r-muh *ee*shtoo]
   where can I wash . . .? onde posso lavar . . .?
   [*o*nduh possoo lavv*a*r]
   washing machine uma máquina de lavar
   [m*a*cky-nuh duh lavv*a*r]
   washing powder detergente [deter-jent]
wasp uma vespa [v*e*shpuh]
watch *(wrist-)* um relógio (de pulso) [reloj-yoo
   duh p*oo*lsoo]
   will you watch my bags for me? pode tomar
   conta da minha bagagem? [pod toom*a*r k*o*ntuh
   duh m*ee*n-yuh bag*ah*-jeng]
   watch out! cuidado! [kweed*a*h-doo]

water água [*a*hg-wuh]
   can I have some water? posso beber água?
   [posso beb*air a*hg-wuh]
   hot and cold running water água quente e
   fria [*a*hg-wuh kent ee fr*ee*-uh]
   waterproof à prova de água [ah pr*o*vvuh
   d*a*hg-wuh]
   waterskiing ski aquático
   [shkee akw*a*tikoo]
way: we'd like to eat the Portuguese
   way queríamos comer um prato português
   [kr*ee*-amoosh koom*air* oom pr*a*h-too
   poort*oo*-ge*sh*]
   could you tell me the way to . . .? pode
   indicar-me o caminho a . . .? [pod eendik*a*r-muh
   oo kam*ee*n-yoo uh]
   see **where** *for answers*
we nós [nosh]
   we are English somos ingleses [s*o*-mooz
   eengle*h*-zush]
   we are tired estamos cansados [sht*a*h-moosh
   kans*a*h-doosh]
weak fraco [fr*a*h-koo]
weather o tempo [t*e*mpoo]
   what filthy weather! que tempo horrível!
   [kuh t*e*mpoo o-r*ee*vel]
   what's the weather forecast? qual é a
   previsão do tempo? [kwal eh uh pruvv*ee*z*o*wng
   doo t*e*mpoo]
   YOU MAY THEN HEAR . . .
   vai chover *it's going to rain*
   haverá sol *it'll be sunny*
   o tempo vai melhorar *it'll clear up*
Wednesday quarta-feira [kw*a*rta-f*a*yruh]
week uma semana [sem*a*h-nuh]
   a week today/tomorrow de hoje/amanhã a
   uma semana [dee oje/aman-y*a*ng uh *oo*muh
   sem*a*h-nuh]
   at the weekend no fim de semana [noo
   feeng . . .]

weight o peso [peh-zoo]
well: I'm not feeling well não me sinto bem
[nowng muh seentoo beng]
he's not well não está bem [nowng shtah ...]
how are you? very well, thanks como está?
muito bem, obrigado [ko-moo shtah – mweentoo
beng, o-breegah-doo]
you speak English very well fala inglês
muito bem [fah-luh eenglesh mweentoo beng]
wellingtons botas de borracha [bottush duh
boorah-shuh]
Welsh galês [galesh]
were: you were *(singular)* (você) era/estava;
(tu) eras/estavas [errush/shtah-vush]
you were *(plural)* eram/estavam
see **you**
we were éramos; estávamos [erramoosh;
shtahvamoosh]
they were eram; estavam [errowng;
shtavowng]
west oeste [wesht]
West Indian antilhano [anteel-yah-noo]
West Indies As Antilhas [uz anteel-yush]
wet molhado [mol-yah-doo]
wet suit um fato isotérmico [fah-too
eezotairmikoo]
what o que [oo kuh]
what? a quê? [oo keh]
what is that? o que é isso? [oo kee eh eessoo]
what for? para quê? [para keh]
wheel uma roda [rodduh]
when quando [kwandoo]
when is breakfast? a que horas é o pequeno
almoço? [uh kee oruz eh oo pikeh-noo al-mo-soo]
where onde
where is the Post Office? onde é o Correio?
[ondee eh oo koorayoo]
YOU MAY THEN HEAR ...
vá até ao segundo cruzamento *go as far as the
second crossroads*

vá a direito *straight on*
vire à esquerda/à direita *turn left/right*
lá em baixo *down there*
which qual [kwal]
  which one? qual deles? [kwal deh-lush]
  YOU MAY THEN HEAR ...
  este/esta *this one*
  esse/essa *that one*
  aquele/aquela *that one over there*
whisky o whisky [weeshkee]
white branco [brankoo]
Whitsun Pentecostes [pentuh-koshtush]
who quem [keng]
whose de quem [duh keng]
  whose is this? de quem é isto? [duh keng eh
  ee shtoo]
  YOU MAY THEN HEAR ...
  é meu/minha *it is mine*
  é de você/dele/dela *it is yours/his/hers*
why porquê? [poor-keh]
  why not? porque não? [poorkuh nowng]
  YOU MAY THEN HEAR ...
  porque ... *because* ...
wide largo [largoo]
wife: my wife minha mulher [meen-yuh
  mool-yair]
will: when will it be finished? quando estará
  terminado? [kwandoo shtarah terminah-doo]
  will you do it? faz isso? [faz eesoo]
  I will come back eu volto [eh-oo voltoo]
win ganhar [gan-yar]
  who won? quem ganhou? [keng gan-yoh]
wind *(noun)* vento [ventoo]
window a janela [janelluh]
  near the window ao pé da janela [ow peh
  duh ...]
windscreen o pára-brisas [paruh-breezush]
  windscreen wipers os limpa-vidros [oosh
  leempuh-veedroosh]
windy: it's windy faz vento [fash ventoo]

....

wine vinho [veen-yoo]
   can I see the wine list? posso ver a lista dos
   vinhos? [possoo vair uh leeshtuh doosh
   veen-yoosh]
» *TRAVEL TIP: a unique wine from NW Portugal is
   'vinho verde': a young, slightly sparkling wine,
   served well-chilled (try Alvarinho).
   Port: try white as well as red, preferably 30 yrs
   old; visit Instituto do Vinho do Porto, Rua da
   Misericórdia in Lisbon.
   Madeira: 3 grades: Bual, Sercial, Verdelho.
   Whites: for sweet white try Moscatel; for dry,
   Bucelas, Colares, Vidigueira.
   Reds: best are full-bodied; try Cave Solar das
   Francesas, Periquita, Porta de Cavaleiros.
   Rosé: Mateus
   Sparkling: by far the best – Raposeira.*
winter Inverno [eemvairnoo]
wire arame [aram] *(elec)* um fio [fee-oo]
wish: best wishes com os melhores
   cumprimentos
with com [kong]
without sem [seng]
witness uma testemunha [tushtuh-moon-yuh]
   will you act as a witness for me? quer ser
   minha testemunha? [kair sair meen-yuh . . .]
woman uma mulher [mool-yair]
   women as mulheres [mool-yairush]
wonderful maravilhoso [maraveel-yo-zoo]
won't: it won't start não pega [nowng pegguh]
wood madeira [madayruh]
   (forest) um bosque [boshk]
wool lã [lang]
word uma palavra [palahv-ruh]
   I don't know that word não conheço essa
   palavra [nowng koon-yessoo essuh palahv-ruh]
work *(verb)* trabalhar [trubble-yar]
   it's not working não funciona [nowng
   foonss-yonnuh]
   I work in London trabalho em Londres

[trabal-yoo eng londrush]

worry *(verb)* preocupar-se [pree-ookoopar-suh]
  I'm worried about him estou preocupado por causa dele [shtoh pree-ookoopah-doo poor kow-zuh dehl]
  don't worry não se preocupe [nowng suh pree-ookoop]

worse: it's worse está pior [shtah pee-or]
  he's getting worse está a piorar [shtah uh pee-oorar]

worst o pior [oo pee-or]

worth: it's not worth that much não vale assim tanto [nowng val asseeng tantoo]
  is it worthwhile going to . . .? vale a pena ir a . . .? [val uh peh-nuh eer uh]

wrap: could you wrap it up? pode embrulhá-lo? [pod embrool-yah-loo]

wrench *(tool)* uma chave inglesa [shahv eengleh-zuh]

wrist o pulso [poolsoo]

write escrever [shkruvvair]
  could you write it down? pode escrever isso? [pod shkruvvair eesoo]
  I'll write to you vou escrever-te [voh shkruvvair-tuh]
  writing paper papel de carta [puppell duh kartuh]

wrong errado [eerah-doo]
  I think the bill's wrong penso que se enganou na conta [pensoo kuh see enganoh nuh kontuh]
  there's something wrong with . . . passa-se qualquer coisa com . . . [passuh-suh kwal-kair koy-zuh kong]
  you're wrong está enganado [shtah enganah-doo]
  sorry, wrong number desculpe, enganou-se no número [dush-koolp, enganoh-suh noo noomeroo]

X-ray raio X [rye-oo sheesh]

yacht um yacht [yat]

....

yard uma jarda [jarduh]

» *TRAVEL TIP: 1 yard = 91.44 cms = 0.91 m*

year um ano [ah-noo]

yellow amarelo [amarelloo]

yes sim [seeng]

yesterday ontem [onteng]

    the day before yesterday ante ontem [antee onteng]

    yesterday morning/afternoon ontem de manhã/à tarde [onteng duh man-yang/ah tard]

yet: is it ready yet? já está pronto? [jah shtah pront]

    not yet ainda não [uh-eenduh nowng]

yoghurt um yogurte [yoogoort]

you tu/você/o senhor/a senhora [too/vo-seh/oo sun-yor/uh sun-yoruh]

    I like you gosto de ti [goshtoo duh tee]

    with you contigo [konteegoo]; com você

» *TRAVEL TIP: the word for 'you'/'yours' in Portuguese depends on how well one knows the person; with strangers 'o senhor/a senhora' (the gentleman/lady) is used; with acquaintances the polite 'você'; with good friends the familiar 'tu'*

young jovem [jovveng]

your *see* **you** o teu/a tua; o seu/a sua [teh-oo/too-uh]

    is this your camera? esta máquina é sua? [eshtuh macky-nuh eh soo-uh]

    is this yours? isto é seu? [eeshtoo eh seh-oo]

youth hostel albergue da juventude [albairg duh jooventood]

zero zero [zairoo]

    below zero abaixo de zero [abye-shoo duh . . .]

zip um fecho de correr [feshoo duh koorair]

zona azul parking permit zone

0 zero [zairoo]
1 um [oom]
2 dois [doysh]
3 três [tresh]
4 quatro [kwatroo]
5 cinco [seenkoo]
6 seis [saysh]
7 sete [set]
8 oito [oytoo]
9 nove [nov]
10 dez [desh]
11 onze [onz]
12 doze [dohz]
13 treze [traiz]
14 catorze [katorz]
15 quinze [keenz]
16 dezasseis [duzzasaysh]
17 dezasete [duzzaset]
18 dezoito [duz-oy-too]
19 dezanove [duzzanov]
20 vinte [veent]
21 vinte e um [veent-ee-oom]
22 vinte e dois [veent-ee-doysh]
23 vinte e três
24 vinte e quatro
25 vinte e cinco
26 vinte e seis
27 vinte e sete
28 vinte e oito
29 vinte e nove
30 trinta [treentuh]
31 trinta e um [treent-ee-oom]
40 quarenta [kwarentuh]
41 quarenta e um [kwarent-ee-oom]
50 cinquenta [seenkwentuh]
51 cinquenta e um [seenkwent-ee-oom]
60 sessenta [sessentuh]
61 sessenta e um [sessent-ee-oom]

70 setenta [setentuh]
71 setenta e um [setent-ee-oom]
80 oitenta [oy-tentuh]
81 oitenta e um [oy-tentee-oom]
90 noventa [nooventuh]
91 noventa e um [noovent-ee-oom]
100 cem [seng]
101 cento e um [sentoo-ee-oom]
165 cento e sessenta e cinco
    [sentoo-ee-sessent-ee-seenkoo]
200 duzentos [doozentoosh]
300 trezentos [trezentoosh]
400 quatro centos [kwatroo-sentoosh]
500 quinhentos [keen-yentoosh]
600 seiscentos [saysh-sentoosh]
700 setecentos [set-sentoosh]
800 oitocentos [oy-toosentoosh]
900 novecentos [nov-sentoosh]
1,000 mil [meel]
2,000 dois mil [doysh meel]
4,650 quatro mil seiscentos e cinquenta
    [kwatroo meel saysh-sentooz-ee
    seenkwent]
1,000,000 um milhão [oom meel-yowng]

*NB in Portuguese the comma is a decimal point;
for thousands use a full-stop, eg 4.000*

ALPHABET: how to spell in Portuguese
a [ah] *b* [beh] *c* [seh] *d* [deh] *e* [eh] *f* [ef]
g [jeh] *h* [agah] *i* [ee] *j* [jottuh] *k* [kappuh]
l [el] *m* [em] *n* [en] *o* [oh] *p* [peh] *q* [keh]
r [err] *s* [ess] *t* [teh] *u* [oo] *v* [veh] *w* [veh
dooploo] *x* [sheesh] *y* [eepsilon] *z* [zeh]